Governmentality, Biopower, and Everyday Life

Routledge Studies in Social and Political Thought

For a full list of titles in this series, please visit www.routledge.com

17. Goffman and Social Organization
Studies in a Sociological Legacy
Edited by Greg Smith

18. Situating Hayek
Phenomenology and the Neo-liberal Project
Mark J. Smith

19. The Reading of Theoretical Texts
Peter Ekegren

20. The Nature of Capital
Marx after Foucault
Richard Marsden

21. The Age of Chance
Gambling in Western Culture
Gerda Reith

22. Reflexive Historical Sociology
Arpad Szakolczai

23. Durkheim and Representations
Edited by W. S. F. Pickering

24. The Social and Political Thought of Noam Chomsky
Alison Edgley

25. Hayek's Liberalism and Its Origins
His Idea of Spontaneous Order and the Scottish Enlightenment
Christina Petsoulas

26. Metaphor and the Dynamics of Knowledge
Sabine Maasen and Peter Weingart

27. Living with Markets
Jeremy Shearmur

28. Durkheim's Suicide
A Century of Research and Debate
Edited by W.S.F. Pickering and Geoffrey Walford

29. Post-Marxism
An Intellectual History
Stuart Sim

30. The Intellectual as Stranger
Studies in Spokespersonship
Dick Pels

31. Hermeneutic Dialogue and Social Science
A Critique of Gadamer and Habermas
Austin Harrington

32. Methodological Individualism
Background, History and Meaning
Lars Udehn

33. John Stuart Mill and Freedom of Expression
The Genesis of a Theory
K.C. O'Rourke

34. The Politics of Atrocity and Reconciliation
From Terror to Trauma
Michael Humphrey

35. **Marx and Wittgenstein**
Knowledge, Morality, Politics
Edited by Gavin Kitching and
Nigel Pleasants

36. **The Genesis of Modernity**
Arpad Szakolczai

37. **Ignorance and Liberty**
Lorenzo Infantino

38. **Deleuze, Marx and Politics**
Nicholas Thoburn

39. **The Structure of Social Theory**
Anthony King

40. **Adorno, Habermas and the Search for a Rational Society**
Deborah Cook

41. **Tocqueville's Moral and Political Thought**
New Liberalism
M.R.R. Ossewaarde

42. **Adam Smith's Political Philosophy**
The Invisible Hand and
Spontaneous Order
Craig Smith

43. **Social and Political Ideas of Mahatma Gandi**
Bidyut Chakrabarty

44. **Counter-Enlightenments**
From the Eighteenth Century to
the Present
Graeme Garrard

45. **The Social and Political Thought of George Orwell**
A Reassessment
Stephen Ingle

46. **Habermas**
Rescuing the Public Sphere
Pauline Johnson

47. **The Politics and Philosophy of Michael Oakeshott**
Stuart Isaacs

48. **Pareto and Political Theory**
Joseph Femia

49. **German Political Philosophy**
The Metaphysics of Law
Chris Thornhill

50. **The Sociology of Elites**
Michael Hartmann

51. **Deconstructing Habermas**
Lasse Thomassen

52. **Young Citizens and New Media**
Learning for Democractic Participation
Edited by Peter Dahlgren

53. **Gambling, Freedom and Democracy**
Peter Adams

54. **The Quest for Jewish Assimilation in Modern Social Science**
Amos Morris-Reich

55. **Frankfurt School Perspectives on Globalization, Democracy, and the Law**
William E. Scheuerman

56. **Hegemony**
Studies in Consensus and Coercion
Edited by Richard Howson and
Kylie Smith

57. **Governmentality, Biopower, and Everyday Life**
Majia Holmer Nadesan

Governmentality, Biopower, and Everyday Life

Majia Holmer Nadesan

Routledge
Taylor & Francis Group
New York   London

First published 2008
by Routledge
270 Madison Ave, New York, NY 10016

Simultaneously published in the UK
by Routledge
2 Park Square, Milton Park, Abingdon, Oxon OX14 4RN

Routledge is an imprint of the Taylor & Francis Group, an informa business

© 2008 Taylor & Francis

Typeset in Sabon by IBT Global.
Printed and bound in the United States of America on acid-free paper by IBT Global.

All rights reserved. No part of this book may be reprinted or reproduced or utilised in any form or by any electronic, mechanical, or other means, now known or hereafter invented, including photocopying and recording, or in any information storage or retrieval system, without permission in writing from the publishers.

Trademark Notice: Product or corporate names may be trademarks or registered trademarks, and are used only for identification and explanation without intent to infringe.

Library of Congress Cataloging in Publication Data

Nadesan, Majia Holmer, 1965–
  Governmentality, biopower, and everyday life / by Majia Holmer Nadesan.
    p. cm. — (Routledge studies in social and political thought ; 57)
  Includes bibliographical references and index.
  ISBN-13: 978-0-415-95854-7 (hbk)
  ISBN-10: 0-415-95854-7 (hbk)
  ISBN-13: 978-0-203-89462-0 (ebk)
  ISBN-10: 0-203-89462-6 (ebk)
 1. Power (Social sciences)   2. State, The.   3. Biopolitics.   I. Title.
JC330.N32 2008
320.1—dc22
                                2007052798

ISBN10: 0-415-95854-7 (hbk)
ISBN10: 0-203-89462-6 (ebk)

ISBN13: 978-0-415-95854-7 (hbk)
ISBN13: 978-0-203-89462-0 (ebk)

Contents

Acknowledgments		ix
1	Introduction	1
	Governmentality	6
	Assumptions and Methods	9
	Chapters	13
2	Liberal Governmentalities	15
	Liberal Governmentalities	15
	Neoliberal Enterprise and Neoconservative Governmentalities	29
3	Governing the Self-Regulating Market	45
	Markets, Mercantilism, and Laissez-Faire Government	46
	Nineteenth-Century Markets: Corporatization and Colonialism	55
	Governing Economic Risk: From Laissez-Faire to the Welfare State	68
	Neoliberalism: Enterprise and Risk	77
	Neoliberal Market Government and Biopolitical Crises	89
4	Governing Population: Biopower, Risk, and the Politics of Health	93
	The Birth of Biopolitics and Foucault's Genealogy of Social Medicine	94
	Twentieth-Century Social-Surveillance Medicine	106
	Twentieth-Century Genetics and Genomics	115
5	Governing Population: Mind and Brain as Governmental Spaces	138
	Madness, Criminology and Eugenics: Nineteenth-Century Dividing Practices	140

*Twentieth-Century Biopower: From Normalization
    to Optimization*   149
*Governing the Brain: Behavioral Genetics, Psychopharmacology,
    and Cognitive Neuroscience*   162
*Governing Difference: Self-Government, Disciplinarity,
    and the Society of Control*   178

6 Biopower, Sovereignty, and America's Global Security   183
Foucault, Agamben, and Sovereignty   184
The United States of America: Biopower, Race, and Sovereignty   192
Surveillance, Threat Governmentality, and Precautionary Risk   202
Sovereign Exceptionality   205
Sovereignty and Liberal Governmentality   208

7 "Bad Subjects" and Liberal Governmentalities   211

Notes   217
References   219
Index   245

Acknowledgments

I would like to express my gratitude to Claudia Aradau, George Cheney, Shiv Ganesh, and Thomas Lemke for reading and responding to chapter drafts. I am most grateful for their careful critiques and critical insights. I also wish to express my gratitude to Sohinee Roy for her careful editing. This book is dedicated to my children, Taj and Kamal Nadesan.

1 Introduction

How are human populations governed in contemporary societies? How is the conduct of everyday life in the family, in the school, and in the workplace shaped by social relations of power? How do individuals engage in self-regulation across social contexts? How are recalcitrant or unruly individuals disciplined? How are the state, the market, and the population constituted and entwined in/through particular arts of government?

One framework useful for addressing these questions is Foucault's analytic of governmentality. Foucault used the idea of governmentality to explore the regularities of everyday existence that structure the "conduct of conduct," ultimately giving expression to distinct historical epochs characterized by particular arts of government (or governmentalities), including laissez-faire, social-welfare, and neoliberal governmentalities.[1] Foucault's understanding of neoliberal governmentality extended beyond popularized definitions that center laissez-faire economic policies to encompass the particular logics and technologies of rule operative across varied domains of social life.

Accordingly, governmentality scholarship simultaneously addresses the rationalities of historically specific forms of political government such as neoliberalism *and* the forms of activity and technologies of power shaping everyday interpersonal and institutional life, thereby bridging micro- and macrolevels of analyses (Gordon, 1991). For example, in the contemporary United States, governmentality explains homologies across neoliberal economic policies in the market and the everyday discipline and character-development programs used by teachers in public schools to foster a particular kind of calculative accountability (Nadesan, 2006). Likewise, governmentality provides a framework for analyzing homologies across "employee-driven" corporate human resource policies that shift risk to employees and neoliberal, international economic policies pursued by the World Bank. Governmentality addresses how society's pressing problems, expert authorities, explanations, and technologies are organized in relation to particular kinds of action/policy orientations, problem-solution frameworks, subjectivities, and activities (see Rose, 1999a). Governmentality also explores how individuals are privileged as autonomous self-regulating agents or are marginalized, disciplined, or subordinated as invisible or dangerous.

2 *Governmentality, Biopower, and Everyday Life*

Foucault was particularly interested in how liberal governmentalities target *life* through social and scientific engineering, through expert administration, and through everyday technologies of the self. Life has been a significant problem-solution frame for liberal governmentalities since the eighteenth century. However, understandings and problematics of life have varied significantly across time, reflecting divergences in liberal governmentalities and distinct historical circumstances. Take, for example, the current cultural preoccupation with genetics. Genetic engineering and genetic-based pharmaceuticals, among other biotechnological pursuits, share an approach aimed at identifying and engineering what are seen as the most basic components of life. The molecularization of life accords with neoliberal rationalities by transforming complex phenomena (e.g., human diversity and disease) into biological assets and costs that can be represented and manipulated within marketized calculi of value. Accordingly, complex conditions such as depression, anxiety, and substance abuse are coded as social and economic risks with calculative costs for industry and the state that must be administered. Expert market authorities trained in molecular psychiatry offer pharmaceutical solutions. Older liberal frameworks of knowledge, such as psychoanalysis and social anomie, lose credence among the public, insurers, and the state, their experts marginalized or retrained. How has this shift in perspective and protocol been achieved? The answers to this question are myriad because shifts in the "conduct of conduct" reflect a vast array of new technologies, new subjectivities, and new calculations. And yet, across disparate, heterogeneous, and decentralized transformations in problem-solution sets, one can also discern a particular regularity, a particular frame, focus, or reduction on the "elements" of life (Rose, 2007) and their market capitalization. Foucault argued that efforts to understand and administer the life forces of the population have persisted since the eighteenth century, although formulations reflect changing liberal governmentalities producing historically distinct problem-solution frames.

Foucault developed the idea of biopower to capture technologies of power that address the management of, and control over, the life of the population. Life, as the central focus, is neither purely accidental nor fully determined. Foucault offered historical contingency when explaining how governmental operations cohere around particular sets of problems, technologies, and forms of expertise. By contingency, Foucault meant that the institutionalized matrices and regularities of conduct that define specific historical strategies of biological government are neither (a) fully or necessarily determined by an underlying structural imperative such as capitalist accumulation or technological "progressive development" nor (b) the result of the arbitrariness of voluntary, rational, or even accidental decision making. Rather, social homologies across the conduct of everyday conduct are achieved in relation to governmental rationalities that link societal governance with everyday life by constituting and binding market, population, and state in relation to common sets of problem-solution frameworks (e.g., health), values (e.g., enterprise), and identities (e.g., entrepreneur).

Biopower is arguably the most pervasive form of power engendering the homologies and systemic regularities across the diverse fields of social life. Although neoliberal strategies of government appropriate and utilize older forms of power—sovereign power, pastoral power, and disciplinary power—biopower offers the most effective and appealing set of strategies for governing social life under neoliberalism because it finds its telos and legitimacy in its articulated capacity to maximize the energies and capabilities of all: individuals, families, market organizations, and the state. As a kind of power that concerns itself with representing, explaining, and regulating the life forces of populations, biopolitical forces adapted to neoliberal ends seek to minimize societal risk and maximize individual well-being through scientific engineering and individual technologies of the self.

Biopower is seductive because its logics, technologies, and experts offer, or at least purport to offer, tools for societal *self*-government. Biopower's mantra of the rational administration of life promises means for realizing the elusive cybernetic fantasy of a society of self-regulating individuals. Under neoliberal governmentalities, sovereignty is disseminated amongst society's members as the welfare state sheds responsibility for its pastorate by shifting risk and empowerment to its subjects. Thus, the classical liberal fantasy of a society of self-regulating individuals is invoked as a rationale for the dissemination of risk and responsibility achieved by and though biopower's operations. In essence, the emergence of biopower as a major force in shaping, eliciting, and controlling populations is inextricably linked with historically contingent developments in liberal, and now neoliberal, forms of government.

And yet, there is more to biopower than the productive, cybernetic administration of life. Biopower may also serve the interests of capitalist accumulation and market forces by eliciting and optimizing the life forces of a state's population, maximizing their capacity as human resources and their utility for market capitalization. Biopower can therefore supplement and extend the power of capital to expropriate value from the relations of production. For example, efforts to manage the health of populations through pharmaceutical interventions serve market interests by relying on commodity solutions (e.g., drugs) and by purportedly delivering a healthier workforce without changing the conditions under which workers labor, without changing market commodities consumed by labor (e.g., soda), and without changing industrial pollutants that affect workers' health. In 2005, Americans spent more than $200 billion on prescription drugs (Tone & Watkins, 2007). Of course, in the context of the United States, this example also points to divergences in interests across the state and market, as industry within the United States shoulders rising health-care costs. Efforts by industry to shift risk (e.g., health insurance and pensions) to employees are not necessarily supported by the state, despite considerable corporate lobbying, because the state retains an interest in, and responsibility for, optimizing the health of its population. Accordingly, biopower may be mobilized and promulgated by market forces, but not all expressions of this form of power necessarily serve market interests or express underlying class conflict.

The complex operations of power and the web of entanglements and sites of contradiction and conflict are also evident within the state itself. The state, a loosely coupled matrix of institutions and authorities, is rent by contradiction and antagonism as its various agencies and expert authorities simultaneously cooperate with, and resist, alliances with market and social activists. For example, the United States' Environmental Protection Agency's (EPA) recent efforts to dramatically reduce perchlorate in drinking water in the name of public health were met by fierce opposition from Pentagon officials, and their defense contractor allies, for fear that lower limits would curb arms production and raise costs (Waldman, 2005). Put otherwise, the (bio)power of the state to reduce health risks in the name of public security were met with the sovereign power of the state's repressive apparatuses (see Althusser, 1971).

Thus, although governmentality stresses how common rationalities of government and technologies of power align the institutions, authorities, and technologies of everyday life, the market, and the state (*de jure* governmental apparatuses), it also recognizes discontinuities, sites of divergence, and contradictions within and across social realms. Some of these discontinuities and divergences can be explained historically in terms of the very constitution of these realms as distinct social fields. Accordingly, this project addresses how the market/economy and population and state were constituted as distinct fields of visibility. Governmentality reveals these fields as organized in relation to common rationalities while simultaneously acknowledging historical discontinuities and divergences. Thus, biopower's complex of operations within a given historical period can never be reduced to the logics of a particular liberal governmentality.

Additionally, although neoliberalism typically governs from a distance through biopolitical technologies of the self and remote flexible networks, older forms of power and control are employed across social realms as the authorities of population (e.g., teachers and doctors, therapists), state (e.g., elected officials and government bureaucrats), and market (e.g., hedge funds and CEOs) exercise a kind of dispersed sovereignty in the course of daily decision making. Moreover, whereas technologies of the self are exercised by affluent populaces, more overt surveillance networks and corporeal disciplines are often exercised over poorer populaces, particularly over those seen as incapable of self-government. Fertility testing, treatment, and expert-informed child rearing among the U.S. upper-middle class are matched by the disciplining, surveillance, and incarceration of the children of America's lower classes (Chaddock, 2003). Up-to-date assessments of cardiac risk, including genetic analyses, are available for the empowered, responsible, self-regulating, choosing subjects of the upper classes while in 2003, 44.7 million Americans lacked health insurance (Fuhrmans, 2005). In the United States, the greatest risk for poor health and premature death is posed by "class," which is a determinate ignored by many market-based and state-sponsored biomedical apparatuses (Isaacs & Schroeder, 2004).

Foucault argued that biopower involves both the life politics of population and the harnessing and disciplining of corporeal bodies. Although his later work emphasized the former expressions of biopower in order to address power's productivity and circulation, discipline and sovereignty remain important dimensions of his approach to social analysis. Accordingly, it is my contention that analyses of how biopower operates must remain attuned to the systems of marginalization, exclusion, and discipline that supplement liberal technologies of the self implicated in the production of self-regulating agents. This emphasis on how biopower operates as a technology of power that both privileges and marginalizes, empowers and disciplines, sets this book apart from more optimistic formulations of biopower as a technology of optimization.

Contemporary analyses of power and control must look beyond the disciplines and surveillance technologies of enclosed institutional spaces. Foucault (2007) argued that governmentality extends analysis beyond the inside of disciplinary institutions to the outside, from specific institutional functions to dispersed, networked technologies of power that circulate across all domains of social life. Foucault's shifted analysis to the outside because he saw historical shifts in the technologies and operations of social power.

Gilles Deleuze (1992) coined the idea of "societies of control" (Deleuze, 1992, p. 4) to address contemporary forms of power that circulate dynamically, producing individuals who experience themselves as internally fragmented, or dividuated, by dispersed networks (see also Hardt & Negri, 2000). Circulating networks often involve computerized strategies of surveillance, representation, and control, thereby requiring individuals to succumb to historically novel surveillance modes and disciplines while adopting new kinds of technologies of the self requiring continuous self-modulation. Deleuze argued that market operations and logics have gained disproportionate power within contemporary societies through the iconic figure of the corporation, which encourages competition among individuals while dividing each person "within" with its imperatives for self-modulation (p. 5). The corporation and financial capital circulate almost without limit, exacerbating old social divisions while also producing new forms of inclusion and exclusion.

My work provides a genealogy of the new societies of control and their attendant global market networks in order to explain the dispersion of neoliberal governmentality across social fields that older liberal governmentalities presented and constituted as distinct. Marketized neoliberal governmentalities increasingly shape the problem-solution frames and technologies organizing conduct within state apparatuses and across everyday "private" life. Of particular interest for this project are the ways biopower's operations are transformed by market-oriented neoliberal governmentalities. *Thus, this book emphasizes how neoliberal market logics and technologies present particular biopolitical problematics and opportunities for state, market, and private actors while, simultaneously, shaping governmental approaches to representing and addressing these problematics.* In what follows, I briefly introduce my approach to governmentality before outlining this book's organization across chapters.

GOVERNMENTALITY

Governmentality scholarship is a growing field that embraces a wide range of Foucauldian-inspired interdisciplinary scholarship concerned with societal governance.[2] Methodological analyses of social governance need not be Foucauldian but include a vast array of approaches addressing strategies and procedures for controlling, regulating, or managing global, national, and local "problems" that extend beyond traditional formulations of the state's purview (see Lemke, in press). Put broadly, the governance literature addresses changing regimes of societal administration and institutional and individual conduct.

What sets governmentality apart from other methodological approaches to understanding societal governance is that governmentality takes governance's problem-solution frames as its objects of analysis. In other words, governmentality analyzes historically how problems and technologies of governance are formulated and addressed. Moreover, governmentality rejects the dualism between state and society that so much of the governance literature presupposes (see Lemke, in press), and it does so by deconstructing their existence as preexisting ontological entities.

In effect, governmentality scholarship deconstructs social givens by exploring their historical constitution as objects of government not by totalizing regimes of governance but by circulating and decentering technologies of power. However, although Foucault pursued governmentality to avoid totalizing, institutional, and functional accounts, he did identify distinct regimes or arts of government that carved out social fields of visibility and helped produce regularities of conduct across fields

Accordingly, governmentality scholars suggest that Western understandings of market, state, and population get constituted and articulated within three distinct arts and technologies of government. These regimes include: (a) laissez-faire or classical liberalism; (b) welfare-liberalism or the welfare state; (c) neoliberalism. It is important to stress that the market, state, and population are produced by these regimes, which are organized around various problems of "government" (see definition following). Thus, rather than presupposing their existence a priori, scholarship addresses how distinct authorities employing diverse strategies have delineated state, market, and population as distinct spheres of visibility by/within changing problematizations and technologies of government.

Foucault argued that shifting regimes of government can be identified in part through shifting technologies and strategies of power. Foucault's analyses organized around the emergence of the sovereignty-discipline-government triad:

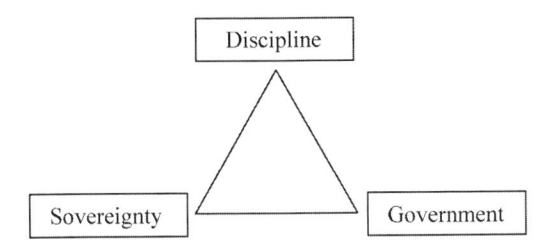

```
            ┌──────────┐
            │Discipline│
            └──────────┘
               /\
              /  \
             /    \
            /      \
┌──────────┐        ┌──────────┐
│Sovereignty│       │Government│
└──────────┘        └──────────┘
```

Foucault's works emphasized the role of sovereignty in premodern time, the development of discipline in the enclosed spaces (e.g., madhouses, prisons, factories) of the eighteenth and nineteenth centuries, and the dispersion and circulation of government (through biopolitics and technologies of the self) that produced the governmentalization of the state. However, Foucault cautioned against viewing sovereignty, disciplinary, and government as constituting a series of substitutions across time. Rather, he argued, they should be understood as eventually constituting a triangle of interconnected systems of government, or governmentality, aiming at security by targeting the population (Foucault, 1979b, p. 19). Thus, the emergence of new expressions of power does not imply erasure of older ones.

Much Foucauldian-inspired scholarship addresses shifting expressions and convergences of these technologies of power across the three regimes of government delineated above, laissez-faire liberalism, welfare liberalism, and neoliberalism. This project adds neoconservatism to an analysis of neoliberalism in the U.S. context but otherwise most closely follows the frameworks of government already articulated.

Before moving forward it is useful to introduce briefly Foucault's diverse but interconnected expressions of power, which include:

- Sovereign Power: The historically specific form of power associated with monarchial sovereignty that involved the right to kill or let live. Sovereign power evolved in relation to philosophical-juridical concerns about the "problem" of sovereignty and in response to specific historical political discourses challenging universal sovereignty (Foucault, 2003). Over time, sovereign power increasingly became subject to juridical concerns pertaining to the rationalization and administration of law (Foucault 1979a, 1979b) and was exercised through the juridical and executive arms of the state through the mechanisms of laws, constitutions, and legislative bodies (Dean, 1999). However, Foucault (2003) claimed that sovereignty in the modern period retains the power of death but has been subject to reformulation so that "the ancient right to *take* life or *let* live was replaced by a power to *foster* life or *disallow* it to the point of death" (p. 80). Sovereign power in this sense is intrinsically tied up with biopower.

- Disciplinary Power: Developed first in the context of institutions such as monasteries, schools, factories, and armies to regulate the bodies of institutional subjects, this form of power was ultimately employed in broader projects aimed at managing and regulating populations within specific territories (Foucault, 1979a). Disciplinary power implies some framework of knowledge about its human subjects and thus is intimately connected with biopolitics as "anatomo-politics" (see following). Although discipline is exercised on the bodies of individuals, the individual simply serves as a way of "dividing up the multiplicity" upon which the discipline is exercised to accomplish an end or objective (Foucault, 2007, p. 12).
- Pastoral Power: Originally expressed in the idea and practice of the Christian pastorate, pastoral power was appropriated and secularized by the state/sovereignty (i.e., government) complex to secure everyday life. Pastoral power is both individualizing and totalizing.
- Biopower: Impelled by the exigencies of governing modern life, biopower refers to knowledge and strategies of power that aim at governing a population's life forces (Foucault, 1990). Emerging in the eighteenth century, biopower is expressed as biopolitics and anatomo-politics (Foucault, 1980):
    - Biopolitics: Implicated in the development of indices of knowledge about populations by expert authorities acting within both public (i.e., state) and private institutions (e.g., hospitals). Population is conceived as a political and scientific problem space. Biopolitics in the modern era operate primarily through security mechanisms rather than disciplinary ones.
    - Anatomo-Politics: Technologies of power that act upon individuals in order to discipline and/or normalize their comportment toward the ends of state security and capital accumulation. Anatomo-politics appropriates disciplinary power for the purposes of managing the corporeality of populations, historically, within specific territories.
    - According to Foucault (2003b, p. 81), the "disciplines of the body and the regulation of the population constituted the two poles around which the organization of power was deployed" seeking to "invest life through and through."
    - Government: An art of government that takes population as its object and governs in the name of individual and state security,

defined both in relation to economic security and social welfare. Foucault used the term *governmentalities* to refer to liberal arts of government, which operate in large part through *"a biopolitics of the population"* (Foucault, 2003, p. 81) and, as Dean put it, seek to "enframe the population" within *"apparatuses of security"* (1999, p. 20). Government is *not* synonymous with the state because it includes regularities of conduct, security apparatuses, and strategies of control that are dispersed across all domains of life. Liberal arts of government, or governmentalities, have increasingly become "globalized" as market-based and biopolitical security apparatuses transverse national spaces.
- Technologies of the Self: Technologies whereby individuals act upon themselves, rendering themselves subjects of liberal/neoliberal government evolving out of liberal government.

For Foucault, the convergence of sovereignty, discipline, and government in the late modern period resulted in a governmentality that combined the individualizing control strategy of pastoral power with the totalizing control strategy of state power, creating in the liberal state a "secular political pastorate that functions both to individualize and to totalize" (cited in Gordon, 1991, p. 8). However, as the apparatuses of the liberal welfare state have been dismantled, privatized, or hollowed out in the last decades of the twentieth century, the secular political pastorate described by Foucault has undergone a series of transformations in government, birthing that regime of government (i.e., that governmentality) described as neoliberalism. Deleuze's (1992) description of the societies of control characterizes key features of neoliberal government, including historically novel forms of networked and often computer-mediated surveillance and control strategies governed primarily by, or in accord with, market objectives. Neoliberalism relies extensively on remote "government from a distance" and biopolitical technologies of the self, but this reliance does not preclude operations of older forms of discipline and sovereignty, particularly as authorities confront biopolitical problems presented by neoliberal governmentalities.

ASSUMPTIONS AND METHODS

As articulated by Rose, O'Malley, and Valverde (2006), analysis of governmentalities entails identification of "distinct styles of thought" and practices in relation to their "conditions of formation" and "contestations and alliances with other arts of governing" (p. 84). Governmentality analysis entails assumptions and methodological practices that require specification.

First, as already mentioned, the analysis of government Foucault described as governmentality extends well beyond state apparatuses. As Thomas Lemke (in press) succinctly explained, governmentality "conceives of the state as an instrument and effect of political strategies that define the external borders between the public and the private and the state and civil society" (p. 1). Thus, although governmentality addresses state apparatuses, it neither begins nor ends with them or with the institution more generally. As Foucault (2007) explicated, governmentality requires the investigator to "move outside the institution and replace it with the overall point of view of the technology of power" (p. 117). Thus, although institutional functions may be of interest, the main analytical focus concerns "the practical dispositions of power, the characteristic networks, currents, relays, points of support, and difference of a form of power, which are, I think, constitutive of, precisely both the individual and the group" (Foucault, 2007, ft. 7, p. 131).

Second, governmentality refuses recognition of "ready-made objects" such as sexuality or mental illness (Foucault, 2007, p. 118). This stance implies that governmentality holds that there is no subjectivity outside of the social; government is *not* seen as an external force acting upon otherwise free agents. Rather, individuals are constituted as such within and by social relations. This position stands in contrast to the philosophical underpinnings of liberalism, which views individuals as more or less rational, autonomous, individualized beings who confront systems of governance in their particularity, complying with or resisting the external forces.

Third, governmentality recognizes that social fields—the state, the market, and population—are in fact heterogeneous spaces constituted in relation to multiple systems of power, networks of control, and strategies of resistance. The state, the market, and population (i.e., society) exist as transactions (Lazzarato, 2005), regulated through disciplinary and security apparatuses, networks of control, logics of government, specific problem-solution sets, and individual value premises. However, although the transactions constituting the fields of state, market, and population reflect and produce shifting liberal regimes of government, not all transactions can be reduced to, or explained by, these shifting regimes. Governmental analysis acknowledges convergences and divergences across the centers and operations of power and influence, embracing the fundamental contingency and complexity of social configurations (see O'Malley, 2004).

In effect, the series of terms that together make up "civil society"—population, society, everyday life—should not be understood as constituting an a priori and privileged field that is colonized from above by externalities of power and control; rather, everyday life is produced through them. Foucault's work addresses how governmental operations are dispersed in the micropractices of the market (e.g., factories) and in everyday practices and familial relationships (e.g., in schools and families). Therefore, analysis neither embraces the totality of all transactions nor holds out a privileged realm—i.e., society—that is viewed as somehow outside of governmental regimes.

Accordingly, this project explores how early modern power relationships (i.e., biopower) that took the population and the body as sites for intervention engendered in the late modern period micropractices, particularly "technologies of the self," whereupon privatized individuals act upon themselves in the course of daily life in manners consistent with expressions of liberal and neoliberal (and neoconservative) rationalities of government.

Fourth, this undertaking diverges from much of the existing governmentality analysis by emphasizing that sovereignty remains an important technology of control. In contrast to technologies of the self that govern through freedom, sovereignty involves more decisive and/or authoritarian expressions of power. Foucault suggested that in the modern era sovereignty is caught up with biopower so that it involves the capacity to deny life. Foucauldian scholars such as Dean (2002a) and Hindess (2001) suggest that sovereignty operates through biopolitics to delineate capable and incapable subjects, rendering the latter "subject to" exceptions to the applications of neoliberal principles of rule (see also Agamben, 2005, 1998). Furthermore, the rise of neoconservative government (and its alliances with American Christian conservatives) has resulted in more formal attention to, and exercise of, the state's sovereign power as neoconservatives and the American Christian right have sought to use state apparatuses to "return" centralized power to ecclesiastic and market authorities.

Fifth, in spite of governmentality scholarship acknowledging the inevitability of social power and *systems* of government, as well as the fundamental contingency of social outcomes, it need not embrace ethical relativism. Systems of power vary in the degrees of expressivity they afford the subjects they constitute as individuals. Liberal governmentalities vary in value orientations, affecting material distributions of resources. Governmentalities vary in their strategies for disciplining unruly subjects and other social "misfits"; while some systems favor punitive measures, others tend toward rehabilitation. Although rehabilitation may ultimately be more "invasive" in terms of the effects of power, it may also be experienced as less onerous by targeted individuals. Some technologies of the self facilitate individual agency while others, under the guise of self-exploration or self-accountability, beget technologies of power that constrain and problematize self-care. All of this is to argue that the inevitability and ubiquity of power and control do not prevent criticism of power's effects because such effects are variably conditioned across dispersed systems of government and localized technologies of the self.

However, the possibility for criticism raises the question of the critic's epistemological stance in interpreting and evaluating governmental systems. Therefore, I address a sixth point concerning governmentality's claims to truth. Following Foucault (1983), this project undertakes a *history of the present* that explores the modes whereby "human beings are made into subjects" (p. 208). As Rizvi (2005) observed, the "history of the present is a history of thought. But this history of thought is strategically situated in the context of its 'own history,' its 'own present,' that is the history which it owns and to which it belongs." Accordingly, this project ponders the history of the present from the stance of the present but does so ultimately to consider alternative histories that might be born by exploring the conditions of possibility for what is. As articulated by Deleuze: "Thought thinks its own history (the past), but in order to free itself from what it thinks (the present), and be able finally to 'think otherwise' (the future)" (1995, p. 119). In other words, this project explores the relationship between government and everyday life in order to consider the possibilities for generating alternative histories.

The final issue to be raised concerns the specific methods adopted in this history of the present. In the preface to his second edition of *Governing the Soul*, Nikolas Rose (1999a) interprets Foucault's genealogical method as entailing concrete and material investigation of the history of the forms of rationality constituting present conditions, including explorations of practices and assemblages implicated in ways of thinking and acting (see p. x). Accordingly, Rose provides a rough set of dimensions for guiding a "history of the present":

- **Problematizations**: the emergence of problems in relation to particular moral, political, economic, military . . . concerns; the authorities who define phenomena as problems . . . ; the criteria in relation to which certain persons, things, or forms of conduct come to be seen as problematic . . . ; the kinds of dividing practices involved. . . .
- **Explanations**: the operative concepts . . . ; the designation of domains of evidence and the criteria of demonstration, proof or acceptability involved, the forms of visibility, remarkability, calculability conferred.
- **Technologies**: the technical assembly of means of judgment . . . ; the techniques of reformation and cure . . . ; the apparatuses within which intervention is to take place. . . .
- **Authorities**: the constitution of particular personages or attributes of authority; the emergence of expertise as a mode of authority and of experts as authorities . . . ; the procedures used to acquire and maintain authority. . . .
- **Subjectivities**: ontological (as spirit, as soul . . . as creatures of pleasure, of habits, of emotions, of will, of unconscious desire . . .); epistemological (as knowable through observation, through testing, through confession . . .); ethical . . . ; technical (what they must do to themselves, the practices, regimens, by which they should act upon themselves. . . .
- **Strategies**: the strategic or governmental aspirations (prevention of degeneration, eugenic maximization of the fitness of the race . . .); the connections and associations with particular political or other programmatics and logics of reform. . . . (pp. xi–xii)

In sum, these dimensions afford the critic a set of tools for exploring the operations of government in terms of the problem spaces carved out by governmental fields, the authorities legitimized to address these spaces, the subjects to be acted upon, and the strategies and technologies guiding such operations.

CHAPTERS

I understand Foucault's governmentality as a genealogy of liberal regimes of government. Foucault's genealogy, articulated in the 1979 essay "Governmentality," addresses state mercantilism, laissez-faire governmentality, welfare-state governmentality, and concludes with the neoliberalism. Liberal regimes of governmentality, or government (as I shall hereto refer to the two terms interchangeably), produce materially and symbolically three distinct fields of visibility: the state, the market, and the population. The technologies of power formulating these fields of visibility vary across liberal regimes, depending upon market strategies of production and biopolitical problematics.

Chapter 2: Liberal Governmentalities introduces my approach to governmentality through a Foucauldian genealogy of liberal governmentalities. The chapter begins with state mercantilism and explains how the population-wealth problematic under monarchial sovereignty provided the conditions of possibility for the formation of the liberal state while birthing that form of power described as biopower. The chapter then addresses the constitution and dislocation of the social fields of the state, the market, and the population across changing regimes of liberal government, including laissez-faire, liberal, and neoliberal governmentalities. This chapter introduces the vast body of governmentality scholarship and prepares readers for the subsequent chapters' more focused, empirical analyses.

Chapter 3: Governing the Self-Regulating Market takes up the market: a field of visibility relatively underexplored in the governmentality scholarship. In this chapter I provide a genealogy of Western market operations across distinct regimes of liberal government, emphasizing how market operations have shaped, and responded to, biopolitical formulations and concerns. The chapter also addresses how corporations emerged as sovereign entities capable of exerting force upon the social field, thereby extending applications of market logics while simultaneously constituting problematics of biopolitical government for the state and population. The chapter concludes by identifying contemporary neoliberal problematics of economic government, which present significant biopolitical exigencies for privatized individuals (e.g., "citizens" or workers) and state authorities even while capitalizing upon the biological life of the population.

Chapters 4 and 5 emphasize the constitution of population and the development of biopower across liberal governmentalities. As a wide range of observers have noted, articulation and institutionalization of the "problem" of public health and the regulation of "madness" played important roles in the development of the modern state (see Porter, 1999; Rosen, 1993). These chapters demonstrate how biopolitical formulations and administrations of the "problems" of public health and madness have changed across time, in accord with changing governmentalities, market imperatives, and particular historical circumstances.

Chapter 4: Governing Populations: Biopower, Risk, and the Politics of Health provides a genealogy of biopolitical operations implicated in the production of "healthy" populations across liberal regimes of governmentality. In particular, I explore how public and private health-promotion agendas and market-driven genomic science cohere under neoliberalism to stipulate constitution of "healthy, responsible" citizen-consumers. These citizen-consumers contrast with those populations denied access to biopolitical technologies and those who are either rendered invisible or are subject to new forms of biosovereignty. Biopolitical operations are as likely to create inclusive fields of agency as they are likely to create invisible barriers between the biopolitical citizens of the liberal state and invisible subjects who are left outside of its (residual) pastoral operations and whose visibility is contingent only upon their perceived social costs and/or security risks.

Chapter 5: Governing Population: Mind and Brain as Governmental Spaces provides a genealogy of liberal governmentalities' disciplinary and biopolitical operations targeting society's dangerous individuals. Once regarded as a problem space, the study of and disciplining of problematic population expanded from the asylum in the nineteenth century, to the mental hygiene movement in the early twentieth century, to behavioral genetics in the twenty-first century. Contemporary market-directed biopolitical innovations in the ability to represent problematic neurochemistry, gene alleles, and neurological states not only promise strategies for targeted government but also suggest possibilities for new strategies of surveillance and control.

Chapter 6: Biopower, Sovereignty, and America's Global Security addresses the visibility of sovereign force and the expansion of military disciplinary apparatuses in the twenty-first century. These trends demonstrate the limits of biopower's more pastoral operations as the capacity to let die and to kill assume renewed significance for contemporary sovereign apparatuses. In addition to exploring the expansion of force, this chapter also explores the social and material construction of war as a neoliberal business enterprise and the attendant cultural "militarization" of the neoliberal American state.

Chapter 7: "Bad Subjects" and Liberal Governmentalities concludes this project by exploring and considering biopower's operations as technologies of power under neoliberal and neoconservative governmentalities. This chapter questions neoliberal governmentalities' capacities to redress biopolitical tensions posed by market imperatives and by racialized cultural imaginings. Most importantly, the chapter concludes by considering the relationship between and across sovereign totalitarian impulses and liberal technologies of freedom.

2 Liberal Governmentalities

What is "the problem of government"? To what extent do governmental technologies cohere across social fields including everyday (private) life, market, and state? How do individuals engage actively in "self-government"? How do sovereign power and discipline supplement (perceived) failures of self-government?

This chapter explores how problems of government have been framed, operative concepts developed, technologies assembled, and authorities constituted (see Rose, 1999a, p. xi). This approach largely follows the Foucauldian scholarship describing "liberal" governmentalities (see Lemke, 2001; O'Malley, 2004; Rose, 1999b), while adding neoconservatism as a strategy of government.

Although laissez-faire, social-welfare, neoliberal, and neoconservative governmentalities correspond with "frames of governance" articulated in political theory and pursued in state initiatives, governmentalities cannot be reduced to the latter. Analyses of governmentalities extend beyond formalized frames of governance to embrace the conduct of conduct across social fields, across everyday life. Accordingly, when describing liberal governmentalities, this and subsequent chapters will draw upon both formalized discourses of governance (e.g., as articulated in theories of political economy) and dispersed technologies of government, particularly biopolitical technologies, that align the conduct of conduct. Although homologies most certainly exist across formalized regimes of governance and the conduct of conduct, the latter's dispersed technologies often produce localized problems and resistance that undercuts the legitimacy and potency of more formal discourses and apparatuses.

LIBERAL GOVERNMENTALITIES

In the introduction to the now classic text *The Foucault Effect,* Colin Gordon stated that Foucault understood government in two senses (Gordon, 1991). First, Foucault viewed government as the "conduct of conduct," by which he meant a form of activity designed to shape personal, interpersonal, and institutional conduct, as well as the conduct of political sovereignty (cited in Gordon, p. 2). Second, Foucault viewed government in relation to specific rationalities of government, rationalities articulating agents, strategies, and subjects of government. Foucault explored how, over time, analytically distinct forms of government became entangled, enabling an upward and downward continuity of government between and across the individual and the state. In unraveling this entanglement, Foucault explored the operations of arts of government across historical contexts, including: (a) "pastoral" government in Greek philosophy and early Christianity; (b) doctrines of government articulating the reasons of the state and state police (or policy) in early modern Europe; (c) doctrines of government articulating early liberalism beginning in the eighteenth century; (d) post–World War II doctrines of neoliberal thought articulated in the United States, Germany, and France (Foucault, 1979b). For Foucault, these arts of government helped structure and shape conditions and possibilities of subjects' actions. I begin with item (b), doctrines of government articulating the reason of the state and state police.

The Liberal State: A Genealogy of Early Modernism

Foucault contended that the emergence of the early modern liberal state depended upon the institution of more diffuse, but ultimately more pervasive, forms of government that slowly replaced the authoritarian and repressive power of the feudal sovereign. In the premodern era—prior to the development of the modern state—power was largely localized in the corporeal body of the *sovereign* monarch, who exercised his or her will absolutely on those within his or her scope of execution, or territory, in the form of the power of life and death (Foucault, 2003b). Foucault observed: "it is at the moment when the sovereign can kill that he exercises his right over life" (2003b, p. 240). However, sovereign power was subtly transformed across time with the development of the modern state through three important developments. First, state and sectional interests motivated by security and wealth extended "governable spaces," beginning in the sixteenth century but particularly in the late eighteenth century. Second, the development of new ways of thinking about government—principally in relation to juridical administration, the state's appropriation of pastoral power over the administration of population, and curtailment of sovereignty over political economy—altered the nature and operations of societal control and power leading ultimately to more diffuse, but simultaneously permeating, technologies of government. Third, these changes realigned sovereignty around the power and the right "to make live and let die" (2003b, p. 241) as sovereignty became entwined with biopower.

Foucault's genealogy of the transformation from sovereignty to government began by exploring how sovereignty and political rule started to be theorized in political philosophy. In particular, Foucault was interested in the development of rationalities of government in the sixteenth and seventeenth centuries that articulated the responsibilities and modes of conduct appropriate for sovereign and patriarchal authorities in the context of the evolution of the early modern state. Foucault specifically focused on how seventeenth-century texts on the art of government created lines of continuity between the government of the family and the government of the state. These lines of continuity addressed the twin problem of maximizing "population-wealth," a dilemma seen as vital for securitizing the territorially delimited nation and central to the administrative practices of police.

Accordingly, Foucault described how the rationalities of government developed during the seventeenth century included (a) "the art of self-government, connected with morality"; (b) "the art of properly governing a family," which belongs to "oeconomy"; and (c) "the science of ruling the state" (1979b, p. 9). Foucault read these seventeenth-century texts as articulating a continuum linking the diverse forms of government. Foucault used the term *police* to describe "the downwards line, which transmits to individual behaviour and the running of the family the sample principles as the government of the state" (1979b, pp. 9–10). In contrast, the proper training of the sovereign—his pedagogy—ensures the upward continuity of the arts of government.

Foucault regarded the seventeenth-century state's *population-wealth problematic* as linking the upward and downward continuums of conduct. He explained that the "central term" of the continuity across these domains was the "government of the family, termed oeconomy," which was modeled on the relationship of the father to his household (1979b, p. 10). Thus, the central problematic of good state government was "how to introduce this meticulous attention of the father towards his family into the management of the state" (1979b, p. 10). Accordingly, the "oeconomy"—understood in terms of the "correct manner of managing individuals, goods and wealth within the family . . . and of making the family fortunes prosper"—served as a model for good state government in the seventeenth century:

> To govern a state will therefore mean to apply economy, to set up an economy at the level of the entire state, which means exercising towards its inhabitants, and the wealth and behaviour of each and all, a form of surveillance and control as attentive as that of the head of a family over his household and his goods. (Foucault, 1979b, p. 10)

In effect, national security and wealth were seen as contingent upon the sovereign's ability to create relationships across disaggregated administrative domains such as trade, agriculture, manufacturing, and so on (Firth, 1998).

Accordingly, in the lecture "Security, Territory, and Population," Foucault described the emergence of "the reason of the state" under mercantilism in relation to "two ensembles of political knowledge and technology" aiming to securitize both territory and population (1997a, pp. 68–69). The first ensemble, a "diplomatico-military technology," ensured development of the forces of the state through alliances and organization of armed apparatuses (p. 69). The second ensemble, "policy [*police*]," addressed the means necessary for making the "forces of the state" increase from within by addressing the health and characteristics of the population (p. 69), thereby transferring to the state functions (e.g., provisions for the poor) that had previously been administered by local authorities including estates, guilds, charities, and ecclesiastical authorities (Dean, 1990). Foucault placed commerce and monetary circulation at the juncture of these two ensembles and connected them to the problem of population as "enrichment through commerce" enabled population expansion (1997a, p. 69).

Foucault (1980a) claimed that the concept of population as a distinct object of inquiry and administration emerged in the eighteenth century in relation to the apparatuses of police:

> The great eighteenth-century demographic upswing in Western Europe, the necessity for coordinating and integrating it into the apparatus of production and the urgency of controlling it with finer and more adequate power mechanisms caused 'population,' with its numerical variables of spaces and chronology, longevity and health, to emerge not only as a problem but as an object of surveillance, analysis, intervention, modification, etc. The project of a technology begins to be sketched: demographic estimates, the calculation of the pyramid of ages, different life expectations and levels of mortality, studies of the reciprocal relations of growth of wealth and growth of population.... (p. 171)

Police power addressed problems of order and security and was exercised through detailed regulations by authorities attempting to redress specific, concrete circumstances (Valverde, 2003). Public health and transportation were historically important problematics for police power.

Although concerns about public health and sanitation predate the liberal state and can in fact be traced at least to the Roman Empire, the eighteenth century witnessed an increasing number of books and pamphlets dedicated to the subject, targeting both state administrators and literate populations. Efforts to describe and administer the health, fecundity, and productivity of the population entailed detailed descriptions of population characteristics using statistical measures because, as Ann Firth summarized, "Population represents wealth because it provides a way of conceptualizing the problem of economic security as the interdependence of different categories of state administration" (1998, p. 24).

Methods for evaluating the strength of the state using statistical measures of the population were developed by the late seventeenth-century physician William Petty (1623–1687). Petty's "political arithmetick" of social facts about the state's strength and security were put into practice and embellished upon throughout the eighteenth century. In *Several Essays in Political Arithmetick,* Petty asserted that the "principal points" of his discourse on political arithmetick included the multiplication of populations in London and the world (1690/1755, p. 7) and "How the City of *London* may be made (morally fpeaking) invincible" (p. 8). Petty wrote that "an exact Account of the People is neceffary in this matter" (p. 8).

The development of political arithmetick roughly coincided with eighteenth-century efforts to dismantle systems allowing the poor and idle to remain outside the circuits of production (Foucault, 1980a). Tudor era reforms that had provided sustenance to the unworking poor were regarded as untenable by eighteenth-century authorities, who sought to maximize the potential of that space, population, revealed by political statistics (see Dean, 1990).

Effort to redress issues of "population-wealth" (including "taxation," "scarcity," "depopulation," "beggary") constituted the conditions of possibility for the formation of political economy as a field of inquiry that would carve out new fields of visibility (Foucault, 1997a, p. 69). Political economy would ultimately serve liberalism as a tool for the critique of state sovereignty, as explained by Foucault in "Governmentality" (1979b):

> It was through the development of the science of government that the notion of economy came to be able to focus onto a different plane of reality, which we characterize today as 'economic,' and it is through this science also that it became possible to identify problems specific to the population; but we can also say that it was thanks to the perception of the specific problems of population, related to the isolation of that area of reality that we call the economy, that the problem of government finally came to be thought, reflected and calculated outside of the juridical framework of sovereignty. (p. 16)

In this reformulation, the family became an element internal to population rather than the model for population. As the family was thought internal to population, it became possible to think of the economy as a field outside of, but related to, the population. As will be explained in Chapter 3, the delineation of the economy as a distinct field served to test, and provide the grid of intelligibility for, the principles of liberalism.

By opening up the economy as a distinct field of intervention, political statistics and political economy ultimately created a field of possibility for problematizing the state's absolute sovereignty over economic transactions. Accordingly, thinkers such as Adam Smith began to conceive of economic government outside of state sovereignty, resulting ultimately in limitations on state authority as the relationship between the state's maximization and societal wealth was severed (Ilpo, 2000). Thus, Foucault considered Smith's work as transforming the relationship between knowledge and government by affecting a "critique of state reason" emphasizing wise restraint of state authorities (Gordon, 1991, p. 15). The market played "the role of a test" for critique (Foucault, 1997c, p. 76). As Katherine Hayles explained, "Because systems were envisioned as self-regulating, they could be left to work on their own—from the Invisible Hand of Adam Smith's self-regulating market to the political philosophy of enlightened self-interest" (1999, p. 86).

Under this new regime of laissez-faire government, statistics, which under mercantilism worked for the monarchial administration, became a "major technical factor" for representing and understanding government's object—population (Foucault, 1979b, p. 16). Accordingly, the newly emerging liberal state accepted some restraints against direct action over the economy and instead sought to provide the conditions of possibility for market expansion and stability. The state also acquired new authority as it assumed further responsibility for securing societal processes over labor and social welfare, over the population, and the administration of life. As Foucault argued, "population comes to appear above all else as the ultimate end of government, that is the welfare of the population since this end consists not in the act of governing as such but in the improvement of the condition of the population, the increase of its wealth, longevity, health, etc." (Foucault, 1979b, p. 17). By assuming responsibility over the economy's supplement—civil society/population—the state (through its policies and institutions) *enabled* the seeming independence of economic transactions while also promising prosperity for the society as a whole. In the process of securitizing both the economy (indirectly) and civil society (directly), the state effectively extended its operations over everyday life, opening up new spaces for state surveillance and government but ultimately affecting (ideological and material) constraints on its formal purview of authority.

Thus, the population-wealth coupling under state mercantilism eventually engendered a conceptual dislocation of the three distinct fields of visibility: *State—Population—Market*. New forms of power, control, and ideas about societal government contributed to the division of these social spheres and were, in turn, shaped by the sphere's dislocations. For example, the liberal (self-governing) critique of the state not only helped produce the economy as a distinct field of visibility but also transformed medieval understandings of state sovereignty, which slowly ceded to legalistic-rational governmental apparatuses aimed at securing the conditions of possibility for economic self-regulation and for engineering the health of the population, birthing biopolitics.

Before moving forward, it is important to note here that Foucault did *not* suggest that sovereignty disappeared with the ascendancy of liberal government. In "Governmentality" Foucault wrote that "the problem of sovereignty was never posed with greater force than at this point" as the state sought what "juridical and institutional form, what foundation in the law could be given to the sovereignty that characterises a State" (1979b, p. 18). Moreover, the notion of a government of population also rendered discipline all the more significant: "discipline was never more important or more valorised than at the moment when it became important to manage a population" (p. 19).

Sovereignty and discipline enabled constitution of the nation-state as a (seemingly) unified political entity. In the *Lectures at the Collège de France*, Foucault (2003b) described how the society of the Middle Ages, permeated by warlike relations, was gradually "replaced by a State endowed with military institutions" (p. 267), affording the state monopoly over legitimate violence. Government of this monopoly over legitimate violence entailed that first ensemble discussed previously, the "diplomatico-military technology" that ensured development of the forces of the state through alliances and organization of armed apparatuses (p. 69). However, the state's monopoly over violence did not extinguish conflict internal to the state as armed and discursive battles raged within the emerging apparatuses of the state.

The emergence of the early modern liberal state entailed the hegemony of a universalizing and collective identity—nationalization of a racialized identity—that disciplined and unified those within its territory against external enemies. Bridging Foucault's disparate discussions of discipline, biopower, and sovereignty, Julian Reid (2006) explained that the emerging state cultivated and disciplined the life forces of its population internal to the state while engaging in interstate war to securitize the "racialized" national way of life. According to Reid (2006), "Foucault distinguishes between how power over life functions through discipline to induce peace within its boundaries by subduing the natural life of the individual body while constituting the species life of populations in exacerbation of war intersocially"; thus, "modern regimes induce peace simultaneous with war" (p. 134). The cultivation and disciplining of the nationalized state identity thereby implicates interstate war in the name of preserving life. The sovereign power over death was justified to ensure peace and preserve life for the territorially defined nation.

The integral connections across race, life, sovereignty, and interstate war are the focus of Chapter 6. For present purposes, however, discussion will focus on how the emerging nation-state simultaneously legitimized and securitized its operations internally through the cultivation, administration, and disciplining of life itself.

Foucault (1997c) argued that *biopolitics*, the science and technologies pertaining to the management of populations, grew out of the early modern state's need to legitimize and securitize. In "The Politics of Health in the Eighteenth Century," Foucault (1980a) described how the health of the population emerged as a problem of government. He stated that (a) whereas power in the Middle Ages concerned the monopoly of arms and the arbitration of lawsuits and punishments of crimes, and (b) the end of the Middle Ages founded the reason of the state and political economy, (c) "Now in the eighteenth century we find a further function emerging, that of the disposition of society as a milieu of physical well-being, health and optimum longevity" (p. 170). Foucault coined the term *biopower* to address that form of power which takes population as its object and operates primarily through the norm (biopower bridges biopolitics and anatomo-politics).

As explained above, driving this new expression of power was the need to securitize the state internally and to maximize its economic resources while, eventually, appearing to abstain from direct intervention in economic "market" government.

Foucault described the nineteenth century as a period characterized by the extension of biopower as new knowledge formations and institutional divisions supplemented and/or replaced former systems of societal control. The elaboration, extension, and institutionalization of the eighteenth century's framework of political arithmetick affected a transformation of social control characterized by the increased significance of the "action of the norm" in contrast with law (Foucault, 1990, p.144). As Foucault explained:

> Such a power has to qualify, measure, appraise, and hierarchize, rather than display itself in its murderous splendor; it does not have to draw the line that separates the enemies of the sovereign from his obedient subjects; it effects distributions around the norm. I do not mean to say that the law fades into the background or that the institutions of justice tend to disappear, but rather that the law operates more and more as a norm, and the judicial institution is increasingly incorporated into a continuum of apparatuses (medical, administrative, and so on) whose functions are for the most part regulatory. A normalizing society is the historical outcome of a technology of power centered on life. (p. 144)

Thus, the externality of the law was supplemented and replaced by the internality of norm as the judicial institution was incorporated into a variety of regulatory "apparatuses" (e.g., medical and administrative) which established and enforced new regulative norms concerning the population's health and productivity. Population emerged as "both the object and subject of these mechanisms of security" (Foucault, 2007, p. 11).

Foucault argued that although sovereign entities such as the monarch or executive authorities (in France and the United States) still retained a degree of repressive power over their populations (e.g., through laws and police power), power succumbed to a profound transformation in its operations and spatial dispersions. Power was no longer restricted to a repressive force: power now also assumed a productivity as its (biopolitical) operations aimed at securitizing the health and economic yield of the population. In achieving securitization, private and public governmental authorities not only produced and disseminated new *disciplinary spaces* (hospitals, clinics, institutions, public schools) and practices (sanitary science, hygiene, exercise) constituting everyday panopticons of surveillance and social control, but also generated *technologies of the self* premised in the idea of individuals as self-governing agents.

Over the course of the nineteenth century, premodern sovereign power was therefore supplemented, replaced, and transformed. In *Madness and Civilization* (1965) and the *Birth of the Clinic* (1994a), Foucault chronicled the shifts in knowledge and expertise and the transformations in social space that engendered extensions of governmental power and *biopolitical* control over the life forces of the population. In *Discipline and Punish* (1979a), Foucault focused on the disciplining of life forces (i.e., *anatomo-politics*) in the new disciplinary spaces (prisons, schools, factories) by new authorities (guards, teachers, factory personnel) using new technologies of power (criminal rehabilitation, pedagogies, machines). Together, biopolitics and anatomo-politics would transform social control as population emerged as a target of government, leading to the dispersion and circulation of technologies of government, what Foucault described as governmentality.

With governmentality, social control/government became less centered and more productive. The early modern state's appropriation of pastoral power and its convergence with *police* to govern population would engender new regimes of social government (through biopower) of the everyday conduct of conduct. Over time, the extension of government through biopower ultimately refigured practices of government in relation to the state by dislocating their close coupling. Accordingly, by the mid-twentieth century, pastoral power was found less in the conduct of state authorities than it was, and continues to be, exercised by bureaucratized and/or privatized experts and professionals. Foucault explained that the governmentalization of the state rendered government (in the Foucauldian sense) both internal and external to the state by creating public and private distinctions and by limiting the scope of activities viewed as within the state's competence.

The state, the "private sphere" of the population, and the economy must therefore be regarded as representational spaces and fields of action whose constitution and delineations are contingent upon the rationalities of rule specific to distinct regimes and technologies of government. Discussion so far has traced the constitutions of these fields within the classical liberal framework of government. I now turn to discuss how the birth of biopower constituted the population as an object for study and intervention, first by the state and subsequently by diverse and often privatized biopolitical authorities. I trace the rise of pastoral power to the heterogeneous pastoral apparatuses of the twentieth-century liberal welfare state.

Pastoral Power, Biopower, and the Liberal Welfare State

When tracing how the state took population as its object, Foucault not only emphasized the science of police (discussed previously) but also addressed the state's appropriation of the Christian "pastoral" ethic. I briefly trace how the Christian "pastoral" ethic and practices were appropriated by the liberal state as the ethos for biopolitical practice, ultimately engendering the welfare state.

In the premodern period, geographical and logistical constraints limited the monarchial sovereign's power, but social control was also executed through the pastoral power of the religious order, particularly as expressed in Christianity. The transformation of "pastoral" power by the institutions of the modern state played an important role in legitimizing and extending "modern" forms of social control, primarily through biopolitical means.

The purported goal of *pastoral power* in the premodern era was to "assure individual salvation" through paternalistic guidance (Foucault, 1983, p. 214). Thus, pastoral power addressed both the community and each individual, throughout the entirety of his or her life. It was exercised through tools such as the "confessional" that revealed the "insides of people's minds," "their souls": thus pastoral power implied "a knowledge of the conscience and an ability to direct it" (p. 214). Christian pastoral power emerged as "salvation oriented," "oblative," "individualizing," and "linked with a production of truth—the truth of the individual himself" (p. 214).

Prior to the eighteenth century, the sovereign exercised a degree of pastoral control through his national stewardship (Firth, 1998). As explained previously in this chapter, under mercantilism, the sovereign's capacity to coordinate and manage disaggregated administrative areas was critical to national prosperity and security. Over time, however, the state's interest in increasing its population and the productivity of its labor led to the development and application of statistical methods to calculations of mortality, life expectance, and fertility engendering the "book-keeping of the state" or "political arithmetic." In his history of public health, George Rosen (1993) described the state's early authoritarian implementation of public-health concerns designed to increase the population in terms of the concept of "medical police." Eventually, the Enlightenment influence tempered medical authoritarianism, but the rational administration of the population grew in order to ensure its growth and economic productivity.

According to Foucault, the "function" of pastoral power spread in the nineteenth and twentieth centuries as it was formally incorporated in the forms of governance and institutions associated with the modern liberal state in terms of its administration and securitization of "population." However, this incorporation by the modern state subtly transformed the old Christian ideals and practices of pastoral power. The objective of pastoral power was reoriented toward ensuring both economic securitization and individual salvation in this world, rather than the next one. Likewise, the meaning of salvation transmuted to encompass "health, well-being (that is, sufficient wealth, standard of living), security, protection against accidents," and so on (Foucault, 1983, p. 215). The officials of pastoral power came to include the populations of public institutions such as the police, schools, and welfare societies, as well as private benefactors. These officials engaged in practices of knowledge production and application that simultaneously legitimated the end of the modern state—to ensure national prosperity and social welfare—and extended its realm of application into the intimacies of everyday life decentering liberal operations of government.

Expansion of the various state institutions in the nineteenth and twentieth centuries was accompanied by new forms of knowledge—knowledge formations that aided, abetted, and legitimated the new forms of societal governance and individual government that came to constitute the modern liberal-welfare state that emerged at the turn of the twentieth century. As explained by Foucault (1983), "the multiplication of the aims and agents of pastoral power focused the development of knowledge of man around two poles: one globalizing and quantitative, concerning the population; the other, analytical, concerning the individual" (p. 215).

Biopolitics was the term Foucault used to describe the development and subsequent operations of this knowledge aimed primarily at dividing, categorizing, and acting upon populations in order to securitize the nation. In the nineteenth century, the emerging fields of medicine, psychiatry, psychology, and education all provided knowledge used to represent, divide, and govern populations according to standards of normality and pathology. Within nineteenth-century disciplinary societies, individuals were thus constituted in relation to the norms or "administrative numeration" of a "mass" (Deleuze, 1992, p. 5). But across time, the older binary standards of normality and pathology, individual and mass, would become fractured as biopolitical knowledge generated more nuanced representations of populations. Increasingly nuanced representations of populations mandated more expert authorities capable of managing proliferating categories of social deviance or concern. More experts led to the multiplication of therapeutic protocols, techniques, and strategies. Likewise, progressively refined representations of economic risk and gain engendered ever more dispersed strategies of surveillance and calculation, creating new forms of economic and biopolitical expertise.

The enclosed spaces of the late nineteenth century had served as early laboratories for the application of biopolitical expertise, supplementing the disciplines of the body—anatomo-politics—aimed at exhorting or disciplining corporeal energies. For example, schools were an important institutional space for biopolitical surveillance and instruction. Eventually, however, applications of biopolitical knowledge would extend well beyond institutional spaces as individuals were instructed in ever more hygienic and marketized technologies of the self. But across contexts, biopolitical practices and authorities sought to discipline and socialize, rendering subjects both "useful and compliant" (Rose, 1999c, p. 233).

Late nineteenth- and early twentieth-century efforts by state and private philanthropic authorities to socialize as well as discipline individuals were prompted by new articulations of liberty, freedom, and social stability, ideas developed and promulgated by new cadres of experts—experts of education, psychology, psychiatry, and medicine. By the close of the nineteenth century, the assemblages of expert knowledge about problematic and/or unruly populations, coupled with the detrimental social effects of nineteenth-century *laissez-faire* economic policies, persuaded some liberal thinkers, as well as philanthropists and other social activists, that the liberal state must take a more active role in producing the rational, autonomous agents presupposed by liberal, democratic capitalism. Thus, the state assumed and transformed for its own purposes "pastoral" power. Biopower, the science and art of managing populations in order to elicit and administer life forces coupled with an array of disciplinary practices, would become the new mode of pastoral operations.

As Plant (2004) explained in "Neo-liberalism and the Theory of the State: From *Wohlfahrtsstaat* to *Rechtsstaat*," this shift in the state's realm of responsibility was marked by a new conception of liberty, a "positive" perception wherein the state's responsibilities were expanded to include the responsibility to "enable" citizens with the means and wherewithal to maximize their individual liberty. Therefore, freedom stood as the ultimate telos of twentieth-century liberal government (Rose, 1999c). Liberal (welfare) forms of government developed around the turn of the twentieth century and later governed through freedom by *producing*—socializing/inscribing—individuals whose rational, autonomous choices resulted in a well-ordered, cohesive society. Foucault argued this telos simultaneously legitimized the state's power while expanding the scope and specificity of its execution: the modern liberal-welfare state utilized biopolitical knowledge and expert authorities to expand its power at the level of the population (harkening to the city-game) while simultaneously these forms of knowledge operated to individualize and subjectify citizens as particular kinds of subjects (the shepherd-game; see Olssen, 1999, p. 30).

Cadres of experts who populated newly emerging professions and social institutions assisted citizens' autonomous self-regulation. Any impingement on personal liberty affected by such experts was tolerated because their authority was seen as "arising out of a claim to knowledge, to neutrality and to efficacy" (Rose, 1996, p. 39). In a sense, sovereign power over life was dispersed throughout the social field as the emerging professionals articulated biopolitical standards of normality and difference and mandated particular forms of therapeutic interventions by the state and/or by biopolitical authorities (e.g., psychiatrists, psychologists, teachers, social workers, etc.). Mitchell Dean (2002b) described the dissemination of sovereignty throughout everyday life as the "delegation of sovereignty" (p. 124) in order to capture how parents, families, health experts, counselors, and other members of everyday society enact decisions about life and death, in part by rendering decisions about what constitutes normality, security, and the conditions of public order. Sovereignty was thus intimately connected to biopolitical frameworks of interpretation and techniques of the various expressions of liberal government.

Exemplifying this project of engineering freedom was the effort by civil engineers and other expert authorities to develop rational urban planning. In the late nineteenth and early twentieth century, the modernist project of "rational planning of ideal social orders" (Harvey, 1989, p. 35) was adapted to the purposes of the liberal state insofar as it undertook the planning and administration of urban centers (see Joyce, 2003). As explained by

Joyce (2003), within the liberal city, a sort of "political economy of infrastructure" was sought, setting up "the conditions of possibility in which freedom might be exercised" (p. 11). Pipes, sewers, clean and well-lit streets all aimed at enabling the liberal person freedom in movement, association, and in the opportunities to engage in self-monitoring and self-government. Although this project was incomplete in scope and application, the idea of rational urban planning aimed at maximizing liberties, efficiencies (and increasingly securities) captured the imagination of Americans in the early modern period and helped legitimize the incredible expansion of government operations throughout the twentieth century.

For Foucault, the institutional and professional cultivation of self-governing citizens throughout the twentieth century entailed new forms and technologies of power. Foucault (1988) described the emergence of "technologies of the self" that "permit individuals to effect by their own means or with the help of others a certain number of operations on their own bodies and souls . . ." (p. 18). Techniques of the self incorporated the telos of pastoral power as expressed by the liberal-welfare state but transformed the agency of operation such that individuals ultimately sought to engage actively in *their own self-cultivation*. The techniques of the self became increasingly important as the late twentieth-century liberal-welfare state governed less through coercion and control and more through, as Rose (1999c, 2007) put it, technologies of freedom and optimization. According to Rose (1999c), twentieth-century problematics of liberalism in Western industrialized nations strove to achieve a balance between governing *enough* to produce a well-regulated, seemingly autonomous society while simultaneously striving to avoid governing *too much* for fear of destroying those social phenomena that liberalism presupposes to exist. Accordingly, political authorities sought to "act at a distance" upon the desires and social practices of citizens primarily through the promulgation of biopolitical knowledge, experts, and institutions that promised individual empowerment and self-actualization (Rose, 1998, p. 73).

Within the United States and the United Kingdom, concerns about the liberal-welfare state governing "too much" were heightened by the demand-focused economic government adopted in the 1930s. In 1936, John Maynard Keynes (1883–1946) published *The General Theory of Employment, Interest, and Money* in which he argued for the primacy of demand in shaping the economy (since he believed that demand created its own supply). Given the importance of increasing demand by reducing unemployment, he proposed that some external force—such as that constituted by government action—be brought to bear upon the problem of unemployment. Favoring public-works projects that reduced unemployment, Keynes emphasized an enhanced role for the liberal state in ensuring individuals "positive freedom," seen as a mechanism for fostering economic and, ultimately, social stability. Keynesian economics articulated the problem spaces attacked by the New Deal reforms and policy initiatives.

However, the slippage between the stated goals of the twentieth-century liberal-welfare state and the material effects of its policies, institutions, and practices has preoccupied biopolitical authorities throughout the late twentieth century. Concomitantly, this slippage has been fodder for social critics of both the left and the right (who might also be regarded as biopolitical authorities). The power effects of expert knowledge and state institutions have been subject to considerable research and condemnation even while critics vary considerably in their interpretations of causality and their proposed solutions or alternatives. In particular, American economic conservatives saw the formal apparatuses of the liberal state as producing dependency and dampening the economic initiative of its citizenry. In contrast, American leftists saw the "welfare state" as preserving capitalism even while the state's repressive apparatuses disciplined populations deemed unfit for self-government.

Marxist critics of the liberal-welfare state suggest that Foucault and the governmentality scholarship understate the extent to which state and market domination supplemented liberal governmentalities. For instance, Bruce Curtis (1995, 2002) argued that Foucault did not go far enough in developing his analysis of how twentieth-century technologies of power utilized the police (in the modern sense of term) and military to augment pastoral power. In particular, Curtis (2002) claimed that while Foucault developed a triadic formula for addressing governmentality in his 1979 piece on governmentality, he ultimately failed to explore how the discipline and regulation of populations are shaped by the military-diplomatic relations existing in the systems of states.

By emphasizing how liberal technologies of the self produce self-governing individuals, some of the governmentality scholarship obscures the roles played by the sovereign state and economic institutions in disciplining unruly subjects (whether those subjects be individuals, groups, or renegade states; see Poulantzas, 1978). Dean attempted to redress this criticism by arguing that economic government and sovereignty are two (internal) dimensions of governmental rule that provide liberalism with the means for curtailing the "norm of the optimization of life" (1999, p. 100). Dean's argument is supported by a close reading of Foucault's essay "Right of Death and Power" wherein Foucault described sovereignty in relation to biopower's underside: "the power to expose a whole population to death is the underside of the power to guarantee an individual's continued existence" (Foucault, 2004, p. 80). As the underside of biopower, sovereignty has the capacity to, as Foucault put it, "disallow" life (2004, p. 80). Still, critics suggest that the binding of biopower and sovereignty may not adequately facilitate analysis of how violence, conflict, and resistance test the limits of the pastoral state and biopower's capillary capacities to regulate the life energies of populations (see Curtis, 1995), particularly when the question of sovereignty is applied to interstate relationships (see Hindess, 2005). These criticisms will be relevant in relation to neoliberal and neoconservative government and to subsequent chapters, particularly Chapter 6, which addresses biopower, sovereignty, and the state. Before developing these objections further, discussion turns to Foucault's genealogy of neoliberal government.

NEOLIBERAL ENTERPRISE AND NEOCONSERVATIVE GOVERNMENTALITIES

By the closing decades of the twentieth century, formalized and state-sponsored liberal technologies designed to produce self-governing subjects and to securitize the market were under attack for governing too much. The liberal capacity to "steer from the centre" was suspect, as was the liberal state's success in producing self-governing subjects (Rose, 2000, p. 159). Neoliberal reforms sought to disperse liberal centers of government and to empower "market" mechanisms, thereby targeting the "excesses" of liberal government. In effect, neoliberal governmentalities extend liberal strategies of government or "action at a distance" (Latour, 1987, p. 219; Miller & Rose, 1990, p. 9) by further deterritorializing the operations of power, particularly through the extension of biopower and through circulating market networks. Foucault and others expanded on how the assemblages and technologies of biopower operate on populations through geographically diffuse technologies that render populations increasingly visible in particular ways using expert knowledge and interventions while simultaneously encouraging individuals' self-regulation and "optimization" (Rose, 2007). In order to know and regulate the health of populations, biopower pursues greater knowledge about, and regulatory mechanisms over, populations, which are themselves fragmented along increasingly nuanced lines of divisibility (see Deleuze, 1992). As shall be demonstrated, the degree of surveillance implicated in neoliberal governmentalities and the progressively demanding requirements for risk reduction and social and economic success have complex effects that often increase social control while encouraging self-regulation. In contrast, neoconservative governmentalities strive to reinvigorate older forms of state sovereignty in order to remoralize the population while securitizing global circuits.

Neoliberal Government: Enterprise and Risk

The neoliberal objective of maximizing individual freedom hinges on the key role afforded market forces in regulating and enabling individual choice. Although neoliberal authorities vary in the degree to which they recognize and advocate for state protection of individual liberties, all neoliberal proponents share the belief that capitalist market freedom is the ultimate medium for the expansion and realization of individual liberty. Expert knowledge therefore seeks to identify strategies for marketizing the institutions and operations of the welfare state, while fostering individual responsibility and accountability in the conduct of everyday life.

A key figure responsible for articulating the terms within which neoliberalism would be debated was Friedrich A. Hayek (1976, 1960, 1944). In *The Road to Serfdom,* Hayek (1944) argued that western liberalism is in crisis, threatened by socialist impingements against economic and personal liberty:

> We have progressively abandoned that freedom in economic affairs without which personal and political freedom has never existed in the past. Although we had been warned by some of the greatest political thinkers of the nineteenth century, by De Tocqueville and Lord Action, that socialism means slavery, we have steadily moved in the direction of socialism. And now that we have seen a new form of slavery arise before our eyes, we have so completely forgotten the warning.... (Hayek, 1944, p. 13)

In *Economic Freedom,* Hayek (1991) elaborated on the limitations of socialism and, even Keynesian macroeconomics, in defense of his laissez-faire approach to economic freedom, which he saw as undergirding personal freedom. Although Hayek acknowledged the limitations of market logics, he viewed a decentralized marketplace as the best mechanism for distributing resources and market-related information:

> The market is the only known method of providing information enabling individuals to judge the comparative advantages of different uses of resources of which they have immediate knowledge and through whose use, whether they so intend or not, they serve the needs of distant unknown individuals. This dispersed knowledge is *essentially* dispersed and cannot possibly be gathered together and conveyed to an authority charged with the task of deliberately creating order. (Hayek, 1988, p. 77)

Hayek's absolute distrust of centralized planning would influence the direction of state reforms of market government, enhancing corporate autonomy and sovereignty at the close of the twentieth century.

Milton Friedman, another noted and contemporary neoliberal thinker, shared Hayek's optimism about the role of market capitalism in ensuring and begetting individual freedom. Indeed, Friedman began his (1962/1982) *Capitalism and Freedom* by condemning John F. Kennedy's famous "Ask not what your country can do for you—ask what you can do for your country." Friedman suggested that while the first half of the statement is overly paternalistic, the second half invokes a falsely "organismic" view of government. In contrast to these articulations of the relationship between government and citizens, Friedman argued that "the scope of government must be limited. Its major function must be to protect our freedom both from the enemies outside our gates and from our fellow-citizens: to preserve law and order, to enforce private contracts, to foster competitive markets" (p. 3).

Moreover, he argued, "government power must be dispersed," localized, and decentralized (p. 3).

Plant's (2004) distinguished twentieth-century liberal and neoliberal thought by elucidating each framework's distinct understanding of freedom. Plant explained that classical liberal thinkers such as T. H. Green and A. Toynbee understood freedom not merely as the absence of coercion, understood as "negative liberty," but also in terms of "positive freedom," understood as the "ability or capacity to do things and to make the best of oneself" (p. 25). As explained previously under the discussion of liberalism, the pastoral ethic of positive freedom shaped attitudes about the state's telos and source of legitimacy. Positive freedom implicitly mandated that the state concern itself with the allocation of resources, and so in this fashion freedom and social justice were coupled.

It is precisely this coupling of social justice and freedom the neoliberal approach rejects. According to Plant, neoliberalism rejects the idea of positive freedom, seeing freedom only in relation to negative liberty. From the neoliberal perspective, the state's role as the defender of liberty resides almost exclusively in its capacities to ensure noncoercion and impartiality in relation to individual liberty and market operations. Coercion is understood strictly in terms of intentional coercive acts. Because individuals are seen as reasoning utility maximizers, neoliberalism holds that self- and society-optimizing behaviors require only guarantees against coercion and partiality. Thus, within the neoliberal framework, individual rights are defined as "negative rights," understood only in terms of the absence of coercion: individuals possess no entitlements other than the guarantee of freedom from coercion and partiality (Plant, 2004, p. 31). Accordingly, neoliberals reject the state's role in promoting positive freedom in favor of a restrictive role for the state, limited to the protections of negative freedom.

However, the degree to which neoliberalism actually diverges from the philosophical foundations of liberalism is debatable. Following Foucault, Barbara Cruikshank (2004) suggested that neoliberal reforms merely tip the state that governs "too much" toward privatization and subjectivization (i.e., further individualized self-government) without actually producing entirely new forms of power or subjects. In effect, neoliberalism sustains liberalism's valorization of individual liberties but recasts the role of the welfare state in enabling them. Nonetheless, neoliberals' rejection of positive freedom does have important material consequence, particularly in relation to the economy/market and the state's efforts toward distributive justice.

Neoliberal refusal to endorse *distributive justice*—which aims to ensure adequate conditions of possibility for individual self-government—constitutes a marked shift away from mid-twentieth-century liberal practices of state government. Hence, the economic implications of the neoliberal view of freedom, defined negatively in relation to the absence of coercion, are that the state is absolved of responsibility for equitable distribution of society's resources. From the neoliberal perspective, distributive justice, advocated by liberals such as John Rawls (1972), is simply wrongheaded. Neoliberal thinkers argue for the primacy of the unrestrained market in distributing society's rewards. Although many neoliberals acknowledge that the market rewards according to no principle at all, the market is seen as the most impartial and efficient medium for distributing resources (Plant, 2004). Moreover, "market disciplines" are seen as both enabling and ensuring utility-maximizing behaviors by both individuals and corporate entities. Thus, the unrestrained market is seen as the most impartial and efficient medium of distribution, particularly because aggregate outcomes cannot be foreseen (Plant, 2004).

Given this emphasis on unrestrained markets, it is not surprising that neoliberal authorities reject both the aims and operations of the Keynesian economics of the welfare state. Government planning, regulation, and spending are seen as inefficient and as impinging upon unrestricted market operations, if in no other way than by limiting private enterprise's access to resources. Moreover, neoliberal authorities believe government spending on social welfare inhibits individuals' utility-maximizing behavior. Welfare and other forms of social spending hurt economic growth by creating disincentives for employment and entrepreneurialism, fostering instead dependency and inefficiency. State spending also is seen as diverting limited resources away from opportunities for economic investment and growth and toward bureaucratic inefficiencies that do not reward individual utility maximization. The market's role in producing inequality is an unfortunate, unforeseen, and unintended consequence that should not be redressed through government intervention, which would impinge both on individual and market freedoms. The market's role as impartial arbitrator, coupled with the entrepreneurial activities of utility-maximizing individuals, together define and ensure the optimal guarantee for freedom. Private philanthropy should serve as society's safety net.

When studying the evolution of neoliberal principles of government in the works of Hayek and Chicago School economists such as Friedman, Foucault and subsequent governmentality scholars argued that neoliberalism as a body of knowledge, strategies, and practices of government seeks to divest the state of paternalistic responsibility by shifting social, political, and economic "responsibility" to privatized institutions and economically rationalized "self-governing" individuals. Thomas Lemke's (2001) work illustrates how the state attempts to divest itself of "responsibility" for its citizens by recasting them as rational, self-responsible/choosing agents:

> The neoliberal forms of government feature not only direct intervention by means of empowered and specialized state apparatuses, but also characteristically develop indirect techniques for leading and controlling individuals without at the same time being responsible for them. The strategy of rendering individual subjects "responsible" (and also collectives, such as families, associations, etc.) entails shifting the

responsibility for social risks such as illness, unemployment, poverty, etc. and for life in society into the domain for which the individual is responsible and transforming it into a problem of "self-care." The key feature of the neo-liberal rationality is the congruence it endeavors to achieve between a responsible and moral individual and an economic-rational individual. (p. 201)

By stressing "self-care," the neoliberal state divulges paternalistic responsibility for its subjects but simultaneously holds its subjects responsible for self-government. As Nikolas Rose (1993) explained, the neoliberal state does not seek to "govern through 'society,' but through the regulated choices of individual citizens" (p. 285). Further: "All aspects of *social* behaviour are reconceptualized along economic lines—as calculative actions undertaken through the universal human faculty of choice," and choice is itself articulated with a rational calculus of costs and benefits (Rose, 1999c, p. 141). Within this neoliberal framework, the social and economic burden of risk shifts from employers and the state to individuals, who must assume the responsibility for rational risk management.

Thus, the neoliberal regime refigures individual "choice" within an economic context of meaning. This frame and its attendant "entrepreneurial" ethic led to the dissolution of the older, "classical" liberal distinction between the private domestic and economic spheres of life and between the state and the market. In sum, the neoliberal regime casts individuals as deliberate actors who strategically maximize their interests while the social realm in its entirety is itself recast in relation to economic rationality, including risk and calculative costs (see Massumi, 2005).

The operations of pastoral power take on new significance within neoliberal regimes of government. Although Foucault himself died too soon to elaborate much on the transformation of pastoral power within neoliberal regimes, other thinkers, including Burchell, Gordon, and Miller (1991); Cruikshank (1999); Dean (1999); Marshall (1996); Peters (2001); Smart (2003); and Rose (1999c), among others, provide compelling accounts of such transformations—including the metamorphosis of educational and fiscal regimes, the privatization of the governmental institutions of pastoral power including social welfare and risk, and the relocation of governmental "experts within a market governed by the rationalities of competition, accountability and consumer demand" (Rose, 1993, p. 285). Deleuze's (1992) work on societies of control explores the ascendancy of market regimes, characterized by corporate power and dispersed networks of surveillance and control.

Prominent market techniques associated with the neoliberal regime—budget disciplines, accountancy, and audit—point to the logic for the relocation of expertise away from the former centers of governmental authority (Rose, 1993, p. 295). These techniques distance experts from political apparatuses and invoke "marketization" as the impartial jurist of value: "In its ideal form, this imagines a 'free market' in expertise, where the relations between citizens and experts are not organized and regulated through compulsion but through acts of choice" (Rose, 1993, pp. 296–297). Cruikshank (1999) described such practices of government in terms of "technologies of citizenship" that engage individuals as free and responsible economic agents, although their agency is inextricably produced in the context of their subjection/subjectification (Foucault, 1980b).

As articulated by Dean (1999), the neoliberal subject is one "whose freedom is a condition of subjection" (p. 165). Of course, regimes of government do not fully "determine" forms of subjectivity—rather, they "elicit, promote, facilitate, foster and attribute various capacities, qualities and statuses to particular agents," and their success is measured by an individual's experiences and performances of self in relation to these regimes (p. 32). Individuals who fail to take "responsibility" for their self-government, or whose modes of comportment violate normative or modality-specific standards, are subject to various forms of guidance and discipline exercised by various "expert" authorities (see Dean, 2002a). Should rehabilitative efforts fail, punitive disciplinary reforms may be availed. Remnants of an older expression of sovereign power, now embodied in state authorities and dispersed by biopolitical actors, may be exercised to incarcerate or otherwise operate upon maladaptive individuals in the name of public order, security, and life itself. The complex operations of heterogeneous forms of power—biopower, pastoral power, and disciplinary power—are all employed to guide and discipline unruly individuals.

A wide range of governmentality scholarship suggests that neoliberal strategies for anticipating and managing the risks posed by potentially dangerous individuals diverge from those found in earlier periods (see Garland, 2001; O'Malley, 2004; Rose, 2007; Valverde & Mopas, 2004). Late-nineteenth-century authorities sought to identify and normalize dangerous individuals through case histories and diagnostics. Later, social-welfare authorities analyzed aggregate data to target dysfunction in order to normalize the entire population. In contrast to these normalizing approaches, neoliberal authorities couple widespread surveillance with "targeted government" to identify and *manage* risk (Valverde & Mopas, 2004, p. 232). Therapeutic normalization cedes in importance. Moreover, perceived threats to the welfare of the larger population are seen as justifying exceptional and often punitive interventions. In this sense, neoliberal (and neoconservative) government forgoes proactive projects of social engineering.

In a sense, neoliberal government presupposes an impossibility—the rational, self-governing neoliberal agents who always act (or learn to act) responsibly in accord with neoliberal value orientations—*and the ruptures that point to the impossibility of the neoliberal fantasy result in ever more invasive efforts to properly produce, manage, and discipline neoliberal subjects.* Expert knowledge, employed by private and governmental agents, is extended and refined to better represent and act upon recalcitrant and/or risky populations who belie the neoliberal fantasy. Moreover, forceful and disciplinary authority is called upon to manage risks. And herein lies the paradox of neoliberalism. Neoliberalism purports to govern through individual freedom, yet it employs diverse and heterogeneous forms of power to establish and preserve "a comprehensive normalization of social, economic and cultural existence"; and thus neoliberalism "attempts to govern as much through 'domination'—a word that covers a myriad of conditions—as it does through freedom" (Dean, 2002b, p. 129). Normalization, as described here, does not necessarily entail therapeutic adjustment but, rather, containment and extrication of risk. Concerns for "responsibility" and "obligation" outweigh freedom and rehabilitation (Dean, 2002b, p. 133).

Sovereignty shapes everyday life through the constitutions of law and through the policing of populations. Sovereignty is demonstrated through delineation of exceptions to the rule of law and by the capacity to deny conditions necessary for life. As Carl Schmitt argued, "Sovereign is he who decides on the exception" (1985, p. 5). Sovereignty underscores the gaps between liberalism's fantasies and the effects of its technologies of government (Agamben, 2000). When government from a distance fails, sovereignty's solution is the radical purge of those entities—people—who belie the liberal fantasy although they are constituted in relation to it (see Agamben, 2000). Public risk management legitimizes this eradication (see Rose, 2007). The widespread practice of incarcerating juvenile offenders, particularly African-Americans, in the United States illustrates this daily operation of sovereignty (Human Rights Watch, 2002). The decision for exclusion finds justification in the logics of risk management and public safety.

Sovereign power is in fact the necessary supplement of the more dispersed and invisible operations of government from afar. Sovereign power as the underbelly of biopower supplements when biopolitical knowledge and expert authorities fail to produce self-regulating agents, but such supplementation must be legitimized with recourse to life itself. And although the state is not the only agent capable of exercising sovereign power, its monopoly over the "legitimate" use of force and its willingness to enact force effectively promulgate neoliberal policies at home and abroad.

A growing body of governmentality scholarship has addressed the issue of "global government" in relation to the contradictory tendencies toward dispersion and consolidation of neoliberal government. In what follows I briefly introduce this idea before moving to situate neoconservative government.

From a Foucauldian perspective, global government entails representational practices and governing technologies aiming to visualize and shape transnational regimes of economic, cultural, environmental, and political government. The character of global government strategies is increasingly inflected by neoliberal objectives and rationalities utilizing market mechanisms to govern. New forms of risk management and sovereign authority are produced as transnational corporations and financial institutions assume the capacities to dictate the conditions of life, including the capacity to let die. Although transnational corporations and financial institutions often use instruments and technologies of government that operate from "afar," they may also rely on overt and repressive apparatuses to curtail local dissent (e.g., private "security" forces).

Strategies of global political government, according to Barry Hindess (2005), emerged in response to the formation of the nation-state system as the legitimate, global framework of systems organization. Hindess argued the European Westphalian state system imposed few constraints on "recognized states" acting against "those who inhabited territories not covered by these agreements and who were thought to possess no sovereign states of the European kinds" (p. 408). The effect was that much of the globe was subject to colonial control by the beginning of the twentieth century. Classical colonial strategies of government employed the concept of race to mobilize populations to support colonial agendas, militias, and technologies of government.

Kalpagam's (2000) "Colonial Governmentality and the 'Economy'" illustrated how the colonial system's use of representational technologies created problem spaces for colonial administration and exploitation. Specifically, discursive practices of colonial government, including technologies of measurement, accounting, and classification, essentially created the Indian "economy." Statistical representational strategies rendered the problem space of economy open to exploitation by colonial interests.

In the contemporary milieu, global economic rationalities of government are increasingly preoccupied with "risk" (Beck, 2006). Ulrich Beck's position held, "Being at risk is the way of being and ruling in the world of modernity; being at global risk is the human condition at the beginning of the twenty-first century" (2006, p. 330). For instance, efforts to regulate economic risk involve the perceived impetus to identify and respond to newly created and discovered risks, the development of frameworks for managing and regulating risk, and the increased use of risk instruments as the organizing framework for decision making (Rothstein, Huber, & Gaskell, 2006). New informatic technologies increase risk through real-time global connectivities while simultaneously striving to manage risk through automated protocols.

Although risk analysis can tend toward political or technological realism, the governmentality scholar has addressed how risk operates as a governmental rationality (see Larner & Walters, 2004; O'Malley, 2004). Neoliberal economic rationalities seek to manage and exploit risk through representational strategies and control technologies that render "global supply chains" and financial transactions visible and manageable. Simultaneously, neoliberal market reforms aiming to unlock regulatory protections domestically and abroad compound risk while shifting the costs and benefits derived from these new risks to specific firms and individuals. The growth of nongovernmental organizations and philanthropy illustrate deterritorialized neoliberal approaches to biopolitical risk management (see Ganesh, 2007). For example, the privately sponsored Grameen Project shifts risk and responsibility to individuals by encouraging entrepreneurial self-government by poor women in Bangladesh with offers of microcredit (Gangemi, 2004).

Neoliberal governmentalities' approach to risk can conflict with older social welfare rationalities employed (at times at least) by certain institutions such as the United Nations. For example, Dillon and Reid (2001) emphasized the social-welfare biopolitics of global government when explaining, "Global liberal government is substantially comprised of techniques that examine the detailed properties and dynamics of populations so that they can be better managed with respect to their many needs and life chances" (p. 41). The United Nations Human Development Report, published in 1999, illustrates a social-welfare biopolitics. This report was generated through extensive surveillance over the life and economic statistics of nation-states across the globe and provided detailed demographic and economic profiles of the economic infrastructures and biopolitical risks facing specific populations. The report encouraged particular kinds of biopolitical interventions designed to reduce risks and maximize life in poor nations. For these reasons, the report and the various development projects motivated by these objectives can be regarded as illustrating social-welfare (liberal) governmental objectives because they aim to engineer the overall health of the global population. In contrast, biopolitical projects are more properly regarded as "neoliberal" in strategy when framed in terms of "partnerships" that shift risk and responsibility to the subjects targeted for intervention (see Rose, 2000, p. 158).

Although global neoliberal government often operates "at a distance," the agents of global government, economic, governmental, and nongovernmental entities (e.g., "relief" organizations), may also exercise sovereignty by overtly and forcefully implementing policies, interventions, and technologies. The U.N., international lending organizations, and regional trade agreements such as NAFTA often stipulate conditions for participation and membership, and increasingly these conditions involve laws, codes, policies, programs, and protocols premised in neoliberal policies and programs (see Latham, 2000). Thus, sovereignty is exercised through the capacities to specify conditions of contract and to deny the sustenance of life (funds).

Melinda Cooper (2004) suggested that the dissemination of neoliberal economic principles of governmentality involves the "right to violence of deregulated capital," which overrides "the power of the decision of the state" (p. 530). The effect of the prioritization of deregulated capital is that "*The decisionism of the sovereign state is mobilized in the service of a prior economic insecurity*" (p. 530). Cooper's analysis points to the potential and capacity for violence to inhere in, or from, neoliberal principles of government from afar while also pointing to the ways whereby neoliberal government subsumes state sovereignty to neoliberal economic agendas and/or expands the privatized space of the market through, for example, enforced "free-trade" zones that operate largely outside of the state's regulatory apparatuses.

As mentioned previously, the nature and role of sovereignty and overt force under neoliberal rationalities of rule have become the center of considerable analysis and debate within the governmentality scholarship. Under neoliberalism, sovereignty is often rationalized in relation to life itself, but that rationalization does not preclude repressive force. Of relevance here is Foucault's observation that the principle defining the strategy of states is that "one has to be capable of killing in order to go on living," potentially exposing whole populations to death (2004, p. 80). The role of *force* by states (e.g., the U.S.) and other such institutions (e.g., privatized security apparatuses) and overt coercion (e.g., by the U.N., the World Bank, the IMF, and the WTO) in mandating and implementing neoliberal agendas make visible the limits of governing from a distance, inviting the use of repressive force. Thus, although global government governs in the name of security and individual welfare, it has also a "martial face" (Dillon & Reid, 2001, p. 44).

The martial face of global (neo)liberal government remains relatively untheorized within the governmentality scholarship. Neoliberalism's martial face has become increasingly visible as American neoliberal logics and programs have become entwined with "neoconservative" ones. In what follows, neoconservatism will be introduced as a reformist rationality of governance, which finds its moral guidance and governmental objectives in the Christian pastorate and America's founding mythos of Manifest Destiny.

Neoconservative and Christian Pastoral Government

Neoconservatism is primarily an American-articulated and -promulgated rationality of government, but such is American influence in the world today that its effects are global. The neoconservative rationality is an odd blend of principles and value orientations derived from classical laissez-faire economic liberalism and American conservative and libertarian thought. Importantly, neoconservative authorities reject the welfare state and reject what they perceive as dangerous liberal-inspired individualism in "private" life, while simultaneously embracing rugged individualists, particularly of the market variety (see Micklethwait & Wooldridge, 2004). In the last twenty years, neoconservative authorities have made alliances with conservative Christians, particularly with right-leaning evangelical Christians. It is therefore not surprising that neoconservative discourse is heavily inflected by a self-conscious Judeo-Christianity and its governmental operations are often unabashedly theological.

The guiding ethos of the neoconservative-Christian nexus is a sense of cultural exceptionalism and a willingness to invoke sovereign authority, guised in pastoral terms. To get a sense of the governmental implications of this pastoral sovereignty, it is instructive to turn to Foucault's genealogy of the concept. Foucault argued that outside of archaic Greek texts, the ancient West tended to lack the idea of a "pastor-sovereign, a king or judge-shepherd of the human flock" (1997a, p. 67). However, this formulation of authority was eventually articulated and promulgated through the West by the ecclesiastical pastorate of the Christian church. Foucault described the shepherd's pastoral power in the following terms:

> The shepherd's power is exercised not so much over a fixed territory as over a multitude in movement toward a goal; it has the role of providing the flock with its sustenance, watching over it on a daily basis, and ensuring its salvation; lastly, it is a matter of a power that individualizes by granting, through an essential paradox, as much value to a single one of the sheep as to the entire flock. (1997a, p. 68)

As described previously in this chapter, under the discussion of liberalism, pastoral authority was appropriated by the emerging liberal welfare state and *secularized* as a means for securitization under the amalgam of knowledge and techniques Foucault described as *police*. Biopolitical knowledge was developed and employed to assist in securitization. As instantiated by the liberal state, pastoral power tended to work from afar, although the institutions and agents of its propagation (e.g., schools, teachers, social workers) might explicate their aims directly in relation to the goal of producing the citizens of the liberal democracy (see Marshall, 1996).

In contrast, neoconservative-Christian government wishes to return to an older sense of pastoral sovereignty, one that articulates securitization not simply in secular terms and one that does not shy from using biopower's underbelly, the sovereign capacity to disallow life. Within the purview of neoconservative-Christian government, new "problems" are rendered visible and new authorities granted, new technologies developed, and new disciplines enacted as its discourses organize "epistemo-political" fields of visibility and expressivity, controlling the production of righteous meaning and action (Lemke, 2004, p. 553).[1] The emerging problem spaces address how to remoralize citizens, how to unleash market disciplines, and how to suppress localized resistance. New authorities must be created and new technologies developed to transform the state, reining in its excesses while simultaneously exercising new disciplines upon wayward elements (e.g., activist judges and secular public entities such as teacher unions). Furthermore, "willed communities" must be fostered that "nourish freedom" by enforcing personal responsibility and virtue (Gerson, 1996b, p. 11).

Although neoconservatism and neoliberalism are united by their support of classical liberal economic policy, they diverge sharply on the matter of the state's relationship to its subjects. Neoconservatives radically reject neoliberalism's secular agnosticism and express caution regarding citizens' capacities for autonomous self-regulation. Neoconservatives embrace religion and advocate for the state's sovereign role in fostering the spiritual morality of its citizens through state-supported philanthropy and through sovereign efforts to unleash market disciplines.

Irving Kristol, an important founder of neoconservatism, identified the tradition's intellectual founders as disillusioned liberals who grew up during the 1930s and 1940s (see Gerson, 1996b), although others dispute this account of the movement's roots (see Norton, 2004). According to Kristol, neoconservatives' experiences with the Great Depression and the 1960s counterculture significantly shaped their attitudes about welfare, the state, and American culture. Neoconservative attitudes about these issues serve to differentiate their position from neoliberalism, even while both schools of thought hold similar positions on the economy and market.

As explained by Kristol, neoconservatives share neoliberals' faith in the economy and the market as the ultimate mechanism for the distribution of societal information and rewards. The neoconservatives believe market capitalism is intrinsically linked to the morality of citizens since capitalism requires trust between business associates and fosters self-discipline (Wilson, 1995). However, according to Kristol, the neoconservatives' experience with the social and economic effects of the Great Depression made them *more open to state intervention* and regulation than either neoliberals or traditional conservatives. Thus, neoconservatives do *not* share traditional conservative "antistate" attitudes and steadfastly favor the cultivation of national patriotism. Moreover, although neoconservatives favor tax cuts, they are more tolerant of budget deficits than traditional conservatives and neoliberals (see Gersan, 1996a; Kristol, 2003).

However, the neoconservative readiness to accept some provisions of state planning and the welfare state discovered its limits in the expansion of welfare services characteristic of President Johnson's War on Poverty and Great Society programs. Kristol (1995) felt these programs engendered a culture of dependency and "corrupted the souls of its recipients" (p. 89). Accordingly, the neoconservatives believe that American culture has achieved a pervasive state of moral degradation, fostered by the welfare state, cultural universalism, and personal narcissism. As Kristol (2003) explained:

> The steady decline in our democratic culture, sinking to new levels of vulgarity, does unite neocons with traditional conservatives—though not with those libertarian conservatives who are conservative in economics but unmindful of the culture. The upshot is a quite unexpected alliance between neocons, who include a fair proportion of secular intellectuals, and religious traditionalists. They are united on issues concerning the quality of education, the relations of church and state, the regulation of pornography, and the like, all of which they regard as proper candidates for the government's attention.

Neoconservatives favor the use of the state to dissolve welfare-state apparatus, thereby redressing the culture of dependency through market disciplines.

In this regard, President George W. Bush's "Ownership Society" aims to rewrite the social contract between the American government and its citizens (Calmes, 2005). At issue are social security, health care, and housing, among other issues (Calmes, 2005). In the neoconservative vision, government assistance would be aimed at expanding people's choices and fostering their personal responsibility so they take "ownership" for their own welfare. In a sense, this "ownership" society is less about capital ownership—at least for the poorer classes—and more about fostering personal ownership of situation, welfare, and morality. Thus, Cruikshank (2004) distinguished between neoconservative and neoliberal logics by arguing that, unlike the latter, neoconservative logics favor a strong role for the state in "remoralizing" citizens using Judeo-Christian ethics to combat moral decline and economic malefaction (see also Brown, 2006).

Starting in the 1980s, neoconservative authorities began forging alliances with Christian social conservatives based on a common desire to remoralize citizens using Judeo-Christian values. Christian organization such as the Traditional Values Coalition, the Family Research Council, and the Christian Coalition helped politicize Christian citizens, who elected neoconservative officials during the 1990s and early 2000s. Neoconservative political authorities subsequently used state apparatuses to implement desired reforms, particularly in relation to state-supported religious philanthropy, religious education, and the regulation of sexuality. Moreover, neoconservative political actors appointed Christian conservatives to a wide range of political posts in the federal and state governments (Krugman, 2007).

Unlike nineteenth-century Christian reformers, contemporary Christian conservatives affirm wealth and private industry. Although conservative Christians often express concern over the fetishization of secular market goods and the capitalization of (biological) life, they have become avid consumers of an ever-growing segment of Christian lifestyle goods and services (e.g., Christian bookstores, clothing, music, television programming, etc). Wealth is understood in terms of God's recognition and reward. Accordingly, conservative Christian attitudes toward wealth and business can be described as a discourse of "evangelical capitalism," promoting individual responsibility and market discipline, while simultaneously working against government-sponsored programs believed to foster dependency (Nadesan, 1999a). The discourse aligns with neoliberal and neoconservative renditions of personal accountability by affirming the individual's responsibility to adapt to contemporary economic relations. Moreover, the discourse of evangelical capitalism invokes ideas of America's Manifest Destiny (discussed presently), thereby theologically inflecting expansion of America's market (see Frank, 2000).

The ideals and lifestyles of Christian conservatives circulate across the geography and cultural imagination of late-twentieth-century America. In particular, the therapeutic, moral pastoralism of evangelical Christianity appeals to Americans seeking guidance and meaning in the context of rapid social and economic change. Evangelical megachurches provide community, rules and norms, and social support for converts, as illustrated by this *New York Times Magazine* article on a 55,000-square-foot megachurch in Surprise, Arizona:

> In sprawling, decentralized exurbs like Surprise, where housing developments rarely include porches, parks, stoops or any of the other features that have historically brought neighbors together, megachurches provide a locus for community. In many places, they operate almost like surrogate governments, offering residents day care, athletic facilities, counseling, even schools. (Mahler, 2005, p. 30)

Evangelical gospels are not restricted to the enclosed spaces of megachurches but are also disseminated widely through technological means including television, live satellite feeds to local churches, and through the Internet (Salmon & Harris, 2007).

Conservative Christian attitudes profoundly permeate America's larger cultural consciousness. One recent poll found that 55 percent of Americans believe mistakenly that Christianity was deliberately written into the U.S. Constitution ("Founders," 2007). Half of the poll's respondents believed that public-school teachers should be allowed to use the Bible as a factual historical text while support for religious freedom of expression for non-Christians (particularly Muslims) declined. The appeal of Christian pastoral governmentalities extends beyond those individuals who identify as conservative or evangelical Christians as many Americans identify with Christian efforts to "strengthen" traditional patriarchal structures viewed as central to producing moral, self-regulating subjects. Accordingly, many Americans favor reinvigorating the state's role in legislating morality and favor extending surveillance over private life (particularly sexuality). Many also favor using the state to transfer many of the concrete operations of pastoral power back to "private" institutions. The church, the family, private schools, and philanthropy are elevated rhetorically in contrast to "degrading" welfare-state supports.

The theologically inflected political doctrine of Manifest Destiny offers a pastoral model of global governmentality for neoconservative and Judeo-Christian citizens who believe in America's cultural and spiritual exceptionality. The doctrine of Manifest Destiny was articulated in 1845 by a journalist but drew and elaborated upon the American governmental ethos, what Coles refers to as American "civil religion" (Coles, 2002). Manifest Destiny functioned explicitly and implicitly as a racialized narrative articulating the moral superiority of American-style liberal, democratic capitalism. Manifest Destiny traded upon the idea that the United States of America was "exceptional" among other societies and before God (Coles, 2002; Stephanson, 1995). As Stephanson (1995) described it, American nationalism was, and continues to be, understood as both "prophetic" and "universal" (p. xiii).

The early doctrine of Manifest Destiny formally articulated a prophetic mission to spread through intervention (and war) the American way of life, although subsequent articulations at times emphasized "mission by example" (Coles, 2002, p. 407). Across time, direct and indirect appeals to America's "Manifest Destiny" have served to articulate national (i.e., racial) unity against internal and external threats to the economic security and (imagined) racial (i.e., "white") purity of the state, even when political actors have been motivated by sectional interests. In effect, although the meanings attributed to Manifest Destiny have changed across time, it has served as an organizing signifier for Americans' racialized national identity and cultural exceptionality.

Within the contemporary United States, Christian conservative, neoliberal, and neoconservative foreign-policy principles, practices, and problems of government find legitimacy in appeals to racialized constructions of origins and the doctrine of Manifest Destiny. In particular, the precepts of America's Manifest Destiny blend with Straussian political precepts in neoconservative approaches to domestic and foreign policy. As Norton (2004) argued in *Leo Strauss and the Politics of American Empire,* the Straussian-influenced neoconservative policy agenda has directly shaped U.S. intervention in the Middle East, engineering its policy toward Israel, and its efforts toward regime change in Afghanistan and Iraq (see also Drury, 1999; Postel, 2003).

Students of Strauss, such as Harvey Mansfield, instructed Francis Fukuyama and William Kristol, while another student, Joseph Cropsey, taught Paul Wolfowitz and Abram Shulsky (Norton, 2004). Within the academy, within conservative think tanks, and within the political apparatuses of the second Bush administration, these neoconservative thinkers and activists have endeavored to remake America and the world according to neoconservative and neoliberal principles of government (see Chapter 6). Neoconservative governmentalities favor the use of military apparatuses to supplement market and philanthropic-based technologies of global government. In effect, neoconservatives favor reinvigorating older conceptions and practices of sovereignty.

Conservative Christians' belief in "End Times" theology, as recently narrated in the *Left Behind* novels (see Standaert, 2006), has fostered support for neoconservative policy initiatives in the Middle East and unilateral support for Israel. The series, conceived by religious activist Tim LaHaye, sold over 70 million copies over the last decade (Standaert, 2006). Its paranoid depiction of a United Nations controlled by the forces of evil contributes to conservative Christians' support for unilateral policy agendas and hostility toward secular approaches to global government. Neoconservatives have cynically appealed to Christian conservative anxieties and paranoia when peddling policy initiatives.

Christian paranoia and neoconservative imperial designs have produced significantly illiberal strategies of global government, which will be discussed in detail in Chapter 6. More relevant, for Chapters 3 through 5, is the tendency for neoconservative/Christian governmentality to reinforce and amplify the disciplinary force adopted by other liberal governmentalities toward those seen as incapable of self-government. An authoritarian and punitive ethos especially inflects turn-of-the-twentieth-century neoliberal logics and strategies of government, supplementing government from a distance. This increasingly punitive ethos echoes nineteenth-century strategies for governing the poor, the criminal, and the mad; its operations obscure the roles played by market and biopolitical forces in producing liberal distinctions between capable and incapable, responsible and irresponsible, moral and deviant, subjects.

Diffusions

What follows explores empirically the diffusion of liberal governmentalities across social fields. Chapter 3 addresses the integral relationship between economics and biopolitics within and across liberal governmentalities. Chapter 3 emphasizes how liberal market logics and technologies have produced particular biopolitical concerns; simultaneously, the chapter explicates how population has served as a site for capitalization by liberal economic interests and technologies. Chapter 3's empirical analysis foreshadows those problematics of population—health and vitality, sexuality, madness, and deviance—that served as explicit nexuses of biopolitical concerns and economic expropriation from the eighteenth century forward. Chapters 4 and 5 address these biopolitical nexuses empirically, emphasizing how liberal governmentalities distinguish among subjects based upon their health or unhealth, normality or abnormality, and optimality or riskiness. Chapter 6 explores empirically how the perceived failure of liberal governmentalities to "govern" risk and deviance from a distance have resulted in the resurgence of older, authoritarian expressions of sovereignty, which threaten to undermine liberal expressions and technologies of freedom.

3 Governing the Self-Regulating Market

Key to liberalism is the idea of the self-regulating market. Foucault's genealogy of liberalism investigated how this idea emerged in eighteenth-century laissez-faire philosophy and tactical strategies of government. Foucault traced how laissez-faire logics and tactics of government (i.e., governmentalities) carved out distinct fields of visibility—market, population, state—that came to be regarded as ontologically distinct social fields. Liberal governmentalities fostered the presumptive reality of these fields by governing the conduct of everyday conduct, shaping everyday actions and values. In effect, biopolitical expertise and technologies of the self are fundamentally entwined with liberal economic governmentalities (see Larsen, 2007).

Readers may discern echoes of Marxist political philosophy in this account of Foucault's genealogy of liberalism. However, there is an important distinction between Foucault's theory of governmentality and most Marxist accounts of economy and society. That is, whereas Marxism saw the private sphere and the state as predicated on the modes of economic production, Foucault saw the private sphere of domestic life, the state, and the operations of capital as integrally structured by shared rationalities of government. These rationalities of government changed across time, organizing fields of visibility and problem spaces specific to evolving frameworks of governmentality. Thus, contrary to Marxism's offer of an uninterrupted genealogy of capital, Foucault's governmental analysis offered a "polymorphous universe" of technologies of power, of which capital accumulation is but one (Pasquino, 1991, p. 107). Moreover, Foucault rejected dualisms between society and state, market forces and individual agency, in favor of an approach that explored how these diverse fields were constituted as such and how their operations are traversed by heterogeneous technologies of power. As explained by Lazzarato (n.d.), "political economy, as a syntagm of biopolitics, encompasses power dispositifs that amplify the whole range of relations between the forces that extend through the social body rather than, as in classical political economy and its critique, the relationship between capital and labor exclusively."

This chapter addresses the delineation and constitution of the market and its biopolitical relations to the population and state within and across distinct governmentalities including (a) state mercantilism; (b) laissez-faire or classical liberalism; (c) welfare liberalism or the welfare state; and (d) neoliberalism. This chapter demonstrates empirically and philosophically the integral connections across biopolitical strategies for governing populations and economic practices of government. Liberal market logics and technologies have historically presented biopolitical problems for state authorities and populations, including social infrastructures, labor availability and vitality, poverty, and consumer demand. Correspondingly, biopolitical concerns have shaped market logics and operations, particularly by prompting state intervention, regulation, or military action, thereby altering the trajectories of liberal governmentalities. At the turn of the twenty-first century, biopolitical concerns pertaining to the optimal vitality of the population have produced fertile spaces for market capitalization (e.g., biocapital), but, simultaneously, neoliberal market logics and operations present new biopolitical problematics, which threaten the integrity of liberal principles of government.

MARKETS, MERCANTILISM, AND LAISSEZ-FAIRE GOVERNMENT

This section explores how the market emerged as a distinct governable space as emerging mercantile powers sought to expand their wealth by encouraging trade and by raising revenues with early securities and taxation. However, although sovereign power played an important role in market expansion, it was everyday market agents who rendered the market visible and subject to calculation through development of various financial and commercial technologies.

Markets, Mercantilism, and Circulation

Karl Polanyi's (1957) genealogy of Western markets, *The Great Transformation,* documents the transformation of the European economy from a feudal to a market-based system (where markets were understood as producing networks across towns). According to Polanyi, markets "played no important part in the economic system" until the end of the Middle Ages (p. 55). In contrast, from the sixteenth century forward, (extended) markets were not only "both numerous and important" but also highly regimented as a "main concern of government" (p. 55). The idea of a self-regulating market would not occur until the eighteenth century. Even then, the apparent self-regulation of the market was indebted to enabling state policies, particularly in the government of labor and, eventually, contract.

Drawing upon Polanyi, Arturo Escobar (2005) described how pre-sixteenth-century efforts by capitalist wholesalers to integrate markets regionally met resistance from local merchants and towns seeking to protect their particular markets. Eventually, facilitated by the traditional municipal system, the emerging European states forced protectionist localities to accept the expanded market system in the fifteenth and sixteenth centuries. Sovereign consolidation of power over local municipal administrative apparatuses was therefore essential to market expansion.

Expanding markets created greater circulation of money, replacing or supplementing the barter economy (Braudel, 1981). By the fifteenth century, Europe had developed a small financial market as Florentine bankers expanded their operations (Goetzmann, 2005). The Florence-based Medici bank, founded in 1397, had become one of the most powerful institutions in Europe by the fifteenth century (Gabel & Bruner, 2003). The growth of financial institutions required new technologies for rendering finance visible, particularly after the loosening of usury restrictions in the late 1500s (Goetzmann, 2005). Profitability in lending hinged on the development of mathematical formulations capable of rendering visible value analysis.

Mercantile control over the disposition of things within territorial boundaries also increased the circulation of people. Efforts to enforce regional and national market integration involved dissolution of feudal, petty modes of localized production, resulting in the exclusion of the majority of the populace from their land. This process of divorcing the producer from the means of production, of "primitive accumulation" in the Marxist sense, facilitated market integration while ultimately generating the productive power necessary for industrialization. But this process also increased circulation of dangerous individuals, of beggars, vagrants, and thieves, leading to the "great enclosure" of the poor, mad, and delinquent during the seventeenth century in hospitals, madhouses, and workhouses (Braudel, 1981). Consequently, Foucault (2007) argued, the mercantile sovereign essentially became an "architect of disciplined space" as well as the "regulator of a milieu" by making possible and guaranteeing circulations while simultaneously creating enclosures that governed dangerous flows (p. 15).

Accordingly, Foucault (2007) argued the *logic* of government that emerged during state mercantilism aimed at "the superimposition of the state of sovereignty, the territorial state, and the commercial state" (p. 15). The *problem* of government thus concerned ensuring "maximum economic development through commerce within a rigid system of sovereignty" (p. 15). In effect, under mercantilism the seat of sovereignty was simultaneously the "central point of political and commercial circulation" (p. 15). Yet, sovereign control over the disposition of economic flows was far from complete as financial markets grew in complexity and importance, particularly through the formation of new institutional forms such as the joint-stock company.

Seventeenth and Eighteenth Centuries: Joint-Stock Companies, Trading, and Law

As argued by Hicks, "the evolution of the institutions of the Mercantile Economy" was "largely a matter of finding ways of diminishing risks"

(1969, p. 48). Expanding markets produced new investment opportunities requiring new technologies for rendering financial gains and risks visible and new contractual forms that enforced agreements among investors. Contemporary financial markets derived from these new technologies and contractual forms.

Long-distance trading, which played a vital role in producing mercantile economies, was often organized into partnerships formalized through sovereign recognition. The Company of Merchant Adventurers of London, as chartered in 1505, illustrates an early partnership granted monopoly rights by sovereign authority (Harris, 2000). The Russia Company, founded in the 1550s, was the first major English joint-stock trading company, followed closely by the Levant Company in 1581. By the seventeenth century, stock markets had developed allowing wealthy individuals to purchase and trade ownership in joint-stock companies.

The stock and bond markets were lucrative but highly speculative enterprises in the late seventeenth century and posed distinct problems for pricing (Davies, 1952). Although bond sales by municipalities and states can be traced to the thirteenth century (Pezzolo, 2005), the origin of modern stock exchanges specializing in creating secondary markets in corporate securities is attributed to the formation of the United Netherlands Chartered East India Company (VOC) in 1602, founded for the purposes of war finance (Neal, 2005). Unlike the competing British East India Company also founded in 1602, the VOC allowed anyone to purchase stock in the trading at the open-air Amsterdam Bourse; however, the initial share price of 3,000 gilders was a substantial sum (Stringham, 2003).

Although incorporation required state approval, early trading of stock often operated extralegally. For example, after 1610, contracts involving uncovered trading in joint-stock companies were not enforceable in the government courts of Amsterdam. Additionally, the government passed a series of ordinances designed to diminish and regulate market speculation. Despite efforts at regulation, by 1688, active trading of VOC shares was pursued by specialized brokers, dealers, and speculators (Neal, 2005). It appears the VOC also financed expansion by issuing debt on its credit. A "forward market" for actual transfer of stock title had developed by the eighteenth century (p. 173). Merchants began to purchase VOC shares as collateral for loans, and the lenders of VOC stock may have purchased options (Gelderblom & Jonker, 2005).

By 1695, there were approximately 100 joint-stock companies in England alone with organized share trading occurring in London (Poitras, 1996). The complexities of investments and hedging begot new forms of expertise as skilled financiers who specialized in stock investment emerged. The British eventually emulated many Dutch innovations within the Bank of England, the British East India Company, and the South Sea Company; ultimately creating the most successful long-term capital market in the early 1700s (Neal, 2005). Many seventeenth-century observers saw sovereign restraint (i.e., "economic freedom") and peace as enhancing capital accumulation while diminishing speculative risks. In contrast, seventeenth-century state governments continued to view the emerging stock market suspiciously and were at times inclined to limit speculation, particularly futures trading (Stringham, 2003).

Still, mercantile authorities were not above state financial speculation, particularly in times of war, and increasingly targeted the population for capitalization during the sixteenth and seventeenth centuries with annuities including "fixed income securities . . . annuities with sinking funds, life annuities, lottery bonds and tontines" (Poitras, 1996, p. 8). Age-contingent annuities were created after the development of political statistics in the second half of the seventeenth century. In 1671, Jan De Witt published *Value of Life Annuities in Proportion to Redeemable Annuities*, providing comparative valuation of life annuities using the concept of present discount value for specific income streams (Poterba, 2005). De Witt looked at the life annuitants registered at The Hague in conjunction with an analysis of the mortality statistics of life annuitants from the Amsterdam register for 1586–1590 (Poitras 1996). In 1672, Amsterdam began offering age-contingent pricing of annuities, but this practice became more widespread after Edmond Halley published "An Estimate of the Degrees of Mortality of Mankind . . ." in 1694 (Poitras, 1996, p. 18), leading private investors to seek out and contract with long-lived individuals (Poterba, 2005). However, life-contingent annuities were complicated by the need to ascertain proof of survival in order to receive annual payment (Poitras, 1996). This requirement increased the need to document life and death and thereby contributed to the statistics available for those who took population as an object of study and intervention.

Statistics emerged as the preeminent tool for representing and valuing new forms of capitalization and risk deriving from novel business relationships and market transactions. Seventeenth-century political statistics created more refined representations of the characteristics and valuations of populations in order to link them to measures of national wealth. Simultaneously, financial statistics rendered risk "calculable" and "collective" through probability tables establishing the regularity of specific events and the "calculus of probabilities applied to that statistic," yielding probability of that class of event occurring (Ewald, 1991, pp. 201–202). As observed by Ian Hacking (1990), development of probability generally, and statistics specifically, eventually transformed societal understandings of chance by "taming chance," thereby undermining deterministic views of causality while still affording a sense of order and regularity about the world.

As the opportunities for accumulating wealth through risky undertakings grew in importance, so also did the importance of debt, both in material practices and in the popular imagination (Leyshon & Thrift, 1997). Speculative, unregulated investment opportunities made the fear of debt more relevant, even to the wealthier classes. For example, crazed late-seventeenth- and early-eighteenth-century investment ultimately resulted in the ruinous South Sea bubble of 1720, which originated from market manipulation of South Sea Company stock (Poitras, 1996). New conceptions of personal liability produced new rules, or contracts, for formalizing relationships among individuals.

The expansion of financial opportunities and risks for individual investors led to formal agreements among brokers designed to enforce contracts. For example, in response to a stock crash in 1792, the Buttonwood Agreement was signed among New York securities traders on Wall Street (Sylla, 2005). Although the specifics of the Buttonwood Agreement are debated, the agreement illustrates early extralegal efforts to formalize rules for securities trading. In 1817, in order to formalize rules for settlement, a group of brokers met to constitute a "Board or Association of Brokers" and adopted the name of the New York Stock and Exchange Board (p. 309). In effect, increasingly complex financial transactions coupled with the specter of personal liability required new types of social relationships formalized through agreed-upon rules. These agreed-upon rules governed many types of business transactions until statute law was expanded in English-speaking nations during the nineteenth century.

The establishment of national banks created more secure investment opportunities for risk-averse investors while extending mercantile state sovereignty over monetary circulation. The Bank of England was founded in 1694, effecting a transformation in state finance that would be followed by other nations (Leyshon & Thrift, 1997). Alexander Hamilton (1755–1804), the first treasury secretary of the newly founded United States, created a plan for the Bank of the United States, whose initial public offering of bank stock occurred on July 4, 1791 (Sylla, 2005). Hamilton's treasury minted currency backed in gold and silver, making it convertible among the other major world currencies of the time. More than thirty European investment trusts emerged across the 1780s and 1790s aimed with the single objective of speculating on the future credit of the United States (Rouwenhorst, 2005, p. 262).

In sum, expanded markets led to new forms of capitalization, finance, and partnership. Population was constituted as a space for capitalization through annuities. Finance emerged as a space of visibility requiring precise mathematic representation. Business transactions among individuals were formalized through explicit designations of sovereign authority, thereby helping to constitute new forms of market-defined relationships. The sheer increase in wealth and economic opportunities for certain sectors of the population guaranteed state mercantile control would meet resistance. Indeed, the political philosophy of liberalism illustrates a formalized critique of the state's power to police market transactions using the idea of personal property as a strategy for critiquing state sovereignty. The next section explores how the individuals' control over, or lack thereof, property and wealth would dictate their status of governmental subjects in laissez-faire political economy.

Laissez-Faire Government: A Philosophy of Wealth and Poverty

From Foucault's perspective, liberalism birthed the idea of the autonomous market as a critique of state sovereignty. Foucault (1997c) remarked in "The Birth of Biopolitics" that the "market as a reality and political economy as a theory played an important role in the liberal critique," although "liberalism is neither the consequence nor the development of these" (p. 76). For Foucault, the market played "the role of a 'test'" for excessive governmentality (p. 76). He observed that the market's relevance as test stemmed from the "basic incompatibility between the optimal development of its economic process and a maximization of governmental procedures" (p. 76). Thus, the liberal critique of excessive government settled on the market freeing "reflection on economic practices from the hegemony of the 'reason of the state'" (p. 76).

By focusing on the market, the liberal philosophers hoped to dislocate the mercantile formulation of the sovereign as the seat of power *and* economic administration, freeing the circulation of goods and control from the sovereign reins of power. Accordingly, seventeenth-century merchants and financiers heeded the call of individuals such as Sir Dudley North, who advocated "Peace, Industry and Freedom that bring Trade and Wealth and nothing else" (cited in Davies, 1952, p. 284). These aspirations would be fully articulated in eighteenth-century political economy, which articulated rights within a semantic context of individual ownership. The emerging philosophy of liberalism critiqued sovereign authority over market transactions but, simultaneously, called upon the state to securitize those transactions through legal and transportation infrastructures. The state was also called upon to police the poor, to govern those who were viewed as ungovernable or as requiring government (Dean, 1990; Driver, 1993).

John Locke (1623–1704) helped delineate the market as a distinct social sphere by articulating a natural right to property outside of sovereign interference. Locke's *Second Treatise of Government* (1689/1982) contended the natural state of mankind was equality: "Men living together according to reason without a common superior on earth, with authority to judge between them, is properly *the state of nature*" (p. 12). Society emerged, from Locke's perspective, to avoid the state of war. But the right to property precedes society; property implicates self-ownership—"every man has a *property* in his own *person*"—and property is entailed in each man's ownership of his "*labour*" (p. 18). Moreover, property includes ownership over objects drawn from the commons by labour: "the *labour* that was mine, removing them out of that common state they were in, hath *fixed* my *property* in them" (p. 19). Thus, property precedes (sovereign) government, and from this principle Locke concluded the state lacks grounds for absolute authority over the disposition of its subjects' estates, although it holds responsibility for the protection of property, for making laws, and for the "defence of the commonwealth from foreign injury" (p. 2). In effect, Locke articulated rights in relation to a conception of property predicated upon self-ownership.

This model of rights based in property had obvious appeal for merchants and propertied classes seeking to limit sovereign authority over their economic holdings and transactions. According to John Maynard Keynes (1926), the language of laissez-faire was first articulated by the Marquis d'Argenson in about 1751: "The Marquis was the first man to wax passionate on the economic advantages of governments leaving trade alone. To govern better, he said, one must govern less." Keynes pointed out that the political and economic appeal of laissez-faire was enhanced by the tendency for late-seventeenth- and early-eighteenth-century authorities to align public advantage to private interests: "The individualism of the political philosophers pointed to laissez-faire. The divine or scientific harmony (as the case might be) between private interest and public advantage pointed to laissez-faire" (Keynes, 1926).

Adam Smith's (1723–1790) "invisible hand" spiritualized the divine harmony between private (economic) interest and public advantage, aligning population and market within a common logic of government. In *The Wealth of Nations,* first published in 1776, Smith rejected sovereign control and intervention over the economy in favor of the "invisible hand." For Smith, the "invisible hand" was implied from the apparent truth that individuals' intentionally self-interested labor effectively promotes the "public interest": "By pursuing his own interest he frequently promotes that of the society more effectually than when he really intends to promote it" (p. 572). Thus, Smith argued against state-directed mercantilism in favor of a mostly unregulated free market guided by the "invisible hand" of supply and demand and individual self-interest, thereby rejecting the model of oeconomy.

Government, from Adam Smith's perspective, ought to enforce contracts, maintain state security in relation to competitor nations, and provide public goods such as roads. Government should be funded in taxes. Government should restrain from policies that could adversely impact market mechanisms. Specifically, government should not impact the availability of free labor by enabling idleness. Smith held that the degree of "industry or idleness" found within a country is contingent upon the proportion of funds "destined for the maintenance of industry" as opposed to "the maintenance of idleness" (1976, p. 428). Accordingly, Smith, among others, felt sovereign authority should be deflected away from constraints on the ownership and transactions of property toward regulation of those lacking property. The poor thus emerged as the proper objects of sovereign government.

Reading early liberal theory, Giovanna Procacci (1991) observed that poverty, as the "counterpart to abundance," appears as the "backcloth against which the discourse on wealth is developed" in the work of early political economists (p. 154). Poverty operates as a "theoretico-practical support for the prospect of increasing abundance," signifying a "market without limits" (p. 154). Poverty is the human "reservoir" whose energies fuel the market expansion (p. 154). Early political economy held the government of poverty should not extend beyond protecting the labor market, unburdening the taxpayer, and making wage labor the generalizable means of subsistence.

But poverty also posed specters that threatened the fantasy of indefinite market expansion. As embodied in Thomas Malthus's (1766–1834) destitute Irish peasant, poverty's extreme—pauperism—pointed to the crisis of underconsumption and the possibility of subversion by subjects who refused transformation into pliable workers/consumers (Procacci, 1991). Pauperism thus required a more extensive kind of government, justified and understood within a moral economy, represented with statistics, managed through rules of hygiene in the workplace and homes, and controlled through childhood education as a "vehicle for socialization" (p. 166). Thus, the poor were transformed into a problem space requiring new calculi of representation and new strategies of administration.

Accordingly, during the mercantile period (roughly 1700s–1800s), concerns about the poor, particularly the idle poor, prompted surveillance and finer distinction among populations. Foucault described the creation of a "finer grid of observation of the population and the distinctions which this observation aims to draw between the different categories of unfortunates to which charity confusedly addresses itself" (1980a, p. 169). Within this finer grid, the pauper gave way to "a whole series of functional discriminations" and, thus, "a complete utilitarian decomposition of poverty is marked out and the specific problem of the sickness of the poor begins to figure in the relationship of the imperatives of labour to the needs of production" (p. 169).

Hence, the poor were targeted for increased economic efficiency within a moral vocabulary vilifying their indolence. Concerns extended even to classes of poor formerly understood as deserving of public charity. A treatise published in 1737, titled "A new scheme for reducing the laws relating to the poor into one act of Parliament, and for the better providing the impotent poor with necessaries, The Industrious with Work and for the Correction of Idle Poor," urged "there is hardly an Perfon fo impotent, but fomething may be produced from his Labour towards his Support. This will depend upon the good Government of the Workhoufes" (p. A4). Likewise, in the early 1800s, the Society for Bettering the Condition and Increasing the Comforts of the Poor offered a treatise describing the desirability of gainful employment in "straw-platting" for "young persons of eight years of age, the infirm, the aged, the cripple, and the blind" (p. 6). Elimination of indolence required reforms in the government of workhouses.

In 1796, Jeremy Bentham (1748–1832) published *Management of the Poor: A Plan, Containing the Principle and Construction of Establishment, in Which Persons of Any Description are to be Kept Under Inspection*, which outlined his "panopticon" inspection house (p. 1). His plan addressed populations associated with penitentiary houses, prisons, houses of industry, work-houses, poor houses, manufactures, mad-houses, and hospitals. Bentham proposed a "panopticon" design for workhouses within which the poor, criminal, and insane would reside; leading to "Morals reformed—health preferved-induftry invigorated—inftruction diffufed—public burthens lightened—Economy feated as it were upon a rock—the Gordian knot of the Poor-Laws not cut but untied—all by a fimple idea in Architecture!" (Bentham, 1796, p. 1).

In Dorothy Porter's (1999) view, Bentham viewed industry houses not simply as a solution for destitution but also as a "'social experiment' in the scientific management of communal life, regimentation of labour and provision of economy security—a miniature society organized for the production of wealth and the improvement of living standards" (p. 60). Industry, security, and happiness were articulated as contiguous in the liberal imagination.

In *Discipline and Punish,* Foucault (1979a) observed the importance of Bentham's morally inflected panopticon stemmed from the new form of surveillance and discipline it helped engender, an "intense, continuous supervision" (p. 174). Surveillance over the poor, the insane, children, and all manner of persons became, as Foucault put it, "a decisive economic operator both as an internal part of the production machinery and as a specific mechanism in the disciplinary power" necessary for producing a well-ordered, docile population across the nineteenth and twentieth centuries. Although the surveillance-disciplinary apparatus would eventually transverse the limits of the formal institution to circulate across society—as Foucault (1990) made clear in *The History of Sexuality*—the poor and the young were its most ubiquitous targets.

Felix Driver's *Power and Pauperism* analyzed targeted government of poor populations focusing on how the British state policed the "free-market" in human labor using the 1834 Poor Law (1993, p. 20). The Poor Law was designed to foster the "independence" of free labor by eliminating relief through forcing labor into the market. Moreover, the law substituted the language of rights associated with the old Poor Law for the language of contract. The language of contract inscribed the laissez-faire moral ideology of "individual self-exertion, the sanctity of private property and the vices of political centralization" (p. 20). This ideology obscured the de facto increase in state power and centralized administration during the Victorian period. The relationship between Poor Law reforms and the centralization of state power should not be underestimated: As Edwin Chadwick wrote in 1864, the Poor Law should be considered as "a measure of police, and of extended penal administration" (p. 494).

Although labor regulations differed in the United States, the rights of property and obligations of servitude were carefully delineated and preserved in the United States from the colonial era onward (Tomlins, 2004). Indentured servants and slaves, or "unfree labor," played an important economic role in early colonial America, leading to local laws that delineated status between free and unfree labor and controlled mobility and conditions of service

(p. 149). By the early years of the nineteenth century, most white Americans were free of indentured status but their legally recognized freedoms were constricted throughout the nineteenth century in response to their employers' expanding legal rights to "exert the magisterial power of management, discipline and control over others" (p. 150). Developments in nineteenth-century law restricted and restrained the "freedom" of employees by replacing more local delimited approaches to the relationship between master and servant with more universalizing laws that emphasized the rights of property holders and employers. Legally delimited relationships between employers and employees would become more important with growing industrialization.

As illustrated by Poor Laws and the refinement of contract governing employees, laissez-faire government found its limits in the government of the poor. The expanding apparatuses of the administrate state provided the labor and legal and transportation infrastructures necessary for market expansion across the nineteenth century, as can be demonstrated through the case of the United States.

NINETEENTH-CENTURY MARKETS: CORPORATIZATION AND COLONIALISM

The early-nineteenth-century state sought to expand market operations through legal and financial enablement, primarily by granting charters for industrial and transportation activities. Over time, however, the state would take a more active role in creating legal, banking, and military infrastructures that reduced the risks associated with investment and finance domestically and abroad. Ironically, the economic/legal entity that emerged from these efforts—the "corporation"—would ultimately contest state sovereignty, particularly when the state acted in the biopower mode to cultivate the health of the population.

By the early twentieth century, the corporation would assume sovereign authority over market operations, fulfilling to an unprecedented degree the governmental dream of controlling the disposition of things. Thus, in a sense, corporations replaced the sovereign as seats of economic governance. But unlike sovereign administration, corporate governance was decentered, fragmented, conflicted, and circulatory. Corporate control over the disposition of things derived as much from new technologies of government involving expansion of the monetary economy, contractual wage-labor, and development of identities defined by consumption as it derived from sovereign control over the internal space of the workplace.

Still, emergence of new "corporate" expressions of sovereign authority would not entail the erasure of state sovereignty. In the late nineteenth century, the state would extend its governmental operations to protect markets abroad more diligently and systematically using military apparatuses. Colonial undertakings required new administrative technologies for representing and governing foreign populations. Finally, as will be developed in further detail in Chapter 5, market-driven colonial expansion also required symbolic systems that represented colonizer and colonized within racialized narratives of origins.

The following discussion traces how economic government was fundamentally transformed in the late nineteenth century by the legal-economic constitution of the new governmental agent, the corporation, using the American corporation as exemplar. Discussion then addresses how states established and protected markets abroad, emphasizing the use of repressive (military) and disciplining (gold standard) apparatuses.

A Genealogy of the American Corporation

In the United States, early-nineteenth-century industrialization was often supported by states seeking to increase their economic bases by offering credit and subsidies to entrepreneurs and firms (Hilt, 2006). But charters of industrial incorporation offered by states in the early nineteenth century were typically quite regulated by state authority, and the charters tended to stipulate government institutions, including the types of products the corporation could produce. The "moneyed incorporations" of banking and insurance companies were more tightly legislated, and early bank charters often restricted the interest rates that could be charged on loans. Most of these corporations had relatively few employees and directors were often involved in the day-to-day supervision of the firms.

Despite the growth of privately held business and incorporation across the early nineteenth century, most Americans were involved in agriculture and most corporations were chartered by state governments for the purposes of transportation, including the creation of canals and, beginning in the 1830s, railroads. Railroads served as the prototype upon which the privatized American corporation was modeled (Chandler, 1965) as well as playing an important role in expanding the American capital market and stock exchange (Pontecorvo, 1958). Although chartered by state governments, railroads were initially heavily subsidized by local towns to stimulate economic activity (Roy, 1997). Railroad privatization during the second half of the nineteenth century derived from a series of historical contingencies involving political mobilizations rather than any inevitable outcome of economic expediency. Once privatized, the railroads operated as powerful sovereign agents that helped mobilize political opinion against government intervention in the "private economy," thereby obscuring the critical role state and local governments had played in the industry's formation and development (Roy 1997, p. 93). As explained by Roy, the railroads played an active role in the very constitution of the categories of public and private in the American imagination.

During the first half of the nineteenth century, railroad securities were akin to other publicly marketed securities used for government finance

(Roy, 1997). But from the 1850s onward, railroads became increasingly dependent upon investment banks to issue new securities, and many of these investment institutions were affiliated with, or branches of, European centers. Consequently, the railroad industry's economic dynamics were predicated on the "dynamics of finance capitalism" including

> profiting from speculation, a short-run autonomy from dependence on revenue when new securities could be sold, but a long-run instability leading to periodic depressions, and finally the easy merger and building of large economic empires through the manipulation of financial instruments. (p. 100)

Until the 1890s, railroad profits derived as much from construction and mergers as from operations.

Although the railroads were among the first to privatize as incorporated corporations, a number of other private companies grew in tandem with the railroads, including steel and finance. Andrew Carnegie moved from employment by the Pennsylvania Railroad to the steel industry, founding the J. Edgar Thomson Steel Works in about 1872–1873. Carnegie's company used innovative production (Bessemer steelmaking) and administrative procedures, enabling significant economic efficiencies. To reduce uncertainties related to supplies, Carnegie purchased the coke fields and iron-ore deposits providing his raw resources, a pattern of vertical integration that would characterize American industrial ownership for decades. In 1889, Carnegie consolidated his holdings in the limited partnership, Carnegie Steel. In 1901, Carnegie sold his steel company to J. P. Morgan's newly formed U.S. Steel Corporation for $250 million (DeLong, n.d.).

As illustrated by the case of Carnegie Steel, during the closing two decades of the nineteenth century, the emerging corporate form countered economic uncertainty with consolidations of ownership. Late-nineteenth-century legal innovations facilitated incorporation, lessened liability, and disadvantaged labor activism against unrestrained corporate sovereignty. Although the state would retain sovereign power over corporations through laws of incorporation and licensing (Valverde, 2003), economic interests often dictated their constitution and enforcement.

Many of the legal innovations that would create the framework for twentieth-century corporate capitalism were legislated in England before being adopted in the United States. Joint-stock companies were easily incorporated in England following the Joint-Stock Companies Act of 1844, although investors held unlimited liability until the Limited Liability Act of 1855. The 1896 legal case *Salomon v. Salomon & Co.* in Britain by the House of Lords formalized the idea of the corporation as an independent legal entity, a construct that had been articulated in the 1862 Companies Act (Ireland, Grigg-Spall, & Kelly, 1987). Together, these rulings replaced the previous view of an incorporated company as "people merged into one body" with the view of a corporation as a depersonalized, reified entity (p. 150).

In the United States. the federal government left the chartering and control of corporations up to the states, excepting the incorporation of national banks, until 1887, when the Interstate Commerce Act was passed, which gave the federal government control of interstate railroad rates (Dodd, 1936). Most states within the United States. offered limited liability by 1860. The state-expanded freedoms from liabilities encouraged incorporation across the closing decades of the nineteenth century. In 1890, under precedents established by the states of New Jersey and Delaware, laws that limited controls on mergers and acquisitions were loosened (Bakan, 2004). Moreover, laws limiting corporations from owning stock in other corporations were abolished. However, this loosening of government controls was accompanied by new federal measures aimed at ensuring a "free market."

In particular, the Sherman Anti-Trust Act passed in 1890 resulted in greater federal discretion over corporations, trusts, and the various forms of business partnerships. The act was passed in order to preserve "free-market" competition (Dodd, 1936). However, the Sherman Anti-Trust Act reorganized ownership, leading to market consolidation, which occurred due to the federal prohibition of industry pools (Roy, 1997). Midsized companies had used the pools to control competition and stabilize prices. With the passage of the Anti-Trust Act, midsized companies were forced to merge or face unrelenting competitive pressures. Thus, passage of the act had the ironic effect of substituting one set of market controls for another by "imposing its [state's] own definition of what was 'natural'" market behavior "onto the economy"—for example, contracts between producers and retailers were deemed natural while contracts among producers were viewed as "unnatural" (p. 184).

By prodding midsized and entrepreneurial industry into a new "corporate" order through the combination of capital holdings easily sold as parcels, the Sherman Act and other legislation not only provided investment opportunities and stabilized competition but also created an order within which the modern corporation would operate in accord with the "dynamics of investment capital at least as much as technical rationality" (Roy, 1997, p. 250). Investment capital became more important as industry sought capital to finance market consolidations, thereby enhancing their government of market competition.

Late-nineteenth-century federal statutes contributed to the evolution of the corporate form. Thus, by the close of the nineteenth century,

> large-scale business enterprise in every major commercial jurisdiction had come to be organized in the corporate form, and the core functional features of that form were essentially identical across these jurisdictions. Those features, which continue to characterize the

corporate form today, are: (1) full legal personality, including well-defined authority to bind the firm to contracts and to bond those contracts with assets that are the property of the firm, as distinct from the firm's owners; (2) limited liability for owners and managers; (3) shared ownership by investors of capital; (4) delegated management under a board structure; and (5) transferable shares. (Hansmann & Kraakman, 2000–2001, p. 440)

Although individual entrepreneurs and partnerships continued to play a role in the economy, late-nineteenth-century corporation laws transformed the market to such an extent that by 1900 approximately 60 percent of American manufactured products were produced by corporations (Dodd, 1936).

By 1912, six industries accounted for half of all manufacturing capital listed in the 1905 *Manual of Statistics,* and U.S. Steel accounted for "a third of all common stock, followed by tobacco, railroad cars, leather, chemicals, and foundry and machine shop products" (Roy, 1997, p. 24). Roy observed that this industrial consolidation arose from two important factors. First, financial capital turned to manufacturing after investors turned away from their nineteenth-century investments in railroad securities. Second, late-nineteenth-century large-scale incorporation prompted by antitrust efforts created an economy bifurcated between "big" and "small" businesses.

Just as corporations sought to extend government over the market, so also did they seek to control the internal space of the workplace using new forms of bureaucratic and technical government. Newly codified principles of management offered by early gurus such as Henry Fayol (1841–1925), coupled with Frederick Taylor's (1856–1915) "scientific" engineering, rendered the internal space of the corporation visible, calculable, and manageable. Additionally, by the early twentieth century, consumers emerged as a market space requiring investigation and the development of strategies of control.

Public perceptions about the emergence and power of the corporate entities in the late nineteenth century may have been influenced by the Darwinian idea of natural selection. Market competition among corporations could be understood akin to the "natural" processes of species selection and adaptation, obscuring the role of the state in shaping the conditions and expressions of industry operations. For instance, industry pools were viewed as impinging against market evolution. Furthermore, Darwinian ideas about natural selection could be used to explain and justify rigidifying class structures in a time when ascribed social hierarchies were increasingly denaturalized by the liberal, Enlightenment ethos of self-government. Finally, social Darwinism also conveniently legitimized imperialist undertakings, even when such undertakings rather blatantly contradicted laissez-faire economic principles by using state apparatuses to create "protected markets."

Governing "Protected" Markets

As Polanyi (1957) observed, throughout the nineteenth century, the powerful Western countries exercised "an unrelenting pressure to spread the fabric of market economy and market society elsewhere," a universalizing governmental/economic imperative which existed uneasily with nineteenth-century national monetary sovereignty based on the gold standard (p. 253). The state, through charters and financing, and later military support, would provide the conditions of possibility for "laissez-faire" market expansion.

The British had embraced "free trade" in 1846 with the repeal of the Corn Laws and, throughout much of the nineteenth century, imported more than they exported. Demands for inexpensive imported food, cotton, rubber, and oil eventually legitimized the need for state-protected "sheltered markets" (Palmer & Colton, 1984, p. 612). Cheap imports, coupled with shipping and insurance services (e.g., Lloyds of London), enabled England to maintain a favorable "balance of payments" within a neomercantilist calculus of value (p. 595).

Most foreign investment up until 1870 was passive or "portfolio" investment, whereupon the investor financed a foreign operation through stock or securities but had little or no direct control over the operation (Gabel & Bruner, 2003, p. 25). However, between 1870 and 1914, when much of the world was drawn into the international economy, foreign direct investment expanded to include more active control over "resource-seeking" colonial investments (e.g., minerals and agricultural products) in developing countries and "market-seeking investments" (e.g., manufacturing, banking, and transportation) in industrial countries (Gabel & Bruner, 2003, p. 25). In many cases, the state assumed military responsibility for securing and/or protecting these investments. As both Uday Mehta (1999) and Jennifer Pitts (2005) document, colonial empires captured the late-nineteenth-century liberal imagination and governed late-nineteenth-century market and diplomatic-military objectives and strategies.

By 1914, the British, French, and Germans had an approximate total of $35 billion in foreign investment, which often reaped higher rates of return than domestic ones (Gabel & Bruner, 2003). This imbalance of returns led to concern about the need for more state government of internal, domestic economics. For example, John A. Hobson's *Imperialism: A Study* (1905/1972) concluded British imperialism demanded huge outlays of public resources to secure colonial possessions, but benefited only sectional interests because such outlays did not, in fact, result in industrial development within England, nor did they lead to expanded export trade. Concerns such as those expressed by Hobson would eventually lead imperial states to erect protections against economic competitors (other colonial nations) while still enabling imports from state-supported "protected markets" abroad.

U.S. colonial expansion followed a different path from many of its European counterparts because it was primarily (albeit not exclusively) limited to the Americas and the Caribbean until after World War II. The 1823 Monroe Doctrine had been designed to protect the Americas from further European colonialism but was used subsequently in relation to the doctrine of Manifest Destiny as grounds for U.S. colonial expansion across the North American continent and, with the 1904 Roosevelt Corollary, Latin America. During his presidency, Theodore Roosevelt also declared that the Monroe Doctrine might dictate the United States "to the exercise of an international police force" in order to safeguard economic investments in Latin America because of the doctrine's prohibition against European interference (cited in Palmer & Colton, 1984, p. 619). U.S. foreign direct investment in Latin America was both government funded, as illustrated by the Panama Canal, which opened in 1914, and privately funded, as illustrated by United Fruit in Central America. The United States' colonial interests eventually expanded to include the Philippines and interests in China.

Late-nineteenth-century Americans viewed imperialist policy in the Philippines, Hawaii, Cuba, Guam, Puerto Rico, and Mexico as spreading "free trade" and "economic integration" (Crinson, 1996, p. 2). Laissez-faire economic ideologies were bolstered by a discourse of "civilization" and "progress" used in political rhetoric and consumer advertising (Domosh, 2004). Coupled with Darwinian-inspired ideas about social evolution promoted by the emerging biopolitical authorities of anthropology and sociology, the civilizing discourse of market colonization vindicated and extended American Manifest Destiny.

By the late nineteenth century, the globalizing economy predicated largely on colonization required technologies of integration and risk management. The "gold standard" served both functions by providing a universal standard of exchange while disciplining inflationary processes domestically (Leyshon & Thrift, 1997). Gilles Deleuze argued that "minted money that locks gold in as numerical standard" iconically illustrated defining characteristics of the late-nineteenth-century disciplinary society (1992, p. 5).

Gold Standard Market Government

Britain had decoupled currency from its fixed metallic standard at the close of the eighteenth century but returned to the gold standard in 1821, a move followed by most of the Western European powers (Leyshon & Thrift, 1997). The gold standard meant economic disciplining would be achieved by what Leyshon and Thrift described as a *"fractioning logic, which imposed the discipline of money directly upon those economic agents involved in the overextension of production and credit"* (1997, p. 64). The gold standard privileged the interests of lenders and financers over industry as it combated inflationary pressures.

Centralization of authority for producing notes backed in gold contributed to the development of neo-state-mercantilism (Leyshon & Thrift, 1997). The Bank Act of 1844 gave the Bank of England regulatory authority over the British financial system by enabling it exclusive power to issue notes, which had to be backed in gold. This move not only helped consolidate a degree of state power over finance but also produced a new kind of money described by Keynes as "state credit money" (cited in Leyshon & Thrift, p. 19). These developments contributed to the growing self-awareness of nation-states as "reflexive, competitive entities in their own right" by the close of the nineteenth century (Leyshon & Thrift, p. 66).

The gold standard thus encouraged states to consider themselves as distinct sovereign entities outside of the old monarchial view of sovereignty. The gold standard also served to delineate the boundaries of the modern-state system because, as Polanyi (1957) explained, "The realm of fixed foreign exchanges was coincident with civilization" (p. 252) since "only countries which possessed a monetary system controlled by central banks were reckoned sovereign states" (p. 253). Those outside the purview of the gold standard could be colonized or incorporated as a protected market by a sovereign state.

However, the disciplinary effects of the gold standard and colonial imports contributed to uneven domestic economic development within sovereign states. Accordingly, in their analysis of the spatial geography of money, Leyshon and Thrift (1997) argued the development of the modern nation-state as a reflexive economic entity existed in tension with the restrictive and disciplining power of the internationally recognized gold standard. By the close of the nineteenth century, growing domestic economic instability encouraged states to implement controls over domestic market transactions. As Britain, Germany, and the United States each sought to protect their markets from foreign encroachments, a new form of nationally regulated capitalism involving protectionist barriers to trade and capital began to emerge. State-erected protections created a "regulative boundary between an internal, domestic market enclosed within the borders of the state, and an external, international market which existed beyond these territorial boundaries" (p. 67). This type of regulated capitalism would become more important during the first half of the twentieth century but would dissipate with the floating exchanges and circulatory networks of late-twentieth-century markets.

Leyshon and Thrift identified a second important development that occurred at the close of the nineteenth century involving "disjuncture in the basis of economic competition" as the United States and Germany encroached upon markets controlled by the British (p. 67). Whereas the British had controlled markets through "capital widening," the United States and Germany tended to compete on the basis of comparative advantage. In particular, the United States' comparative advantages stemmed from innovations in labor production by Taylor and Ford and administrative changes wrought by Sloan at General Motors. The increased economic competition among states, coupled with the desire to create protected markets and access to oil in the Middle East, would eventually culminate in World War I, signaling closure of nineteenth-century problematics and strategies of economic government. These problematics are rehearsed before moving forward to the development of the twentieth-century liberal welfare state.

Nineteenth-Century Problematics of Government

In the contemporary imagination, nineteenth-century liberalism lacked government intervention. The state, it is believed, lacked regulative control. But as explored previously, the contemporary imagination misunderstands the nineteenth-century laissez-faire ethos in Britain and the United States. In both contexts, the state assumed more responsibility for providing the conditions of possibility for market autonomy by shaping and controlling the technologies of incorporation. The state also played a vital role in ensuring the availability and fitness of labor power through intervention in the problem space of population. The state's interest in population would lead to interventions in the areas of public health and hygiene, education, and in articulating the conditions of possibility for market operations, including legislating rules regarding labor contract. At a philosophical level, state interventions in the arena of population were designed to stabilize society by securing expectations and disciplining unruly forces and agents, particularly in relation to labor availability. At a material level, the state's investments in the infrastructures necessary for market autonomy would ultimately contribute to formation of a new form of sovereign entity, the modern corporation. The corporation would in turn produce and disseminate technologies of the self adopted by the population in the pursuit of happiness and self-government.

The foundations for the idea that government should securitize expectations had been foreshadowed in Jeremy Bentham's *Principles of Civil Code*, first published in 1843. Bentham held that government securitizes rights and property through law but in so doing creates obligations and responsibilities. Although Bentham's thoughts emphasized individual obligation and duty, they also mandated the role of government in the constitution and securitization of rights designed to afford the greatest level of happiness to the greatest number of people, as articulated in his 1776 *Fragment on Government*. Government regulation of market operations and the formalization of contract laws previously unenforceable under common law illustrate state efforts to securitize expectations.

Nineteenth-century social critics and reformers sought to expand the role of government and private institutions in securitizing expectations for both rich and poor while disciplining the unruly and wasteful: society's wastrels and degenerates. Social observers grappled with the dilemmas posed by conflicting nineteenth-century necessities and values: How to maximize the happiness of the greatest number while protecting the freedom of the individual, of property, and of the market? How to expand markets and reduce market risks while maintaining a laissez-faire approach to economic government? The nineteenth-century imagination produced a seemingly contradictory tableau characterized by individual self-interest and self-regulated markets framed against the backdrop of an organic societal totality, the racialized nation-state, demanding oversight and government.

As will be explained further in Chapter 4, the territorially defined nineteenth-century colonial nation-state was imagined in racialized terms. Britain, for example, was not merely a sovereign state; it was also understood as populated by a national race, the health and well-being of which required hygienic cultivation, particularly in the second half of the nineteenth century. Consequently, as Pat O'Malley (2004) argued, the "social" was constituted as an organic, collective entity characterized as the source of individual obligations and rights and also as entity, a space of visibility, subject to sociological, anthropological, and economic analysis (p. 29).

Herbert Spencer's (1820–1903) *Social Statics: or, the Conditions essential to Human Happiness specified, and the first of them developed* (first published in 1850) and *The Man versus The State* aptly illustrated how laissez-faire economic and political principles were conjoined with a view of society as an "organic" entity (Spencer, 2003, p. 32). Spencer believed society entailed evolutionary processes requiring individual adaptation. He held that modern democratic society required a particular kind of adaptation based on the molding of character and habit because the "greatest happiness is obtained only when conformity" to government and culture are "spontaneous" (p. 35). Accordingly, he wrote:

> The social state is a necessity. The conditions to greatest happiness under that state are fixed. Our characters are the only things not fixed. They, then, must be moulded into fitness for the conditions. And all moral teaching and discipline must have for its object to hasten this process. (p. 35)

Spencer argued this molding and discipline should aim at, and be developed, as much as possible through the exercise of "self-government" (p. 86). Self-government, Spencer argued, was absolutely essential for democracy because, as he put it, "Conduct has to be ruled either from without or from within" and the "chief faculty of self-rule being the moral sense" (p. 106). From this Spencer concluded, "the degree of freedom in their institutions which any given people can bear, will be proportionate to the diffusion of this moral sense among them" (p. 106).

Spencer felt many among the poor lacked self-government and that the Poor Laws had, for generations, cultivated "habits of improvidence" (p. 314). Spencer suggested "much" of the poor's suffering was in fact "curative, and prevention of it is prevention of a remedy" (p. 314). Spencer railed against the idea that the state should assume responsibility for alleviating this kind of suffering. Spencer's view of the curative properties of the poor's misery no doubt echoed the Malthusianism formulation that overpopulation was checked only by war, famine, pestilence, or self-engendered reproductive control. The state, from Spencer's perspective, served its function by giving "formal sanctions and better definitions" of men's rights, namely the right of property that he believed (against Bentham) predates government itself (p. 393).

The ethos of self-government articulated by Spencer, among others, fostered disciplinary regimes aimed at instilling self-control in the home, in the emerging institutions of the public school, in the prisons, and in the workhouses. Particularly, surveillance and discipline operated together in the nineteenth-century colonial plantations, domestic factories, workhouses, and schools to produce docile bodies from whose labor capital could be accumulated. Such docile bodies were regarded as having cultivated the ideals of self-government proper for their stations.

It is of course a simplification to regard labor as necessarily docile or to represent nineteenth-century laborers as succumbing to Spencer's ideology. Yet, the ideals of self-government promulgated across nineteenth-century cultural apparatuses, coupled with nineteenth-century surveillance and disciplinary institutions, enabled labor's adjustment to the new kind of sovereign authority that emerged in force during the nineteenth century, the corporation.

The late-nineteenth/early-twentieth-century corporation's embodiment of sovereign authority was markedly distinct from monarchial sovereignty or even the secular pastorate of the emerging state apparatuses of public health (see Chapter 4). In the United States, the emerging corporation sought to exercise government over the market through consolidation and vertical integration, often entailing colonialism as illustrated by Henry Ford's "Fordlandia" rubber plantations. Within its enclosed spaces, corporations implemented new disciplinary regimes, extorting the energies of docile bodies with technological and bureaucratic disciplines. Overt "sovereign" expressions of punishment were less visible as the practices and technologies of self-government (self-discipline), surveillance, and institutional disciplines were dispersed across society, although late-nineteenth- and early-twentieth-century corporations occasionally used brute force upon the bodies of recalcitrant workers. On the whole, power increasingly became mundane and anonymous. Moreover, the social operations of power were obscured by laissez-faire ideals, including the principles of self-ownership, self-discipline, and contractual labor. Laissez-faire ideals implied that the rational actor of economic theory who willingly entered contracts in a free market to exchange labor for money was also the rational citizen of the liberal state; therefore, the citizen deserved recognition of the rights implied from the Lockean idea of self-ownership. This ideology promoted transformation of paupers into self-reliant, "independent labourers" through Poor Law reforms (see Dean, 1990, p. 14). Later, the evolving knowledge and disciplines of "scientific management" inspired by Taylor in the United States produced an "anatomo-politics" of the human body, rendering more aspects of the labor process visible, calculable, and subject to expert intervention and bodily elicitations.

The institutional surveillance and disciplines exercised over contracted workers in enclosed spaces were reconciled, in the popular imagination, with the ideals of democratic personhood. Mitchell Dean (1990) suggested the solution to the dilemmas posed by liberal imperatives of freedom on the one hand, and greater social control by market forces on the other, lay in a particular constitution of the private sphere. The private sphere emerged as a separate sphere in response to "a multitude of state and other governmental interventions which loosely cohere around the objective of the promotion of a specific *form of life*" (p. 13). The private sphere was constituted in terms of economic responsibilities, particularly so for "the social agent, the male breadwinner" who bridged the disparate "private" arenas of the home and the workplace (p. 13). Marxist critics have often cited the contradictions between the liberal philosophy and capitalist practices of the period, but, in contrast, Dean suggested that "the problem must be repositioned not so much as a contradiction between theory and practice but as the complex and subtle confrontations between a universalistic, ethical discourse of rights and the particularistic, practical logics of government" (p. 13).

The "private sphere" also operated to address societal risks posed by nineteenth-century urban conditions and economic exploitation. Jacques Donzelot's (1979) *Policing of Families* explains how a philanthropic complex aimed at disseminating desired social norms of conduct across the social body emerged in the nineteenth century. As Donzelot argued, the philanthropic complex, which entailed privatized "assistance" directed at the family, facilitated social government without challenging the laissez-faire economic order. Philanthropic efforts revolved around three "poles": (a) the "assistance pole"; (b) the "medical-hygienist pole"; and (c) the "tutelary complex" (Donzelot, 1979, pp. 55–56, 96). The "assistance pole" directed welfare assistance through the private sphere, thereby preserving the liberal bifurcation of the public and private spheres. In contrast, the "medical-hygienist" pole sought to address the problems incurred by the industrialization of society, thereby functioning to sustain the resources required for industry, which was itself tied to state security. The tutelary complex would address the socialization of youthful paupers both at risk to and from society. These three poles converged in their focus on the family: "Hygienist philanthropy evaded a political challenge to the economic order by transforming it into a challenge to family authority by way of the norm" (p. 73). The philanthropic complex helped secure society from dangers posed by extreme poverty while preserving the seeming separation of public and private spheres.

Corporate-sponsored welfare programs had long participated in this philanthropic complex (Brandes, 1976). By the mid-1800s, companies such as the Waltham Watch Company were expending considerable funds for employee housing while other companies contributed to civic infrastructures including streets, sewage systems, and church schools. As Stuart Brandes explained, in the United States, the "gospel" of corporate welfarism was promoted by Christian reformers, private social-service leagues, industrial societies, and American universities, among others.

But turn-of-the-twentieth-century reformers were not always satisfied with the scope of the emerging apparatuses of corporate welfare. Some private charitable organizations pressed for more direct state intervention to preserve society from the dangers of population and, even, from predatory corporations. In the United States, the late-nineteenth-century social progressives, in particular, felt public authorities ought to take a more active role in fostering individual self-government; one important avenue involved addressing the adverse economic conditions that fostered social degeneracy. Contributing to this perspective was the "Gospel of the Germs," which will be outlined in Chapter 4 (Tomes, 1998), which linked all of humanity in relation to the contagion of transmissible disease. Poverty, criminal degeneracy, and other expressions of social malaise increasingly came to be viewed within Progressive politics and philosophy as societal risks requiring governmental interference to securitize society, the economy, and the nation-state. The growth and professionalization of the positivistic social sciences around the turn of the twentieth century provided the cadres of experts need to create new ways of representing the social body in terms of its norms and deviations.

These biopolitical authorities at times worked directly for corporations but were also at times willing to critique market practices and corporate government when they were perceived as threatening public health or employees' capacities for self-sufficiency. The collapse of widespread corporate welfare during the 1930s would create opportunities for biopolitical authorities to agitate for state-sponsored welfare reforms.

Although the apparatuses of the welfare state altered the strategies and practices of corporate welfare, corporations would develop new strategies for cultivating populations with the rise of consumer culture. Moreover, the marketplace of goods that developed during the early decades of the twentieth century provided a new social context for the articulation and expression of liberal rights of personhood in manners consistent with corporate interests. The social ideal of the citizen as consumer offered a semiprivatized sphere for autonomous choice while also ameliorating the economic perils of overproduction. The enhanced productive capacities of the emerging large corporations, organized bureaucratically and in accord with the principles of scientific management, demanded increased consumption. The citizen-consumer neatly resolved the seeming contradictions between (a) personal autonomy and (b) the economic and political sovereignty of industrial barons and their disciplinary spaces (see Ewen, 1990). Workers' mobilization by the liberal discourses of consumption is revealed by their demands for a "living wage" commensurate with their needs as citizen, breadwinner, and consumer (Glickman, 1999). Advocates promoted "consumption unapologetically, not as a site of embourgeoisement but as a locus of political power" (p. 6).

The consumer psyche would emerge in the early twentieth century as a new space to be investigated by biopolitical authorities employed by corporations, engendering still new forms of surveillance and technologies of visualization and government. The technologies of the self that would emerge as the intersection of advertising appeals and consumer self-government would transform personhood across the twentieth century.

But the new form of sovereign authority that emerged, the modern corporation, also engendered considerable risks to economic and social stability. The next section illustrates these risks and the new strategies of state government that arose in response, forging a nexus of corporate and state government described as the welfare state.

GOVERNING ECONOMIC RISK: FROM LAISSEZ-FAIRE TO THE WELFARE STATE

The transition to the twentieth century was marked by conflict in Western liberal-market democracies as market uncertainties, risks, and crises were regarded by many as destabilizing of society and the market (O'Malley, 2004). Western liberal capitalist nation-states increasingly sought means beyond the gold standard to reduce the risks associated with global markets and resistant (labor) populations. Also, new government issues arose within modernizing corporations as ownership increasingly was severed from management. By the mid-1930s, effective measures for protecting investors were sought, entailing new legislative government by the state (Dodd, 1936). By the 1940s, new international government institutions were created to temper the risks associated with international trade and finance.

New government structures were also required to address the new liabilities stemming from the consolidation of economic activity within large corporate forms. Labor unrest and outright resistance forced state action, eventually undermining the principles of individualized "free-market" labor contracts with the legislation of collective bargaining rights. Further, the population's demonstrated capacity for volatility encouraged market and state investment in knowledge formations and practical technologies aimed at pacification and the development of more pastoral corporate government, as illustrated through the human relations movement in management and through private and public foundations such as the Rockefeller Foundation (Lemov, 2005). In the home and in schools, moral training and self-discipline strategies bolstered workplace strategies and reforms.

The End of Laissez-Faire and the Welfare State

World War I marked the end of the hegemony of laissez-faire ideology within Western industrial nations. In the war's early days, the British, French, and Russian governments had agreed to pool financial in addition to military resources (Hudson, 2003). Within domestic economies, government interference in trade and economic planning was widespread with industrial rationalization as the primary goal (Chambers et al., 1983). Unionism in the United States was stifled by calls to patriotic duty (Marchand, 1998), and existing and emerging media forms (e.g., motion pictures) were employed to foster patriotic compliance with industrial rationalization. Increasingly, the biological and psychological health of the nation was linked to national security and economic market prosperity in a tight nexus of closely coupled relationships.

World War I offered new opportunities for close alignments between sectional economic interests and national policy in the form of war profiteering. World War I was funded in part by U.S. private investors, who financed arms purchases. Upon entry into the war, the U.S. Congress voted to use government funds to pay for arms loans to the allied powers (Hudson, 2003). The war was quite profitable for many American investors and industries, expanding the strength of the nation within a neomercantile calculus of value (Crossen, 2005). For instance, DuPont, then the nation's largest munitions maker, sought a guaranteed profit of $1 million from U.S. government contracts. However, by the early 1930s, American munitions makers were accused of being "merchants of death" in response to a Senate Munitions Inquiry that found "the arms makers and bankers had grown rich while the fighting men suffered" (cited in Crossen, p. B1). Proposed legislation limiting wartime profits eventually lost momentum. Wartime profiteering soon wound down but would resume during World War II, forming the foundations of the postwar military-industrial complex.

The 1920s industrial expansion and development of consumer culture were threatened with overproduction crises and the stock-market crash of 1929, resulting in risks to and from the population. The technological and labor innovations wrought by scientific management and Ford's assembly line had not delivered a population prosperous enough to consume the vast array of newly produced goods. Business expansion financed on credit declined. Agricultural goods harvested in Europe, the United States, and the colonies were underconsumed to the extent that in 1930 a bushel of wheat sold for the lowest price in 400 years (in terms of gold; Palmer & Colton, 1984). By 1932 the world's industrial production had dropped to two-thirds of what it had been in 1929, and unemployment reached more than 13 million in the United States and 3 million in Great Britain (Chambers et al., 1983). State efforts to control currency values by rejecting the gold standard destabilized currency exchange and trade, exacerbating contraction (Palmer & Colton, 1984). The world economy disintegrated into highly competitive national economic systems.

By the 1930s, the economic depression and its attendant threats to state security had reconstituted the domestic market as a space to be regulated and controlled, particularly in relation to the operations of private financial institutions and securities sales. In the United States, President Franklin D. Roosevelt's New Deal reforms brought the space of the economy under greater federal control while retaining privatized ownership and protecting private property (namely finances and securities). On March 4, 1933, the federal government enacted legislation allowing it to become the principal regulator of all banks within the Federal Reserve System (Dodd, 1936). Legislation also disallowed all banks of deposit from selling securities. The Glass-Steagall Act of 1933 created the Federal Deposit Insurance Corporation and kept banks out of the stock market. A Federal Communications Commission was established in 1934, providing the federal government regulatory power over telephone and telegraph companies. The Securities Act of 1933 required issuers of securities to "file with a federal commission and make available for investors an amount of information about the issuer and the security to be issued which far exceeds in volume and completeness of detail anything required by state law" (p. 54). Compliance failure could result in prohibition against future sales, civil liability of issuers and directors, and criminal penalties. The Securities Exchange Act of 1934 extended these provisions to interstate security markets and formed the Securities and Exchange Commission. In 1938, the exchange announced a fifteen-point program aimed at improving protections for investors.

Yet, these extensive efforts at market government by the federal government affected corporate sovereignty in only limited ways, primarily by regulating financial and securities transactions. In 1936, Dodd completed his review of statutory business corporation law by observing that even under the New Deal Congress, the federal government was reluctant to supersede the states as the primary sources of corporate law and that the states were reluctant to regulate corporate governance:

> As matters now stand, the states are largely engaged in bidding against one another for the favor of the promoters of corporate enterprises and concern themselves only to a limited extent with the practical consequences to the investor of an economic system under which the average stockholder is a mere passive contributor to an enterprise controlled by potentially self-seeking groups vested with almost unlimited powers. (p. 57)

Dodd observed the federal government was "wholly without responsibility for the general character of our corporate mechanism" and was instead "seeking to regulate corporate publicity, corporate accounting, proxy solicitation, managerial profits from stock trading, and control of reorganizations by 'protective' committees" (p. 58).

Perhaps the primary area where corporate sovereignty *was* constrained concerned the contractual obligations between the corporation and its employees. Due to industrial labor militancy, labor reforms were also enacted by New Deal legislation, including the Wagner Act, which afforded manufacturing unions in the North guaranteed rights to collective bargaining. These labor reforms were mandated by popular unrest and the growing realization that market autonomy could only be preserved by the introduction of some constraints on corporate sovereignty over workers, as the very existence of the domestic free market was viewed as at risk by worker resistance.

Efforts by sovereign states such as the United States to exert government over domestic economic activities eventually prompted efforts, in the aftermath of World War II, to enact global economic government institutions aimed at reducing the crises and risks associated with "unregulated" capitalism in order to preserve the "free-market" economy. In particular, the philosophy of John Maynard Keynes (1883–1946) outlined a governmental approach to securitizing national economies and pointed to strategies for reducing the risks of global markets.

Keynes's economic ethos, which emphasized aggregate demand for goods, informed a new approach to international economic governance. This was formalized in July 1944 at the Bretton Woods Conference, otherwise known as the United Nations Monetary and Financial Conference. Participants seeking to create a globalized system for governing economic risk for the "developed" Western nations created the International Bank for Reconstruction and Development (i.e., the World Bank) and the International Monetary Fund (i.e., IMF). Although Keynes had argued for development of a new international currency, the U.S. dollar emerged as the world's reserve currency (Gokay, 2005). The dollar was not fully convertible to gold because this convertibility was limited only to foreign governments (Gokay, 2005). The dollar became the preeminent technology for stabilizing global currency exchange and trade.

Bretton Woods participants also hoped to guarantee open international markets through prohibition of trade blocks and protected economic spheres of influence. The leading Western industrial nations were tasked with governing the system and were required to lower barriers to trade and the movement of capital. Creation of an International Trade Organization was proposed but was never ratified by the U.S. Senate. However, the General Agreement on Tariffs and Trade, signed in 1948, created 45,000 tariff concessions, influencing over $10 billion in trade, or approximately 20 percent of the existing global market ("GATT," n.d.). GATT was designed to ensure states could use trade to address balance-of-payment deficits (Leyshon & Thrift, 1997).

Additionally, to guarantee the viability of liberal democratic capitalism in Western Europe, the United States adopted the Marshall Plan in 1948.

The Marshall Plan strategized state security through engineering economic stability, in part through engineering aggregate demand. Military "security" for the new space of the international market was guaranteed through the creation of the North Atlantic Treaty Organization (NATO) in 1949. The United Nations, founded in 1945, replaced the League of Nations (1919).

The United States' national government and market dominated the post–World War II landscape. During the war, the United States had demanded gold as repayment for its supplies to the allies, and, by the end of the war, the U.S. held 80 percent of the world's gold (Gokay, 2005). It also controlled 40 percent of the world's production (Gokay, 2005).

The post–World War II Cold War between the United States and the Soviet Union facilitated political and economic intervention in a developing world that had after World War II tried to free itself from the "sheltered markets" of Western colonialism. In the 1950s, anticolonization movements in the developing world had led to nationalization of commodity firms such as rubber and bauxite, followed in the 1970s by nationalization of oil concessions in Saudi Arabia, Kuwait, and Venezuela (Yergin & Stanislaw, 1998), leading eventually to formation of the OPEC oil cartel. Authorities of developing countries challenged Western liberal ideals and operations of free-market government in the name of developing world autonomy and pan-nationalism. But resistance and independence efforts posed by the developing world were undermined by internal conflicts and Cold War covert political interference. The Non-Aligned Movement, coined by Indian Prime Minister Nehru in a speech in 1954, and the 1964 formation of the Group of 77 developing nations under U.N. auspices, faced significant challenges posed by the political economy of finance and by U.S. and Soviet machinations.

In particular, international finance would serve as a primary technology whereby the international "market" and transnational corporate authorities would acquire control over the internal space of developing nations' economies. As will be discussed presently, the authorities capable of engineering the shift in governmental ethos and capital ownership were neoliberal and neoconservative economists, financiers, and speculators. To explain how neoliberal authorities assumed control over international finance, it is necessary to explore the rise and fall of finance and Fordist production in the mid-twentieth-century U.S. welfare-security state.

Finance, Fordism, and the Welfare State

In the post–World War II context, the Bretton Woods system was designed to stabilize international finance by linking the U.S. dollar to gold. Other nations' currency could be converted to dollars. Thus, the tightly coupled U.S. economy and government exerted global power in part through monetary technologies as the world's currency reserve. But, as explained next, this arrangement changed in response to a number of structural contradictions.

In the 1950s, American corporations and financial institutions began to invest in Europe and abroad to avoid domestic regulations and taxes on repatriated earnings as well as to take advantage of the opportunities for economic growth in the postwar period (see Brenner, 2006; Sassen, 1991). These moves extended the post–World War II space for foreign direct investment by American corporations and American banks soon followed. Profits earned by U.S. corporate and financial investments in Europe and abroad were largely retained in banks residing in Europe, creating "Eurodollars." Eurodollars were then invested in U.S. treasury bonds, U.S. corporate stock, and in loans to developing nations (Engdahl, 1993; Sassen, 1991). Eurodollars were also loaned to U.S. banks, providing a source of low-interest loans that helped fuel U.S. domestic expansion in the post–World War II era (Leyshon & Thrift, 1997).

Accordingly, post–World War II American economic expansion was largely financed by inexpensive oil and low interest rate loans from the Eurodollar market. The Fordist accumulation regime made possible by these phenomena, coupled with the lack of competition to U.S. industry, was characterized by "intensive accumulation" of capital with "monopolistic regulation" of the economy by large corporations (Amin, 1994, p. 9). Underpinning the technologies of Fordism were electromechanical technologies based primarily on (cheap) oil and petrochemicals. Fordism entailed the proletarianization of work; standardization, intensification, and mechanization of production; scale economies; oligopolistic competition; protected national markets; vertical integration; coordination of the institutions of banking, industry, and the state; mass consumption; and rising rates of capital concentration (Amin, 1994; Harvey, 1989).

The Fordist economic regime in the United States was coupled with the development of social programs aimed at securitizing the population through full employment, education, and welfare. Alessandro de Giorgi (2006) summarized how the nineteenth-century model of disciplinary control reached its zenith under Fordism:

> It is particularly in the first half of the twentieth century that the project of a perfect articulation between the discipline of the body and the regulation of whole populations came to completion, embodied as it was in the economic regime of the factory, in the social model of the *welfare state* and in the penal paradigm of the 'correctional' prison. (p. x)

The anatomo-politics of the factory conjoined with the normalizing discourses and practices offered by biopolitical (social-welfare) and consumer authorities conjointly articulated while the "correctional" prison promised reform through the inculcation of bodily and psychic disciplines.

Social security ("police") apparatuses in the U.S. welfare state included military-security complexes enabled by cheap credit (Leyshon & Thrift, 1997). Cold-war defense spending contributed to the production of a military-industrial complex that fueled domestic economic growth and shaped techno-scientific innovation, significantly shaping developments in the U.S. economy.

In 1949, President Truman's national security staff called for major increases in defense spending, believing these would invigorate the economy by stimulating industry while redressing unemployment (Wehrle, 2003). Military-industrial expenditures constituted more than 50 percent of total U.S. government expenditures across the second half of the twentieth century (Boies, 1994). Both "hard" and social sciences conducted in universities and "private" foundations were extensively funded by military and intelligence sources, producing a "science-security complex" as the state sought to outgun and outpsychologize the Soviet Union, North Korea, and China (Moreno, 2006, p. 22).

Labor unions saw the military-industrial buildup as creating opportunities for equitable economic growth and, with the onset of the Korean War, leveraged war mobilization to address depressed areas and industries (Wehrle, 2003). Again, after the Soviets launched Sputnik, labor worked in concert with the defense industry to promote spending. In *City of Quartz,* Mike Davis (1992) described the rise of Los Angeles in relation to the military-industrial complex, illustrating how military-Keynesianism contributed to the urban geography and political economy of America's West Coast cities. Domestic military-Keynesianism was gradually supplemented with military spending abroad: By 1969, military aid and "security assistance" constituted 52 percent of U.S. foreign aid (Hudson, 2003, p. 221). American arms manufacturers also sold weapons abroad, making the United States the biggest international arms dealer (Boal, Clark, Matthews, & Watts, 2005). The military-industrial complex thus helped delineate and produce the liberal welfare state in America.

But the post–World War II economy was not characterized by indefinite expansion (see Brenner, 2007). Recessions occurred intermittently across the last half of the twentieth century. The reasons are complex, but many observers point to lack of corporate investment in the U.S. industrial infrastructure, including industries such as auto manufacturing and steel production. American capital was growing accustomed to higher rates of return on foreign investments (in the 1950s and 1960s) and on financial speculation (by the mid-1970s), resulting in less investment in manufacturing (K. Phillips, 2006). Moreover, the American domestic economy was increasingly understood and calculated in relation to mass consumption by the population (see Aitken, 2006), which was mediated by plastic credit (Marron, 2007), eventually leading to high rates of household indebtedness and bankruptcy and low levels of savings. Sustained efforts by economic conservatives (even within the "Democratic" party) to undermine labor power also undermined any growth in real household wages of the working class by the early 1970s (Brenner, 2007).

In the 1970s, the U.S. government responded to domestic recession with increased government spending on the military-industrial complex. During this period, the United States produced more dollars, rather than raising taxes, to meet spending needs for the Vietnam War and Johnson's War on Poverty. Domestic "Keynesian" defense and social spending produced inflation and triggered demands by foreign investors for U.S. dollars to be converted to gold. In August 1971 the U.S. Federal Reserve decoupled the link between gold and the dollar in response to its inability to meet the demands of foreign banks to convert dollar reserves into gold (Gokay, 2005). The dollar then "floated" in the international currency market, lacking backing other than U.S. government credit (p. 44).

Petrodollars helped bolster the U.S. dollar in the early 1970s as the U.S. government persuaded Saudi Arabia to accept only dollars for oil (Gokay, 2005). OPEC subsequently accepted this agreement as well. The U.S. dollar thus acted as the global reserve currency for the oil trade, thereby ensuring high demand for the dollar. The accumulation of U.S. dollars by petro-producers was directed into U.S. Treasury bonds and bills, the funds from which the United States used to address its international deficits. Petrodollars were also loaned to developing nations. In conjunction with the International Monetary Fund and the World Bank, the transnational banks exerted global financial hegemony by crowding out other profit-seeking private financial flows (Leyshon & Thrift, 1997). The circulating, floating dollar helped produce the dispersed market networks of neoliberal societies of control.

The transnational banks' importance grew in the 1970s as the 1974 OPEC price hike increased nations' dependence on lending. Developing nations were hit hard by the OPEC hike, coupled with a drought that hurt agricultural production, and were subsequently forced to assume more debt (Engdahl, 1993). Paul Volcker's move in the United States to tighten the money supply, paralleled by a similar move in Great Britain, made dollars more expensive and thereby exacerbated the developing world's indebtedness (as payments for OPEC oil had to be made in U.S. dollars). A consequent international recession dropped the prices on commodities exported by developing nations, hampering their ability to make loan payments.

Transnational banks responded by granting further loans, financed by OPEC revenues. Spurred by the desire to avoid regulatory controls and enabled by advances in information and communication technology, many of the lending banks operated offshore, thereby having no lender of last resort (Sassen, 1991; Leyshon &Thrift, 1997). Consequently, the transnational bank lenders accrued large, unregulated, and unguaranteed debt.

The convergence of low commodity prices, high oil prices, and high interest rates on U.S. dollars plunged the developing world into a level of debt to the transnational banks that could not be financed. Developing countries would by the 1980s be forced to privatize formerly state-nationalized economic interests in order to receive debt relief from international lending agencies such as the World Bank and the IMF. For the developing world, the debt crisis would unravel efforts to steer from the center as neoliberal reforms ushered in a new era of government.

More generally, the global-system effects of debt crisis coupled with the inflationary spending of the United States would destabilize the "international regulated space" that had emerged in the post–World War II context, "comprised of a constellation of nation states linked one to another through reciprocal flows of money, goods, and services, complemented by a set of international institutions which existed to manage processes of adjustment within the international economy" (Leyshon & Thrift, 1997, p. 71). The internal regulated space would be replaced by decentered networks of capital; managed largely but not exclusively by corporations, financial institutions, and security exchanges; characterized by packaging and trading of debt (Deleuze, 1992).

Leyshon and Thrift (1997) identified three primary contradictions as straining the post–World War II regime, thereby precipitating the collapse of regulated domestic spaces:

1. There was a critical contradiction between the "disciplining role attributed to money at an international level and the pursuit of welfarist-oriented accumulation strategies on a national level," particularly in the U.S. context in which the demand for dollars allowed the United States to pursue expansionary growth in military and social spending.
2. There was "a critical contradiction between the role of the US as both the governor and guarantor of this regulatory order on the one hand, and its position as a competitive geographical-political jurisdiction in its own right on the other."
3. There was a critical contradiction stemming from the "geographical configuration of the postwar regulatory order, which was based upon a system of nation states, each of which was deemed to be both politically and economically sovereign" and the growing tendencies toward "internationalization of accumulation . . . as producers resorted to production within foreign markets to avoid the effects of spiraling tariff barriers." (pp. 71–72)

These incongruencies were unmasked by the financial crises of the 1970s. Consequently, transnational commercial banks lost hegemonic control over *international* financial activity during the 1980s as credit moved into security markets and other financial services (Leyshon & Thrift, 1997; Sassen, 1991). Although banks still controlled international payment mechanisms, they increasingly competed with security firms, insurance companies, and other financial institutions (e.g., institutional investors such as pension funds) providing a wide range of services, especially stockbroking (investment portfolio management; Sassen, 1991, p. 66). Direct competition in the United States was made possible by President Clinton's 1999 repeal of the Glass-Steagall Act. Securities transactions grew during the 1990s with an explosion of corporate finance through debt and stock issues (Brenner, 2007). The sum results of these and other changes included "growth of cross-border acquisitions of financial firms and sharp increase in the internationalization of mergers, acquisitions, and joint ventures among financial institutions" as well as the formation of an international equity market (Sassen, 1991, p. 66).

The rise of alternative financial institutions and investment opportunities outside the international banking system helped delineate the transition away from the welfare-state regime and Fordist patterns of capital accumulation toward neoliberalism (Sassen, 1991). Geographically centered, nationally identified, and bureaucratically regulated corporations (even if transnational in operation) would cede to new microcircuits of capital more regulated through a wide range of international financial institutions and hedge funds using automated technology to manage risks.

Ideological frameworks promoting liberalization of trade and financial regulations encouraged neoliberal reforms. The next section addresses the institutional forces and technologies, authorities, and strategies of the neoliberal regime of government.

NEOLIBERALISM: ENTERPRISE AND RISK

In "The Birth of Biopolitics," Foucault distinguished the "Ordo-liberalism" of the German Federal Republic from the "American neoliberalism" associated with the Chicago School but argued these approaches shared "a critique of the irrationality peculiar to 'excessive government'" and advocated "a return to a technology of 'frugal government'" (1997c, p. 78). According to Foucault, both approaches

> cited the danger represented by the inevitable sequence: economic intervention, inflation of governmental apparatuses, overadministration, bureaucracy, and rigidification of power mechanisms, accompanied by the production of new economic distortions that would lead to new interventions. (p. 78)

Although emphasizing their similarities, Foucault observed an important distinction between Ordo-liberalism and American neoliberalism in that the former requires a "vigilant policy of social interventions" to ameliorate social risks. American neoliberalism, in contrast, "seeks rather to extend the rationality of the market, the schemes of analysis it proposes, and the decision making criteria it suggests to areas that are not exclusively or primarily economic" (p. 79).

American-style neoliberalism rejects the equation between population and wealth. As articulated by a column in *The Wall Street Journal,* the "principle measure" of state success is the "Gross Domestic Product" (Grove, 2007, p. A15). But, against Keynesianism, the state's role in ensuring GDP growth is restricted to providing the conditions of possibility—openness, transparency, contract, and competition—for market operations. The state has no legitimate role in stabilizing markets, engineering demand, or directly subsidizing industry or populace.

Under neoliberal regimes of government, the state should seek only to protect the market and capitalists from overt "illegal" activity that hampers transparency and good corporate government. For example, the Public Company Accounting Reform and Investor Protection Act of 2002 (a.k.a. Sarbanes-Oxley) was passed to protect investors from corporate fraud in response to the Enron, WorldCom, and Tyco International scandals, among others. Although neoliberals disagree over optimal governance operations, they concur that shareholder value is the only value that should matter in the marketplace. Milton Friedman's (2005) essay "The Social Responsibility of Business Is to Increase its Profits" asserts corporations have no responsibility beyond maximizing shareholder value.

Accordingly, within neoliberal rationalities of government, the market is the primary mechanism for societal government and the state operates primarily to securitize "open" markets and (shareholder) expectations through articulation of the mechanisms for, and enforcement of, transparency, contract, and competition. American-style neoliberal reforms in the United States and Great Britain seek to disperse liberal centers of government and to empower "market" mechanism, thereby targeting the "excesses" of liberal government (see Harvey, 2005). American neoliberalism emphasizes the rational-choice "prudentialism" of risk-assuming, self-governing subjects (O'Malley, 1996, p. 199) and calls upon the state to construct itself in market terms (Brown, 2006). Moving forward, this chapter addresses itself only to American-style neoliberal government in contrast to Ordo-liberalism.

As Melinda Cooper (2004) explained, neoliberalism targets opportunities for profit in "the space of systemic economic risk opened by the integrated world market" (p. 527). Thus, neoliberal governmentalities seek to eliminate barriers to the free flow of finance and capital globally. Second, they strive to create new technologies for representing and leveraging risks/opportunities stemming from international flows. Strategies for representing, anticipating, and hedging risk are regarded as integral for neoliberal market expansion because risk aversion is viewed as economically destabilizing (Ip & Whitehouse, 2007).

As addressed in Chapter 2, a key figure responsible for articulating the philosophical terms within which American neoliberalism would be debated was Friedrich A. Hayek (1944, 1960, 1976). Hayek's absolute distrust of centralized planning would influence the direction of state reforms of market government, enhancing corporate autonomy and sovereignty at the close of the twentieth century.

In the American context, the emerging neoliberal ideology was taught in the schools of economics and business at the University of Chicago, MIT, Harvard, and Yale (Babb, 2004). References to this new market ethos emerged in the political rhetoric and financial policy of the Reagan administration. Neoliberal principles were applied to the policies and practices of the World Bank, the IMF, the U.S. federal government (e.g., Friedman's monetarism), and to governmental reforms in Chile and Mexico. Neoliberal authorities acted in concert with neoconservatives to push economic and social reforms.

U.S. Neoliberalism

In the 1990s, U.S. domestic reforms were aligned with neoliberal rationalities of government, as illustrated by the financial reforms previously discussed and by NAFTA. President Clinton signed the North American Free Trade Agreement (NAFTA) in 1994. Multilateral negotiations such as NAFTA aim for market efficiencies and investor security, helping to increase cross-national flows while reducing risks to corporate entities and individual investors (Longworth, 1998). The United States and other nations rely on the WTO, which replaced GATT in 1995, to adjudicate competing neoliberal trade imperatives. The WTO stresses elimination of tariffs, subsidies, and regulatory barriers while protecting intellectual property rights, particularly in the context of counterfeiting in the developing world (Goozner, 1999). Although liberal governmentalities have always valued intellectual property rights, the problem-solution frame of securing patents has achieved heightened significance for economically developed nations attempting to protect innovations, particularly in the areas of entertainment, biotechnology, and computing.

Neoliberal political reforms in the United States have included privatization of state operations and institutions. Privatization has comprised public infrastructures of highways, bridges, and airports (Thornton, 2007) while other "public goods" such as national parks are targeted for privatization (Ruskin, 2005). The U.S. prison complex has increasingly outsourced operations to private contractors and relied extensively on private prisons to address overcrowding (Smith & Hattery, 2006). Public schools are subject to neoliberal regimes of accountability while public universities are forced to embrace "enterprise" models of self-sustainability in the face of sharply declining public support. Still, the U.S. science-security complex perpetuates through private and public funding of university and foundation research, particularly in the area of biotechnology, which is seen as vital to the future competitiveness of U.S. capital.

Driven by the ethos of personal responsibility, President Clinton instituted welfare reform with P. L. 104–193, the Personal Responsibility and Work Opportunity Reconciliation Act, in 1996. President Bush followed by offering an "Ownership Society" wherein citizens would assume more risk while reaping the promised benefits of personalized homeownership, control over retirement savings, tax credits or vouchers for education, job training, and health insurance (Calmes, 2005). As explained in *The Wall Street Journal,* "The emphasis would be on the individual, supplanting a seventy-year-old approach in which citizens pool resources for the common good—and government doles out benefits" (p. A1). Ironically, although the welfare reforms and the ownership-society programs forced the poor into the workforce, thus reducing welfare spending, other government programs grew, providing food and medical subsidies for poorly compensated workers, leading to "record numbers" of the populace relying on public aid (Ohlemacher, 2007, p. A5).

Neoliberal domestic reforms were strategically packaged for U.S. populations by appealing to cultural values, such as personal responsibility, and a revitalized Judeo-Christian theological ethic. Specific programs designed to appeal to white middle-class suburbanites entailed tax cuts and tax credits for private education, including religious education. Robert Brenner (2007) detailed how the U.S. Republican Party, in particular, was able to expand its base in the socially conservative, antiunion but industrialized American South by appealing to these privatized, and often racially and religiously inflected, policies.

Globalizing Neoliberalism

In the closing decades of the twentieth century, neoliberal economic advisors working in private firms and institutes, as well as in the global monetary governing agencies such as the IMF and World Bank, viewed trade and currency liberalization and export-oriented production as the primary strategies for fostering economic development in the developing world or, more cynically, as an effective strategy for capital expropriation (see Harvey, 2005). For instance, the IMF shifted from "'adjustment' of balance of payments problems to addressing structural economic crises in third world countries" through "liberalizing" structural adjustment programs (Panitch & Gindin, 2003, p. 53). Private enterprise, market freedom, and corporate autonomy were celebrated value orientations, and this rationality of government shaped biopolitical statistical representations and projections. Thus, the World Bank estimated in 2002 that the elimination of all trade barriers and subsidies would "lift 320 million people above the $2 a day poverty line by 2015" (Blustein, 2005, p. D1). In 2005, the World Bank scaled back these projections but maintained its neoliberal commitments.

Privatization and deregulation of state resources and industries were seen as vital for economic development (see Davis, 2006). During the 1970s and 1980s, the IMF and World Bank began hinging development loans on nations' willingness to adopt neoliberal reform policies aimed at privatizing national industries, reducing barriers to foreign direct investment, and reducing state subsidies for national industries and social welfare. National resources were also targeted for privatization by foreign direct investment, including basic ones such as water and electricity (Esterl, 2006). Mike Davis's (2006) *Planet of Slums* described the deleterious social effects of neoliberal reforms, in concert with corruption, upon the denizens of the world's most populous and poorest cities. Markets, however, both legal and extralegal, find great opportunities in such cities through the trading and exploitation of resources, including commodities and human bodies.

Although global inequality poses opportunities for profit, it also presents risks. Neoliberal and neoconservative authorities offer free trade, private philanthropy, and microenterprise as solutions for documented inequalities. In 2005, Paul Wolfowitz, a prominent neoconservative whose economic policies were consistent with neoliberal agendas, pledged to promote free trade after assuming leadership of the World Bank (Hitt, 2005). Responding to criticism that the World Bank emphasizes big-business interests, Wolfowitz promised to promote small-business loans and microenterprise, thus promoting privatized market-based solutions to global problems such as poverty. Wolfowitz also promised to improve "government" in poor countries (Andrews, 2005). But for many of the world's impoverished, the most lucrative and viable opportunities for microenterprise often exist outside of the parameters of "legitimate enterprise" and good government (trafficking of drugs, people, arms, etc.).

In sum, neoliberal reforms and policies, coupled with new financial, communication, and transportation technologies, have expanded extralegal markets while transforming the zones of qualification for participation in formal or legal market operations. Changes consist of globalization of finance and production processes contributing to unparalleled levels of market integration (through supply chains, trade, and finance), with the concomitant exclusion of nations and peoples unwilling or unable to participate in the neoliberal rules of good government (U.N., 1999), producing vast "shadow" circuits and economies that foster and undercut "legitimate" transactions (Nordstrom, 2000). Funds generated by illicit trading fuel global resistances, including terrorism (Simpson & Faucon, 2007).

"Aggressive competition" exists inside the imagined spaces of advanced national economies (Liagouras, 2005, p. 22), leading to corporate consolidation (Gabel & Bruner, 2003). In contrast, the developing world derives its economic significance in relation to commodity markets, manufacturing supply chains, and exploited human labor (Klare, 2004). Additionally, elite groups in developing countries are increasingly targeted by marketers as part of a global consumer class; simultaneously, poor nations are regarded as convenient dumping grounds for substandard products originally destined for richer markets.

Deregulated and extralegal capital flows and trade have produced new risks and opportunities for corporate entities, market investors, illicit agents, and various biopolitical authorities. These new risks and opportunities require new technologies for representing, calculating, and controlling flows, contingencies, and effects. What follows addresses some of the new "risks" to, and by, populations arising from neoliberal economic governmentalities.

Neoliberal Authorities, Risks, and Global Flows

Specialized information and communication services are required for globalized financial exchanges and complex manufacturing supply chains to "manage and control global networks" (Sassen, 1991, p. 11). Over the 1980s and 1990s, complex new enterprise-resource services and specialized applications were developed (e.g., SAP, Oracle, People Soft) to manage flows of goods and services, creating new infrastructural technological zones and outsourcing practices. The pervasiveness of enterprise-resource systems mandates digital identification codes for a "machine-readable world" (Dodge & Kitchin, 2005, p. 851), creating new metrological zones for standardizing, managing, and controlling regional and global flows of information/commodities/finance (Barry, 2006).

New "metrological zones" also enable global financial transactions entailing the production, evaluation, and commodification of assets whose ownership is dispersed internationally. For instance, global finance is increasingly organized around "securitization," which entails aggregation of large pools of assets by financial firms such as Lehman Brothers, as well as by major banks such as Citigroup (Penner, 2007, p. A11). These financial agents sell securities backed by collective asset pools, primarily (but not exclusively) in the form of bonds, whose ratings are evaluated based on their risks and returns. Advocates see securitization as democratizing capital through its availability and attendant geographic dispersion. However, the technologies or valuation models used to render the securities' risks and returns visible and calculable have limited capacities and are not transparent to consumers. "Trust" thus helps mediate the global metrological zones produced by the trading of these securities. Any "fragility" in balance sheets of security firms or markets ruptures trust and subsequently upsets entire metrological zones, destabilizing highly interconnected global markets (Penner, 2007, p. A11).

Consumer debt is an asset commonly pooled and securitized. Marron's essay "Lending by Numbers" illustrates a valuation technology used to assess the risks of consumer debt through statistical credit-scoring technologies. Statistical means for assessing credit have replaced older focal points such as "character," offering abstract, generalizable, and seemingly objective means for assessing risk, thus reifying individual creditworthiness as something (ostensibly) existing independent of the act of measurement while displacing social power divisions that shape individuals' economic status (2007, p. 104). Additionally, credit technologies extend the scope of risk through behavioral scoring that monitors individual credit on a continuing basis. Debt evaluated in this manner can be pooled in aggregate based on "objective" accounts of riskiness and subsequently securitized. But, as so clearly dramatized by the subprime-mortgage meltdown in the summer of 2007, statistical scoring technologies are limited by the peculiarities of their heuristics.

As demonstrated by this discussion of securitization, new technological and financial practices have transformed the spatial configuration and circulation of finance globally. The import of these changes grows as finance increasingly dominates global market transactions. Within the United States, financial-sector profits exceeded those of manufacturing by the mid-1990s; by 2004, financial firms commanded nearly 40 percent of all U.S. profits, primarily by managing, packaging, and trading debt and credit instruments (including household debt) and managing debt-related corporate restructuring (K. Phillips, 2006, p. 266). The extent of private credit and debt undermine traditional efforts to evaluate the nation's money supply using the traditional focus on the Federal Reserve Board's estimates.

Jia-Ming and Morss (2005) summarized specific instruments and institutions transforming late-twentieth-century financial markets. They argued that during the twentieth century the following revolutions in finance occurred.

1. The institutional revolution.
2 The risk-adjustment industry.
3. Changing money mechanisms.
4. Changing criteria for a strong currency.
5. Changing criteria for a good investment (p. 204).

Each of these changes will be discussed briefly.

Over the last twenty years *new financial institutions have emerged and/or been transformed in response to new forms of financial activity* including "insurance companies, pension funds, stockbrokers, investment banks, mutual funds, venture capitalists, and financial management" (p. 205). Pension funds, mutual funds, and insurers hold the largest portion of the world's financial assets ($59.4 trillion), but Asian central banks, hedge funds, private-equity funds, and petrodollars are gaining in importance (Wessel, 2007). Opportunities for investment proliferate as new information technologies and financial forms produce new forms of value, such as new groups of securities linked to derivatives (see Aglietta & Breton, 2001). Bundled securities are sold piecemeal across the globe, dispersing risk, but also creating it by fostering global interdependencies (Slater & Karmin, 2007).

Institutional investors and new investment vehicles have transformed global finance and, accordingly, global economic trends, including foreign direct investment. For example, public capital to developing nations has declined relative to the growth of private capital. In 2005, assets in investment funds aimed at emerging market exchange-traded funds and mutual funds exceeded $103 billion (Farzad, 2006). In the face of speculative trends, *Business Week* cautioned private individual/corporate investors that "emerging-market" risks include: (a) "incomplete reforms" as developing nations fail to "curb the state's role in the economy"; (b) "political perils" as developing nations' "fiscal discipline may waver" during elections; (c) "debt default"; and (d) "nationalization," as illustrated by the case of Venezuela, which will be discussed later in this chapter (Engardio, 2007, p. 42). These "risks" all derive from developing nations' perceived failures to adequately implement neoliberal reforms.

Given the ubiquity of risk, market authorities strive to develop surveillance networks and informatic technologies to render risks visible and calculable, allowing leverage. Indeed, some investment mechanisms seek out risky, but potentially lucrative, opportunities produced by the neoliberal flows governed by new metrological technologies. Hedge funds and private-equity pools thrive on risky investments abroad and domestically, leading former Federal Reserve Chairman Alan Greenspan to state: "Risk is no longer perceived as a major risk, at least as it was in years past, and that, I must say, I find disturbing" (cited in Farrell, 2007, p. 40).

U.S. and British officials' overall reluctance to employ the state to regulate capital risks reflects the neoliberal turn to market forces. *Risk-adjustors, privatized entities that help capital manage risk, have emerged as powerful global institutions* (Jia-Ming & Morss, 2005). Wikipedia provides a concise definition of financial risk management as "the practice of creating value in a firm by using financial instruments to manage exposure to risk" ("Financial Risk," n.d.), requiring technologies for identifying and measuring risks. Jia-Ming and Morss (2005) reported risk-adjustment activities are the leading business in the financial-services sector, surpassing even mobilization of savings for investment. Risk-adjustment activities are viewed as a market-based solution to market-generated risks.

Changing money mechanisms have contributed to the creation of new risks addressed by risk-adjustors. The rise of credit cards, e-money, and other forms of electronic finance weaken monetary policy pools and state regulation, complicating the process of determining the quantity and source of monetary supply (Jia-Ming & Morss, 2005). Meanwhile, a host of derivative instruments lets "investors spread cash across different asset classes and countries like never before" (Lahart, 2007, p. C1). Capital flows create new centers of power as investment managers of private funds—mutual funds and hedge funds—assume unprecedented influence in the developing world through their advisory authority (Torres & Vogel, 1994).

National governments have limited abilities to control domestic or globalizing economies through monetary policy and interest rates due to the rise of securities and other private sources of credit, in addition to the globalization of finance and production. Thus, Jia-Ming and Morss (2005) concluded *the strength of a currency no longer hinges exclusively on trade balance and domestic rate of inflation*. International economic theory has failed to address the growing importance of capital flows, particularly in the form of bundled securities, because of its continued focus on commodity flows.

Nevertheless, neoliberal authorities regard the lack of centralized steering capacities as relatively unproblematic. Moreover, they contend state agents such as central banks should refrain from efforts to steer or correct markets to avoid undermining market disciplines. In the summer of 2007, central banks in Europe, the United States, and Japan were tested by the credit crunch caused by the subprime-mortgage implosion. Fearing credit infusion by central banks would produce "moral hazard" by bailing out risky investments, neoliberal market authorities called upon central banks to exert restraint in their lending and interest rate cuts (O'Driscoll, 2007, p. A11). Yet central banks are also responsible for ensuring "orderly" markets and thus face conflicting priorities and risks.

Assuring "orderly" markets is further problematized by growing extralegal "shadow" economies (Nordstrom, 2000). Unprecedented global flows include a wide range of extralegal market operations that escape direct state surveillance and control, including unregulated factories, drug and human trafficking, counterfeit goods, and so on. Extralegal and illicit market operations tend to remain invisible to formal economic analyses, yet profoundly shape the livelihoods of people while significantly impacting actual currency and commodity flows.

Efforts by state actors to control extralegal flows typically entail eradication through brute suppression or involve expanding formal recognition to already existing extralegal operations. Widespread piracy leads to calls for stricter enforcement of intellectual-property laws through government seizures of counterfeit goods (Richards, 2004). Extralegal cross-border flows are legitimized with "free-trade zones" modeled after NAFTA. Designed to create "protected" zones for economic investment and trade, these free-trade zones often forgo more traditional labor protections and make few concessions to environmental concerns. Free-trade zones illustrate new "zones of qualification" for neoliberal market participation by individuals, corporations, and states (Barry, 2006, p. 240) with "antipolitical" effects (Barry, 2002, p. 268). Recently, U.S. politicians called for the creation of an American Free Trade Agreement (AAFTA) that would include North America, Central and South America, and the Caribbean. Sweetening the sell is the promise that such a program would promote "trade, open societies, development and democracy . . . in concert with immigration reform" (Zoellick, 2007, p. A17).

The narrative used to sell the proposed AAFTA mirrors the changing criteria for assessing investment strategy. As Jia-Ming and Morss (2005) noted, *new criteria for assessing value have recently emerged.* In the past, short-term earnings' potential dictated commercial banks' loan policies and equity valuations. But recently, short-term earnings' potential has lessened in import for banks that simply earn a commission by selling off their assets onto a secondary market without having to worry about long-term prospects. This phenomenon, coupled with the asset value increase realized when private companies go public with initial public offerings (IPO), has contributed to a new way of assessing value based in storytelling by experts. Stories emphasizing how a particular corporation "fits into a technological revolution" are particularly popular (p. 213), as illustrated by Google's IPO. Managerially directed stories and value orientations also operate internally to produce normative systems of employee control (Cheney, 1991; Deetz, 1992; Mumby, 1993). Researchers studying management, corporate culture, and public-issue management have detailed how image management emerged as a prominent technology across the twentieth century. Image management "sells the market" to employees/consumers/investors by linking laissez-faire market government and consumption to democracy, by adding value to goods whose origins are mystified by complex supply chains, and by interpellating preferred identities and lifestyles (Aune, 2001; Ewen, 1990).

Neoliberal Policy, Corporate Government, and the Population

Around the tide of neoliberal business and economic practice, a discourse of enterprise, articulating workers and citizens more generally as entrepreneurial agents, has arisen (duGay, 1996; Nadesan, 1999b, 2001). Growing individual and public indebtedness justifies neoliberal disciplines, further legitimizing dismantling of welfare-state apparatuses while shifting risk and responsibility to individuals.

But neoliberal state apparatuses such as those in the United States and Great Britain face challenges resulting from neoliberal regimes of government. While new investment vehicles and new technologies have created substantial national wealth, biopolitical census technologies designed to reveal the contours of that wealth find the extent of its inequitable distribution poses new risks for social stability and the health of the population. Moreover, the transference of societal risk management from government to privatized institutions and individuals exacerbates those risks. Over the 1990s and early 2000s, income inequality grew in the United States, culminating in "near all-time highs" in 2004 with 50.1 percent of national income going to the top 20 percent of households while only the top 5 percent of households experienced real income gains ("Life," 2005). As of November 2006, U.S. consumers' spending exceeded their disposable income by 1 percent (Whitehouse, 2007). In Europe, governments' efforts to render labor laws more "flexible" resulted in labor unrest despite claims that recovery hinges on such measures (Walker, 2006, p. A1). What follows explores the new risks for citizen workers.

Neoliberal economic "reforms," globalization, and automation have transformed U.S. conditions of work. Labor is increasingly separated into a core sector, with higher job security and benefits, and a periphery sector, which often lacks both (see Ong, 1991). The peripheral sector is characterized by "flexibilization" and underemployment, often in low-skilled, low-wage service occupations (Clinton, 1997). The manufacturing labor force was reduced by a fifth between 1995 and 2005, while the financial sector grew from about 25 percent to about 40 percent of corporate profits (Brenner, 2007). As summarized by De Giorgi (2006), the new political economy of work entails

> the growing precarisation of work, the flexibilisation of employment and the constant overlapping between the 'legal' economy and the many hidden, informal and illegal economies producing a gradual fusion of work and non-work, mixing the labouring and dangerous classes [of past formulations] together and making any rigid distinction between the two almost impossible. A paradigmatic example is offered by the migrant labour force. (p. xi)

These dangerous classes are neutralized through risk-management technologies, including "surveillance, urban seclusion and mass confinement" (p. xi). I would add the additional risk-based technology of high-interest financing, which promises consumer goods to low-income populations but delivers a new kind of debtor servitude (Grow & Epstein, 2007).

Wal-Mart illustrates the problematics posed to the state by corporate sovereignty and neoliberal market governmentality. Wal-Mart Corporation is the largest employer in the United States and in the world. In 2006, it employed 1.8 million people and it was second in revenues (CNN, 2007). Yet in the United States, many Wal-Mart employees are eligible for state-sponsored health care and other benefits due to their low wages.

Wal-Mart manages complex global supply chains contracting with factories in more than sixty countries to produce its goods ("More Breaches," 2006). To manage complexity, Wal-Mart developed its own in-house enterprise resource system. Companies wanting to do business with Wal-Mart must implement technological systems that can coordinate with Wal-Mart's in order to, as one article put it, "handle project accounting capabilities such as activity-based costing (ABC), lean manufacturing, and specialized electronic data interchange (EDI) and radio frequency identification (RFID)," thereby producing new metrological zones (Girard, 2003).

Wal-Mart has recently applied lean manufacturing principles (i.e., flexibilization) to its human-resources policy. Wal-Mart is currently attempting to "wring costs and attain new efficiencies" in staffing through "implementation of scheduling-optimization systems that integrate data ranging from the number of in-store customers at certain hours to the average time it takes to sell a television or unload a truck" to predict how many workers are needed at any given hour (Maher, 2007b, p. A11). These "labor-optimizing" systems schedule workers in response to variable need, subjecting them to fluctuating scheduling, and requiring some to be "on-call." In 2006 the company implemented wage caps for workers and increased reliance on part-timers (Greenhouse & Barbaro, 2006). Suppliers providing services for Wal-Mart also implement lean production in human resources by exploiting immigrant labor (Greenhouse, 2003).

Wal-Mart's emphasis on flexibility precludes workplace unionization. In 2007, Human Rights Watch accused Wal-Mart of using security cameras to spy on employees who were perceived as pro-union and of planting spies to monitor these workers' activities (Maher, 2007a). In 2005, Wal-Mart closed a Canadian store that was about to become the first ever to achieve a union contract (Geller, 2005).

As argued in *Fortune* magazine, Wal-Mart "is changing the rules for corporate America" (Useem, 2003, p. 65). For instance, Wal-Mart's entry into the grocery market has significantly altered that industry (Bianco & Zellner, 2003) and forced the major players, including Safeway and Kroger, to wring wage and benefits concessions from their unionized employees. Critics coined the term *Wal-martization* to refer to Wal-Mart's economic and social impact (cited in Stringer, 2005, p. B3). Greg Denier, spokesman for the United Food and Commercial Workers International Union, described Wal-martization as a threat to prosperity: "The future is bleak if the future of America is a Wal-Mart job" (cited in Stringer, 2005, p. B3).

Wal-Mart's demonstrated capacities to adversely shape the conditions of work for employees, contractors, and workers abroad, coupled with its market impact, have resulted in bad publicity for the company. In 2005, Wal-Mart responded to negative press with an aggressive public-relations campaign that primarily targeted consumers, using TV ad spots and full-page newspaper ads in more than 100 leading U.S. newspapers (Stringer, 2005). Wal-Mart's low prices, its provision of "cheap-chic" fashion (some of which are counterfeit; Useem, 2003, p. 72), low-cost prescription drugs (McWilliams & Martinez, 2006), and its "Americana" cultural imagery appeal to consumers, undercutting critics' arguments that Wal-Mart poses security risks to the American way of life.

Wal-Mart represents the market risks and opportunities of neoliberal market economics. Wal-Mart offers its investors and senior executive officers financial incentives for lean-production techniques. Labor is a cost to be managed. But Wal-Mart does not rely simply on enclosed disciplinary spaces to wring efficiencies from workers' bodily operations. In addition to utilizing older disciplinary means, Wal-Mart employs a wide range of surveillance and labor-optimizing devices that operate from a distance to increase worker visibility and manageability, ranging from surveillance cameras to the sophisticated and technological supply-chain and labor-optimizing information-management systems. These technological strategies for representing and managing costs circulate geographically while centralizing the capacity to "see" and engineer new efficiencies. Employee and community dissent and resistance engender media spectacles. But commodities, advertising, and public relations entice consumers with affordable goods packaged in American cultural iconography. Wal-Mart's neoliberal efficiencies and nostalgic "Americana" iconography invade new terrains globally. And yet, Wal-martization also poses new challenges for self-governing neoliberal citizens and for nation-states that still retain some level of pastoral responsibility for the welfare of their population.

NEOLIBERAL MARKET GOVERNMENT AND BIOPOLITICAL CRISES

A vast array of biopolitical authorities working in national and global government institutions such as the United Nations and nongovernmental agencies (NGOs) suggest significant risks threaten future global economic security. These risks range from the environmental risks of expanded markets and industrialization (e.g., global warming) to the political perils of global inequality (Davis, Lyons, & Batson, 2007). This section concludes this chapter by addressing the rise of a new philanthropic complex that, akin to nineteenth-century philanthropic complex, aims to securitize the population and economy while preserving the vital liberal distinction between spheres of government.

The perils posed to and by marginalized and impoverished countries are now unmistakable. Even countries experiencing GDP growth from neoliberal reforms face new biopolitical risks. Mexico's small farmers were economically devastated by NAFTA, leading to rising rates of poverty (Borden, 2003). China's experimentation with state-sponsored capitalism contributes to a growing chasm between rich and poor, fueling dangerous levels of social unrest (Cody, 2005) and pollution, threatening the well-being of the nation. India's economic boom has led to inflationary pressures imperiling the nation's poorest (Wonacott, 2007). Russia's population has been so jeopardized by neoliberal reforms that it faces declining life spans despite economic growth (Koretz, 2003). Ironically, hunger rates rise worldwide despite increased production of the world's food supply (Thurow & Solomon, 2004). Disciplinary organizations such as the IMF threaten sanctions against countries that run up debt on social spending. Even within prosperous nations such as the United States, global flows threaten social stability as more professional work (e.g., accounting, programming, legal) is offshored, and as the populace swells with poor immigrants escaping poverty, unrest, and/or seeking entrepreneurial opportunities.

In the developing world, social inequality and frustration with the seemingly "interested" nature of neoliberal economic reforms have created populist resistance and a desire for many for a return to centralized state sovereignty. A United Nations report released in 2004 found that "a majority" of Latin Americans would support authoritarian governments if said governments bettered their personal circumstances (Tobar, 2004, p. A15). Not surprisingly, populist presidents were elected, including Venezuela's Hugo Chávez and Bolivia's Evo Morales. Chávez's policies signal a return by some developing nations to centralized steering. In early 2007, Chávez pledged to nationalize Venezuela's largest publicly traded private companies, including CANTV, which is controlled by the United States. Verizon Communications (Silver, Slater, & Millard, 2007) and Electricidad de Caracas are controlled by the U.S. AES Corporation. In Bolivia, Morales began nationalization of the country's natural-gas industry.

Neoliberal authorities recognize the necessity for addressing global risks arising from global inequality, environmental degradation, and energy depletion. Failures to develop strategies for managing these risks raise the apparitions of environmental catastrophe and rising authoritarianism globally. Neoliberal authorities, however, rely primarily on nineteenth-century solutions to stabilize the market and population in times of global risks.

Public outcry in Western industrial nations about labor abuses in the developing world prompted creation of globalized nongovernmental agencies such as the Fair Labor Association, established in 1997. Such agencies promise to counter the "abuses" of economic globalization through direct and indirect factory oversight but rarely succeed in altering the basic premises and operations of neoliberal governmentality. Rather, such agencies offer a pastoral biopolitics aimed at curbing the worst abuses of capitalist sovereignty in developing nations.

Individual and corporate philanthropy offer, in the neoliberal imagination, the most promising strategies for addressing those problems identified by biopolitical authorities as posing risks to the economic, social, and environmental stability of a nation. Corporate philanthropists such as Bill Gates tackle "social problems" such as poverty, literacy, and health by granting funds only to agencies that demonstrate fiscal accountability and calculable outcomes (Hechinger & Golden, 2006). News periodicals hail the "birth of philanthrocapitalism" ("The Business," 2006, p. 8). In contrast to older philanthropists, this new breed tends to "chop and change" instead of passively awaiting changes from their social investments (p. 9). Philanthrocapitalists strive to apply market disciplines to "professional philanthrocrats" in order to achieve measurable outcomes more efficiently (p. 9).

Christian evangelicals and conservatives, many of whom have historically viewed Christ as an enterprising businessman, have long pursued philanthrocapitalism. As one news report explained: "Welding business savvy to spiritual needs is an evangelical tradition. As early as the 19th century, born-again pastors preached prosperity and received in return the support of influential businessmen" (Driscoll, 2006, p. A16). Barton's (1925) *The Man Nobody Knows* represented Jesus as the founder of modern corporate business. Today, megachurch founders refer to themselves as "spiritual entrepreneurs" (Driscoll, 2006, p. A16), promising their flock spiritual satisfaction and economic well-being.

In this context of meaning, microenterprise is viewed among philanthrocapitalists and evangelical business missionaries as the primary strategy for alleviating poverty. Privately funded microenterprise is valued for fostering enterprise and independence while maintaining the neoliberal distinction between state and economy. Contemporary philanthrocapitalist renditions of microenterprise echo nineteenth-century admonitions to the poor that they seek gainful employment through "straw-platting."

Neoliberal enterprise and its philanthropic supplements, however, are not always successful in pacifying alienated or marginalized populations. The technologies of production that have facilitated global flows have also produced populations much more aware of their economic deprivation and marginalization (Brzezinski, 2004). Brute force is often called upon to discipline those unwilling or unable to find their place within neoliberal governmental regimes. Accordingly, enclave elites in developing countries and transnational corporations wishing to protect their foreign interests do not hesitate to enlist private security contractors who suppress resistant populations using old forms of brutality. For example, private security contractors operate in Nigeria to protect oil production and transportation from the resistance of impoverished local populations. Although privatized security illustrates a neoliberal solution to risk, it does not imply the demise of state power. Private security is often funded or supplemented with state resources. For example, Nigeria is a principal recipient of U.S. security assistance in West Africa, and in 2004 it became eligible for surplus U.S. military arms (Klare, 2004). Likewise, the government of Colombia funded right-wing paramilitary groups accused of gross human-rights violations while receiving substantial financial support from the U.S. government, including approximately $4 billion in antidrug and military aid since 2002 (Forego, 2007). Thus, neoliberal government often entails sovereign force and repression when states' economic and political security are understood as "at risk." Chapter 6 will take up the relationships among population, market, and sovereignty in further detail.

In conclusion, neoliberal market governmentality faces contradictory imperatives. On the one hand, neoliberal governmentality operates from a distance through dispersed, capillarylike technologies that expand the reach of neoliberal financial and commodity markets. On the other hand, the neoliberal imperatives toward market expansion produce security risks that require development of risk-management strategies, many of which entail prudential leveraging of opportunity and risks. But the risks posed by dispossessed populations stymie microenterprise and neoliberal philanthropy. Those same technologies of production that enabled market expansion breed discontent and alienation while offering oppositional groups means for resistance. Brute, sovereign force is used against resistant populations, further fueling dispossession and alienation, heightening market risks while begetting more forceful repression by both state apparatuses and outsourced militias. Thus, neoliberal governmentality is rent by its own contradictions. Chapter 6 will return to these contradictions, but I now turn to address the constitution and governmentality of population in Chapters 4 and 5.

Chapters 4 and 5 address the "conduct of conduct" governing the biological and mental health of populations across liberal governmentalities. As shall become clear, biopolitical problematics are simultaneously economic ones. The population—its health and vitality—and the market—its opportunities and risks—are integrally structured in accord with shifting liberal governmentalities.

4 Governing Population
Biopower, Risk, and the Politics of Health

Chapter 4 explores how the biopolitical government of population emerged as a significant problem with the constitution of the modern, Western liberal state (see Porter, 1999; Rosen, 1993). Michel Foucault recognized the importance of changing understandings of disease, health, sanitation, hygiene, and mental pathology as he saw their formulations and treatment regimes shaped public life and individual practice. Indeed, Foucault's analysis of governmentality examined how linkages between (a) the health of the population and (b) the economic and political security of the state resulted in distinct "biopolitical" strategies for representing and acting upon populations across liberal governmentalities. For Foucault, biopolitical strategies were not simply imposed from above but were adopted as practices of self-government in everyday routines and disciplines.

Biopolitics is a form of power that addresses the species bodies of the population and therefore supplements the corporeal disciplines of anatomo-politics, although the two are inextricably conjoined in that each requires the other. Foucault acknowledged concerns about health and sanitation predated liberalism but observed in "The Birth of Social Medicine" that "starting in the eighteenth century human existence, human behavior, and the human body were brought into an increasingly dense and important network of medicalization that allowed fewer and fewer things to escape" (Foucault, 2003c, p. 320). Foucault's interest in the medicalization of society was multifaceted and included somatic developments in medical understandings, public sanitation and medical charity toward the poor (2003c), and psychiatric power (2003a, 2006). Foucault argued that although medical technologies of government change across time, they tend to cohere around security problematics posed to, and by, the vitality, fecundity, and productivity of the population. Liberal regimes of medical government claim to optimize freedom by securitizing/regulating the conditions of life. Regimes of medical government involve state apparatuses, private experts, and individual technologies of the self.

Foucault saw biopolitics as intimately connected with the uncoupling and transformation of sovereignty and state government because, as the eighteenth-century state assumed pastoral authority for the health and welfare of its population, it helped produce new and more diffuse institutional apparatuses aimed at maximizing national vitality. Over time, health apparatuses, including evolving medical and psychiatric institutions, produced new institutional spaces such as institutes of public health, hospitals, clinics, psychiatric institutions, homes for indigent children, and so on. Biopolitical authorities—alienists, physicians, public-health experts, social workers—also produced new "disciplines" that shaped the practices and value orientations of the population, including sanitary sciences, domestic hygiene, and medical hygiene.

By the twentieth century, the convergence of sovereignty, discipline, and government blending the "city-game" of government with the "shepherd-game" affected, and was constituted through, significant changes in biopolitical operations that shifted the focus of discipline/government from the outside (e.g., from law and the forceful disciplining of the body) to the inside (e.g., the disciplining and cultivation of the mind), as older disciplinary regimes were either supplemented or replaced by a biopolitics of population and by technologies of the self (Gordon, 1991, p. 8).

Within contemporary neoliberal governmentalities, biopolitical technologies are increasingly understood within marketized formulations of value and technologies of care. Efforts to rationalize health-care costs produce wide networks of surveillance, responsibilized individuals, and targeted governance of risky persons whose unhealth threatens national vitality. Simultaneously, the neoliberal imagination constitutes health-related biotechnology as a vital space for market capitalization and strategy for national competitiveness, generating resistance from leftist and socially conservative biopolitical authorities.

This chapter traces liberal regimes of health government, emphasizing how changing understandings and health practices have been inscribed by, and produced, biopolitical distinctions between (desirous) healthy and (dangerous/polluted) unhealthy populations, between those (a) deserving of health education and support and (b) those requiring targeted surveillance and segregation or disciplining.

THE BIRTH OF BIOPOLITICS AND FOUCAULT'S GENEALOGY OF SOCIAL MEDICINE

Chapter 2 explained how the concept of population as an object of inquiry and administration arose in the eighteenth century as the early liberal state began considering the economic potential of its populace. Inspired by the coupling of population and wealth, William Petty's political statistics (1755) revealed the population, "with its numerical variables of spaces and chronology, longevity and health," as a space demanding not only surveillance but also intervention (Foucault, 1980a, p. 171). Statistical measures of fertility, health, and productivity revealed problem spaces requiring state intervention and/or private philanthropy.

Foucault (2003c) described these biopolitical representations and interventions as *"state medicine,"* citing them as the first phase of social medicine. He traced state medicine to the authoritarian "medical police" that emerged at the close of the sixteenth century in Germany (my italics, p. 323). Developed within mercantilist logics, state medicine linked national wealth to the population's vitality. State medicine in Germany entailed: (a) "observations of sickness gathered from the hospitals and doctors of different towns and regions"; (b) "standardization of medical practice and medical knowledge"; (c) "an administrative organization for overseeing the activity of doctors"; and (d) "creation of medical officers, appointed by the government" (p. 324). State medicine was most regimented and authoritarian as practiced through German medical police.

State medicine did not, however, simply act from above. The eighteenth century witnessed an increasing number of books targeting literate populations, interpellating them as responsible for their own health and well-being. As Foucault explained:

> Different power apparatuses are called upon to take charge of 'bodies,' not simply so as to exact blood service from them or levy dues, but to help and if necessary constrain them to ensure their own good health. The imperative of health: at once the duty of each and the objective of all. (1980a, p. 170)

For example, in 1733 *The Art of Nursing: Or the Method of Bringing up Young Children According to the Rules of Physick For the Prefervation of Health, and Prolonging Life* hoped to "oblige the Publick" by publishing "The true Way of bringing up young Children," among other treatises (Brotherton & Gilliver, p. 3). Likewise, in 1794, William Moss published an essay titled *An Essay on the Management, Nursing and Diseases of Children, from the Birth: And on The treatment and Diseases of Pregnant and Lying-In Women*, which was "defigned for Domeftic Ufe , and purpfely adapted for Female Comprehension" (title page). Issues pertaining directly to the growth of the population, including midwifery, nursing, treatment of childhood diseases, and the practices of foundling hospitals were of central importance in these texts.

As the fecundity of the population and the regulation of its health and sexuality were constructed as problem spaces, older modes of governing populations were supplemented with, or substituted by, new biopolitical strategies. New corporeal disciplines and sanitary regimes targeted physical health and, significantly, psychic health or "happiness." Public and privately funded sanitation schemes would play important roles in the second type of social medicine Foucault identified.

Foucault (2003c) argued the second form of the development of social medicine, *"urban medicine,"* addressed health in terms of urban sanitation (my italics, p. 326) followed closely by "labor-force" medicine. Late-eighteenth- and nineteenth-century urban medicine arose out of the need to unify the city in "a coherent and homogeneous way" governed by a "single, well-regulated authority" while addressing the tensions within the city caused by overcrowding and industrialization (p. 326).

Prior to the close of nineteenth century, the origins of diseases were believed to exist in the weather, the soil, air vapors—in short, in the physical environment. Quarantine was therefore the primary mechanism used to halt disease transmission. Public "health" efforts therefore focused primarily on surveillance and segregation of the ill, disposal of sewage and garbage, and occasionally street cleaning (Duffy, 1990; Porter, 1999).

Nineteenth-century industrialization in Europe and the United States exacerbated urban squalor and disease, prompting more systematic efforts to relieve congestion and disorder, concentrating on the circulation of air and water and the institution of sanitary boundaries. Urban medicine targeted the "zones of congestion, disorder, and danger within the urban precincts" believed responsible for breeding disease (Foucault, 2003c, p. 330). Thus, urban medicine was less about bodies and more about a medicine of "things—air, water, decompositions, fermentations" (p. 332).

Sanitary science developed in relation to the concerns of urban medicine. In England, the 1842 "sanitary idea" entailed creation of a central public-health authority to direct local boards to improve urban sanitation including drainage, cleansing, potable water, and the sanitary regulation of dwellings, commerce, and so on (Porter, 1999). The social body itself was viewed as sick (Petersen, 1999) and the poor were targeted as primary sources of contagion, mandating greater surveillance and policing. The poor's mere existence posed moral and biological threats to national vitality.

Thus commenced the third direction of social medicine, "*labor force medicine*," which targeted the poor and workers (my italics, Foucault, 2003c, p. 333). Foucault saw labor force medicine as a nineteenth-century innovation that originated out of urban medicine but was characterized by distinct modes of operation including control of vaccination, organization of records of epidemics and diseases, development of mandates for reporting dangerous illness, and localization of unhealthy places requiring oversight and intervention. In England, health services for the poor were guided by the same logic as the Poor Law: the poor required surveillance and administrative oversight in order to maximize their productive capacities.

Foucault's genealogy of social medicine should not be read as implying a simple series of substitutions. The institutions and practices of these three dimensions of medicine were entwined, particularly during the nineteenth century, when state security was linked to the expansion of markets and the securitization of labor and military recruits. However, evolution of the institutions and practices of social medicine point to changing technologies of social government as *security* problematics and apparatuses slowly replaced or supplemented *disciplinary* ones, even in the context of public health. For example, Foucault (2007) compared sixteenth-century plague regulation, which involved imposition of partitioning grids upon regions and disciplining of movement, with smallpox inoculation practices that began in the eighteenth century.

Smallpox inoculations securitized the population less through quarantine than through medical campaigns. Inoculation practices were based on detailed statistical representations of populations and targeted the population as a whole. Extant disciplinary apparatuses were employed to facilitate compliance. Thus, security drew upon the "old armatures of law and discipline" to foster national vitality (Foucault, 2007, p. 10).

Foucault (2007) found the eighteenth-century practice of variolization (inoculation) remarkable because it was foreign to prevailing medical theories. He concluded the development of population statistics provided mathematical support for a practice that could not be explained, indeed was "unthinkable," within prevailing medical understandings (p. 58). Variolization represented a very early security mechanism aimed at the population, legitimized by statistical representations of the population, which was widely practiced despite its discontinuity with medical knowledge. The next section considers medical understandings which, until the close of the nineteenth century, were largely predicated on the environmental accounts of disease origins informing urban medicine and sanitary science.

The Diseased Body: Transformations in Understanding

In 1611, the governor of the early Virginia colonists ordered citizens to keep their houses "sweete and cleane" (cited in Duffy, 1990, p. 11). The logic informing the governor's order was that of the *cordon sanitaire* of quarantine, which viewed disease transmission in relation to the contamination of space by illness and therefore relied on enforced boundaries between spaces to halt the dissemination of disease (Armstrong, 2002). Medical authorities worked to secure boundaries to prevent the spread of contagion but lacked understanding of the nature and causality of pathology (Foucault, 1994a).

Prior to the end of the nineteenth century, medical practice was largely informed by this logic of contaminated spaces. Disease was believed to stem from individuals' susceptibilities to adverse environmental conditions, and treatment aimed to halt epidemics. But the study and treatment of disease changed radically across the eighteenth and nineteenth centuries as medical investigation moved from the two-dimensional study of overt disease symptoms to a three-dimensional model of clinical investigation of underlying disease pathology. The three-dimensional model of the diseased body would serve as a condition of possibility for the development of "germ"-based theories of disease at the close of the nineteenth century.

In the very early eighteenth century, the study of disease tended to be disassociated from medical practice and entailed abstract understandings of disease species in relation to classificatory schemes:

The nosological picture involves a figure of the diseases that is neither the chain of causes and effects nor the chronological series of events nor its visible trajectory in the human body. This organization treats localization in the organism as a subsidiary problem but defines a fundamental system of relations involving envelopments, subordinations, divisions, resemblances. (Foucault, 1994a, pp. 4–5)

A kind of "philosophical" knowledge was required for the study of disease (p. 5) as analogies "defined essences" (p. 6).

Medical practice in the eighteenth century was directed less toward the concrete body of the patient and more toward the signs differentiating one disease from another. Accordingly, as David Armstrong (1995) interpreted Foucault, the practice of "bedside medicine" by early-eighteenth-century physicians was predicated on a two-dimensional system where illness was "coterminous with the symptoms" reported by patients such that the "overt symptom was the illness" (p. 394; see also Jewson, 1976). Physicians' medical examinations monitored the surface sequence of symptoms. Patients were often accommodated in physicians' homes (Foucault, 1994a).

In response to the concerns of state medicine (explained previously), publicly funded medical hospitals and private clinics began to be opened in the eighteenth century, offering new venues for treatment and observation (Foucault, 1994a). Early public hospitals in France and England housed orphans, the aged, and the poor infirm, although they were eventually to serve a wider variety of functions. Physicians used the hospitals for bedside observation and instruction, providing a spatial context for a more systematic study of disease.

However, clinics provided the most important locale for developments in practices studying and understanding disease. Early clinics were established in the eighteenth century for pedagogical purposes in France and Austria as counterpoints to hospital instruction. Foucault (1994a) saw the clinic as instrumental in producing a particular medical gaze, the "anatomo-clinical perception" (p. 174) that would ultimately expand medical investigation by addressing the corporeal body directly. After the French Revolution, clinics played a pivotal role in educating doctors in France and emerged as institutions of scientific discovery.

Late-eighteenth-century clinical investigators drew upon nosological understandings when examining patients who were perceived as afflicted by particular diseases. Although investigation was initially guided by abstract nosologies and the desire to impart instruction to aspiring physicians, the synthesis of medical nosologies and clinical examination eventually prompted closer investigation of disease relationships and underlying causal connections as the patients' bodies became more central (Armstrong, 1995). This shift occurred with a radical transformation of the clinics as they were reorganized as sites for medical discovery. By the early nineteenth century, medical understandings were codified and statistical data collected to test and confirm tentative hypotheses.

New interest in the characteristics of the diseased body—its specific abnormalities, pathologies, and lesions—transformed the two-dimensional model of eighteenth-century medicine, eventually replacing it with a three-dimensional model in the early nineteenth century as medical authorities began to think of disease in terms of "symptom, sign and pathology" (Armstrong, 1995, p. 394; see Foucault, 1994a, pp. 159–170). The significance of the new three-dimensional model of disease was that the symptom was no longer equated with the disease, but rather the doctor was called upon to infer from the symptoms "signs" of some *underlying* pathology/lesion (Armstrong, 1995). Observation of bodily effects sometimes bypassed patients' self-reports as clinicians sought to "identify the exact nature of the lesion from the telltale indicators or signs it left within the body" (Armstrong, 2002, p. 58).

Foucault described nineteenth-century medicine as regulated in relation to normality: "it formed its concepts and prescribed its interventions in relation to a standard of functioning and organic structure, and physiological knowledge . . ." (1994a, p. 35). Consequently, this medicine operated according to a "medical bipolarity of the normal and the pathological" (p. 35). Normative models of functioning or appearance served as the basis upon which medical deviance and pathology could be identified. The article, "An Account of the Organic Chemical Constituents or Immediate Principles of the Excrements of Man and Animals in the Healthy State," illustrates the "scientific" pursuit of normality and pathology: "To extend our pathological knowledge, and afford new means of diagnosis, by applying a method of analysis to healthy evacuations, thus affording to physicians and pathologists an opportunity of examining these matters in a morbid state" (Marcet, 1854, p. 265).

Surgery and autopsy were used to render the inside of the pathological, diseased body visible within the clinical space (Long, 1992). In Europe and the urban United States, the poor largely provided physicians with the bodies explored through surgery and autopsy. Physicians thus began to link epidemics to poor living conditions, realizing from their statistical data the poor were more likely to fall ill and die than the rich (Kurzweil, 1977), thereby creating the impetus for labor-force medicine.

While actual medical practice by physicians varied widely in application and locale,[1] social medicine, as described by Foucault, grew over the nineteenth century as public-health authorities embraced a new regime of hygiene based on the correlation between sanitation and illness implied by the higher rates of disease among the urban poor. But nineteenth-century social medicine also drew upon the new understandings of the diseased body. As Armstrong (2002) explained:

> Instead of a *cordon sanitaire* between potentially coalescing geographical spaces the new regime of hygiene monitored a line of separation between the space of the body and that of its environment. At the same

time, the internal characteristics of this corporal space were also being dissected and studied in the newly emergent medicine of the clinic and the hospital; yet it was public health that grappled with the fundamental question of body boundaries, of the line that demarcated a corporal space from a non-corporal space.... (pp. 7–8)

The new regime of hygiene that separated the body from the environment was disseminated throughout the culture in the form of everyday sanitation practices. At first, sanitation was seen as combating moral degradation by creating a barrier between disease and purity; later, by the close of the nineteenth century, sanitation practices (i.e., hygiene) were understood as combating germ transmission as disease was increasingly thought to inhere within the body's interior.

Social Medicine: From Sanitary Science to the Science of the Germ

Across the nineteenth century, the state slowly assumed more direct responsibility for monitoring and regulating public sanitation in urban spaces, leading to the institutionalization of public health in government establishments. By the close of the nineteenth century, public-health policy and oversight were seen as critical for bridging individual and social health because the emerging logic and practices of sanitary science emphasized the social costs of products imbibed and expelled by individual human bodies, including air, water, and human waste.

Although Foucault did not elaborate on this point, the impetus for social medicine rested in part on its very obvious links to state security. The integral connection between individual health/sanitation and state security was in no place better dramatized than in the military, where cholera and bacterial infection of wounds crippled armies. The British experience in the Crimean War (1854–1856) dramatized perils to troop health through the terrible mortality wrought by cholera and wound infection. Mobilized by the obvious implications for security, the British Army began reforming and enhancing its medical services, although it was not until 1898 that the various components of the Army Medical Services amalgamated to form the Royal Army Medical Corps (Pearce, 2002).

During the American Civil War (1861–1865), the North sought to avoid the British experience in the Crimean War by forming the U.S. Sanitary Commission; however, typhus, malaria, and wound infections were rampant and contributed significantly to causalities (Pearce, 2002). The number of casualties during the war and the lack of medical facilities at its close led the U.S. secretary of the treasury to commission a post–Civil War study examining the state of the marine hospitals, which had been founded in 1798 to aid sick and disabled seamen. Reforms prompted by this study led to a centrally controlled Marine Hospital Service headquartered in Washington, D.C. (Parascandola, 2006). In 1878, as a result of the National

Quarantine Act of 1878, the Marine Hospital Service assumed responsibility for administering all federal quarantines. The health of the military, the population, and the state were contiguously constituted, requiring expansion of all dimensions of social medicine.

However, the linkages drawn across sanitation, health, and state security were not restricted to public spaces. Nancy Tomes (1997, 1998) described the role of sanitary science in the American context, focusing in particular on how the domestic sphere came under the purview of sanitary authorities. "House diseases," the literate public was warned by sanitary experts, could be abated through individual hygiene. Not only was personal sanitation seen as combating disease by separating the impure from the pure; it was also understood by middle- and upper-class Americans of the nineteenth century as a "reflection of individual 'enlightenment' and self-discipline" (1997, p. 507). Popular periodicals directed at women such as *Godey's Ladies Book* and *Ladies' Home Journal* (established 1883) instructed women (those affluent enough to purchase the publications) in the practices of home sanitation, or as Tomes phrased it, "the gospel of home hygiene" (1998, p. 54), which constituted social norms of righteous domestic behavior. In a social context in which morality was linked to individual sanitation, people voluntarily adopted many of the sanitarians' prescriptions for good health and proper living.

Many of the public and domestic normative practices of sanitary science continued to be performed throughout much of the twentieth century as they remained relevant after development of the "germ" theory of disease (Tomes, 1998). Prior to the 1870s, the idea that disease and its lesions were caused by living organisms, the "animacular hypothesis," was widely disbelieved until Robert Koch's (1843–1910) and Louis Pasteur's (1822–1895) findings concerning the bacterial origins of disease established empirical support for the model (p. 5). As shall be demonstrated, "discovery" of the "germ theory" of disease amplified the significance of public health, necessitating surveillance over the "social" mechanisms of disease transmission, even while many of the nineteenth-century practices of sanitation (including quarantine) continued to be practiced.

Acceptance of the "germ theory" of disease was made possible by refinements in technologies for representing previously invisible biological spaces. Whereas the clinic had revealed the hidden interiority of the diseased body to medical investigators, suggesting hidden pathways of causality, the microscope offered a technology for rendering newly disclosed spaces visible in novel ways.

An essay by George Adams published in 1787, *Essays on the Microscope*, argued the microscope was invented around the year 1680. Microscopes were first used to examine the visible world more closely. For example, in 1665 Robert Hooke (1635–1703) published a book of drawings of insects as seen through a microscope (Jacker, 1966). However, early-eighteenth-century microscopic innovations allowed access to the previously invisible world of cells and bacteria. The study of life at the cellular level, *cytology*, emerged as an important nineteenth-century science in Europe and the United States, revealing for scrutiny the most minute and previously invisible elements of life. Thus, it is hardly surprising some felt the microscope allowed for the emancipation of the mind from errors and prejudices, leading to the path toward truth itself.

Late-nineteenth-century innovations in microscopic technology refined understandings of the multiplicity of pathological agents lumped together in the late-nineteenth-century public imagination as "germs." In the 1870s, Robert Koch (1843–1910), a country physician, found tubercle and cholera bacilli. His work helped produce the study of medical bacteriology (Rosen, 1993). Koch's postulates of proof for infectious diseases included the idea the agent had to be present in every case of the disease and could be isolated from the host and grown in vitro.

Although Koch's postulates were not always applicable to the study of viral diseases, they defined subsequent research objectives and methodologies. Accordingly, two lines of research ensued: (a) the development of technical methods for the cultivation and study of bacteria, and (b) after 1877, the study of mechanisms of infection and implications for prevention and treatment of contagious disease (Rosen, 1993, p. 288).

The new science of bacteriology was formalized in the United States with the establishment of a bacteriological laboratory in 1887 within the Marine Hospital Service (MHS; National Institutes of Health, n.d.). Formed in 1798, the MHS provided medical care for merchant seamen but also screened passengers on arriving ships for infectious disease. The MHS's purview was extended to the general population as the organization applied newly derived knowledge about bacterial contamination to contain a cholera epidemic in New York City. In 1891 the MHS assumed responsibility for medical inspections of newly arrived immigrants (Parascandola, 2006). Jewson (1976) coined the idea of "Laboratory Medicine" to capture the importance of this phase of medical investigation (Armstrong, 1999). The MHS eventually evolved into the U. S. National Institutes of Health.

Nineteenth-century sanitation science evolved in relation to new understandings of disease mechanisms and transmission. For example, in response to concerns about bacterial infection of food, in addition to unscrupulous adulteration practices, the chief chemists of the U.S. Department of Agriculture campaigned in the 1880s and 1890s for legislation regulating food purity. By 1898, states across the United States began legislating food standards. By 1909, federal meat standards and inspections were mandated (U.S.F.D.A., 2005). These developments illustrate how sanitation science evolved as a security apparatus as its programs aimed less at containing disease and more generally at securing the health of the population through prevention. This evolution was made possible by greater surveillance of disease transmission within and across specific populations.

Public and expert surveillance of vectors of disease transmission soon also included the human body. By the end of the nineteenth century, bacteriologists had proven healthy individuals could carry pathogenic organisms, inadvertently spreading disease through contagion. Enabling this insight were the new understandings of the human body fostered by the sanitary science and matured by the germ theory of disease. Public-health officials and medical authorities rapidly sought to educate the public about the causes and prevention of the germ theory of disease (Rosen, 1993; Tomes, 1998). Moreover, medical inspections of public schools, a project that had begun sporadically in the 1870s, was formally established and institutionalized by the mid-1890s in order to screen children for infectious diseases (Rosen, 1993). Although the poor were initially targeted for heightened medical surveillance, as described by Foucault's labor-force medicine, turn-of-the-twentieth-century social-surveillance medicine soon embraced all of the population within its surveillance networks.

The Surveillance Model of Medicine: From the Germ to Eugenics

Interest in the role of interpersonal relationships in spreading germ-born diseases ushered in what Armstrong (1995, 2002) described as a "social-surveillance" model of medicine and public health at the turn of the twentieth century, emphasizing systematic observation of the population, including seemingly healthful populations. Armstrong (2002) observed social medicine differed from the medicine of the clinic and laboratory because it addressed a space "outside the body" in relation to basic ideas about health and illness (p. 52). While Armstrong's model extended Foucault's approach to social medicine, the former identified a unique configuration of events and understandings that shaped early-twentieth-century public-health programs:

> The danger now arose from people and their points of contact. It was people who carried ill-health from the natural world into the social body and transmitted it within. The epidemiological gaze therefore began to shift from the environment to the mode of transmission between people and to ramifications of social relationships. (Armstrong, 1983, p. 10)

The new "social-surveillance" model of public health extended preventive medicine beyond questions of environment and sanitation to "the minutiae of social life" including personal hygiene habits such as spitting and sneezing (p. 11). Social space was mapped first in relation to surveillance over transmittable diseases (e.g., tuberculosis and venereal diseases) and subsequently, in the beginning of the twentieth century, in relation to a "psychosocial" space, which will be unpacked presently (p. 153).

Public schools, in particular, became a primary space of investigation for the social transmission of disease. In this context and others, the practitioners of social medicine sought to understand and maintain hygiene "across the mingling space" of social relationships that threatened health with biological contagion. Over time, with the extension of psychoanalytic ideas into the medical imagination, the threats posed by social spaces would expand to include psychological ones as well.

Understanding interpersonal norms of transmission and prevention of bacteria-transmitted diseases constituted only one component of the public administration of social health. The public administration also slowly began assuming responsibility for overseeing and *engineering* the overall *health* of populations. Rising disease rates in the 1870s and 1880s in Europe and the United States raised concerns about the vitality of the population (Tomes, 1998). Declining birth rates beginning in the 1870s and high infant mortality rates, particularly during summer months, were of particular concern.

A 1906 essay titled "Physical Degeneracy or Race Suicide?" published in *Popular Science Monthly* illustrates the grave concern with which these issues were regarded. In the face of statistics establishing declining birth rates in nearly all Northern European countries, the author advocated measures to encourage higher fertility among otherwise "thrifty, foreseeing, prudent and self-controlled parents" as well as policies and programs aimed at reducing infant mortality and child paupers (Webb, 1906, pp. 528–529). "Unlimited medical attendance" for childbearing mothers and children and "feeding of all the children at school" were also encouraged (p. 529). These efforts were together aimed at producing "worthy citizens" (p. 528) and avoiding "race suicide" (p. 529). By 1912, Theodore Roosevelt's campaign pledges included compulsory health insurance, believing it would curtail sickness as a cause of poverty (Crossen, 2007).

Accordingly, the turn-of-the-twentieth-century science of eugenics strove to engineer the health of the population through selective breeding and pro-natalist policies for desired populations. Undergirding this science was a simple model of heritability predicated on the direct transmission of "heritable traits" and diseases. Given the prevailing tendency to view intelligence, criminality, and alcoholism, among other "traits," as heritable, eugenic policies also included sterilization and seclusion as strategies for removing elements from the population pool. Chapter 5 will explore eugenic practices in more detail.

The poor health of many young men screened for military service in England at the close of the nineteenth century and in the United States early in the twentieth century strengthened the perceived link across state security, racial degeneracy, and the health of the population. The nation was itself cast in biological and racialized terms (Rose, 2007). Rosen (1993) observed concern over the nation's health at the close of the nineteenth century coincided with the reappearance of mercantilist ideas and policies, including colonizing efforts aimed at securing resources and markets.

Racial ideas and the eugenics movement helped bolster colonialism abroad and motivated concerns about health and contamination domestically. As demonstrated by the article on race suicide, racial purity constituted an important subtext of the health and hygiene movements in Europe, the United States, and Australia. Eugenics, microscopy, and health statistics were motivated by common concerns and employed common technologies to identify sources of biosocial contamination to the purity of the nation (Stern, 1999). In the United States, the National Quarantine Act was passed in the late nineteenth century to screen immigrants, who were often believed to be morally and biologically degenerate. Likewise, Alison Bashford's (2004) *Imperial Hygiene: A Critical History of Colonialism, Nationalism and Public Health* explored policies and practices of race and health management in Australia in the early part of the twentieth century aimed at producing an "imagined white (read: pure, clean, uncontaminated) Australia" (p. 4). Bashford's reading of immigration and health policies as forms of racial purification in Australia has relevance for similar practices and policies pursued in the United States. As explained by Tomes, the "The specter of infection served nativists and racists well in their efforts to legitimate immigration restriction and racial segregation" (1999, p. 11).

In the context of these concerns and efforts, it is not surprising child mortality and health became critical public-policy issues. Public authorities from politicians to public-health officials saw their duty not only in relation to the prevention of disease but also in relation to improvement of the white population stock to prevent "race suicide." Contaminated food, parental ignorance, and malnourishment effectively became problem spaces subject to expert analysis and governmental policy (Rosen, 1993). In the United States, safe-milk campaigns instituted at the close of the nineteenth century had helped initiate widespread public-health campaigns. The stations set up in urban American cities to provide "safe" milk eventually assumed responsibility for "educating" mothers on home hygiene and child rearing. The safe-milk campaigns and the hygiene movement owed their developed to the germ theory of disease but were inflected by racialized fears about the national stock.

By the early 1900s, the germ theory of disease and the practices of the hygiene movement had dispersed more widely across the culture. During the 1880s and 1890s, avoiding germs had been primarily the obsession of prosperous urban families. In the early 1900s, however, reformers sought to bring hygienic enlightenment to all Americans in order to emancipate the whole society form the fear of infectious diseases. To that end, the gospel of the germs coupled with surveillance medicine (Armstrong, 1995) were taken up by an "impressive array of Progressive-era institutions," including municipal and state health departments, life insurance companies, women's clubs, settlement houses, Boy Scouts and Girls Scouts, YMCAs and YWCAs, labor unions, and agricultural extension programs (Tomes, 1998,

p. 9). The hygiene movement in all of its expressions sought to improve the health and productivity of the nation. Although the movement professionalized social workers, home-health workers, nutritionists, visiting nurses, and other experts, it also interpellated everyday wives and mothers as its agents in order to improve the population stock (Porter, 1999; Tomes, 1998).

In sum, innovations in understandings about disease mechanisms and vectors across the eighteenth and nineteenth centuries—from Bedside Medicine to Hospital Medicine to Social-Surveillance Medicine and the Gospel of the Germ—contributed to the development of what Nikolas Rose, following Foucault, described as "medico-administrative" knowledge of a "human and 'biological' space of society, of its health and sickness, of the relations of these to housing, to moral habits, to types of labour and the like" (1999b, p. 56). Toward the close of the nineteenth century "the task of government was thought within a medical vocabulary" (p. 56), entailing the "medicalization of social space" (p. 64), leading ultimately to twentieth-century epidemiological medicine and the mental-hygiene movement.

Moreover, as illustrated by Tomes's (1998) account of domestic sanitary science, the task of medical government also entailed what Rose labels a "hygienic transformation of the family" (Rose, 1999b, p. 64). Nettleton's (1991) work on dentistry and Dorey's (1999) work on "better baby contests" illustrate the hygienic transformation of the family as mothers looked to biopolitical authorities for guidance on healthful child-rearing practices during the early decades of the twentieth century.

As described by Rose (1999b), medical government entailed two central axes of police:

> There was the axis of *statistics,* which mapped out the population as a territory to be known, with its rates of birth, illness and death, which were stable enough to be known yet varied across time and space ... And there was the axis of *administration,* which sought to invent the mechanisms for regulating events in widely dispersed and heterogeneous locales, forms of conduct and types of difficulty, not merely to avert illness, but to promote well-being. (p. 55)

The axis of statistics arose from the eighteenth century's political arithmetic while the axis of administration, particularly the centralization of administration, entailed development and institutionalization of the professionals and social spaces dedicated to cultivating the health of the population.

TWENTIETH-CENTURY SOCIAL-SURVEILLANCE MEDICINE

Across the early twentieth century, public-health authorities collected and analyzed epidemiological data in order to develop risk profiles for somatic diseases first, and subsequently in relation to risk profiles for mental health, criminality, alcoholism, and so on. The collection, analysis, and publication of epidemiological data became a critical component of the governmental apparatus of public health, precipitating a crisis in nineteenth-century clinical medicine (Petersen & Lupton, 1996). The creation of disease profiles based on analysis of population aggregates slowly replaced a medicine of professional case-by-case diagnostics. The shift reduced the uncertainty associated with nineteenth-century diagnostics; although the nineteenth-century patient could solicit a second opinion, his or her diagnosis was never certain (O'Malley, 2004).

Aggregate population statistics replaced uncertainty with the seemingly more exact and objective science of probability, legitimizing and institutionalizing "epidemiological" medicine predicated in population surveillance and the statistical creation of risk factors and risk profiles (Castel, 1991; Foucault, 2007). While nineteenth-century medicine simply treated the patient identified as ill, twentieth-century epidemiological medicine sought to identify "risks" for disease outbreaks and mental illnesses across the general population. The creation of risk factors and profiles stimulated further surveillance aimed at prevention.

By the 1920s in the United States, hygienic successes over germ-borne illness ushered in a new era of medicine that addressed chronic, noninfectious ailments including heart disease, kidney disease, and cancer (Tomes, 1998; Petersen & Lupton, 1996). These new categories of disease required more extensive social surveillance and expert analysis, dissolving distinct clinical categories of health and illness as everyone came to be embraced within expert networks of visibility (Rabinow, 2005).

Today, the level of surveillance characteristic of epidemiological medicine essentially deconstructs the patient as a distinct subject because the field of medical visibility entails the compilation and combinations of "factors" likely to produce biological and "mental health" risks across the population (Castel, 1991). As Castel explained:

> A risk does not arise from the presence of particular precise danger embodied in a concrete individual or group. It is the effect of a combination of abstract *factors* which render more or less probable the occurrence of undesirable modes of behaviour [or biological and mental illnesses]. (1991, p. 287)

Whereas risk in the nineteenth century resided in concrete and often "dangerous" individuals, risk in the twentieth century was constituted at the level of the population. This transformation aimed to reduce direct, forceful interventions by maximizing the preventive, administrative management of populations seen as at risk by virtue of their collection of risk factors.

Elaborating on Castel's formulation of risk, Rabinow (2005) explained how twentieth-century surveillance strategies project (socially) determined risk factors onto the population: "This new mode anticipates possible loci of dangerous irruptions, through the identification of sites statistically locatable in relation to norms and means" (p. 187). Computer technology would eventually facilitate decontextualized, impersonal assessment of populations at risk and their disease costs.

Under mid-twentieth-century social-welfare liberalism, the state assumed responsibility for managing and securing health risks to the population. Thus, state-sponsored biopolitical authorities anticipated risks and acted to avoid or manage their detrimental effects, while simultaneously cultivating the health of the population through education and health-promotion programs. In the United States, social-welfare health programs remain firmly entrenched within contemporary life in the institutional edifices of the Center for Disease Control, the National Institute of Health, Medicare, and state-sponsored health-welfare programs.

Unlike much of Europe, the United States did not assume control for the entirety of the nation's health as large private employers subsidized employees' health insurance. Employers contracted with private health insurers for rates based on aggregate employee characteristics and often helped subsidize employees' health costs. Individual underwriting was required for small employers or those self-employed.

However, neoliberal strategies of government increasingly shape the biopolitics of health as individuals are exhorted to assume responsibility for insuring, monitoring, and acting upon their own health statuses. In the United States, health insurance has become an individual responsibility as workplaces shed this "benefit." Simultaneously, marketized actuarial strategies produce finer gradients among risky populations using increasingly nuanced health-screening technologies (see Dillon & Lobo-Guerrero, in press). Populations designated as risky are penalized for their health status unless they are insured through large corporate workplaces. Efforts by corporate entities that underwrite employee insurance to reduce their "health burden" lead to new disciplinary technologies that threaten to dissolve liberal distinctions between public and private realms (Zoller, 2003, 2004). Health-care costs mesmerize the neoliberal imagination and are represented as economic burdens which must be captured in precise statistics and disciplined through efficiencies and individual responsibilization.

"Health" also mesmerizes the conservative imagination. Health, purity, and American virtue are cast in contiguous terms by conservative religious authorities seeking to remoralize the nation. Sexuality is a particularly salient object of conservative health discourse, requiring endless examination and exhortation. Consistent with neoliberal imperatives, conservative authorities offer personalized technologies of the self designed to produce spiritually "healthy" bodies. The following section briefly illustrates these trends in understanding and producing national "health."

From Social-Welfare Governmentality to Neoliberal Technologies of Health Government

The neoliberal shift in health management is aptly illustrated by government and employer responses to rising rates of diabetes. Health management of this disease calls upon individuals to monitor their personal "environmentally" mediated risks, including body weight, stress, and level of exercise. Simultaneously, public-health officials' efforts to reduce the aggregate economic and social costs of diabetes involve targeted government of at-risk populations involving new types of health surveillance.

In the United States, public-health officials' pastoral efforts to manage the spread of diabetes illustrate decontextualized, impersonal assessment of populations at risk, as illustrated by this recent article from *The New York Times*:

> An estimated 800,000 adult New Yorkers—more than one in every eight—now have diabetes, and city health officials describe the problem as a bona fide epidemic. Diabetes is the only major disease in the city that is growing, both in the number of new cases and the number of people it kills. And it is growing quickly, even as other scourges like heart disease and cancers are stable or in decline. (Kleinfield, 2006)

The 2002 "cost to the country" for diabetes was estimated at $132 billion; however, because diabetes increases risks for other diseases, extrapolated costs are much higher (Kleinfield, 2006).

Today, nearly 41 million Americans have been identified as "at risk" by public health statistics because of their "prediabetic" status. Ethnicity has been designated a primary risk factor. The U.S. Center for Disease Control and Prevention predicts one in two Latino children will eventually develop diabetes compared with one in three across the general population. Native Americans stand at even greater risk.

Identification of specific population as "prediabetic" illustrates the idea of a "protodisease" (Rose, 2007, p. 85). Protodiseases entail risk-based identification and targeted preventive treatment. According to Rose, protodiseases tend to be articulated within an economy of hope in that prepatients are encouraged to adopt treatment regimes to stave off undesirable diseases or health conditions. However, individuals' failure to engage in preventive regimes can lead to punitive consequences, as will be discussed presently.

In order to produce a protodisease, researchers must first use epidemiological research to identify risk factors at the level of the population. Once factors for protodiseases are established, populations must enter surveillance networks that monitor their risk status. Additionally, public-health campaigns must be employed to educate the public on those technologies of the self most likely to reduce disease risks while encouraging submission to routine surveillance by health authorities. For example, New York City Department of Public Health officials mobilized to identify specific risk factors in targeted neighborhoods in the hope of developing particular strategies for self-management by populations in those areas (Kleinfield, 2006).

Health-surveillance networks increasingly target children at risk for "protodiseases." The American Academy of Pediatricians asked pediatricians to "routinely monitor how active patients and their parents are each day to help conquer obesity" as a preventive measure against Type II diabetes (Tanner, 2006). Public schools in the United States have also adopted surveillance techniques to identify children believed to be at risk for future diabetes, relying largely on the child's weight as a predictive factor, generating resistance from outraged parents who see their children as targeted by school officials and peers (Chaker, 2007). Weight becomes a personal and moral liability as individuals are held responsible for managing their health to minimize their social/economic costs.

Today, vigilance is demanded of family-practice doctors, schoolteachers, and parents, all of whom are required to monitor children and one another for susceptibility to environmental dangers posed by "fat," lack of exercise, diet, television consumption, drugs, cigarettes, and so on. Understood as jeopardizing the inner sanctity of the body and mind, these threats are believed to derive from lifestyle choices involving diet, peer selection, daily activities, and so on (e.g., as illustrated by the "scientific finding" that having an overweight friend increases one's own risk!). The costs of these "social contagions" are taken up within an economic calculus that includes health care, mental-health care (e.g., for depression), lost wages, disability costs, and the nation's long-term economic productivity. But it is individuals who are encouraged to take responsibility for these costs by managing their own health. In addition to a vast corpus of books and magazines dedicated to technologies of health, Web sites that tally personal disease risks using "calculators" and offer prevention strategies are increasingly popular resources for responsibilized individuals (Parker-Pope, 2006, p. B1).

In addition to the school, the workplace is a primary site wherein individuals are subject to health surveillance and health "training," particularly through "wellness" programs (McGillivray, 2005). U.S. employers who sponsor employee health care often aggressively encourage them to know and manage their personal health risks (Zoller, 2003, 2004). For instance, Scotts Corporation requires employees to complete "exhaustive health risk assessments" or pay higher insurance premiums. Scotts also fired employees who smoke (Conlin, 2007, p. 64). As Heather Zoller's (2003, 2004) research demonstrates, corporate interest in employee health can produce new surveillance and disciplinary apparatuses that impinge against liberal understandings of privacy while rendering individuals responsible for health outcomes. Corporate health surveillance arguably *dissolves* the liberal personal sphere as more and more "lifestyle" factors are linked with health outcomes.

As the range of risk factors expands, more and more of the population are subject to surveillance by public-health officials and corporate agents for "risk factors," thereby contributing to the proliferation of threats while simultaneously producing highly nuanced understandings of "health" or wellness (e.g., healthy heart, healthy bones, healthy brains, etc.). Lifestyle, diet, and social and biological environmental hazards expand categories for identifying and calculating risk, while individuals are interpellated as responsible for monitoring and acting upon these dangers (Armstrong, 2002). And as illustrated by the case of diabetes, disease symptoms and signs derive significance as risk factors for additional illnesses (Armstrong, 1995).

Although risk factors multiply, neoliberal calculi of value encourage targeted governance of health expenditures. Accordingly, state-sponsored preventive health-care regimes typically target poor populations who are believed incapable of monitoring and acting upon their own health. Moreover, in the popular imagination, such populations are often vaguely perceived as threatening national vitality. For instance, the vast flow of immigrants produced by neoliberal "reforms" in developing nations are frequently represented in the press as accountable for spreading "third world" diseases such as tuberculosis (Kenyon et al., 1999), although tuberculosis already exists in U.S. prison populations (Farmer, 2005). Additionally, ethnic minorities within the United States are often depicted as failing to take responsibility for increased genetic risk for diseases such as diabetes. Such individuals are cast as economic burdens, gobbling gains in GDP growth, threatening the national vitality.

Conversely, in addition to being targeted by corporate-sponsored wellness programs, more prosperous consumers are targeted by an ever-expanding range of market agents offering products and techniques for maximizing health, ranging from organic products and vitamins to fitness training. Indeed, affluent populations often flaunt their wellness as a form of social currency (e.g., in reference to personal trainers, product selection, etc.) and, as will be discussed later in this chapter, technological savvy (e.g., in relation to genetic testing). Most importantly, prosperity alone guarantees access to the health insurance which operates as a necessary precondition for liberal life (see Lobo-Guerrero, 2007).

Conservative Government of Health Risk

In the age of generalized anxiety (Dunant & Porter, 1996), concerns about the corruption of American morality by minorities, homosexuals, welfare mothers, and liberals, among others, constitute a visible space for conservative health government. Gay, sexually amoral, irresponsible, lazy, unpatriotic Americans are constituted as "others" in need of surveillance and intervention in the neoconservative and religious imaginations. Additionally, the moral malaise of America is demonstrated by diseases such as AIDS and other sexually transmitted diseases (STDs), as well as by contraception and abortion.

Socially conservative angst about these phenomena can be located within the extension of a biopolitical matrix of power that originated in the eighteenth century. Accordingly, Foucault argued "four great strategic unities" emerged in the eighteenth century, forming "specific mechanisms of knowledge and power centering on sex": "a hysterization of women's bodies," "a pedagogization of children's sex," "a socialization of procreative behavior," and "a psychiatrization of perverse pleasure" (1990, pp. 103–105). The first unity, "a hysterization of women's bodies," entailed the saturation of women's bodies with sexuality and their insertion first, within medical practices (by reason of the bodies' pathologization) and, second, in the social body (by ensuring regulated fecundity). Hystericized female bodies were also inserted into the family space, wherein they assumed "biologico-moral responsibility" for children (p. 104). The second unity, "a pedagogization of children's sex," entailed the "double-assertion" that all children "indulge or are prone to indulge in sexual activity," and yet that activity "posed physical and moral, individual and collective dangers" (p. 104). The third unity, "a socialization of procreative behavior," entailed

> an economic socialization via all the incitements and restrictions, the 'social' and fiscal measures brought to bear on the fertility of couples: a political socialization achieved through the 'responsibilitization' of couples with regard to the social body as a whole . . . and a medical socialization carried out by attributing a pathogenic value—for the individual and the species—to birth-control practices. (pp. 104–105)

The fourth unity, "a psychiatrization of perverse pleasure," entailed isolation of the sexual instinct as a distinct biological and psychical entity requiring clinical analysis of its anomalies and "assigned a role of normalization or pathologization with respect to all behavior; and finally, a corrective technology was sought for these anomalies" (p. 105).

While it is beyond the purposes of this chapter to explore these unities in detail,[2] the U.S. cultural preoccupations with sexuality, abstinence, gay marriage, and abortion can be located within modern permutations of these four great strategic unities. Socially conservative "health" discourses are fundamentally normalizing in that they presuppose heterosexual, patriarchal ideals against which social pathology (e.g., moral risk) is measured and targeted for discipline.

Conservative actors often identify pathology and moral risk by appropriating and reinterpreting the biopolitical statistics generated by established health institutions, such as the National Institutes of Health, within moralizing, normalizing, and disciplinary frameworks. For instance, conservative authorities utilize crime and poverty statistics to pathologize child rearing by working mothers and by female-headed households. Likewise, organizations such as Focus on the Family use biopolitical data about sexually transmitted diseases to affirm God's design for monogamous sexuality, sanctified by marriage.

Women's unregulated sexuality and access to abortion are of particular concern for social conservatives because they are linked to societal decline and degradation (Lake, 1984). To combat decline, conservative activists educate women on the detrimental effects of premarital sex, which they link to depression and low self-worth, and on "syndromes" such as the "post-abortion syndrome" (Bazelon, 2007). Rejecting the wider society's model of biopolitical expertise, many antiabortion activists are regular women who claim to suffer from the syndrome they describe (Bazelon, 2007). Biopolitical resistance against society's relaxed social mores occurs as Christian conservatives disseminate "health" information reinforcing preferred value orientations.

Evangelical and Christian conservatives' efforts to regulate women's sexuality also entail more forceful measures. The current Bush administration, favoring abstinence-only education, blocked Surgeon General Dr. Carmona from promoting contraception use (Harris, 2007). Additionally, social conservatives pressured state legislators to block proposed requirements that adolescent girls receive a new vaccine for cervical cancer. More locally, Christian health-care providers, particularly pharmacists, refuse to fill and occasionally confiscate women's contraceptive prescriptions and rape victims' morning-after pills (Jones, 2004).

Christian conservatives repeatedly condemn homosexuality as an aberration against God and nature. In 2006, Bishop Serratelli of New Jersey, chairman of the U.S. Conference of Catholic Bishops, stated his church views same-sex relations as "objectively disordered" because "they do not accord with the natural purpose of sexuality." He clarified that although "simply experiencing a homosexual inclination is not in itself a sin," homosexual acts are "sinful . . . never morally acceptable," and "do not lead to true human happiness" (Cooperman & Whoriskey, 2006, p. A1). The 2007 Bush nominee for the post of surgeon general had, in 1991, argued gay sex was abnormal, unhealthy, and dangerous ("A Nominee," 2007).

Hysterization of women's sexuality and normalization of heterosexuality are elements of government strategies seeking to combat the nation's alleged descent into moral decay. More generally, righteous Americans view the very existence of sexual "choice" as part of a more general social illness threatening moral security. Abstinence, compulsory heterosexuality, and Jesus-inspired self-discipline are viewed as purifying solutions to the unhealth of the nation (Shorto, 2006).

Public funding under the current Bush administration mirrors these imperatives as U.S. overseas money is tied to antiprostitution pledges (Phillips, 2005) and nearly one quarter of grants to combat AIDS were allocated to religious groups (Beamish, 2006). The Republican-led Congress mandated in 2006 that one third of prevention money be dedicated for abstinence and fidelity programs and that condom promotion must include abstinence and fidelity messages (Beamish, 2006).

Conservative health government elevates the paternalistic family as the optimal place for healthy development. Accordingly, Bush appointee Wade Horn, head of the federal Administration for Children and Family, adapted "marriage promotion" to a wide array of federally funded child-welfare programs (Meckler, 2006). Ironically, conservative health government promotes nineteenth-century formulations of the preferred Malthusian couple for poor populations domestically and abroad (see Greene, 1999), even while favoring abstinence-based contraception, illustrating Foucault's third unity.

Yet, Christian conservatives also actively promote sexual activity within the confines of the devout, responsibilized heterosexual family. Christian wives' sexual responsiveness contains male heterosexual impulses, contributing to social and economic stability (Kintz, 1997). In analyzing writings by evangelical women, Kintz observed the evangelical wife preserves her husband's faith by containing and satisfying his sexual needs. Griffith (1997) described the paradox of the evangelical wife's empowerment through her total submission to God's plan (for domestic arrangements) and her husband's desires. Workshops, retreats, and self-help literature assist evangelical women. For example, the Web page "The Marriage Bed: Sex and Intimacy for Married Christians" (n.d.) recommends frequent and loving sexual intercourse for married couples and relies on scripture to provide guidance and prohibitions.

In the United States, morally righteous individuals are encouraged and exhorted to engage in self-surveillance and self-work in order to maintain the boundary between the pure self and threatening environments. Assisting the righteous is an expanding array of Christian self-help literature and "Christian" medical practices. Although the alternative self-help literature is long established, the growing range and popularity of Christian self-help and "Christian wellness" (Sataline, 2007) demonstrate the degree of social anxiety about the purification of bodies and souls. Sample titles of Christian self-help material include:

The Surrendered Wife by Laura Doyle (2001).
Fit for God: The 8-Week Plan That Kicks the Devil OUT and Invites Health and Healing IN by La Vita M. Weaver (2004).
Holy Smokes: Inspirational Help to Kicking the Habit by Jean Flora Glick (2004).

Self-surveillance, self-discipline, and pastoral control over family members are the primary technologies for eradicating the softening and decay of national morality. Individuals and groups who are viewed as lacking control or resisting purification efforts must be targeted for more coercive control strategies, including using state apparatuses to deny services.

Paradoxically, perhaps, these fears of moral malaise and social contagion coexist with a growing social anxiety about the internal threats posed by susceptible bodies, bodies with weakened immune systems, and/or susceptibility genes. Media reports of scientific findings suggesting that addiction, fat, obsessive behaviors, homosexuality, among other social vices, have "genetic" components cannot always be easily reconciled with understanding these phenomena as social contagions and moral failings. Supporting biogenetic accounts are late-twentieth-century medical technologies, which render visible previously obscured "molecular" aspects of biological, mental, and social illness.

Moreover, recent technological advances enabling science to address risk at the level of the population genome have again subtly altered understandings, shifting the focus of analysis from specific *genetic* risks posed by genetic mutations or alleles (such as those implicated in cystic fibrosis) to more amorphous *genomic risks*. The model of Mendelian genetic risk posits a more direct and linear relationships between genotype and disease phenotype, while the model of genomic risk seeks a more loosely coupled relationship between the two, inviting individuals to pursue technologies of the self, such as lifestyle modification, to combat disease susceptibility (Novas & Rose, 2000; Saukko, 2004). The next section explores the emergence of molecular medicine and the attendant ascendancy of genetic biopolitics and the kinds of technologies of the self that emerge in the context of the neoliberal marketization of health.

TWENTIETH-CENTURY GENETICS AND GENOMICS

As demonstrated previously, the governmental fields of molecular biology and genetics coexist uneasily with environmentally constituted threats and social displacements. One prominent strategy for their reconciliation entails the susceptibility gene, which neatly embraces environmental and genetic risk using probability formulations. In what follows, I trace the development of the susceptibility gene and genetic government. Robin Bunton and Alan Petersen coined the phrase "genetic governance" to refer to how genetic technologies and envisioned changes will impact individual bodies (i.e., through technologies of the self), social communities, and political and economic environments (2005, p. 1). Since all fields of visibility entail representational technologies, I shall begin with those that enabled development of the idea of genetic causality and, eventually, genetic susceptibility.

To govern—society, the family, the self—requires a visible field of action. Thus, strategies of government always imply representational technologies. In the eighteenth century, representational technologies using political arithmetic rendered visible "population" as a problem space. The microscope, epidemiological statistics (Petersen & Lupton, 1996), and brain scans (Dumit, 2004) have all served as important twentieth-century governmental technologies. Governmental regimes are constituted in relation to matrices of knowledge and technology that make forms of life visible and subject to intervention.

Technological innovations in the capacity to "see" facilitated the search for the basic hereditary elements of life itself in the context of nineteenth-century eugenic concerns. In 1879, chromosomal behavior was observed microscopically, providing the basis for molecular biologists' accounts of mitosis, as described in Edmund B. Wilson's 1896 *The Cell in Development and Inheritance*. In 1902, Richard Zsigmondy developed the ultramicroscope, which could study objects below the wavelength of light. In 1909, the term *gene* was coined to denote the "particles" believed to inhere in the chromosomes. Although some scientists believed these hypothetical genes were the locus for the material of inheritance, other scientists viewed the cells' proteins as a more likely site (Hubbard & Wald, 1999).

In 1910, Wilhelm Johannsen (1857–1927) articulated a new way for viewing heritability—a "genotype conception"—that drew upon and blended Gregor Mendel's work on peas and microscopic studies of cell biology and embryology (Johannsen, 1911, p. 131). Johannsen described the vehicles of genetic transmission as inhering in cells transmitted to zygotes. He understood the word *gene* as simply "a very applicable little word, easily combined with others, and hence it may be useful as an expression for the 'unit-factors,' 'elements' or 'allelo-morphs' in the gametes, demonstrated by modern Mendelian researchers" (p. 132). By "genotype," Johannsen meant "the sum total of all the 'genes' in a gamete or in a zygote" (pp. 132–133). "Phenotype" referred to "'types' of organisms, distinguishable by direct inspection or only by finer methods of measuring or description" (p. 134).

Whereas speculations on phylogenetics (evolution) had previously relied on "morphology, supported by the huge collections of the museums" (Johannsen, 1911, p. 134), genotype analysis would evolve across the twentieth century from mere measurement of phenotypic characteristics (e.g., the color of flowers) to molecular analysis of the character of genes. Ernst Ruska's 1931 coinvention of the electron microscope, which uses electrons accelerated in a vacuum, made genotype analysis possible for twentieth-century geneticists.

The microscope became iconic as *the* technology for studying life, as explained by Lily Kay (1993) in *The Molecular Vision of Life*. Beginning in the 1930s, the Rockefeller Foundation began funding the emerging discipline of "molecular biology." Kay outlined key features of this emerging field that shaped the problem space wherein life was conceptualized throughout much of the first half of the twentieth century:

- The new biology emerging in the 1930s would focus on the "unity of life phenomena common to all organisms" (p. 4).
- Phenomena would be approached at their most minimalist levels leading to employment of bacteria and viruses as probes and models.
- Research aimed at discovering "physicochemical laws governing vital phenomena" that were cleaved from host organisms, leading to an

almost exclusive focus on "mechanisms of upward causation, ignoring the explanatory role of downward causation" (p. 5).
- Research defined the locus of life phenomena primarily at regions between 10^{-6} and 10^{-7} cm, requiring an "imposing technological landscape" of microscopes, ultracentrifuges, X-ray diffraction, etc (p. 5).
- "Research problems were often defined by the instruments designed to examine them" (p. 5).

This matrix of research practices and technologies engendered a view of life that tended toward mechanistic and linear accounts of chemical "building blocks" (i.e., proteins), largely ignoring how synergistic and/or environmental phenomena might impact molecular operations. Genomics and biological psychiatry are today the pinnacle achievements of this legacy with respect to their desire to understand life, disease, and mental pathology in terms of physical processes and chemical structures.

The simplicity of this framework for understanding life at the molecular scale may have contributed to its ideological appeal in the social context of political upheaval in the 1930s. The Rockefeller Foundation viewed molecular biology as a means of social control and as a successor science to eugenics (Kay, 1993), and had financed, during the 1920s and 1930s, behaviorist social-science research pursuing these ends (Lemov, 2005). Molecular biology promised a more objectively "scientific" approach to social control by rendering visible and calculable the most basic elements of the human body and psyche.

Herbert Gottweis's (1998) *Governing Molecules: The Discursive Politics of Genetic Engineering in Europe and America* extended Kay's work, explaining that in the post–World War II era, the U.S. National Institute of Health replaced the Rockefeller Foundation as the major source of funding for molecular biology. In the postwar context, molecular biology assumed importance in relation to its promised capacities to improve the health of the population by uncovering the "genetic" elements of disease and health and by fostering national economic competitiveness through the commercial applications of research innovations.

X-ray crystallography and biochemical assays painstakingly revealed the shape of DNA, protein sequences, and the mapping between DNA codons and amino acids in protein synthesis (Mackenzie, 2003). James D. Watson and Francis Crick offered their model of the structure of DNA, the double helix, as the locus of hereditary material in 1953. According to the model provided by Watson and Crick, the gene was conceived as a stretch of DNA dictating the composition and synthesis of proteins, which mediate heritable traits (Hubbard & Wald, 1999). The idea of genetic mediation and the subsequently articulated processes of transcription, translation, and replication utilized the cybernetic model of information transfer. As Gottweis (1998) explained:

Genes were now interpreted as consisting of DNA, which was seen as 'encoding' information that determined the process of replication and protein synthesis. Linguistic tropes such as 'code' and 'information' became naturalized with the scientific and cultural discourses of the postwar era to the point that it became virtually impossible to think of genetic mechanisms and organisms outside the discursive framework of information. Molecular biologists came to view organisms and molecules as information-storage-and-retrieval systems. (p. 53)

Life was distilled as information through abstraction of genetic sequence data. The cybernetic, self-replicating gene assumed central importance as the locus for life and as an integral component of the Cold War "knowledge-power nexus" (p. 53). Genetics promised economic returns on commercially applicable genetic innovations in health and agriculture and, simultaneously, promised to maximize the health of the population.

Introduction of computer programs such as FASTA and BLAST in the 1970s and 1980s allowed for automated comparisons of sequence data, heralding the era of bioinformatics (Mackenzie, 2003). Today, a wide range of systems capable of integrating data sources and processing techniques exists. Roche Holding's 454 Genome Sequencer currently offers the least expensive option for sequencing a person's genome, costing about $300,000 (Winstein, 2007). However, most genetic analyses do not sequence whole genomes; rather, they scan for specific alleles or groupings of alleles (i.e., alleles are alternative forms of a genetic locus). Machines capable of scanning for 500,000 genetic variations are now available, enabling researchers to identify "suspect" alleles that can be subsequently *correlated* with diseases such as diabetes or autism, or perhaps even with behavioral or cognitive traits such as memory, usually through comparisons of populations (Regalado, 2006a).

It is important to stress that genomic sequencing does not necessarily reveal how genes function. As explained by Mackenzie (2003), the software used in sequencing comparisons "treat the problem of sequence alignment as an editing problem: how many single character edit operations would be needed to transform a given sequence file into another given sequence file" (p. 322). However, "the level of abstraction" allowing for comparison of sequence data "does not translate into ready visualization of the biological function of the sequence" (p. 324). Significant computational challenges impinge against "direct mapping between protein sequence data and knowledge of protein shape and biochemical function" (p. 325). In other words, the various types of genetic sequencing studies (e.g., associational and linkage studies) do not necessarily provide any insight into how genes operate unless researchers can draw upon other data that have explored how the genes in question operate to produce proteins.

It is useful to examine briefly the foundations of genetic theory in order to better understand mid- to late-twentieth-century ideas about genetic determinism, genomic analysis, and genetic engineering.

Genes, Genetic Analysis, and Genomic Analysis

Standard Understandings:

The standard description of the human genome involves the following information. Typically located inside the nucleus of each human cell are forty-six chromosomes, consisting of twenty-two pairs of autosomes and one pair of sex chromosomes. Each chromosome is made up of two "arms," a short arm (called "p" for petite) and a long arm (called "q"). Each arm is composed of base pairs, forming rungs of the DNA ladder. Each base pair is constituted by the binding of two nucleotides by hydrogen bonds. DNA, or deoxyribonucleic acid, therefore is essentially organized into strands constituted by millions of nucleotides linked together. Nucleotides are comprised of the following:

- One of four nitrogen bases—Adenine (A), Guanine (G), Cytosine (C), or Thymine (T).
- Deoxyribose (a five-carbon sugar).
- A phosphate group.

Nucleotides are named after which of the four nitrogen bases present, A, G, C, or T, as shown in Figure 1 from the National Genomic Research Institute (n.d.):

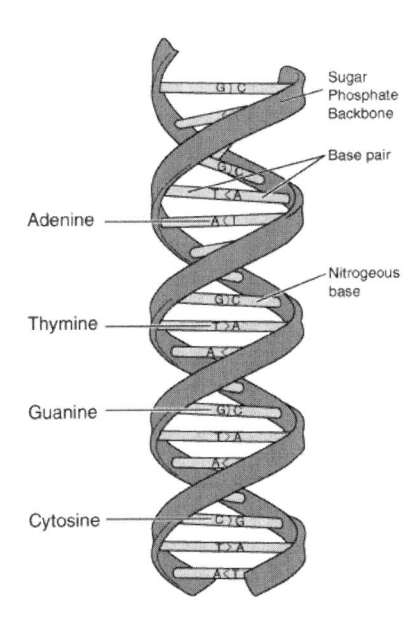

Figure 1. Nucleotides
Courtesy: National Human Genome Research Institute

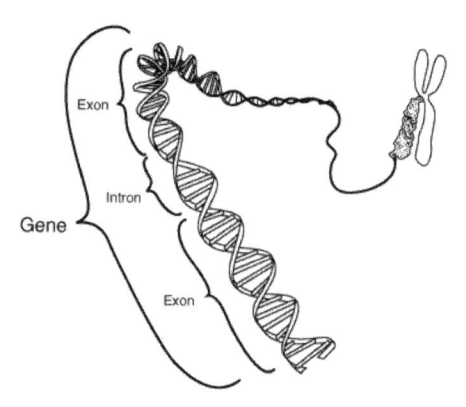

Figure 2. Introns and exons
Courtesy: National Human Genome Research Institute

As generally understood, a gene is a piece or span of DNA varying in size from about 10,000 base pairs to up to 2 million (Rabinow, 2005). However, the very definition of what a gene *is* remains subject to dispute (see Cambridge Healthtech Institute, n.d.).

As spans of DNA, genes contain regions known as *exons* and interspersed regions known as *introns*. Introns are regarded as "junk DNA" because they are "spliced out" of transcription to mRMA. The introns typically contain about 90% of the DNA sequence of each gene, as illustrated by Figure 2 from the National Genome Research Institute (n.d.):

The process whereby genes "produce" proteins is typically represented accordingly: a section of DNA is transferred to an assembled piece of messenger RNA (introns spliced out), which moves outside of the cell nucleus into the cytoplasm where it is bound by a ribosome. There, the mRNA is "translated" into proteins. However, translation is not always directly "faithful" and is subject to mediation and "error."

Genes as Information:

As illustrated by this explanatory account of genetic transmission, genetic reproduction is framed as a process of information storage (i.e., in the DNA sequencing), transmission (i.e., mRNA), and retrieval (i.e., in the production of proteins). Globalized research efforts to faithfully represent the sequencing of base pairs are spurred by the tantalizing possibility of identifying SNPs and errors associated with disease. SNPs are the most common form of DNA variation. A SNP is a single-base substitution of one nucleotide for another, as illustrated by the polymorphism A/G across the two possible sequences GAACCT in person A and the sequence GAGCCT in person B (Perkinelmer, 2006). The difference between a SNP and a genetic "error" is decided by the frequency of the variation across the population:

> SNPs and point mutations are structurally identical, differing only in their frequency. Variations that occur in 1% or less of a population are considered point mutations, and those occurring in more than 1% are SNPs. (Cambridge Healthtech Institute, n.d.)

Despite the great interest in SNPs, most people share the same gene sequences: 99.9 percent of one individual DNA sequences will be identical to that of another person. Of the 0.1 percent difference, over 80 percent will be SNPs.

SNPs are thought to occur every 100–300 bases. Over 4 million SNPs have been identified of the approximately 10 to 30 million thought to potentially exist. Efforts to identify additional SNPs may be facilitated by the discovery that SNPs might be present in alleles in block pattern, termed *haplotype* blocks. Decades of research on the heritable transmission of disease using genetic sequencing reveals that few diseases are *directly* caused by SNPs or genetic errors.

Genetic Heritability:

Genetic analysis in the decades following the "discovery" of DNA typically posited a model of direct genetic heritability of disease. Accordingly, geneticists sought to identify alleles and mutations causing disease expressions in clear and direct ways. Genotype and phenotype were closely coupled within this model. One example of a disease that was "discovered" to be caused by a clear genetic origin is cystic fibrosis.

Cystic fibrosis, a disease found most frequently in people of European descent, was transformed from a syndrome of symptoms to a disease by the discovery of genetic causes (Hedgecoe, 2003). Commonly, in cystic fibrosis, there is a deletion in a gene sequence on the long arm of chromosome 7 so that instead of the "normal" sequence ATC AT CTT T GGT GTT, there is ATC ATT GGT GTT. "CTT" is missing in the flawed sequence illustrated here. However, over 1,000 different mutations of the gene at issue have been identified. The conventional wisdom is that in order to develop the disease, individuals must inherit a defective sequence from each parent, although phenotypic expressions of the disease are highly variable.

Geneticists often represent cystic fibrosis as "easy" because inheritance of two flawed sequences directly causes the disease. However, Adam Hedgecoe (2003) demonstrated new forms of ambiguity stemmed from geneticization of cystic fibrosis. He explained how the classification criteria relied on a set of exclusions that obscured evidence that carriers (with one defective sequence) are at risk for a host of other medical conditions, contradicting the conventional wisdom that one gene alone fails to affect the phenotype. For Hedgecoe, these examples demonstrated the social contingency of medical classifications and the ambiguity stemming from efforts to link disease conditions to genetic first causes, even in the case of the "easiest" of genetic-linked diseases.

Excepting examples such as cystic fibrosis, the promise of finding gene sequences that directly cause diseases has been relatively unfulfilled because most diseases are not directly heritable. For instance, a disease such Alzheimer's can result from (a) different mutations of the same gene or (b) from mutations of different genes (Insel & Collins, 2003). Moreover, often the same mutation in the same gene can result in variable phenotypic manifestations. Finally, the "extent of pathology, the location of pathology, or the age of onset can be influenced by modifier genes, by environmental factors, or by poorly understood effects that contribute to differences in severity" (p. 617). Genes rarely cause diseases in direct ways; rather, genes confer susceptibility.

Consequently, current endeavors to link disease to genes often pursue genomic analysis of alleles or haplotypes that confer or reduce risk. As mentioned previously in the chapter, genomic analysis differs from earlier forms of focused genetic analysis because it scans entire genomes for genetic polymorphisms or mutations linked to disease susceptibility using new representational and computing technologies. Genomic analysis therefore allows researchers to identify a range of genetic variations statistically correlated with a disease. The statistical correlation does not equate with a model of genetic determinism: rather, it suggests "risk" or susceptibility. Identification of susceptibility genes also suggests disease pathways that previously escaped investigative attention.

Genetic science has also moved beyond studying sequences to address dynamic processes. Research on epigenetic change has profound implications for taken-for-granted assumptions about the relationship between the genotype and phenotype and points to the limited value of sequencing data to conclusively predict disease or disease expression. Epigenetics involves regulation of gene expressions, entailing:

> the regulation of changes in gene expression by mechanisms that do not involve changes in DNA sequence. Epigenetic changes encompass chromatic structure modulation, transcriptional repression, X-chromosome inactivation, genomic imprinting, and the suppression of the detrimental effects of repetitive and parasitic DNA sequences on genome integrity. (National Cancer Institute, 2006)

Epigenetics explains why identical twins afflicted with cystic fibrosis might have significant divergences in the expressions of their disease. Accordingly, Reiner Veitia (2005) suggested the very idea of a clone needs to be rethought as a consequence of the degree of phenotypic variation expressed in an organism not encoded in its genome. Conceptualizations of clones (based on sequenced comparisons) involve a "statistical over-simplification representing a series of individuals having essentially the same genome but capable of exhibiting wide phenotypic variation" (p. 21).

Complementing the study of epigenetic processes is proteomics, the examination of how proteins are expressed under different biochemical conditions. Proteomics studies posttranslational modification to proteins and therefore extends beyond analysis of epigenetic regulation of gene expression (Strohman, 2002). Other areas of research, including study of networks of glycolysis and mitochondrial oxidation reduction, require research to address dynamic systems of interaction across molecular environments. Taken together, epigenetics, proteomics, and the study of metabolic networks (e.g., metabolomics) decouple mechanistic linear formulations of the genotype-phenotype relationship and demonstrate the limits of sequencing data's capacities to reveal the dynamics of living bodies.

The emerging "dynamic" sciences linking DNA sequences with translation and posttranslation processes again implicate environmental threats. For example, although some epigenetic factors may be internal (endogenous) to the organism, many are not. As the article from the National Cancer Institute (2006) explains, "A variety of chemicals, certain base analogs, radiation, smoke, stress, hormones [such as estradiol], butyryl cAMP, bromobenzene, other agents [such as nickel, arsenic, cadmium], and reactive oxygen species can alter the phenotypes of mammalian cells epigenetically." The most commonly observed epigenetic change occurs when chemical groups attach to DNA, resulting in silencing of a nearby gene (Winstead, 2005). Research suggests dietary alterations can produce changes in DNA methylation, which can impact the phenotype (Waterland & Jirtle, 2003). It is believed epigenetic changes play a role in cancer development, particularly when they affect genes that suppress tumors and/or regulate growth (see Begley, 2004a).

By stressing factors regulating gene expression and the production and regulation of proteins, new research has the potential effect of expanding the perception and calculation of risk to encompass environmental forces. The study of dynamic biological processes also offers opportunities for interventions designed to regulate gene expression, protein production, and metabolic processes. For example, researchers suggest targeting unwanted epigenetic changes (e.g., methylation) may be far easier in the long run than reversing genetic mutations (Winstead, 2005).

Genetic Ambivalence:

However, Mendelian genetic analysis haunts contemporary genetic science. For instance, a posting by the Cambridge Healthtech Institute (n.d.) explains how the Mendelian logic of direct heritability haunts contemporary discussions of genetic risk:

One of the most unfortunate legacies of Mendelian genetics is the lumping together of gene defects and genes. People with various genetic defects may or may not manifest a disease phenotype . . . classical genetics was so firmly based on gene defects that only recently have we begun to determine what "normal" or wild-type genes really are. Careful reading and/or listening will often reveal that people use the word gene and a number of related words and phrases (mutations and other variants) very loosely and interchangeably. And we are only starting to realize the full extent of the diversity which characterizes "normal" variants.

Wild-type is defined as the "normal" version of a gene. However, recent genetic research revealing the "normal" SNP variation within the population genotype, coupled with errors in each person's genotype, call into question the viability of the idea of a standardized, universal genome. And yet, the Mendelian legacy of direct inheritance of "deviant" genes haunts contemporary nomenclature as observed by the Cambridge Healthtech Institute: "some fairly common words (allele, polymorphism, wild-typing) may carry an explicit (or more frequently implicit) connotation of 'normal' and/or functional, dating from the early days of genetics when only mutant phenotypes revealed the presence of genetic variations." In other words, this haunting impinges against geneticists' capacities to express contemporary appreciation for "normal" genetic variation as the vocabulary implies that variation necessarily confers risk or pathology.

As a discipline, turn-of-the-twenty-first-century genetics is torn by its legacy: its desire for the capacity to represent and control and an evolving appreciation for genomic complexity and contingency. On the one hand, the biosciences as a whole demonstrate on their Web sites and in personal testimonials a profound appreciation for the diversity of life and its unyielding complexity. Researchers seem to reject biological determinism in favor of a loosely coupled, nondeterministic model of the genome and risk and susceptibility. Such a model views genotype and phenotype as loosely coupled and regards with skepticism efforts to impute direct causality from statistical correlation.

On the other hand, pervading genomic research aims, grant funding, and published research studies are the modernist desire to capture, represent, calculate, and govern the range of human variation, as embodied in the Human Genome Project (HGP). The roots of the HGP can be traced to a U.S. Department of Energy initiative charged with developing new energy resources and technologies ("The Human," n.d.). The HGP's goal was "to generate a high-quality reference DNA sequence for the human genome's 3 billion base pairs and to identify all human genes" ("The Human," n.d.). Thomas Lemke suggested the HGP implicitly constructs and evaluates individual personhood in relation to an ultimately normatively constituted "consensus genome" (2004, p. 553). Riskiness, when assessed in relation to the consensus genome, leads to a new "discourse of deficiency" that constitutes individuals in relation to the risky disposition of their genetic variation against an impossible, imagined mean of normality (p. 553).

The evaluation of difference in relation to an (imagined) normativity permeates much genetic research, including allele-association studies comparing populations for alleles potentially associated with disease. The effect of this imagined normativity is researchers occasionally claim to have identified disease SNPs, which are later found to have no relationship to the disease at issue.

Scientific efforts to extrapolate genetic normativity and difference, and to capitalize on the latter, have raised considerable concerns (see Reardon, 2005). Critics argue technoscience assigns risk values to bodily differences, which are then targeted for government. Moreover, critics contend a primary force driving interest in human genetic difference revolves around the medicalization of susceptibility (through suspect SNPs) engendered by new regimes of genetic surveillance and the proliferation of marketized strategies and technologies for assessing risks and engineering their reduction (see Clarke, Mamo, Fishman, Shim, & Fosket, 2003, p. 181).

Genetic Surveillance

However, advocates of genetic science respond by explaining the kind of surveillance necessary to study susceptibility and identify risk is remote and impersonal (Rabinow, 2005). The HGP and other such projects operate an impersonal and ultimately hopeful biopolitics aimed at representing the scope of human genetic variation and linking variation with discernable risks or benefits (see Rose, 2007). A new project launched by the Children's Hospital of Philadelphia, the oldest pediatric hospital in the United States, provides an example of how surveillance can be achieved. The project entails collecting and analyzing detailed DNA profiles on as many as 100,000 of its patients (Regalado, 2006b). The hospital will use a DNA scanner to map each patient's genes, focusing on 500,000 genetic markers. The genetic, informatic maps will be stored anonymously. The hospital's president explains the project's objective: "The ultimate goal is to discover predictive diagnostic markers and later use them on every child in the future" with the hope of preventing or treating disease (cited in Regalado, 2006b, p. B2). However, commercial applications also motivate the rush to collect and store patients' genetic data: "By linking genetic information to electronic medical records, hospitals are well placed to obtain research funds and patents and to strike partnerships with drug firms" (p. B1). The Children's Hospital of Philadelphia states it plans on patenting "their discoveries" (p. B2).

And yet, assessing risk is a challenging project in the era of post-Mendelian genetics because, as discussed above, geneticists recognize several or many genes will be implicated in susceptibility for a given disease, and susceptibilities will be modulated by environmental factors. However, the potential commercial applications of genetic susceptibility drive clear risk assessments within medicalized interpretive frameworks. The need for risk assessments propels further genetic surveillance.

But genetic surveillance does not simply occur by market agents and public-health officials. Every day individuals are mobilized to engage in genetic self-surveillance. Popular media indirectly promote personal surveillance by fostering genetic medicalization of disease while minimizing perceptions of complexities and contingencies. Most media accounts represent gene alleles as playing pivotal roles in *causing* disease, as opposed to conferring susceptibility as measured at the level of population risks.

Consequently, members of the American public now desire access to information about their personal genetic profiles. Private laboratories currently offer individual consumers, in addition to medical clients, an increasing range of genetic screening tools. Recently, *The Washington Post* announced: "Labs Turn DNA into Personal Health Forecasts" (Cha, 2005, p. A1). Genetic diagnostics have become so pervasive that consumers can now order home-based DNA kits which allow them to "test" their personal DNA for suspect alleles linked with disease (Lueck, 2005). Growth of the medicalization of susceptibility led the Council for Responsible Genetics to criticize the use of home-based genetic tests and the subsequent targeted marketing of medicine or lifestyle advice to the presymptomatic at-risk consumers (Wallace, 2005).

But the promises of personalized medicine based on genetic profiles are seductive and suggest opportunities for medical government beyond lifestyle adaptations. Adam Hedgecoe's (2004) study, *The Politics of Personalized Medicine: Pharmacogenetics in the Clinic,* provides a case analysis of the sociological implications of personalized, genetic-based medical practices focusing on Alzheimer's disease and breast cancer. Pharmacogenetics involves genetic testing to develop and prescribe drugs and is premised on the idea that genomic-based somatic differences can be used to differentially target drug forms or treatment regimes. Yet, Hedgecoe found a gap between clinical practice and genetic screening stemming from the economic and technical complexities of actual medical practice. Still, popular interest in pharmacogenetics is bolstered by media reports, as illustrated by this newspaper headline: "New Genetic Tests Boost Impact of Drugs: Cancer Screens and Moves by FDA Help Finally Launch Era of Personalized Medicine" (Winslow & Mathews, 2005, p. D1). Critics suggest popularized "personalized medicine" shapes social expectations unrealistically by simplifying uncertainties and obscuring the technical and economic complexities inherent in pharmacogenetic testing (e.g., Pollack, 2006). But the varied promises of genetic engineering are economically and socially seductive.

Genetic Engineering

The promises of personalized medicine and genomic science more generally rest in genetics' success in learning to understand exhaustively and govern genetic operations. Genetic engineering is not about simply producing genetically engineered products (e.g., tomatoes) and genetically tailored pharmaceuticals. Human gene therapy is suggested as a possible mode of treatment for genetic diseases such as cystic fibrosis. Proposed treatment protocols would entail inserting "normal" DNA sequences into the DNA of cells with flawed genetic sequences. Gene therapy has also been proposed for treating other forms of disease not necessarily genetic in origin. Epigenetic-related engineering promises to find genetic-based treatment regimes for cancer patients. The use of recombinant DNA and cloning technologies to "knock out" genes has revealed gene sequences associated with both the development and suppression of breast cancer tumors (Wells, 2004).

In effect, genetic engineering, genetic modification (GM), and gene splicing represent a wide range of efforts to shape genetic expressions, usually of proteins. Genetic engineering of plants and animals most often entails two basic forms of alteration to the processes of DNA replication: (a) addition or (b) deletion of functions. In principle, to add a function to a cell, geneticists need only to introduce a gene that codes for the desired function. To delete a function, engineers must "knock out" a gene or introduce an "antisense" gene to interfere with the cell's ability to express a specific gene. Genetic engineering may target somatic, "nongermline" cells, which will not affect the genetic makeup of future generations or target "germline" cells, which will affect the genetic makeup of future generations. Viruses are currently seen as useful tools for genetic engineering because they can serve as "vectors" capable of delivering selected genes to targeted cells, although they can produce undesirable effects, including toxicity, immune and inflammatory responses, and gene control and targeting concerns (Hanna, 2006).

Genetic engineering has existed since the 1970s. In 1972, the first successful recombinant DNA experiment was achieved. Recombinant DNA entails joining DNA from different species and subsequently inserting the hybrid DNA into a host cell, typically a bacterium. Recombinant DNA technology was patented in 1980 by Stanley Cohen and Herbert Boyer, who cofounded Genentech, Inc. in 1976. In 1973, a segment of frog DNA was fused with the bacterium *E. coli*. The fused DNA was placed back into an *E. coli* cell, wherein a specific frog protein was copied. The phrase *genetically modified organism* (GMO) references any organism produced through recombinant technology. Genetically modified mice are today being used to develop insight into genetic behavioral predicates (Godinho & Nolan, 2006). Frankenstein-like mice are subject to both genetic mutagenesis and pharmacological manipulation in order to observe targeted neurochemical systems.

Genetic engineering, involving recombinant DNA and cloning, is employed to develop new forms of "biocapital," as explicated recently by Kaushik Rajan (2006) in his genealogy of postgenomic bioengineering. Recombinant DNA has produced bioengineered agricultural crops such tomatoes, rice, and cotton. Opportunities for biocapitalization today govern genetic engineering's approach to studying human diseases, susceptibilities, and "traits." Consequently, pharmaceutical applications dominate bioengineering agendas pursued by both biotech and pharmaceutical companies. As explained by Rajan, "upstream" research, which identifies lead compounds, is primarily pursued by biotech companies; while "downstream" research, which manufactures and markets therapeutic molecules, is primarily pursued by established pharmaceutical companies (p. 21).

Bioengineering is a highly contested terrain. On the one hand, biotechnology promises to produce innovative products to enhance the nation's health and economic vitality, creating jobs and enhancing national economic competitiveness. From this perspective, public resistance to genetic engineering is understood as a threat requiring government. On the other hand, biotechnology is politicized by safety risks, economic costs, and environmental perils. In 1974, the U.S. National Institute of Health instituted the Recombinant DNA Advisory Committee (RAC) in response to public concerns about the safety of genetic engineering. But activists regard this committee as insufficient for redressing genetic dangers and risks. Critics observe that recombinant DNA therapy has resulted in the death of experimental human subjects, probably because of the toxicity of the vector viral agents used to deliver the genetically engineered DNA (Liebert, 2002) and inadequate regulatory protections for patients receiving gene therapy (Weiss, 2007). Concerned scientists argue more generally that transgenic animals and plants introduce new risks by exposing extant life to potentially virulent viruses used as vectors and/or by exposing the world's plant and animal genomes to potentially dangerous mutations (see Schurman & Kelso, 2003). Despite this politicization, public risk management of transgenic processes focuses primarily on threats posed by contagion, entailing invocation of old barriers, the *cordon sanitaire,* to prevent contamination (Kerr, 2003). The next section elaborates on the construction and government of genetic risk.

Genetic Biopolitics

Genetic research and engineering are highly politicized endeavors deriving their meanings from public rhetoric and debate as much as scientific practice (see Condit, 1999). The very existence of an organization labeled "The Council for Responsible Genetics" points to politicization and the perceived need for public education and activism and enhanced regulatory oversight and control. Genetic research and engineering are sites wherein America's social conservatives part company with the neoliberals, resulting in explicit debates about genetic government. The Christians believe life, in all of its forms outside of labor, is not a marketable resource. They fear risks to the sanctity of life and fear risking God's wrath for trespassing in his purview. Environmentalists and political leftists are oddly aligned with Christians in their concerns about genetic engineering and marketization.

Leftists either abhor the commercialization of life or the unequal distribution of its innovations. Environmentalists fear risks posed by transgenic mutations to the larger ecosystem. Neoliberal authorities, on the other hand, fear the economic risks to the nation posed by these objections.

Throughout the 1970s and 1990s, restrictions on genetic engineering in the United States were largely under the purview of expert governmental authorities (Gottweis, 2005a, 2005b; Kerr, 2003), although the public was invited to "express" opinions. In the context of neoliberalism, the public's rights to express concerns are inviolate; however, weighing and adjudicating concerns are the province of expert authorities who calculate future benefits and risks. And so, over the last thirty years, religious conservatives, environmentalists, and disability-rights activists have raised risks for expert adjudication.

As observed by Carlos Novas and Nikolas Rose (2000), the institutions, rhetoric, and expert authorities of the new genetics have responded to the myriad concerns raised by new genetic technologies. For example, in the United States, the National Institute of Health established the Recombinant DNA Advisory Committee in 1974. In 1990, the Ethical, Legal and Social Implications (ELSI) Program was established as part of the Human Genome Project to identify, analyze, and address the ethical, legal, and social implications of human genetic research while the research is being conducted. Moreover, in 1996, the United States passed the Health Insurance Portability and Accountability Act (HIPAA), which prohibited insurers from excluding Americans from group coverage due to genetic predispositions but did not preclude insurers from genetic testing nor from charging higher rates based on genetic profiles (National Genome Research Institute, n.d.).

Carlos Novas and Nikolas Rose (2000) suggested regulatory responsivity, coupled with constitution of the public as active agents, mark the divergence between the new and old eugenics. Others, however, express less certainty about the utopian promises of genetic engineering. In particular, three prominent criticisms are leveled in relation to human genetic technologies and engineering:

1. Risky Genes: Risky genes in the context of disease susceptibility and recombinant engineering.
2. Capitalization of Life: The costs and benefits of human genetic technologies and engineering are not evenly distributed.
3. Marketization of Cure: Market-based products may serve market interests before those of the population.

Risky Genes

"Risk" is the frame organizing the first set of objections to genetic research and engineering. Discourses about risk are ways "of ordering reality, of rendering it into a calculable form" (Gottweis, 2005b, p. 119). Formulations and assessments of risk are inherently contingent upon political processes that reflect cultural values and preoccupations. Because this chapter has already addressed the concerns associated with genetic engineering, this section addresses those genetic "risks" linked with concerns about a new eugenics.

Herbert Gottweis (2005a, 2005b) observed genetic discourses are increasingly transversed by, or countered with, ethical concerns. For example, the 2003 report produced by the U.S. President's Council on Bioethics stressed the ethical dilemmas recently posed by genomic science (Kass, 2003). Likewise, recent popular accounts of genetic engineering are likely to report risks as well as benefits (see Park, 2006). However, across these various types of reporting, ethical ambivalence and undecidability are not presented as insurmountable hurdles; rather, the dangers and contingencies of genetic research are simply presented as new problem-solution frames that must be carefully evaluated using both technocratic and ethical-moral frameworks of interpretation (Gottweis, 2005a, 2005b). Accordingly, Gottweis (2005a) described "an emerging political-regulatory discourse on genomics that deals extensively with the ethical ambivalences and moral dilemmas created by these lines of research and the exploration of their meaning, applicability, impact and implications."

One of the greatest apprehensions fueling ethical ambivalence about the benefits of genetic research stems from the current gap between risk assessment and treatment. Even scientists involved with Iceland's famous DeCODE genetics project expressed unease about the uncertainty deriving from the gap between (a) the capacity to identify "risky" disease susceptibility genes and (b) available treatment protocols (Hjörleifsson & Schei, 2006). Two concerns stem from this gap: the first relates to personal "responsibilization" for genetic risk while the second suggests possibilities for a new kind of personalized eugenics.

In popularized medical and genetic discourses, patients actually given feedback about aspects of their DNA profiles, who are assessed of their risks, are presumed to be rational, autonomous agents who will willingly engage in strategies and lifestyle courses designed to reduce their genetic risk for developing diabetes, heart disease, or cancer (see Petersen & Bunton, 2002). Individuals who fail to act by modifying their diets, lifestyles, or other health risks after learning of genetic susceptibility may therefore be deemed responsible for personal health outcomes and may be accordingly disciplined. Critics also warn of a nascent, informal, and personalized eugenics that could occur as individuals become responsibilized for their offspring's health outcomes.

The economically and medically privileged agents of liberal democracies have at their disposal a wide range of prenatal testing protocols designed to identify genetic risks in themselves or their future offspring but few means for treating genetically linked diseases. Technologically hip and financially equipped prospective parents can request genetic screening to determine whether they "carry" known disease susceptibility genes even before pregnancy occurs. In this fashion, individuals engage in technologies of the self—they work upon themselves—in order to discover or reduce risk. Motivating these technologies for the self is a concern for, and sense of responsibility toward, other family members (Novas & Rose, 2000), particularly future offspring.

Future dilemmas stemming from the risks posed by susceptibility genes are aptly illustrated by the case of autism. Autism is a very heterogeneous condition lacking a unified phenotype (i.e., lacks unified expression of symptoms). Autistic individuals may experience significant cognitive, behavioral, and somatic "deficits" or may be relatively "normal" in their function despite difficulties with social relationships and communicative pragmatics.

Efforts to identify autism susceptibility genes are well financed and well publicized. Often, researchers conduct genetic analysis of large collections of families in which more than one child has autism (linkage analysis). Autistic siblings are compared at intervals along each chromosome for similarities or differences using genetic markers. Additionally, whole genome analyses using a set of 300–400 polymorphic markers have identified suspect alleles (Klauck, 2006). Yet, the micromolecularization of autism has yielded ambiguity and uncertainty. Researchers often fail to replicate findings across autistic populations as the number of susceptibility genes proliferates. Moreover, researchers find family members of autistic people exhibit genetic variations yet do not suffer from autism. Accordingly, as is the case with nearly all genetically linked phenomena, the expression of autism susceptibility genes is fundamentally open to an indeterminate range of influences.

But autism advocates fear the search for autism susceptibility genes will eventually yield prenatal screening technologies aimed at identifying embryos "at risk" for developing autism ("Autism Prenatal," n.d.). Indeed, a state-funded $7.1 million research project aimed at creating autism diagnostic tests was recently launched by TGen and the Southwestern Autism and Resource Center in Arizona (SARRC; Synder, 2006). Since autism can be detected by trained observers in the first year of life, the test has primary relevance for prenatal assessment. Reportedly, TGen and SARRC also intend to "use the money as leverage to raise $50 million in private and public funds to develop autism-related drugs" (Synder, 2006, p. B1).

The possibility that any autism-diagnostic test might be used for prenatal testing raises ethical issues which are today addressed primarily in the context of individualized decision making. Because families bear the economic and social costs of caring for disabled individuals, they may "choose" to abort embryos or fetuses testing positive for the risk of autism, even when risks are small and outcomes unpredictable.

Dumit and Davis-Floyd argued biotechnical knowledge and biotechnological applications aiming at the *production* of perfect babies imply a "technocratic emphasis on the baby-as-product" (1998, p. 5). Amniocentesis, ultrasonography, alpha-feto-protein (AFP) testing, among other screening devices, apply biopolitical knowledge and technology to facilitate production of perfect beings: the perfect babies who will grow up to be the self-regulating and responsible citizens of the neoliberal state. These expert forms of technocratic knowledge and technologies offer the implicit promise of weeding out beings possibly lacking the future potential to self-regulate.

Recent testing advances enabling very early prenatal detection of Down syndrome and autism prenatal tests demonstrate biopolitical operations on the unborn (see Tremain, 2005). Couched in relation to risk and arbitrated in relation to parental "choice" (Dumit & Davis-Floyd, 1998, p. 2), these technologies ultimately aim to securitize the nation through the scientific engineering of its citizenry while risks and costs are shifted to individual citizens. Joan Rothschild's *The Dream of the Perfect Child* (2005) explored how the discourse of human perfectibility permeates contemporary reproductive medicine, inadvertently producing a coincident discourse of the imperfect child.

Concerns about the creation and institutionalization of (eu)genetic technologies raise the specter of a new form of biosovereignty. However, in contradistinction to the liberal fantasy of a sovereignty dispersed in the self-instituting and self-limiting populace, the kind of biosovereignty at issue here concerns the growth of power over the instrumentalization and destruction of life itself (Mbembe, 2003). Anne Caldwell (2004) differentiated biosovereignty from traditional sovereignty by the former's operations, described in relation to the logic of exception rather than the law, its application to material rather than to juridical life, and its global biopolitical terrain. Achelli Mbembe referred to this kind of biosovereignty as "necropolitics" when addressing its "capacity to define who matters and who does not, who is *disposable* and who is not" (2003, p. 27). Although Mbembe and Caldwell applied their discussions of necropolitics and biosovereignty to the dispossessed subjects of racism, colonialism, and war, these ideas can be applied also to the eugenic effects of reproductive technologies used (or promised) to screen for biopolitically determined differences, or "risks," rendering particular expressions of life disposable.

According to Shelley Tremain (2006), this kind of biosovereignty actually constricts the scope of social autonomy. Specifically, Tremain argued genetic screening technologies demonstrate a form of power that impinges upon, rather than expands, the field of action:

> the constitution of prenatal impairment, by and through these practices and procedures, is a widening form of modern government that increasingly limits the field of possible conduct in response to pregnancy. Hence, the government of impairment in utero is inextricably intertwined with the government of the maternal body. (p. 35)

Biosovereignty need not entail the centralization of power in a sovereign entity/body but can also be dispersed throughout the populace as technologies of the self shape biopolitical decisions and outcomes.

But biosovereignty meets "biosociality" (Rabinow, 2005, p. 186) as privatized individuals join forces to agitate on behalf of their (perceived) shared biology. For instance, children with Down syndrome have recently attempted to change negative perceptions of their disorder as a new prenatal test becomes available; currently, almost 90 percent of women given a Down syndrome diagnosis abort (Harmon, 2007). Disability-rights activists' biosociality finds support from Christian conservatives, who are troubled by the scientific government of life itself and have used political lobbying to block government-funded stem-cell research. Neoconservatives also register concerns against technocratic biosovereignty and have even called for state regulatory action to combat dehumanizing experiments conducted by private actors (see Fukuyama, 2002).

As dramatized by the debates outlined in this section, the political dimensions of genetic governance and biosovereignty stem not only from the direct power over life and death but also from the formulation of the problem of risk itself. Are "risky" genes to blame for disease or risky lifestyles and/or environmental hazards? Do recombinant genetics pose environmental risks, or does the failure to develop recombinant and cloning technologies risk the long term economic and social security of the nation? Do genetic-based medicine and testing pose risks for "humanity" itself? The framing of these questions and the attentions afforded them point to political contestations over forms of economic, genetic, and personal government.

However, although undecidability pervades discourses about biotechnology, within the United States the neoliberal imperatives for individualized adaptations and market freedom have tended to constrain the practical relevance of public debate as societal investments are increasingly privatized and individualized. As Forbes (2006) noted, "The neo-liberal 'hollowing out' of the state has dissipated both powers to act and the institutional knowledge of how to initiate a wide range of actions in the face of new technologies, such as novel technologies" (p. 73). For example, public debate about government funding of stem-cell research and cloning has little impact on the majority of research studies conducted in these areas because the research tends to be privately funded and often commercial in orientation (e.g., see Hart, 2003).

As commercial calculi of value drive private research exploration, shaping trajectories of genomic scientific discovery and product development, critics herald the dangers of genetic capitalization as well as the possibility for new health inequalities.

Genetic Capitalization

The economic promises of genetic capitalization as well as ethical dilemmas are demonstrated by DeCODE. In 1998 the parliament of Iceland passed a bill enabling creation of a centralized database of the Icelandic people's genealogical, genetic, and personal medical information (Hlodan, 2000). DeCODE, a biomedical company, was afforded an exclusive contract to the database. DeCODE had previously contracted with Hoffman-LaRoche, a Swiss pharmaceutical corporation. In 2002, DeCODE purchased MediChem Lifesciences, a U.S. pharmaceutical company. The Icelandic government guaranteed a $200 million loan to DeCODE to help move MediChem's operations to Iceland (Eerlingsson, 2002). DeCODE promised economic opportunities (e.g., jobs) and financial returns to the Icelandic people but simultaneously transformed their national genome into a commercial commodity over which they had little control.

Critics express concerns over the commercial patenting of the human genome. In 2005, *The Wall Street Journal* reported at least 18.5 percent of human genes were covered by U.S. patents (Westphal, 2005). *Science Magazine* concluded many patents were granted improperly and in "an overly broad manner," consequently limiting research on gene sequences by those other than the patent holder (Paradise, Andrews, & Holbrook, 2005, p. 1566). Critics fear commercial patenting will limit the scope of medical investigation to only those research trajectories promising significant financial returns.

Currently, utility patents are available for the following biotechnological innovations:

- A process of genetically altering or otherwise inducing a single or multicelled organism to:
- Express an exogenous nucleotide sequence.
- Inhibit, eliminate, augment, or alter expression of an endogenous nucleotide sequence.
- Express a specific physiological characteristic not normally associated with that organism.
- Cell-fusion procedures yielding a cell line that expresses a specific protein (e.g. monoclonal antibody).
- A method of using a product produced by the above manipulations. ("What can be," n.d.).

Plant patents can also be granted to anyone who invents or discovers and asexually reproduces distinct and new varieties of plants. In September 2005, a U.S. Court of Appeals for the Federal Circuit upheld a previous ruling that patents could not be granted on DNA strands binding genes whose functions are unknown (Kintisch, 2005). In a dissent, federal Judge Rader claimed the decision would harm support for early-stage research providing "a cognizable benefit for society" (cited in Kintisch, 2005, p. 1799).

Not surprisingly, the patenting of life forms, whether human, animal, or plant, DNA or RNA, produces considerable controversy. Are the basic elements and processes of life subject to capitalization? U.S. courts have ruled affirmatively. In 1976, the state of California's Supreme Court concluded a cancer patient, Mr. Moore, had no control over a cell line called "MO" that had been removed from his spleen because products of nature are patentable once isolated to produce forms not found outside of laboratory conditions (Council for Responsible Genetics, 2000). The abstraction of the sequence in the form of "information" renders the process impersonal and almost "virtual" and has the odd effect of depoliticizing the commoditization because of these characterizations.

The market potential of genetic innovations results in huge capital investments by for-profit corporations (mainly pharmaceutical, biotechnology, and genomic start-up firms) and by public universities seeking to subsidize their operations through government grants and private research funds. Justification for genetic capitalization comes in all forms. Pharmaceutical companies will develop drugs for previously untreatable diseases such as cancer. Biotechnology companies will genetically engineer bacteria capable of breaking down pollutants (Fialka, 2004). Economic security, national competitiveness, and health maximization are represented as contiguous terms in neoliberal formulations of health marketization.

Marketization of Cure

Despite these promises, uncertainty and ethical ambivalence continue to grow around the tendency for health innovations, particularly those associated with genomic science, to be driven largely by market agents concerned only with commercial applications. Among countless concerns are three sets of criticisms. The first set of criticisms concerns questions about what types of research will be funded when commercial designs dictate research agendas. The second set of criticisms addresses the degree to which pharmaceuticals and biotechnology can actually "cure" or prevent disease and the dangers of overprescribing the products of bioengineering. The third set of criticisms addresses health access. Together, these criticisms point to the cultural politicization of "health" governance and to the dispersion of genetic government across the realm of everyday concerns.

The first area of criticism addresses the effects of market government of health research. Cuts in public funding limit exploratory medical/genomic research (as illustrated by cuts in National Institutes of Health [NIH] funding; Begley, 2006a). Commercial ventures, increasingly governing research agendas and practices, are less inclined toward exploratory studies. Consequently, "new" drugs brought to market are often not new at all but variations on already existing drugs (see Angell, 2004). Moreover, purportedly "new" drugs often target conditions already treatable with existing drugs without significant improvements in outcomes or reductions of side effects. In 2004 the U.S. Department of Health and Human Services issued a report titled "Innovation/Stagnation" outlining concerns about "pipeline" problems in drug and health innovation. These issues problematize market government of health research.

The second set of criticisms addresses the growing medicalization of everyday life and questions whether the benefits of biotechnology are overstated in public-relations and marketing hype. At a general level, critics challenge the growing pharmaceutical government of protodiseases as well as the medicalization of "lifestyle" conditions such as insomnia and stress (see Weintraub, 2007). In 2005, Americans spent more than $200 billion on prescription drugs (Tone & Watkins, 2007). Pharmaceutical spending on advertising in the United States totaled $5.3 billion in 2006 alone (Mathews & Kiang, 2007). Recent media reports of the dangerous side effects of a wide variety of drugs exacerbate concerns about overprescribing and efficaciousness, particularly for conditions that can be treated by other means. The promises of biotechnology have been particularly clouded as a growing number of drugs operating at gene levels have been associated with safety risks (e.g., Avandia, manufactured by GlaxoSmithKline). Finally, critics charge drug-safety tests are compromised by commercial conflicts of interest (e.g., see Armstrong, 2006a, 2006b). Chapter 5 will take up these concerns more specifically in relation to the pharmaceuticals produced by brain-based genetic science.

The third group of criticisms ask whether the soon-to-be-achieved benefits of biotechnology (particularly pharmaceuticals) will be available to all or whether they will merely reinforce existing systems of access and marginalization. Critics point to gross disparities in efforts to eliminate treatable diseases as omens of tomorrow's genetic-based medicine. People around the world continue to die of treatable and manageable diseases, including malaria, measles, dysentery, tuberculosis, and AIDS (Farmer, 2005). Poor people's access to drugs in the developing world is often limited to their serving as experimental test subjects. Thus, poor nations view genetic and pharmacological patents as discriminatory. The government of Thailand's recent decision to suspend patent protections over needed drugs demonstrates how public-health concerns can conflict with privatized economic interests and logics (Zamiska, 2007).

Significant disparities in access also occur within the service-dominated flexible U.S. employment market as more people lack employer-sponsored health care (Solomon & Wessel, 2007). Access disparities to health care may help explain why social class significantly predicts life expectancy in the United States (Isaacs & Schroeder, 2004). But even those who carry health insurance worry that health information, particularly genetic information, will be used against, rather than for, patients in the form of higher premiums.

Contesting Health: Biopolitics and Marketization

Health government is not simply imposed from above but is debated in living rooms and privatized medical interactions between patients and health providers. Health activism by everyday people has put pressure on public officials, becoming a volatile political issue in the United States. However, faced with enormous and growing current account deficits, U.S. public authorities urge curtailment of state-sponsored entitlement programs to avoid an encroaching "debt spiral" as health-care costs are estimated to rise to 19 percent of the GDP by 2050 (Ip, 2007). Economists warn private health-care spending threatens to impede the nation's economic competitiveness as private employers are indebted by their retirees' legacy costs.

Corporate-sponsored efforts to make employees savvy and responsible health consumers through "empowering" programs emphasizing consumer research and choice have not captured the public imagination. The federal government and state governments face a growing crisis of legitimacy as their ability to assume responsibility for managing health risks to populations are undermined by federal debt, market imperatives and conflicts of interest, and neoliberal reforms in social-welfare spending.

Simultaneously, health-care and related industries—particularly biotechnology and pharmaceuticals—fuel U.S. economic growth. Within neoliberal logics, health stands as a vital space for market capitalization domestically and abroad. Social-welfare tactics to govern biohealth's marketization are understood within neoliberal logics as threatening commercial innovations and national competitiveness. The problem spaces carved out by social-welfare and neoliberal governmentalities contrast in no other area as sharply.

Contestations over health also offer insight into the purifying agenda of conservative Christianity. Health care is a site of condensation for social anxiety about America's moral decline and the quality of the population stock. Christian self-help literatures offer devout Christians technologies of the self for health surveillance and management. However, conservative governmentality strongly endorses energizing the state in order to remoralize the nation. Government-sponsored religious philanthropy is a favored strategy for implementing moral reform while political appointees in government agencies ensure funding for this program.

Finally, as shall be taken up more specifically in the next chapter, regimes of health government are inscribed by, and produce, biopolitical hierarchies between healthy and unhealthy populations, between deserving and undeserving/risky populations.

5 Governing Population
Mind and Brain as Governmental Spaces

> *"DNA discoverer James Watson caused an uproar in Britain for a remark about differences in intelligence based on race . . . saying he's 'inherently gloomy about the prospect of Africa' because 'all of our social policies are based on the fact that their intelligence is the same as ours, whereas all the testing says not really.'"* (Ritter, 2007, p. A2)

Whereas Chapter 4 explores how shifting regimes and strategies of government have articulated and acted upon the population's "health," Chapter 5 addresses how mind and brain were delineated as governmental spaces demanding representation and intervention across the nineteenth and twentieth centuries and points to those representations likely to dominate the early twenty-first century.

As Foucault (1979a) explained in *Discipline and Punish*, the nineteenth-century disciplinary society identified and contained "threats" to a territorially delimited nation. Externally defined dangers such as immigrants and internally defined ones such as madness, "idiocy," criminality, and other forms of "degeneracy" or "perversion" were understood as threatening to the biological security of the race-nation. Dangerousness and unreason had to be removed from society and contained so as to avoid contagion.

Foucault observed historical efforts to divide and sequester deviant populations created new opportunities for surveillance and, eventually, intervention and regulation. For example, Foucault's work on madness demonstrated how institutionalization enabled refinements in psychiatric understandings of the threats to reason. Various psychiatric reformers applied knowledge gleaned from systematic observation of inmates to their rehabilitation. And so institutionalized surveillance eventually contributed to therapeutic normalization, engendering new kinds of expertise and professional practices

By the close of the nineteenth century, efforts to identify the sources of social and mental deviance had revealed two primary loci: the mind and the brain. Although European and American child savers had addressed the habituation effects of "adverse" social environments, it was the brain as revealed by biological psychiatry, and the mind as revealed by psychoanalysis, which stood in public and professional imaginations as primary sites for surveillance and expert intervention by late-nineteenth- and early-twentieth-century biopolitical authorities.

Early- to mid-twentieth-century efforts to understand and engineer the mind to prevent social deviance (and to shape and elicit the desires of potential consumers) led to the popularization of psychology and psychiatry beyond the bounds of the institution and the clinic. New technologies of the self emerged as individuals were instructed in, and readily adopted, the practices of mental hygiene. Public (e.g., schools) and private (e.g., workplaces) establishments adopted mental-hygiene precepts and the welfare state funded programs aimed at securing the psychological adjustment of the population. Still, psychiatric institutions and prisons remained important disciplinary spaces for enclosing those deemed incapable of self-government due to their overt eccentricities or criminal tendencies. Sovereign power was exercised by psychiatrists, judges, and medical practitioners in their diagnoses, judgments, and treatments of such individuals.

Toward the end of the twentieth century, neoliberal reforms and innovations in genetics and psychopharmacology ushered in an era inflected with possibilities both utopian and dystopian with respect to the identification and management of biogenetic "risk." While much of the existing literature on "health government" addresses riskiness in relation to susceptibility to somatic "disease," the final section of this chapter addresses how riskiness is monitored and measured in relation to mental illness/difference. Forms of surveillance and risk assessment vary considerably across somatic health government and psychiatric "mental government," as do their aims and technologies of power. Assessments for risk for disease are designed to increase the overall health of the population while simultaneously "empowering" the purportedly rational and autonomous subjects of neoliberal government, illustrating both pastoral power and technologies of the self. In contrast, the questions asked by the authorities of mental health and the emerging authorities of behavioral genetics, cognitive neuroscience, and psychiatric pharmacology tend to emphasize characteristics and behavioral dispositions regarded as socially undesirable, thereby suggesting an orientation aiming to integrate surveillance within a disciplinary framework to be applied both to the population and to the individual. Although early twenty-first-century biopolitical authorities of the mind and brain encourage technologies of the self designed to enhance personal government, they do so within what Nikolas Rose (2007) described in *The Politics of Life Itself* as an ethos of personal responsibility and an epidemiology of public safety that can promote a new biology of control. My previous work on the genealogy of autism (Nadesan, 2005) encourages a hermeneutics of suspicion, which flavors this chapter's analysis of the new biological matrices of interpretation and marketized strategies of remediation and control.

Accordingly, this chapter begins with a Foucauldian genealogy of disciplinary and biopolitical practices regulating those deemed "mad" or "degenerate." Discussion traces the emergence of the more pastoral forms of mental government operative across the liberal welfare state of the twentieth century while recognizing historical continuities in efforts to identify, sequester, and discipline those with overt behavioral disturbances. The chapter concludes with a discussion of the new biopolitical and disciplinary apparatuses governing the brain at the turn of the twenty-first century, including behavioral genetics, neuropsychiatry, and cognitive neuroscience. Although these late-twentieth-century innovations promise "optimization" within an economy of hope (2007, p. 15), they do so within neoliberal, marketized formulations of risk, responsibility, access, and therapeutic remediation predicated upon, and leading to, new strategies of biopolitical control.

MADNESS, CRIMINOLOGY, AND EUGENICS: NINETEENTH-CENTURY DIVIDING PRACTICES

In various ways, modernity has attempted to eliminate, enclose, and/or discipline the mad, the criminal, the addict, and the mentally impaired. It is not necessary to romanticize those who have been categorized by these labels, or the conditions labeled, in order to acknowledge that for centuries the apparatuses and authorities of liberal modern states have sought to repress or seclude those who belie the idea that individuals are capable of self-government in accord with liberal principles of rule. One need not romanticize alcoholism or madness to recognize that understandings of these conditions are subject to changing paradigms of knowledge and treatment. Designations of criminality or madness occur within social conditions of possibility, conditions which often contribute significantly to the production of the targeted pathology.

Foucault's critique should not, therefore, be understood as denying the existence of mental illness or excusing criminality. Rather, his objective was to explore how changing knowledge formations, institutions, and biopolitical authorities represented and understood such conditions while emphasizing attendant power effects. The consequences of power include not only overt ideological effects, such as those deriving from nineteenth-century discourses of degeneracy, but also less overt effects derived from the new forms of subjectivity and social relationships engendered by changing governmental operations. This section addresses both the ideological and productive aspects of biopower in the nineteenth century.

Madness: From Moral Pathology to Biological Psychiatry

In *Madness and Civilization,* Foucault (1965) observed that as the medieval threats of leprosy and plague receded in the mid-fifteenth century, madness came to be seen as the primary threat to social welfare. In response to this threat, those seen as afflicted were sometimes confined to ships that sailed without destination, designed merely to rid the land of undesirables. The task of isolating and confining the mad and feebleminded had begun.

Later, by the seventeenth century, vagabonds, particularly mentally ill vagabonds, were regarded with increasing intolerance by industrializing European society. Consequently, institutions emerged in great number to confine the mad, the "fool," and the "somber melancholics," among others, in an effort to force labor and to separate reason from unreason (Foucault, 1965, p. 36). The 1656 decree founding the Hospital General in Paris illustrates the founding of such institutions and the beginning of what has come to be called "the great confinement." Under this reign, madhouse directors exercised significant power over the administration of inmates' lives, who often lived chained and in great misery. Sequestered, the mad and other unfortunates were viewed by the public as both morally and corporeally corrupted. In the era of enlightened reason, madness was seen as the other of reason itself. No efforts were made in these early years of confinement to "cure" inmates of their afflictions.

During this period, the determination of madness tended to be made using molar distinctions. Diagnoses of idiocy, insanity, and dementia involved overt behavioral criteria that largely excluded the subjective (experiential) symptoms of the afflicted individual (Berrios, 1996). Mental disorders or incapacities were regarded as "obvious" in nature (p. 16). Court proceedings were used to assess mental incapacity with evidence from the testimonies of family members or neighbors (Houston & Frith, 2000). Witnesses were interrogated about the habits and behavioral oddities of the person whose mental status was under determination. The court's decision was based on overt and remarkable deviance in behavior. In England, those deemed incapacitated by madness or idiocy were designated as wards of the sovereign (McGlynn, 2005).

Over time, confinement of the unreasoned provided opportunities for expert authorities to observe and act upon inmates. By the close of the eighteenth century, the alienists who presided over the madhouses began to create standardized and systematic descriptions of various forms of psychopathology (Berrios, 1996). Psychiatric distinctions were used to differentiate those patients who might respond to treatment from those who would not. For instance, Phillip Pinel (1745–1826) described *manie sans delire* as a form of mania without delusions that was responsive to treatment (cited in Berrios, 1996).

Pinel used refinements in psychiatric understandings to argue for the release of treatable inmates. Although many observers of the history of psychiatry described Pinel as humanizing the conditions of inmates, Foucault saw Pinel's efforts as motivated by economic imperatives. In the essay "Madness and Society," Foucault (1998) noted Pinel only "liberated" from the madhouse those who were able to work. Those who remained inside were subject to more pervasive and insidious controls as treatment regimes were developed. These sought to instill self-discipline—including disciplined work—so that inmates might learn self-control and self-ministry (Shorter, 1997). The "techniques of cure" were for Foucault (1998) expressions of new forms of power, acting both upon the minds and the bodies of its subjects, and eventually transforming the chaotic space of the madhouse into the disciplined and disciplining space of the nineteenth-century psychiatric institution.

Foucault situated Pinel's efforts within a larger project to "purify" and "neutralize" the threat of unreason and moral contamination posed by the mad and indigent (Foucault, 1965, p. 296). For Foucault, the institutional asylum and its curative moral and biologically inspired techniques were part of a new disciplinary apparatus combining the enclosed institution (with its functions: "arresting evil, breaking communications, suspending time") with other panoptic disciplinary mechanisms that were dispersed capillarylike throughout the society (Foucault, 1979a, p. 209). This diffuse disciplinary apparatus combined surveillance with interventions designed to normalize difference and to harness energies for industrial purposes while stripping Western thought of its recognition and responsivity to the voices of unreason. Foucault concluded that in the Enlightenment institution, "madness will never again be able to speak the language of unreason, with all that in it transcends the natural phenomena of disease. It will be entirely enclosed in a pathology" (Foucault, 1965, pp. 196–197).

As interest in classifying and understanding psychiatric disorders grew, nineteenth-century biopolitical authorities—alienists, physicians, neurologists, and eventually psychiatrists—devised ever more strategies for distinguishing disorders characterized by (a) overt expressions of "mania" involving delusions and hallucinations (psychoses) from (b) more subtle abnormalities of affect, social relations, and subjective experience from (c) forms of "idiocy" (Rafalovich, 2001; Trent, 1994). New labels such as monomania and moral insanity encompassed abnormalities in behavior or affect not characterized by delirium and hallucination (Berrios, 1993).

The sheer variety of approaches toward understanding "insanity" and "idiocy" across the nineteenth century demonstrates the salience of biopolitics to nineteenth-century life and the cultural preoccupation with dividing populations according to gradients of abnormality. Expert authorities, including alienists and individuals representing the emerging specialization of medical psychiatry, offered competing interpretations of the causes and treatments of problematic mental symptoms using case studies and diagnostic evaluations. These data were used to develop understandings of dangerous individuals who could be identified and targeted for surveillance and normalization. As Foucault (2006) argued in *Psychiatric Power*, biopolitical efforts were often directed at rendering the insane (or "idiot") "docile and submissive" (p. 22).

Foucault argued nineteenth-century approaches to understanding, treating, and regulating madness institutionalized and professionalized the apparatuses and authorities of disciplinary power, which substituted the centered control of monarchial authority with a circulating and capillary form of power that was "anonymous, multiple, pale and colorless" (2006, p. 22). Psychiatric apparatuses of discipline typically operated within a moral vocabulary pathologizing the patient's will (first) and biology (later). These apparatuses were appropriated by the human sciences, particularly criminology and anthropology, as will be discussed presently.

Accordingly, early-nineteenth-century "Romantic" psychiatrists such as Johann Christian Heinroth (1773–?) viewed madness in relation to disorders of the soul ("Seelenstörungen") caused by guilt about sin (Steinberg, 2005). Heinroth believed sinful living inspired by unleashed passions would eventually corrupt the soul, leading to mental illness (Shorter, 1997). In effect, mental illness entailed a kind of choice. Thus, within this formulation, mental illness was symptomatic of moral degeneracy.

Other authorities linked mental illness and "idiocy" with disorders of the will without invoking actual transgression or sin. Edouard Seguin (1812–1880), for instance, viewed idiocy as a disorder of will and sought to educate "idiot children" using "moral treatment" (cited in Foucault, 2006, p. 215). Foucault argued in *Psychiatric Power* (2006) that Seguin believed the problem with "idiot" children was their "monarchical will," which entailed a child's refusal to submit to parental authority and refusal to integrate within a system. Thus, the idiot was one who, as Foucault described it, "stubbornly says 'no'" (p. 215). Hence, Foucault asserted Seguin saw the teacher's role as enforcing compliance by becoming the "absolute master of the child," and this mastery must be instantiated and enforced by the impeccable corporeality of the teacher's body, which is capable of subduing and disciplining the bodily energies of his students (p. 216). Seguin's approach to tutelage required transforming the pedagogical social space into an institutional, disciplinary space resembling that found in the institutional asylum.

Although biological psychiatry rejected the moral vocabulary of the obstinate or sinful will, it ultimately expanded the scope for disciplinary power's operations to the interiority of the brain. Nineteenth-century doctors and psychiatrists employed the clinical-pathological method to understand insanity and retardation, reasoning from signs and symptoms, to discern underlying disease lesions (Shorter, 1997). Anatomical knowledge of the human body's interiority, including the brain, had been gleaned by centuries of autopsies, many of which had been conducted publicly in the anatomy theaters that came into existence in the seventeenth century and flourished until autopsies became restricted to professional authorities in the early nineteenth century (Greteman, 2002). By the early 1800s, authorities claimed to link specific mental symptoms and behavioral anomalies to brain irregularities caused by disease, injury, or inborn condition, as illustrated by Everard Home's 1814 article titled "Observations on the Functions of the Brain," wherein Home linked anatomy, behavior, and idiocy with water and blood in the brain's ventricles and adjoining anatomy.

As Foucault (2003a) observed in *Abnormal*, these efforts to explain human pathology in relation to biological conditions had curious juridical-legal effects. Beginning with Article 64 of the 1810 legal code, madness (i.e., dementia) altered legal determination of the criminality of an offense. However, this shift in perspective afforded by medical knowledge had the attendant effect of more closely linking criminality and madness because, with the introduction of extenuating circumstances, the judicial process more closely attended to the "description, assessment, and diagnosis of the criminal himself" (p. 32). Thus, although medical knowledge was used to temper sentencing, it simultaneously constituted the criminal as a particular kind of being: an inherently dangerous or abnormal individual. Biopolitical authorities were charged with the description, identification, sequestering, or disciplining of dangerous and abnormal individuals. To a lesser extent, nineteenth-century biopolitical authorities sought to normalize dangerous individuals, although normalization become a more central objective in early-twentieth-century biopolitics.

In effect, by constituting criminals as particular biological beings, nineteenth-century biological psychiatry inadvertently amplified the moral taint of madness. Benedict Morel (1809–1873) exacerbated this taint through his account of madness and mental retardation as regressive, degenerative, and heritable. While attempting to identify the "natural forces" shaping the human condition, particularly those engendering "incessant progression" of insanity, epilepsy, and crime, Morel observed many psychiatric patients possessed corporeal oddities, which he speculated could be heritable (cited in Shorter, 1997, p. 94). By 1857, he articulated the idea of degeneration to describe intergenerational deterioration. Morel wrote: "Degenerations are deviations from the normal human type, which are transmissible by heredity and which deteriorate progressively towards extinction" (cited in Alexander & Selesnick, 1966, p. 162). By articulating mental illness within a somatic/medical framework and by linking "madness" and "idiocy" with heritable degeneracy in behavior and mind, Morel ushered in a social paranoia of the contagion posed by all those deemed degenerate. The asylum served as a disciplinary space that could contain contagion and thereby protect the health of the larger population.

But the process for identifying degenerates required medical or psychiatric evaluation and often relied on visible symptoms and overt expressions of pathology. In England, Henry Maudsley helped biological psychiatry describe the visible, corporeal features of pathology. In 1870, Maudsley published an article on "Relations Between Body and Mind and Between Mental and Other Disorders of the Nervous System" in which he described the "mental effect" of diseases. However, he linked these mental effects with a wide range of diseased organs and conditions including the "thoracic organs" of the heart and lung, which he believed caused physical changes to the nerves (p. 829). Although a proponent of the disease model,

Maudsley cautioned not all "cases of insanity" could be linked to bodily causes and these *idiopathic* cases probably resulted from "the influence of the hereditary neurosis and in the peculiarities of individual temperament" (p. 831). Yet, Maudsley urged readers to consider that even in the case of these "moral causes of insanity," the individual in question was subject to "a *physical* change," to an "actual wear and tear of nerve-element" (p. 831).

Biological accounts offered by Maudsley and others did not lessen the moral taint of insanity. Indeed, the biology of deviance expanded beyond insanity to include a wide array of deviant or dangerous individuals, as illustrated by Alexander Johnson's (1898) account of "degenerates":

> [the class of degenerates includes] prostitutes, tramps, and minor criminals; many habitual paupers, especially the ignorant and irresponsible mothers of illegitimate children, so common in our poorhouses; many of the shiftless poor, ever on the verge of pauperism and often stepping over it; some of the blind, some deaf-mutes, some consumptives. All of these in varying degree, with others not mentioned, are related as being effects of the one cause—which itself is the summing up of many causes—degeneracy. (pp. 328–329)

Late-nineteenth- and early-twentieth-century society was threatened by this ever-expanding class.

The Biologization of Criminal Degeneracy and the Development of Eugenics

The biological medicalization of madness assumed new meaning in the context of late-nineteenth-century fears about racial health and evolution. In particular, Charles Darwin's (1809–1882) ideas significantly impacted societal attitudes about madness, idiocy, and criminality as late-nineteenth-century biopolitical authorities linked these "traits" to the potential for "selection" toward degeneration. The specter of degeneration was amplified by its close association with the idea of race, thought often in territorial terms. Anthropological and sociological interest in representing and tabulating distinct human "races" in the first half of the nineteenth century created the conditions of possibility for comparing and evaluating the relative health, intellect, evolution, and degeneracy of "races" within an evolutionary framework during the second half of the century.

Early-nineteenth-century travelers and "anthropologists" had begun chronicling diverse peoples, or "races," found in the Middle East, Asia, and Africa, and by the 1860s journals such as the *Journal of the Anthropological Society of London* and *Philosophical Transactions of the Royal Society of London* published articles establishing hierarchies among chronicled peoples. For example, in 1864 James Hunt compared "the anatomical differences existing between the Negro and the ape on the one hand, and between the European and the Negro on the other." He observed that "The brain of the Negro had been proved to be smaller than in the European, Mogul, Malay, American, Indian, and Esquimaux" (p. xv), thereby concluding "the Negro is inferior, intellectually to the European" (p. xvi). Efforts to illustrate biological differences extended to the body's interiority as well, as represented in the article published in 1864 titled "On the Brain of a Bushwoman: And on the Brains of Two Idiots of European Descent," which detailed and compared autopsy results of the aforementioned (Marshall).

European anthropological accounts drew upon Darwinian or Lamarckian evolutionary ideas but often regarded the human "races" as distinctly evolved species, countering Charles Darwin's contention that all humans had evolved by common descent (see Darwin, 1859, 1871). Thus, white Europeans envisioned themselves as a more evolved species. This type of imagining is characteristic of the kinds of distinctions drawn by biopolitical thought: as argued eloquently by Dillon and Lobo-Guerrero (in press), the "political imaginary of species being demarcates and differentiates itself specifically by excluding from its very imagining, the invaluable, the incalculable . . ." (p. 8). Biopolitical ontologies crystallize and legitimize moral-political economies.

Francis Galton (1822–1911) provided one of the most compelling moral economies of his time based on an ontology of heritable human differences *within* populations, further fragmenting the biopolitical continuum. While Galton, cousin to Darwin, may have believed in common descent, he simultaneously believed in a hierarchical continuum of heritability which mirrored established social hierarchies within and between nations.

In 1876, Galton published "A Theory of Heredity" in *The Journal of the Anthropological Institute of Great Britain and Ireland*. Citing Darwin's (1868) *Variation of Plants and Animals Under Domestication*, Galton argued in favor of Darwin's "theory of Pangenesis" to explain the heritability of "inborn or congenital peculiarities that were also congenital in one or more ancestors" (Galton, 1876, p. 329). In his essay "On Blood-Relationship" (1871–1872), Galton provided a diagram of pangenesis as applied to animal and human heritability explaining how parental elements were intergenerationally conveyed to their offspring in the forms of manifest and latent embryonic elements (p. 398). Galton believed his model, which emphasized the "newly impregnated ovum" (p. 395), was superior to the simplified models of generational transmission that had dominated nineteenth-century thought on heritability, although he remained mystified by the exact process by which elements were transmitted to the ovum.

Galton's interest in heritability was motivated by his desire to describe and predict the range of human differences, particularly in relation to intelligence. Galton developed surveys and questionnaires to collect data on human differences that he correlated statistically—a strategy of representation he developed—to provide data for his contention that intellect and other human traits were heritable (see Galton, 1889). Using this data, Galton developed psychometrics, by which he understood the science of measuring mental faculties. Late-nineteenth- and early-twentieth-century psychometrics suggested those individuals with lower scores were more prone to undesirable social traits or behaviors, particularly criminality. Psychometrics provided "scientific evidence" for the theory of degeneracy that had been forwarded several decades earlier.

Galton's work and the work of other late-nineteenth-century statisticians supplied representations of human differences across and within populations, while Galton's interest in embryology pointed to the biological vector for the heritable transmission of these differences. The convergence of these interests would lead to his science of eugenics published in 1904, but even before its articulation the popular and scientific imaginations were captured by the specter of recklessly procreating, dangerous degenerates. In particular, work framing criminal behavior within a biological framework promoted fears about heritable degeneracy.

In 1870, Mr. Bruce Thompson, resident surgeon of the general prison for Scotland, published an article titled "The Hereditary Nature of Crime" in the *Journal of Mental Science,* in which he argued that "on the borderland of lunacy lies the criminal population" (cited in Fletcher, 1891, p. 229). Thompson offered the following propositions:

1. That there is a criminal class distinct from other civilized and criminal men.
2. That this criminal class is marked by peculiar physical and mental characteristics.
3. That the hereditary nature of crime is shown by the family histories of criminals.
4. That the transformation of other nervous disorders with crime in the criminal class also proves the alliance of hereditary crime with other disorders of the mind, such as epilepsy, dipsomania, insanity, etc.
5. That the incurable nature of crime in the criminal class goes to prove its hereditary nature (p. 229).

This approach for understanding criminals as heritable degenerates was popularized by Cesare Lombroso (1835–1909) of the University of Turin, who created physiognomic typologies (i.e., facial attributes) of the characteristic appearance of various types of criminals: for example, he described murderers as often possessing canine teeth and a nervous tic (Fletcher, 1891). In his 1891 review of "The New School of Criminal Anthropology," Robert Fletcher described the wide range of physiological conditions believed to occur frequently among the "criminal class," including "valvular disease of the heart" (p. 226). Anthropologists, psychiatrists, and medical professionals specializing in criminal behavior were excited by the prospect of identifying criminals on the basis of these typologies of physical characteristics and conditions.

The idea that criminal behavior, insanity, and idiocy were heritable converged with Darwinian ideas about natural selection, birthing the discourse known as "social Darwinism." By at least 1887, Darwinism was applied to social phenomena, as illustrated by J. B. Clark's use of the phrase "economic Darwinism" to refer to economic competition (1887, p. 46). Darwinism was linked to Malthusianism by 1888, as illustrated by James Welling's claim in the *American Anthropologist:* "In the emphasis given by Malthus to the 'struggle for existence' (for this phrase is Malthus's before it was Darwin's) we might almost be tempted to say that Darwinism is little more than Malthusianism 'writ large'" (1888, p. 6). By 1892, S. Alexander observed, in the essay "Natural Selection in Morals," that "in the battle of Darwinism the point of hottest fighting has shifted from the world of nature to the world of man" (p. 409). With the fusion of social Darwinism and Malthusianism, the late-nineteenth-century imagination confronted the horrific possibility human evolution would be shaped by degenerate criminals, madmen, and idiots, lowering "the average standard of manhood and womanhood" at levels "both physical and mental" (Johnson, 1898, p. 326).

The specter of degenerate evolution fueled biological science. Embryology and biology identified the vehicles of genetic transmission as inhering in cells transmitted to zygotes (Johannsen, 1911). Gregor Mendel's work on peas, popularized in 1900, provided a more specific account of how natural selection operated across generations, giving rise to the idea of the "genotype conception" of heredity, as articulated by Wilhelm Johannsen (1857–1927) (Johannsen, 1911, p. 131). Early-twentieth-century positivist science promised certainty in understanding intergenerational heritability while the social sciences provided more detailed typologies of the degenerate kinds threatening human devolution.

In this context, Galton published his essay on eugenics, "Eugenics: Its Definition, Scope, and Aims," in *The American Journal of Sociology* (1904), which intended to "bring as many influences as can be reasonably employed, to cause the useful classes in the community to contribute *more* than their proportion to the next generation" (p. 3) with the aim of "improvement" (p. 1; see also Galton, 1901). Although Galton did not dwell on the social degenerates endangering human evolution, subsequent writers emphasized such threats, as illustrated by D. Collin Wells's essay "Social Darwinism" (1907), which elaborated in great detail upon the dangers criminals, "defectives and dependents" posed to society (p. 701).

Turn-of-the-twentieth-century thought had converged to produce biological apparitions threatening social order and the long-term viability of the populations of specific nation-states. Above all, the sciences of man—particularly biology, anthropology, psychiatry, and medicine—had created new hierarchical divisions among and within peoples based in bioevolutionary ontologies. These ontologies divided according to degrees of evolutionary fitness, pathology, and degeneracy.

TWENTIETH-CENTURY BIOPOWER: FROM NORMALIZATION TO OPTIMIZATION

The human sciences would undergo profound transformations in their approaches to the study of "man" across the first half of the twentieth century. Although biological psychiatry and medicine would persist in their study of the interiority of the corporeal body (i.e., brain), psychology, anthropology, and sociology would adopt new understandings of the individual and her or his relationship to "society" that emphasized the social production of the person and the overall health of national populations. While fostered by the "science" and concerns of eugenics, a wide range of academic discourses contributed to this shift toward the social. Although it is beyond the purposes of this project to trace the range of diverse contributions, their conjoined effects were to center social forces and personal experiences in shaping individuals' psychologies and behaviors. While regarded as "humanizing," new formulations of society and the individual also introduced new subjectifying practices, particularly new technologies of the self whereupon individuals willingly operated upon themselves and those in their immediate environment to produce the self-governing subjects of liberal democracy.

Tracing the shift from laissez-faire liberalism to early-twentieth-century welfare capitalism involves not simply the transformations in economic practices addressed in Chapter 3 but also the examination of the new practices of social and mental hygiene adopted by the population. Chapter 4 detailed development and advocacy of hygienic and eugenic "health" practices that were, across the twentieth century, adopted by individuals as technologies of the self. Discussion now turns to describe biopower's operations on the brain and mind in the context of "social" constructions of the relationship between individuals and societies characteristic of mid-twentieth-century liberal, social-welfare states.

Mental Hygiene, Normalization, and Development of Technologies of the Self

While the institutional asylum had assumed importance for sequestering dangerous populations, new methods for measuring mental "failings" and new models of psychopathology had, by the early twentieth century, created new populations of psychically afflicted persons whose less profound pathologies were seen as warranting therapeutic intervention outside the asylum's boundaries.

For example, Sigmund Freud's work in Europe suggested new possibilities for therapeutic interventions outside of institutionalization as he "psychologized" forms of mental illness that had previously been considered organic and incurable while drawing attention to milder symptoms. Freud's formulation of the neurosis in relation to unconscious repression of universal drives revealed the human psyche as a problem space ripe for surveillance and intervention, even while it alleviated some of the moral tainting of mental illness. Freud's psychoanalytic "talking cure" emphasized subjective experience, thereby requiring the patient and analyst to render visible and dissect the hidden interiority of the psyche. Perhaps most importantly, Freud's work on the neurosis and unconscious ruptured the dichotomy between normal and abnormal individuals while also offering the possibility for normalizing behavioral and psychic pathology.

But Freud's work on the psychology of mental pathology had little influence on nineteenth-century biological psychiatry as psychology and biological psychiatry were rather fundamentally split in their understandings of the source of pathology. But in 1908 and 1911, Eugen Bleuler (1857–1939) synthesized Kraepelin's organic concept of dementia praecox with psychoanalytic elements (Hoenig, 1995), leading to a tentative détente between knowledges laying claim to the brain and those laying claim to the mind. Bleuler's psychologization of the symptoms of madness led him to be more optimistic about treatment for the organically disordered, paving the way for the creation of a new institutional space, the psychiatric clinic, designed to help treat those prepsychotics and neurotics afflicted by troubling symptoms not severe enough to warrant institutionalization. Under the mental-hygiene movement, to be discussed presently, normalization was justified to cultivate the health of the overall population.

Public and biopolitical support for this new institutional space was motivated in part by eugenic concerns, which were heightened with the popularization of the idea of "race suicide." Additionally, early-twentieth-century activist efforts to "normalize" mental illness, using personification in sympathetic individuals, helped alleviate the taint of mental illness while offering the possibility of therapeutic normalization. Finally, expert and activist endeavors to explain childhood delinquency in relation to the social contagion of adverse circumstances altered public perceptions about the "truth" of heritable degeneracy.

The idea that mental "degeneracy" might be treated was popularized in the United States by the publication of Clifford Beers's *A Mind That Found Itself* (1908), which humanized the plight of an ex-psychiatric patient. An article on the history of the mental-hygiene movement published in 1931, titled "The Golden Age of Mental Hygiene," argued that next to Sigmund Freud, Clifford Beers was most responsible for fostering a therapeutically medicalized understanding of the human psyche (Adams, p. 93). Beers's personalized account elicited public sympathy and helped to legitimize efforts to treat the mentally ill in a period when they were often regarded as threats to the moral purity and health of the nation.

Beers may have legitimized the idea that madness and other forms of degeneracy could be treated, but the mental-hygiene movement was formalized and institutionalized by medical and psychiatric professionals who combined psychoanalytic principles and biological psychiatry to emphasize treatment and prevention. These twin emphases led to the creation of psychiatric wards in general hospitals and the establishment of community-based clinics, engendering a shift away from full-scale commitment to the late nineteenth century's pessimistic and moralistic organic psychiatry, as the psychiatrists who staffed the new wards and clinics hoped to treat patients who were not yet fully "insane," and further, sought to *prevent* mental illness, and more importantly, social deviance in the community (Horn, 1989).

The physical move away from the asylum therefore engendered a new social program, the *mental-hygiene* movement, which sought to promote mental health and combat mental illness through, in part, community-based psychiatry. Adolf Meyer (1866–1950), a European émigré who founded the Henry Phipps Psychiatric Clinic at Johns Hopkins, coined the label of mental hygiene. The early strength of the movement is demonstrated by the 1909 founding in the United States of the National Committee for Mental Hygiene (Shorter, 1997).

In his clinical work, Meyer incorporated Freudian approaches to psychoanalysis into his developmental, psychobiological approach to psychiatry. In order to identify the early roots of trauma, Meyer and other mental-hygiene proponents were increasingly responsive to studying the various forms of childhood mental, emotional, and criminological deviance, thereby revealing childhood as a problem space for biopolitical surveillance and intervention beyond nineteenth-century philanthropic concerns. Expert authorities were not merely concerned with identifying the precursors to, and early signs of, deviance but were also intent on identifying norms of development against which deviance could be compared and measured.

Work by William Healy was instrumental in fostering both expert and popular interest in the social precursors of mental and behavioral pathologies. In an essay published with Edith Spaulding in 1914, Healy debunked the idea of inborn criminality using a thousand cases of "young, repeated offenders" (Spaulding & Healy, p. 837). Later work questioned the idea immigrant children were necessarily intellectually inferior to native-born citizens (see Jones, 1999). New child authorities suggested (morally inflected) social intervention could combat development of criminal delinquency and adult mental pathology. The home and personal relationships were constituted as primary contexts for expert surveillance and professional and philanthropic intervention. Mothers were eventually educated in childhood "norms," derived from expert surveillance, leading to the diffusion of new technologies that both constituted and governed child "development."

Accordingly, David Armstrong (2002) concluded, in *A New History of Identity,* the early twentieth century engendered a new approach to medical subjectivity centering on surveillance, mental hygiene, the child, and interpersonal dynamics. This approach would evolve over the course of the twentieth century as new dangers to the "psycho-social space of interpersonal hygiene" were discovered everywhere as the medical model of preventive hygiene based on the germ theory of disease was reframed to encompass a loose conceptualization of degeneracy and delinquency as caused by the "contagion" of adverse and/or degenerate social (i.e., "environmental") circumstances. The resulting social-surveillance model extended preventive medicine beyond more general questions of environment and sanitation to "the minutiae of social life," including personal-hygiene habits such as spitting and sneezing (Armstrong, 1983, p. 11).

The objective of the new medical model of subjectivity was to understand and cultivate normalcy in order to improve the health of the population (see Rose, 1999a). Following the lead of Stanley Hall, investigation of "normal," "individual" child psychology appeared in American journals by the late 1890s (see Sharp, 1899) but reached the status of a distinct field of inquiry in the 1930s as the study of "personality and social adjustment" (Murphy, 1937, p. 472). The examination of the normal personality sought to measure norms of intelligence, emotions, and morality while identifying interpersonal and/or social threats to their achievement and maintenance (see Horn, 1989; Jones, 1999).

Social interest in, and support for, the project of understanding and cultivating social normativity reflected a neoeugenic attitude toward population as well as an orientation toward societal risk management. As explained in Chapter 4's discussion of nineteenth-century biopolitics, the exigencies of disease and industrialization led to early twentieth-century concerns for the health and welfare of the domestic population, upon which the state's security rested. Moreover, as Tomes observed:

> Many converts to the germ theory believed deeply in a 'chain of disease,' a 'socialism of the microbe' that linked all member of American society together. If not for simple humanity, then for this reason alone, they argued, the health problems of the poor and the newcomer had to be addressed. (1998, p. 12)

Although immigrants and various degenerates remained "threats" to the population, the public became more receptive to the idea these dangers could be adjusted, normalized, and/or transmuted as opposed to being contained or excised.

The birth of sociology as an academic discipline in the United States reflects this new orientation toward investigating, understanding, and engineering the "social." In July of 1895, A. V. Small initiated the first issue of *The American Journal of Sociology* with the assertion: "Sociology has a foremost place in the thought of modern men" because, *"in our age the fact of human association is more obtrusive and relatively more influential than in any previous epoch"* (p. 1). Small attributed Charles Darwin, Karl Marx, and Herbert Spencer as birthing this new orientation toward reflection upon the social, but it was everyday biopolitical authorities, such as health care authorities and advertising agents, who would develop and disseminate its diverse strategies of government (see Marchand, 1985; Nettleton, 1991).

Widespread dissemination of the practices of mental hygiene and the norms of development and personality, as articulated by biopolitical authorities and the agents of advertising, resulted in new technologies of the self. Adults and children were educated about norms of behavior and affect in order that they might assume responsibility for monitoring their families' well-being. Mental hygiene was presented to mothers as a logical extension of nineteenth-century sanitation practices as they were instructed in how to care for their families. As mothers assumed responsibility for their families' mental hygiene, the locus of governmental relations shifted from the state, the institution, the hospital, and the clinic to the daily micropractices of individuals engaged in their everyday routines (see Nettleton, 1991). From surveillance technologies to development of technologies of the self, the problematics of physical and mental health, and their links to citizenship, became increasingly individualized.

Did this new model of medical subjectivity and new apparatuses of normalization produce a "freer" subjectivity? Although the mental hygiene movement and the development of the study of "normality" deemphasized repressive force, they also ushered in new panopticons of power/knowledge that fragmented old binary formulations of difference and normality with nuanced continuums while implementing new surveillance strategies and technologies of the self that circulated across the spaces and practices of everyday life.

In *The Order of Things* (1994b), Foucault critiqued the metaphysical foundations of psychiatry specifically, and the human sciences more generally, because he saw them as resting on a problematic conception of "man." Foucault argued the category of man was a historically specific understanding that emerged in the early modern period. Foucault maintained this category of understanding has powerful material effects because it channels human inquiry into a recursive logic predicated upon an impossible self-understanding.

Foucault (1997b) argued the modern imperative "know yourself" was (and continues to be) facilitated by the "norms" established by the social sciences (p. 28). One comes to know oneself, one's partners, and one's children in relation to behavioral, cognitive, and emotional norms generated by the social sciences. The dissemination of the principles of mental hygiene, particularly in the form of child-guidance literature and expertise, coupled with the appeals of early advertising, provided the American public grounds for self-assessment and self-knowledge (see Jones, 1999).

The objective of reflexive and rational control over the psychic life of the nation through expert knowledge, administration, therapy, and personal technologies of the self would become the telos of much twentieth-century social and biological science (e.g., see Lemov, 2005; Rose, 1999a). Indeed, projects of social engineering would become institutionally linked with economic government; first through the auspices and funding of private foundations such as the Rockefeller Foundation (Kay, 1993; Lemov, 2005) and later through government-sponsored funding. Under the "liberal" Keynesian ethos, Western liberal democracies engaged in projects of social engineering to ameliorate social conditions seen as most directly linked to criminality and psychopathology in order to foster the overall health and security of the population.

It is important to consider, however, that twentieth-century dissemination of psychologically informed liberal technologies of the self had little relevance for those who were actually institutionalized in psychiatric hospitals. Indeed, neither the mental hygiene movement nor the proliferating authorities of psychological adjustment offered much succor to those incarcerated within the disciplinary apparatuses of twentieth-century psychiatric institutions. Electroconvulsive therapy, insulin shock therapy, frontal lobotomies, and a vast array of restraining devices were used by biopolitical authorities to "treat" individuals subjected to psychiatric confinement from the mid-1930s to the 1950s. The discovery of lithium salts in 1949 as a "treatment" for manic depression ushered in a new strategy for disciplining the unruly subjects of psychiatric institutions (Lakoff, 2005). In 1952 the antipsychotic properties of chlorpromazine were detailed, and in 1957 the first tricyclic antidepressant was developed for severely depressed patients. But the heavily sedating properties of these new drugs were regarded by critics as introducing a new pharmacological straitjacket that merely substituted one form of oppressive control for another. The deinstitutionalization following these psychopharmacological developments would contribute to the impetus to find more market-based products for managing the most overt and/or disturbing symptoms of "mental illness" in the late twentieth century. Although this tendency is taken up and addressed further in the final section of this chapter, the history of the move toward optimization must first be chronicled.

From Normalization to Optimization: Mental Health and Human Development in the Welfare State

Post–World War II societies, shocked by the horrific excesses of Nazi eugenics, grew more receptive to environmental explanations for mental illness and social pathology. Accordingly, under the "liberal" Keynesian ethos, Western liberal democracies engaged in projects of social engineering to prevent irruption of those social conditions seen as most directly linked to producing criminality and psychopathology. Cadres of experts were created and institutionalized around this project. Yet government of mind and brain resided less in the hands of state authorities than it did in the proliferation of biopolitical authorities and in the everyday technologies of the self exercised by self-governing citizens. Biopolitical expertise about mental health in the United States was organized along at least four great divides: psychoanalysis, humanistic psychology, biological psychiatry, and cognitive psychology. Each paradigm of inquiry took up the mind or brain using distinct ontologies and strategies of intervention. Although the primary sites for biopolitical investigation and intervention were the laboratory and the clinic, each paradigm's vocabulary gained popular currency and circulated throughout the social body.

Psychiatry, Psychology, and Normalization

In the post–World War II era, psychology emerged as a professionalized and respected discipline, applying itself vigorously to solving the problems of adjustment in modern society (Napoli, 1981). Moreover, as explored by Nikolas Rose in *Governing the Soul* (1999a), Ellen Herman in *The Romance of American Psychology* (1995), and Rachel Lemov (2005) in *World as Laboratory,* among others, psychological vocabularies permeated everyday life through their inclusion in popular literature, advertising, pediatric screenings, pedagogical practices, and so on. Individuals seeking to optimize their personal well-being, or to explain the lack of well-being of their self or social/familial acquaintances, adopted popular disseminations of formalized psychological frameworks.

Although psychological expertise was primarily developed and disseminated by private biopolitical authorities, within the United States considerable funding was provided by the state during the Cold War (roughly 1947–1989). As explained by Jonathan Moreno (2006), the security state's interests in social adjustment and alienation were twofold: encompassing (a) a concern for engineering domestic stability and (b) a concern for the uses of persuasion and propaganda in Cold War conflicts. Thus, the U.S. government actively supported private university and foundation research on the psychology and psychiatry of persuasion, compliance, and intergroup relations. The psyche effectively became an object of government for a wide range of authorities, including private researchers, advertisers, military security advisors, and everyday individuals seeking advice from psychological authorities in order to facilitate their adjustment to intricate social circumstances.

The psychological complex (Rose, 1999a) provided these diverse authorities with a wide array of tools for understanding and shaping the psyche. In the United States, the American Psychological Association (APA) published the *Diagnostic and Statistical Manual* (*DSM*) to delineate the vast array of afflictions that could disrupt the psyche or its behavioral manifestations. As a classificatory system for diseases or syndromes, the APA aimed "to see, to isolate features, to recognize those that are identical and those that are different, to regroup them, to classify them by species or families" (Crowe, 2000, p. 69). The effect of these codifications was a proliferation of categories of deviance from imagined norms of psychic and behavioral "health." Psychiatric accounts of the threats to normality evolved across the twentieth century. Accordingly, the various revisions of the *DSM* map the transition from (socially mediated) psychoanalytic and psychodynamic accounts of psychic disorders to the current emphasis on biological psychiatry (see APA, 1952, 1968, 1980, 1987, 1994).

The exploration, categorization, and systematization of personality and cognition were not restricted only to those displaying overt "disturbances" but were also applied, in nuanced form, to map the distribution of differences across the entirety of the populace (Paul, 2004; Rose, 1999a). Throughout the twentieth century, personality and intelligence tests that inventoried the psyche and distributed the population in relation to specific characteristics were developed. The most widely used personality test in the United States was probably the Minnesota Multiphasic Personality Inventory (MMPI; Black, 1994). Clinicians designed this test in the 1940s to check for psychological disorders, and it includes scales designed to measure obsessive-compulsiveness, self-concept, sex problems, dominance, authority conflict, cynicism, social anxiety and stimulation, and masculinity-femininity, among others. Later, additional scales were added to measure eating disorders, substance abuse, family function, and readiness for treatment (Black, 1994). In aggregate or isolation, the individual's scores were compared with normative scores provided by the MMPI. Personality tests such as the MMPI served both to objectify the individual within a pregiven calculus of statistically derived "phenotypic" normativities and to provide the individual a technique for self-knowledge so that she or he might better herself or himself (Nadesan, 1997; Rose, 1999a). Additionally, corporate and military authorities widely employed these tests to reduce the risks posed by potentially resistant or alienated workers and soldiers.

Mid-twentieth-century researchers who sought to establish the heritability of the phenotypic traits measured by personality inventories or psychiatric disorders relied primarily on biometric research. Biometric studies addressing the psychobiology of personality and psychopathology required the creation of reliable descriptions of phenotypic characteristics such as intelligence or anxiety. Survey instruments and observations were then used to measure the degree to which close relatives shared the characteristic in question. In order to impute genetic influence, research had to "factor" out environmental variance, which was usually accomplished by using studies of twins (fraternal and identical) and adoptees.

But application of heritability research was limited in contrast to the more obvious policy implications of social-environmental accounts of human development. Accordingly, while some researchers believed in genetic influences, undesirable conditions such anxiety, alcoholism, drug addiction, and mild to moderate depression were widely regarded as problems to be prevented through social conditioning and education, and treated through individual or group therapy at clinics, and so on (if discussed at all). Work by O'Malley and Valverde (2004) demonstrates how socially objectionable pursuits (involving alcohol and/or drugs) were governed at a distance by dispersed biopolitical authorities who represented such activities as anchored in destructive drives and conditions, and instructed "patients" in the management of these impulses.

Biopolitical authorities wishing to restore or manage the psyche could also resort to legally sanctioned pharmaceutical products. Across the twentieth century, drugs were used to manage troubling mental symptoms and problematic behaviors from the early 1900s onward. Sedatives, such as barbital and phenobarbital, were widely prescribed to help reduce anxiety (Trujillo & Chinn, 1996). In 1957, benzodiazepines were developed and replaced many of the early barbiturates. By the early 1960s, market-driven pharmaceutical companies began searching for the physiological bases of a wide range of conditions previously regarded as purely "psychological" in orientation.

The mid-twentieth-century security state at times supported research on the physiology of motivation and affect. Militarized apparatuses experimented with psychological drugs in order to produce fitter soldiers who suffered less from fatigue. Additionally, government-funded experts pursued chemically invasive techniques for revealing the hidden interiority of resistant minds (Moreno, 2006). But this shadowy government-sponsored research fueled popular resistance in the 1960s and 1970s and contributed to popular suspicion about the desirability and/or viability of pharmaceutical government.

As argued by Andrew Lakeoff in *Pharmaceutical Reason*, the "development of psychopharmaceuticals did not lead directly to the institutionalization of pharmaceutical reason" (2005, p. 5), characterized by the equation of mental symptoms with neurochemical deficiencies. Mid-twentieth-century biological psychiatry proved disappointing in its capacities to reveal the interiority of the brain and could not provide models that consistently and persuasively bridged the gap between brain and mind. Moreover, leaked military experiments were notorious for their failures rather than their successes. Psychology therefore remained somewhat agnostic about the biology of emotion and behavior and tended to stress individuals' cognitive or behavioral responses to social stimuli. In the popular imagination, mental illness, dependency, and criminality remained moral failings or were perceived as stemming from "environmental" factors.

During the late 1960s and 1970s, the antipsychiatry movement agitated against biological psychiatry and its pharmaceutical technologies for disciplining unruly psyches. Thomas Szasz (1920–) and Michel Foucault, among others, figured in the movement. Its ideas were popularized in books and films that pathologized the sanity of "normal" society. The antipsychiatry movement suggested biological psychiatry masked social control. Accordingly, Szasz argued, "The classification of (mis)behavior as illness provides an ideological justification for state-sponsored social control" (cited in Sullum, 2000). Moreover, Szasz claimed collaboration between government and psychiatry results in a "therapeutic state," in which psychomedical therapy is used to repress disapproved behaviors, habits, and emotions (1989, p. 212). Szasz's critique of the therapeutic state echoed Foucault's critique of biopolitical control.

Most antipsychiatry-movement critics did not deny the possibility of biologically induced differences in behavior, affect, or cognition but rather critiqued the power effects of psychiatric formulations and practices. Critics were particularly concerned about the horrific treatment of the mentally ill in hospitals and institutions. Other critics of the psychiatric/psychological complex argued its knowledge formations and therapeutic practices psychologized problems that were ultimately social in orientation. For instance, the feminist movement convincingly demonstrated how centuries of "psychiatric" problems in women stemmed from their oppression by patriarchal conventions and values. Similarly, systems theorists suggested even the most pronounced expressions of mental illness were at least in part mediated by social factors (e.g., see Bateson, Jackson, Haley, & Weakland, 1956). Finally, a number of journalists and privatized individuals raised the specter of the possibility of insidious state control through psychological manipulations using reports of widespread experimentation with LSD on soldiers and university students during the 1970s (see Moreno, 2006).

In sum, although biological psychiatry and pharmaceutical government were operative, they were countered with approaches emphasizing environmental conditioning and psychological therapeutic remediation.

Technologies of Transcendence and Optimization

Humanistic psychology emerged in tandem with, and in response to, these powerful critiques against psychiatric/psychological knowledge and practice. Resisting established traditions, humanistic psychology sought to enhance the health of the already healthy (Kyle, 1995). Although humanistic psychology largely rejected the discourse of individual pathology, it did have the effect of extending the twentieth-century project of social adjustment by enhancing the scope of psychological expertise to include what Rose described as "optimization," which aims not simply at adjustment to normalcy but also strives for "enhancement" (Rose, 2007, p. 20). Importantly, optimization technologies do not only act upon individuals but also mobilize individuals to act upon themselves to achieve personal happiness and well-being, among other measures of success. In this sense, humanistic psychology helped created the psychological context for the development of neoliberal rationalities of *self-government*.

Humanistic psychology pushed optimization through its approach to life as a "quest to meet needs, to quiet the anguish of the recognition of personal shortcomings, and to achieve a greater degree of fulfillment than traditional faith had encouraged" (Jorstad, 1990, p. 154). This project of personal self-development achieved social legitimacy by means of its claims to foster the conditions necessary for democratic personhood (Herman, 1995). Accordingly, Gordon Allport, an early humanistic personality theorist, claimed in 1954 that

> Up to now the 'behavioral sciences,' including psychology, have not provided us with a picture of man capable of creating or living in a democracy.... What psychology can do is to discover whether the democratic ideal is possible. (cited in Herman, 1995, p. 264)

Humanistic psychology promulgated ideas about self-directed personal change and actualization that impacted nearly every sector of American life. Humanistic authorities emphasized secular contexts such as the family and the school in order to transform them into sites for individual self-actualization, influencing expert discourse about pedagogy, child development, family counseling, and everyday vocabularies (Jorstad, 1990). Carl Rogers called for changes in social institutions to reflect humanism's goals better. In particular, he argued for removal of obstacles to "normal growth and development" so as to maximize individuals' capacities for self-regulation and personal growth (cited in Herman, 1995, p. 267). The human-potential movement would eventually be appropriated in the 1960s by the New Age movement in the pursuit of personal transcendence and in the 1980s by evangelical Christianity in the pursuit of spiritualized self-actualization (Nadesan, 1997).

The idea of self-actualization was applied to society's most vulnerable members, engendering a subtle transformation in societal attitudes toward the mentally ill and disabled, particularly disabled children. In 1975, the U.S. Congress passed the Individuals with Disabilities Education Act guaranteeing that children with disabilities received free, appropriate education. The nineteenth-century specter of feebleminded children threatening the health and evolutionary fitness of the population had been replaced by the idea of vulnerable children requiring special protection in order to optimize their capacities for self-actualization. Although passage of this act and others (e.g., Civil Rights Act of 1964) aimed at enhancing individual opportunities for self-actualization did not in fact eliminate repressive and marginalizing economic and cultural forces, particularly as experienced by poor and "minority" populations; civil rights legislation did create the *de jure* legal environment within which individuals and groups could challenge those agents and systems denying their capacity for personal actualization.

The scope for application ideas about human potential included not only personal happiness but also embraced mental or "cognitive" ones. Cognitive psychology emerged in the 1970s and 1980s as *the* hegemonic knowledge formation governing understanding and development of the mind in a social context characterized by concern over personal actualization and increased economic competitiveness within and between societies.

Cognitive psychology assumed a problem solution framed by its desire to represent and engineer the problem space of mental operations. This problem-solution frame would ultimately guide neuroscience's inquiry into the brain, as discussed later in this chapter. Cognitive psychology did not simply attempt to understand the mind; rather, it sought to optimize its capacities. By the early 1980s, cognitive psychology had adopted the computer as its primary metaphor for the mind with the objective of discovering stored mental programs (Schultz & Schultz, 1987). The "library of programs" and mental "plans of action" were understood as devices involved in mental "processing" of information.

By the mid-1980s, cognitive psychology's appropriation of the new vocabulary of artificial intelligence (e.g., cognitive "modules" and "distributed" or "connectionist" intelligence) and its alliances with neurology (i.e., in the form of neuroscience) had transformed the psychological discipline into a "science" (see Fodor, 1983). The discipline's salience had grown as policymakers and anxious educators and parents sought to increase U.S. global competitiveness by enhancing the knowledge and intellectual capacities of the population.

Cognitive neuropsychology, in particular, seemed to offer new strategies for engineering and governing the mind. The infant's mind was rendered particularly salient in this governmental discourse as media accounts of early development dramatized parallels between human cognition and computer "programming" (Nadesan, 2002). For example, a 1996 article in *Newsweek* magazine claimed:

> It is the experiences of childhood, determining which neurons are used, that wire the circuits of the brain as surely as a programmer at a keyboard reconfigures the circuits in a computer. Which keys are typed—which experiences a child has—determines whether the child grows up to be intelligent or dull, fearful or self-assured, articulate or tongue-tied. (Begley, 1996, p. 56)

The computer analogy reinforced the implied immutability of early brain formation, principally through the idea of neural wiring. The concept of early programming was extended to explain emotional development, framed either in terms of the stimulation and maturation of "specific neural circuits" or in terms of social learning. Parents were called upon to enrich their children's environments while biopolitical authorities demanded greater state support for early childhood enrichment to maximize the aggregate population's intellectual capacity.

Expert and public interest in the potential for neurological government grew as cognitive neuropsychology and neuroscience promised to reveal the secret interiority of the brain through new imaging technologies. Additionally, developments in new psychiatric drugs promised the capacities for neurological government of troublesome affective states with fewer side effects. For example, U.S. prescriptions for methylphenidate (Ritalin), first marketed in 1955 for narcolepsy, grew by 500 percent between 1991 and 1999 (Singh, 2007).

During the last two decades of the twentieth century, a cognitive and pharmaceutical discourse of engineering and optimizing neurological states slowly supplemented, and then replaced, the psychological discourse of personal adjustment, fulfillment, and self-actualization. Although market and university authorities conducted much of the cognitive-pharmaceutical research, findings were seen as having direct implications for the nation's overall military security and economic competitiveness. New technologies would simultaneously promote human resource optimization and encourage market capitalization. Thus, market logics promoted biopolitical developments, ranging from pharmaceutical products to developmental toys, designed to optimize the nation's vitality, intellectual capital, and international competitiveness.

Children achieved new significance as a site of optimization for middle- and upper-class parents and policymakers as neoliberal market operations demanded highly educated, flexible workers. Whereas the popularized discourses of childhood neuroscience emphasized children's intellectual and emotional *environments,* a wide range of biopolitical authorities expressed new interest in *inborn* mechanisms that rendered individuals more or less capable of developing the capacities for personal self-government (e.g., intellectual and emotional). These authorities often questioned the effectiveness of state-sponsored social interventions designed to improve the aggregate health and welfare of the nation, including many welfare programs. While some of these authorities simply preferred family and philanthropically based social supports, others believed individuals were either irreparably affected by their "adverse" home environments, rendering state support useless, or biogenetically unsuited for rising intellectual and social requirements. *The Bell Curve* (Herrnstein & Murray, 1994) lent popular support to suspicion that state-sponsored social interventions were incapable of overcoming genetically based limitations. The degree to which racist ideas permeated the emerging genetic consciousness is demonstrated by the quote from James Watson cited at the beginning of this chapter.

The final section of this chapter discusses new biopolitical discourses that address the individualized space of the brain. While some remain open to the role of social environments in shaping the problem space of the brain, others emphasize inborn, heritable influences. However, despite contention over the relative influence of "nature" or "nurture," all of the discourses examined in this final section tend to understand the brain physiologically, resulting in very specific types of technologies for representing and acting upon the range of human differences. Thus, the final section of this chapter highlights new strategies of objectification and subjectification stemming from contemporary biotechnological innovations in representation and control.

GOVERNING THE BRAIN: BEHAVIORAL GENETICS, PSYCHOPHARMACOLOGY, AND COGNITIVE NEUROSCIENCE

In the second half of the twentieth century, the (neo)liberal ideology of self-government coupled with the market quest for financial returns have together stimulated development of scientific technologies designed to represent and manipulate the human brain. Behavioral genetics, pharmacology, and cognitive neuroscience all represent technologies aimed at identifying the biogenetic predicates of mind and behavior. Implicit in this pursuit is the unspoken assumption that such knowledge will enable understanding of the source of social deviance and enhancement of individuals' capacities for personal self-government and economic competitiveness. Although operating within distinct fields, these research areas share a common set of ontological assumptions about human nature:

- Phenotypic "traits" or characteristics or symptoms (e.g., anxiety or intelligence) can be objectively and reliably measured and predicted (through their correlation with other "traits" or tendencies) and can therefore be projected onto the population in order to identify sites of risk or susceptibility.
- The behavioral and affective predicates of phenotypic characteristics are encoded in the brain (and/or genes) and therefore can be subject to technologies of visualization that localize and render present the biogenetic predicates of human differences.
- The biogenetic predicates rendered visible through new representational technologies and methodologies—microarrays and fMRIs—can ultimately be subject to technological manipulations that will facilitate self-government by normalizing "pathology."

Whereas behavioral genetics and cognitive neuroscience seek, in distinct ways, to elucidate the mechanisms governing brain states (and, more indirectly, behavior), pharmacology seeks to make an intervention in order to more properly govern the brain's affective states. From a *pharmacological* point of view, genomic mappings will reveal the genetic predicates or correlates of desirable/undesirable behavior and affective states. Once rendered visible, new technologies for acting upon the brain's chemistry can be developed to serve the dual purpose of securitizing the state by engineering normality (or hypernormality) while facilitating pharmaceutical capital accumulation. While pharmacological scientists continue to toil in laboratories searching for molecular agents capable of modulating neurotransmitters, these efforts are supplemented by the work of *behavioral geneticists* who seek to identify the genetic predicates of behavior, emotion, and cognition, often through biometric studies of twins and adoptees but sometimes using advanced genetic-screening technologies such as those employed to identify risks for heart disease or cancer, using either association or linkage studies. *Cognitive neuroscience,* in contrast, uses neural imaging technologies to identify neural normality and deviance and to map mental operations onto the brain. Each of these approaches will be discussed individually.

Despite differences in focus and methodology, all approaches strive to identify the biogenetic predicates of human conduct and, especially, deviant conduct. For critics, these approaches can operate as forms of biosovereignty, or disciplinarity, used against neurologically and/or genetically "deficient" and/or dangerous others. Accordingly, although Castel (1991) viewed the developments of the late twentieth century as affecting a move away from concern with "dangerous" individuals toward a decentralization of risk (projected on the population and operationalized in terms of risky behavior), I argue that to varying degrees pharmacology, behavioral genetics, and cognitive neuroscience have the potential to reinscribe aspects of the nineteenth-century degeneracy discourses while offering private and state authorities new means of exercising power and control over suspect populations. My position stands in contrast to more optimistic accounts offered by some governmentality scholarship.

Behavioral Genetics

Behavioral genetics contends psychopathology and empirical and measurable human "traits" such as intelligence, creativity, and anxiety are heritable. The century-long project of ascertaining heritability has employed diverse technologies, spanning nineteenth-century charts of family pedigrees, twentieth-century biometric methods, and twenty-first-century genomic analysis and experimental manipulations with transgenic animals.

Biometric methods, discussed earlier in this chapter, primarily address the heritability of intelligence and socially undesirable conditions such as schizophrenia and alcoholism. For example, *The New York Times* reported recently, "We know from twin and family studies that about 50 percent of a person's vulnerability to addiction is genetic" (Denizet-Lewis, 2006). But critics challenge the methodological assumptions upon which biometrics rests. As Steven Rose (2001) observed, this type of research must make simplifying assumptions in order to (artificially) partition out genetic and environmental contributions to phenotypic characteristics. However, "if there is a great deal of interaction between genes and environment, if genes interact with each other, and if relationships are not linear and additive but interactive, the entire mathematical apparatus of heritability estimates falls apart" (S. Rose, 2001).

Given the well-rehearsed limitations of biometric methodologies, behavioral geneticists looked eagerly to new findings in the area of medical genetics for directions for proving the heritability of personality traits (e.g., introversion) and psychopathology (e.g., manic depression). Accordingly, today researchers investigating the heritability of personality traits and psychopathology follow the lead of medical research on the genetic origins of disease to explain how phenotypic expressions—disease symptoms or personality traits—can be traced to specific gene alleles or mutations. Particularly of interest are alleles expressed in the brain. Behavioral genetics therefore treats personality traits and biological symptoms similarly in order to trace phenotypic characteristics to genotypic features.

However, in order to employ established behavioral inventories and cognitive measures during the initial empirical measurement of the phenotypic trait under investigation, behavioral geneticists must reject a binary measure of the trait (disease/no-disease) in favor of multifactorial models: with "multifactorial traits" the phenotypes are distributed in a continuum and the (believed) predisposing genetic factors are referred to as quantitative trait loci (QTLs; Craig, McClay, Plomin, & Freeman, 2000, p. 23). Behavioral geneticists hope to identify gene alleles upon which the QTLs can be mapped.

Following medical genetics, behavioral geneticists who study people (rather than animals) typically employ positional genetic analyses—linkage analysis and allelic association—to map QTLs (Neiderhiser, 2001). Linkage analysis looks at related individuals to determine whether they share the same allele(s) for targeted DNA markers and therefore assumes these alleles are somehow responsible for a given phenotypic characteristic without necessarily understanding how the allele is expressed. In other words, researchers merely infer (probabilistically) targeted alleles contribute to the trait without understanding how.

Allelic-association studies focus on the population (unrelated individuals) and aim to correlate differences in disease/trait frequencies "between groups (or in trait levels for continuously varying characters) with differences in allele frequencies at a SNP. Thus, the frequencies of the two variant forms of (alleles) of a SNP are of primary interest for identification of genes" affecting the phenotypic trait under investigation (Cardon & Palmer, 2003, pp. 598–599). Said differently, this research compares two groups, an experimental group and a control group. Distinct differences in (a) the trait frequency and (b) the allele frequency must exist across groups. Then researchers attempt to correlate allele frequency with the trait. However, because the population groups differ, researchers may mistakenly identify a SNP found within the targeted population as contributing to the trait or disease being studied (Cardon & Palmer, 2003). Spurious associations stem from erroneous pathologization of human differences and therefore demonstrate the homogenizing and normalizing tendencies latent within contemporary genomic research (see Lemke, 2004).

Using these forms of genetic analyses, researchers claim to have found the genetic loci for a wide range of human traits and characteristics. For example, in the popular press, headlines read: "Possible link of violence, gene found" (Cooke, 2002), "Scientists link anxiety to specific gene" (Talan, 2002), "Researchers find stress, depression have genetic link" (Vedantam, 2003), and "Manic-depression gene identified, scientists say" (Ritter, 2003). Researchers claim to have developed direct linkages between phenotype (e.g., anxiety) and genotype (e.g., QTLs), although the more sophisticated researchers reject Mendelian models of direct heritability and instead appropriate the language of risk and susceptibility. Still, such connections entail a kind of fixing of the relationship between genotype and phenotype and the reification of phenotypic characteristics as relatively invariant and measurable.

The current biologization of violence and criminality was in part prompted by the U.S. Department of Health's "Violence Initiative" launched in the early 1990s, which applied organic psychiatry and behavioral genetics to the problems of violence and criminality (Allen, 1999). According to Nicole Rafter (2006), today's efforts reincarnate nineteenth-century models of crime, as mediated through the mid-twentieth-century biological psychology. Biologization of criminality produces new forms of genetic surveillance as police across the United States take DNA samples from people convicted of misdemeanors and felonies (Levy, 2006). Police officials recommend also taking DNA from relatives of suspected criminals (Weiss, 2006). DNA samples are sometimes scanned to identify alleles that can be linked with prisoners' crimes (Ossorio & Duster, 2005).

As Nikolas Rose (2007) observed, the geneticization of mental illness and undesirable social tendencies has the potential to produce a new biology of control. Framed from the public-health model of epidemiological disease management, one could imagine a scenario wherein biopolitical authorities seek out potentially dangerous individuals and their relatives based on their genomic profiles. Imagine the dystopian possibilities implied by biopolitical efforts to identify suspect alleles in "at-risk" populations prior to any criminal offense. Although this prospect may seem improbable, public discourse in the aftermath of the 2007 Virginia Tech shooting suggests strong public support for targeted identification and surveillance of suspected "dangerous" individuals. For example, a lengthy opinion piece in *The Wall Street Journal* argued for greater surveillance and incarceration of dangerous individuals, lamenting that "in our well-intentioned quest to maximize personal liberty, we've moved conceptual eons away from taking the concept of dangerousness seriously" (Kellerman, 2007, p. A17). Innovations in the ability to identify and monitor biogenetic riskiness are occurring in a context of heightened fear and suspicion about dangerousness.

Research on the heritability of dangerousness is but one part of a larger project aiming to explain all manner of social differences in relation to biogenetic profiles and predispositions. For instance, Dr. Bruce Lahn's work at the University of Chicago illustrates how genetic research can be employed to naturalize "race"-based differences in social/economic status (Regalado, 2006c). Dr. Lahn's interest in how gene alleles correlate with cognitive ability led him to focus on gene alleles known to be expressed in the brain.

According to Dr. Lahn, genetic changes over the past several thousand years may be linked to brain size and intelligence in certain populations throughout Europe, Asia, and the Americas but not in sub-Saharan Africa (Regalado, 2006c). At issue in Lahn's research are the alleles Microcephalin/G37995C (on chromosome 8p23) and ASPM/A44811G (on chromosome 1q31): defects of these genes result in brains one-third of normal size. Using DNA samples from 1,184 people around the world, Dr. Lahn's research team concluded new (in evolutionary terms) mutations of these genes had spread through some populations, particularly those outside Africa. Dr. Lahn's team inferred the SNPs and associated haplotypes engendered "smarter" brains because the spread of one mutation roughly coincided with the first evidence of cave art while the spread of the second roughly coincided with the development of cities and written language. While Lahn is not explicit about the point, his research alludes that differences in genetically transmitted intelligence explain achievement gaps between Africans and Europeans and between whites and blacks in America.

However, the posited relationship between the alleles at issue and general or specific forms of intelligence is purely inferential. Critics charge the use of genetic analyses to explain the heritability of intelligence, behavior, or personality suffers from problems beyond the challenges faced by genetic accounts of disease susceptibility. At the most basic level, the validity and reliability of phenotypic measures of intelligence, personality traits, and mental illness are subject to dispute. Secondarily, genetic analysis does not provide information on gene expression and cannot provide clear linkages between suspect alleles and phenotypic expressions. Finally, the phenotypic "traits" associated with intelligence, affect, and behavior are all mediated by mind. And mind is mediated by environment.

It is not surprising, given these criticisms of behavioral genetics, that Dr. Lahn's research has been subject to considerable peer scrutiny. For instance, a study titled "Normal Variants of *Microcephalin* and *ASPM* Do Not Account for Brain Size Variability" disputes the premise of Dr. Lahn's research—that these mutations engender larger brains—by measuring the actual brain volume of carriers of the genetic mutation using MRI imaging (Woods et al., 2006). The University of Chicago eventually decided to cancel a patent based in Lahn's research that would purportedly have developed DNA-based intelligence tests (Regalado, 2006c).

The proposed patent illustrates the latent racist biopolitics informing (at least some) efforts to capitalize upon biological life. A review of gene-related patents and patent applications filed since 1976 revealed a significant trend in the use of racial categories in gene-related patents (Kahn, 2006). Although some groups see the explicit use of race in research as an antidote to standards of biological normativity built around Caucasians, many scientists and activists criticize the assumptions, methodologies, and applications of race-based research and clinical practice (e.g., see Kahn, 2006; Reardon, 2005; Rose, 2007).

Dr. Lahn's research also points to the growing import of behavioral genetics in the emerging bioeconomy. Researchers from a broad range of disciplines, including psychopharmacology, cognitive psychology, criminology, and biological psychiatry, increasingly regard genetic influences as shaping personal destiny. For in an article titled "Epidemiology in Neurobiological Research" (2001), heritability of intelligence scholar Robert Plomin suggested, as part of his larger claim that genetic inheritance explains approximately 40 percent of the variance for "g," or general intelligence, that "individuals select or create environments that foster their genetic propensities."

However, a recent study addressing a gene allele expressed in the brain that is purportedly linked to violence demonstrates the environment's role in modulating phenotypic expressions, while also illustrating resistant use of biopolitical data. Researchers studying genetic and biographic data found carriers of a mutation of the MAOA gene were prone to violence *only* when raised in environments characterized by aggression and violence and little parental affection (Begley, 2006c; Kim-Cohen et al., 2006). Moreover, other researchers question whether the gene plays any role in shaping aggression (Morris, Shen, Peirce, & Beckwith, 2007; Ossorio & Duster, 2005). Yet, mediating factors are swept aside in the rush to visualize, explain, predict, and govern the range of human differences. The quest for understanding and control, coupled with the commercialization of technologies for scanning and pharmacologically treating social differences, together create an imposing biopolitical matrix.

As illustrated by Dr. Lahn's work and popularized accounts of the link between the MAOA gene and violence, efforts to provide evidence for the heritability of phenotypic traits increasingly interrogate genes known to be expressed in the brain. A prominent strategy for mediating the relationship between genotype and phenotype involves the brain's neurochemistry. Brain chemistry can purportedly be linked by molecular genetics to suspect gene alleles. Simultaneously, brain chemistry can be used to explain "abnormalities" or "pathologies" of intellect, affect, and behavior. Another strategy, pursued by cognitive neuroscience, calls for developing "neural phenotypes" that can mediate genotype and cognitive phenotype in stable or reliable ways (Ramus, 2006, p. 249). The neural phenotypes at issue need not be restricted to neurochemistry but could also include morphological factors or patterns of electrical or chemical activity revealed through brain-imaging technologies. However, discussion turns first to psychopharmacology and neurochemical government.

Psychopharmacology

Psychopharmacology seeks to reveal the biogenetic predicates or correlates of desirable/undesirable behavior and affective states. Once rendered visible, new technologies for acting upon the brain's chemistry can be developed to serve the dual purpose of securitizing the state by engineering normality (or hypernormality) while facilitating pharmaceutical/biotechnological capital accumulation.

Perhaps the most extensive research conducted on the brain has been pursued by psychopharmacology. As mentioned previously in this chapter, between 1949 and 1959 a series of biological agents were developed to treat the symptoms of manic depression (lithium salts), psychosis (chlorpromazine), and depression (tricyclic antidepressants such as imipramine; Lakeoff, 2005). Foundational to the treatment of patients using these drugs were the ideas that mental states were epiphenomena of brain states and that chemical imbalances in the brain produce mental imbalances. Neurotransmitters—serotonin, dopamine, norepinephrine, epinephrine (adrenalin), and gamma-aminobutyric acid (GABA)—are today represented as a primary coding device for the transmission of neural information and the regulation of affective states because they bridge the gap—synapse—between the brain's neurons. Serotonin uptake, for example, has been implicated as "causing" depression while dopamine has been implicated in behavior regulation and addiction.

In general, psychopharmacology is less interested in making arguments about the genetic heritability of brain states than it is in making an intervention in the brain's biochemistry that will reliably shape individuals' affective states or behaviors. However, this project of biochemical engineering often entails detailed analyses of the molecular genetics of the brain's neurotransmitters, and frequently, although not necessarily, inborn genetic influences—SNPs for example—are believed to explain variability in neurotransmitters.

Since gene therapy is not yet (and may never be) a viable therapeutic option, the treatment for abnormal or undesirable brain states, within the parameters of this configuration, requires manipulation of the brain state through some external, pharmaceutical, agent. Nikolas Rose's (2003) phrase *neurochemical selves* captures the pervasive popular belief that emotional states are caused by neurological chemicals, that unwanted states such as depression derive from their imbalance, and that pharmaceutical interventions can remedy them. Pharmacological government over neurological chemicals is linked in governmental discourse to the reduction of economic and personal risks.

An article on the "science" of addiction illustrates the operative logic of psychopharmacological accounts of the relationships across gene, brain, and mind:

> Recent studies in both animals and humans have indicated that those with low levels of dopamine D2 receptors, which regulate the release of dopamine in the brain, are more likely to find the experience of taking drugs pleasurable. Some researchers, like Volkow, suggest that people with fewer D2 receptors experience a less intense reward signal, causing them to overindulge in order to feel satisfied. (Denizet-Lewis, 2006)

The range of genes implicated in "regulating" dopamine is unclear, but pharmaceutical applications for intervening in dopamine levels and reception already are being created. Indeed, the article discusses at some length the range of commercially developed drugs being explored to govern dopamine and, thereby, addiction.

The ideas that mental states/behavior can be explained directly by brain states (linked to gene states) and that these states are easily subject to chemical engineering hold widespread popular appeal. The medicalization of addiction, depression, and anxiety suggests possibilities for targeted government. But establishing clear and exclusive linkages across mental states, brain states, and gene states is a very challenging set of undertakings. David Healy's work examined some of the difficulties inherent in establishing these relationships. At a most basic level, current understandings of brain chemistry are very incomplete and some basic tenets, such as the serotonin theory of depression, may be inaccurate. More philosophically, molecular accounts of complex emotional states such as depression or happiness ignore synergy across molecular environments, ignore the role of the psyche in shaping brain states, and ignore the role of social environments in shaping psychic states. Consequently, biochemical interventions implying an efficacious "pharmaceutical scalpel" may be destined to failure (Healy, 1997, p. 5). The notion of the pharmacological scalpel harkens back to nineteenth-century positivism, while the idea of a normative neurochemical balance invokes modernist normativity, both in its capacity to identify biochemical norms and in relation to the projection of those norms onto the population in order to identify sources of deviance from normative regulative ideals.

One can argue the governmental impulse to visualize, control, and govern shapes the desire to map the biological chemistry of personality differences and behavioral dispositions. Imagine the pastoral opportunities implied by the identification of the chemicals shaping the expression of anxiety or violence and the linking of such chemicals with genetic predicates. Imagine further the identification of specific haplotypes implicated in the grouping of violence-susceptibility genes and the subsequent mapping of likely irruptions across the population. Whereas past mappings of the social correlates of violence—for example, poverty or child abuse—revealed complicated social-structural relationships not easily modified, the possibilities presented by neural-genetic accounts are (seemingly) more amendable to direct intervention without upsetting existing social and economic institutions. Impersonal, genomic-based epidemiological mappings of addiction, for example, could be projected onto the population and particular population groups targeted for enhanced surveillance and expert intervention.

Synthesizing the projects of behavioral genetics and psychopharmacology, one could imagine a dystopian future in which genetic-based behavioral epidemiologists scan children for haplotypes correlated with addiction, violence, aggression, language disorders, and so on, and then subject them to pharmaceutical interventions to modulate the phenotypic expressions of their heritable genotypes. Of course, in such a world, children bearing recognizably "dangerous" haplotypes would have been "selected out" by concerned, aspiring parents in the process of in-utero screening (e.g., see Zuckerman et al., 2007). Although this dystopian imagining is unrealistic in many regards, it constitutes a logical extension of current efforts to map social attributes onto genetic properties.

Certainly, this dystopian fantasy implies science will succeed in identifying the neurochemical, neurogenetic predicates or risk factors for "undesirable" addictions, behaviors, cognitive characteristics, and personality traits. But success has remained elusive for a wide variety of reasons (e.g., see Insel & Collins, 2003). Pharmaceutical government may ultimately be limited by the undisciplined mediations of mind.

Mental states are not mere epiphenomena of brain states; rather, they have the capacity to shape brain states (see Begley, 2007, 2006b, 2006c). Mental states not only produce conditions of possibility for brain states (e.g., post-traumatic stress) but may also be used strategically to govern unwanted brain states and/or physiological conditions. For instance, considerable research suggests a variety of corporeal and mental disciplines and technologies of the self can be as efficacious as pharmaceuticals in governing the mind. Tourette's patients can be trained to eliminate tics using self-surveillance and mental discipline (Fisher, 2007). Some schizophrenic patients can be trained to "live" successfully with the auditory delusions of "voices" (Smith, 2007; see also Carey, 2006a). The forms of surveillance and discipline required for governing physiological processes illustrate extremes of personal self-control, but they may ultimately be experienced as more freeing than pharmaceuticals since the latter have significant side effects including sexual dysfunction, lethargy, and considerable weight gain, depending upon the type of medication.

The project of social government through pharmaceutical interventions faces challenges beyond the limits of the pharmacological ontology of mind. As mentioned previously, critics of pharmaceutical government question the medicalization of social differences and behaviors. Medicalization of social deviance has been well documented (e.g., see Conrad & Schneider, 1985; Laurence & McCallum, 2003; Miller & Leger, 2003), and the expansion of lifestyle-drug development and marketing by pharmaceutical companies points to the widespread medicalization of a whole range of conditions ranging from depressions to sleep problems and sexual dysfunction (Weintraub, 2007).

According to David Healy (n.d.), pharmaceutical companies create markets by shaping perceptions of mental illness and self-government. Even *The Wall Street Journal* acknowledged, "it is a common marketing strategy for drug companies to advertise a disease before specifically advertising medicine to fight it" (Whalen, 2006, p. B2). Healy's position holds consumer response to drug marketing is conditioned by risk management. Accordingly, Healy's online essay, "Psychopharmacology and the Government of the Self," contends:

The best selling drugs in modern medicine do something similar—they don't treat disease. They manage risks. This is clearly true of the antihypertensives, the lipid lowering agents and other drug. It is true also of antidepressants, which have been sold on the back of efforts to reduce risks of suicide.

Healy has specifically criticized the SSRIs used to treat depression because he believes their tendency to reduce inhibitions can result in suicide among susceptible users, particularly teenagers (see Bernstein & Dooren, 2007).

Critics mainly object to the pharmaceutical governance of more subtle symptoms. Parents may use pharmaceuticals to enhance or optimize their children's normality, extending their use beyond management of overt symptoms of mental illness. Many behavior-management drugs for children are prescribed believing "that these agents will return children within the set of norms that will minimise future risks" (Healy, n.d.). Healy concluded the mapping of the human genome will merely exacerbate these trends given pharmaceutical-driven research and development.

Critics of pharmaceutical governance also suggest commercial interests cloud research objectivity in studies addressing pharmaceutical benefits and risks (e.g., see Armstrong, 2006a, 2006b; Berenson, 2006). For example, close examination of clinical trials indicates half of the patients with depression do not respond to standard antidepressant medications (see Abboud, 2005; "Landmark," 2006; Vedantam, 2006). Moreover, placebo effects cast doubt on even that level of statistical efficacy: one study comparing antidepressants with placebos found only an 11 percent improvement in depression symptoms among those taking the drugs over those taking the placebos (Bernstein & Dooren, 2007). More troublingly, psychiatric drugs often produce undesirable "side effects" (e.g., suicide from antidepressants or dangerous weight gain from Zyprexa and Risperdal; see Abboud, 2005; Berenson, 2006; Medawar & Hardon, 2004; Vedantam, 2006).

The explanatory frameworks and medicalized protocols promulgated by pharmaceutical authorities may obscure alternative approaches to understanding and treating troubling conditions. For instance, commercially funded research on the genetic basis, and neurochemical government of "ADHD," tends to obscure the well-documented role of childhood lead exposure (and potentially smoking) in producing the same general symptoms leading to ADHD diagnoses ("Attention," 2006). A wide range of chemical toxins may cause prenatal or postnatal brain damage leading to diagnosis such as autism (Grandjean & Landrigan, 2006). Brain damage, made evident by increased childhood surveillance, may resist pharmacological correction. Most psychopharmacological agents assume deviant brains that require chemical "normalization," but brains damaged by neurotoxins may require different strategies; for example, whole body therapies to produce new neural pathways. But the dominant neurochemical frame precludes other understandings and trivializes the sometimes significant side effects associated with psychotropic drugs (see Goldstein, 2007; Mathews & Abboud, 2005).

In 2005, approximately 1.6 million children and teenagers were given at least two psychiatric drugs in combination despite lack of understanding of the underlying causes for the symptoms targeted for management (Carey, 2006c; Harris, 2006). Overmedication of children in the pursuit of normalization is a particularly problematic effect of pharmaceutical government. In 2007, a four-year-old girl overdosed on a "cocktail" of powerful psychiatric drugs given to treat the symptoms of bipolar disorder and attention deficit disorder (Carey, 2007). A Medco survey found that teenagers' use of psychiatric and insomnia drugs doubled from 2002 to 2007 ("A Medco," 2007). Widespread medication of children with potent psychiatric drugs has in some cases replaced social-behavioral-cognitive interventions because of their convenience and the dogma of their efficaciousness.

Parents may regard pharmaceutical sedation as a last resort in the context of increasing social intolerance for juvenile crime and misbehavior. Under social-welfare liberalism, social workers and educators drew upon psychiatric, sociological, and psychoanalytical knowledge in order to improve children's environments and, in cases of juvenile delinquency, "forestall the drama of police action by replacing the secular arm of the law with the extended hand of the educator" (Donzelot, 1979, p. 97). However, in the current framework of responsibilization and public safety, youthful offenders are regarded more and more as dangerous individuals requiring incarceration and punishment. Desperate parents are no doubt mobilized by expert authorities and seductive advertising to medicate their children into normality to avoid punishing state apparatuses.

The relative cost-effectiveness of pharmaceutical government, compared to social-psychological interventions, may also appeal to state and private apparatuses with limited budgets facing demands for entitled services. Efforts by pharmaceutical companies and biopolitical authorities to destigmatize mental illness have increased demand for services. Drug companies' medicalized cures for unwanted human emotions are perceived by public and private insurers as cost-effective alternatives to lengthy behavioral/cognitive protocols.

Pharmaceutical government of mental and emotional states has long been of interest to the militarized apparatuses of the security state. Truth serums and drugs that can render soldiers impervious to the need for sleep have been pursued by government-sponsored researchers (Moreno, 2006). Biochemical efforts to repair or sedate the scarred psyches of soldiers diagnosed with post-traumatic stress currently complement efforts to produce biochemically enhanced supersoldiers. Indeed, pharmaceutical government offers a relatively cost-effective means today for addressing the overwhelming number of veterans damaged by their participation in the "war on terror":

> Nearly 64,000 of the more than 184,000 Iraq and Afghanistan war veterans who have sought VA health care have been diagnosed with

potential symptoms of post-traumatic stress, drug abuse or other mental disorders as of the end of June, according to the latest report by the Veterans Health Administration. Of those, nearly 30,000 have possible post-traumatic stress disorder, the report said. . . . (Hull & Priest, 2007, p. A1)

Although pharmaceutical agents may not "cure" these afflicted soldiers, the drugs do promise to govern the excesses of unruly psyches damaged by war horrors.

There is no doubt drugs can productively help adjust people to the stressors and paradoxes of modern life. Moreover, drugs may be vital for suppressing distressing symptoms. To argue pharmacology and behavioural genetics are forms of biopower aimed at representing and regulating the life forces of the population does not imply this biogenetic matrix *necessarily* harms or adversely disciplines the population, nor does it erase efforts by individuals to use these technologies as means of self-government.

However, the commercial incentives for biochemical government—for the capitalization of life—have political effects, including the medicalization of socially rooted pathology and the distraction of resources and attention away from investigating other causal pathways and from developing alternative governmental technologies.

Neurological Visibility

As an emerging type of surveillance over biological bodies, brain-imaging technologies help science bridge the link between heritable genotype and (behavioral or trait) phenotype, although these uses are not necessarily inscribed in the technologies themselves. Brain-imaging technologies provide neuroscience with representational tools for creating the "neural phenotypes" seen as necessary for establishing definitive relationships between (a) brain and mind and (b) brain and gene (Ramus, 2006, p. 249). Using technologies such as fMRI (functional magnetic resonance imaging) and PET (positron-emission tomography), scientists attempt to identify the particular brain sites and processes involved in regulating and/or producing specific cognitive skills, addictions, or emotional/psychiatric predispositions. They also hope to discern "typical" or "normal" patterns of activation/involvement or link patterns of activation (neural phenotypes) with phenotypic traits (e.g., high anxiety). Ultimately, research may point to gene alleles that correlate with specific neural phenotypes, bridging brain and gene (and behavior or trait). In this fashion, complex and ambiguous phenomena such as intelligence are spatially localized in brain centers or processes, which can then be subject to genetic analysis.

Joseph Dumit's (2004) *Picturing Personhood: Brain Scans and Biomedical Identity* argued brain-scanning technologies are used to create at least two distinct types of representations of the brain: one specific to the field of pharmacology, the other based in the distributed-intelligence metaphors of cognitive neuroscience. Dumit limited his discussion to positron-emission tomography (PET), but his analysis points to how assumptions about the brain and its relation to cognition and affect shape observation and interpretation.

PET entails introducing a radioactive substance into the body and using the energy emitted in its decay as the means for creating a three-dimensional image of the brain (Uttal, 2001). PET scans enable insight into the brain's metabolism of specific substances, as well as blood flow into a particular brain region. This technology is useful in providing a representation of brain processes, although it remains unclear whether the site of the greatest metabolic activity (as measured by the PET scan) is necessarily the site for the operation of a cognitive process.

Dumit described how PET technologies are used to interrogate the two distinct models of the brain. The pharmacological model uses the metaphor of "autoregulation," which views the brain as actively engaged in maintaining a homeostatic balance through multiple neurotransmitters. In contrast, the model specific to cognitive neuroscience uses the metaphor of "coding" of information, entailing brain mapping and circuitry (p. 184). While PET operates within both metaphoric frameworks, each implies different and sometimes incommensurable interpretations of data results. Dumit's analysis demonstrates the interpretive work involved in "reading" PET images: "Understanding a PET image of a person with depression requires, then, reflection on categories of people and metaphors of the brain, as well as imaging technologies and practices" (p. 185).

Brain images are therefore fundamentally contingent representations: brain-imaging technologies are not transparent reproductions, and therefore their *meanings* are subject to layers of interpretive processes (see also Uttal, 2001). Hence, some neuroscientists contend imaging studies have failed to advance knowledge of the brain much beyond nineteenth-century understandings of brain functions' localizations (Carey, 2006b). However, in the popular imagination, PET and other neural-imaging technologies have achieved the mythical status of truth-telling devices about the nature, operations, and dysfunctions of the human brain.

PET and other neural technologies (e.g., fMRI) have been used to interrogate depressed, anxious, addictive, and otherwise "disordered" brains. For example, PET is used to see how disordered brains are different, either in their neurochemistry or in the patterns and activation of their neurological circuitry. The idea is that PET and/or other technologies might reveal specific clinical disorders in terms of neurochemical or neurological activity profiles (i.e., neural phenotypes). Observed neurological differences, as represented through brain-imaging technologies, suggest neural centers, which might govern particular behaviors or psychopathologies. For instance, neuroscience recently mapped addiction onto an area of the brain known as the insula ("Spot," 2007). Behavioral geneticists subsequently have been searching for the genes "regulating" brain sites such as the insula.

Efforts to delineate neurological difference have prompted neuroscientists to develop comprehensive profiles of neural normality, as illustrated by this study using MRI data to map developmental stages of neural normality:

> About 400 healthy newborns to teenagers, recruited from healthy families, are having periodic MRI cans of their brains as they grow up. They also get a battery of age-linked tests of such abilities as IQ language skills and memory. The project is funded by the National Institutes of Health. The MRI images measure how different parts of the brain grow and reorganize throughout childhood. Overlap them with the children's shifting behavioral and intellectual abilities at each age, and scientists expect to produce a long-sought map of normal brain development in children representative of the diverse U.S. population. ("Researchers," 2007, p. A19)

Neurological normality provides the grid of intelligibility for identifying, mapping, and measuring differences requiring normalization.

Biopolitical and consumer authorities are enthralled by neuroscience's promise to map human emotion and psychopathology onto the brain while also providing grids of intelligibility for measuring and comparing neurological variations based on delineations of neural norms. Behavioral genetics hopes development of neural phenotypes will point to gene alleles that govern neurological states. Pharmacology is excited by the promise of a future governed through targeted biotechnologies.

Yet neural technologies' success in identifying specific brain irregularities/abnormalities that can reveal or predict anxiety, depression, or mental illness has been mixed (Carey, 2005). Similar or even identical psychiatric symptoms (e.g., hallucinations) may arise from divergent biological processes, calling into question the feasibility of developing distinct neural phenotypes for specific psychiatric labels such as autism or schizophrenia.

More generally, neuroscience struggles to distinguish neural differences that matter (i.e., that cause or are symptomatic of behavioral/cognitive effects) from "normal" neurological variations. For instance, what looks like a site of high activity in one person's brain may be a normal change in another person's brain because of the "normal" range of variation across the population (Carey, 2005). Moreover, individual brains change across time and in relation to experience, exhibiting plasticity (Begley, 2004b). Even when distinct neurological differences are observed in specific populations, it remains unclear whether the brain difference engendered the psychological condition (e.g., depression) or whether the psychological condition engendered the brain difference (Carey, 2005). Neuroscience is inclined to confuse correlation with causality (DeGrandpre, 1999). Despite these limitations, scientific and public interest in the capacity of neural technologies to reveal the inner space of the mind/brain continues to grow, particularly when the research suggests opportunities for market application or capitalization. For example, a recent study reported in the press claimed to reveal the distinct characteristic brain activity of "visionary leaders" using EEG data (Dvorak & Badal, 2007).

Contemporary neuroscience discourses representing brains as transparent often invoke positivist and evolutionary logics. Research projects a grid of visibility for identifying neural mechanisms that localize and (purport to) explain a wide range of observable human differences. Mental states are thus believed to be reducible to specific brain states. Brain is often reduced to genes selected by evolutionary pressures. These formulations echo nineteenth-century discourses of biological degeneracy to the extent that un/desirable human behaviors or conditions are explained within biological and evolutionary discourses essentializing and naturalizing human differences while mystifying the role of social processes in producing and interpreting human variations.

In effect, the reduction of mind to brain and the use of informatic technologies to represent the brain therefore fix and objectify human variability in ways that render them susceptible to calculations of statistic normality and difference. Anne Beaulieu (2001) critically described how informatic "atlases" of the brain used as baselines in brain-mapping studies are associated with particular ideals of knowledge, which shape what counts as "objective" knowledge about the brain (p. 639). Beaulieu explained that efforts to integrate the various disciplines studying the brain engendered standard data formats and common languages, including the idea of the "voxel," derived from the older "pixel" (picture element) used to represent the brain (p. 643). Information, whether physiological or anatomical, can now be attributed to a particular voxel in the brain, thereby allowing translation of all kinds of neural information to a standardized format. A voxel is therefore simply a "digital tool" allowing integration and juxtaposition of various types of neural knowledge by assigning numerical values set in a matrix (p. 643). A voxel-based digitalized brain scan enables statistical averaging, thereby enabling *averaged* representation of *normality* to be generated: "When the voxels in the scans are averaged, areas of greater variability are blurred, while in areas of lesser variability, the image is sharper than it would be in an individual scan" (p. 649). People whose scans are averaged are selected for their "supernormal" status; that is, their normativity is defined by exclusions such that they were untraumatized, unmedicated, unaddicted, nondiabetic, not pregnant, not having any psychiatric or neurological disorders, and so on (p. 646). Digitalized interfaces enable automated standardization of data generated from multiple subjects. Increasingly, these atlases encompass multiple-level structures marked in standardized ways for certain population characteristics such as gender, level of education, and so on, enabling quantification of variability for a population.

The "technological fix" for handling large samples of qualitatively distinct data has profound epistemological and ontological consequences (Beaulieu, p. 668), including informatic abstraction, standardization, normalization, and the quantification of variability from standardized norms. The ultimate goal of this aggregation and standardization is the differentiation of normal brains from pathological ones. Pharmaceutical companies are particularly interested in the commercial applications of this research.

The military-security complex has also actively supported this type of brain research (Moreno, 2006). Neuroimaging technologies serve as a point of condensation for the fantasy of mind reading and mind control. Accordingly, government-supported researchers strive to develop dictionaries of typical neural patterns associated with a particular emotional state like aggression while simultaneously seeking technologies that can remotely scan and identify suspect patterns. It matters not whether typical patterns are viewed as acquired through socialization or whether they are understood as innate. All that is required is the development of statistically averaged patterns against which individuals can be compared in order to identify potentially risky/dangerous individuals. The fantasy of remote surveillance is supplemented by the titillating possibility of actually controlling brains remotely through electromagnetic stimulation. Although these imaginings of the will to power are unlikely to be realized, they demonstrate how efforts to visualize the brain are motivated by and engender problematics of control.

Finally, popular dissemination of informatic and genetic data about the human brain in the popular media propagates new models of the subject invoked by people in their everyday lives to make sense of their experiences. These models include those discussed here: (a) the neurochemical self centering neurotransmitters (Rose, 2003) and the (b) hard-wired circuited self developed by cognitive neuroscience and neuropsychology. Both models of personhood derive their legitimacy from brain-scanning technologies and their representational schemata. Individuals who draw upon the discourses produced around these representational technologies become subjects of the discourse as they draw upon its vocabulary to explain personality quirks or even to recast disability as difference. Biosocial identities (Rabinow, 2005) and advocacy pose interesting and complex objectifying and subjectifying effects.

Autism-advocacy efforts drawing upon the metaphors of cognitive neuroscience and neuropsychology illustrate biosocial subjectification (Nadesan, 2005). Personal testimonials offered on Web pages and in published accounts by people with autism and Asperger's syndrome draw upon neuroscience to recast disability as neurological difference. As illustrated by an Amazon.com review posted by "a reader from Los Angeles" of the book *Pretending to Be Normal*: "Many autistics now feel that we are a positive neuro-variation, possibly an evolutionary step forward from the mob mentalities that now crush this planet." This idea of autism as "neuro-variation" leads to the converse of "neurological typicals." The idea that people with autism share a unique set of neurological differences—rendering them ontologically different in *mind* from the rest of the population of the "neurologically typical"—is both homogenizing and divisive, even while it fosters affirmation by and for people who view themselves as autistic. Divisiveness is demonstrated by the tendency for autism advocates to draw upon the metaphors of cognitive neuroscience and brain-imaging studies when comparing themselves to "neurological typicals" or NTs. And yet, contrary to affirmative efforts to reimagine autism as difference rather than disorder, people living with the disorder know it is a difference that ultimately tends to be devalued and stigmatized in relation to privileged "neurotypical" normality.

Objectification therefore occurs as the dissimilarities affirmed by people with autism are pathologized in psychiatric, medical, and pharmacological representations that together seek to identify the biogenetic causal factors explaining autistic abnormality. Phenotypic accounts of autistic difference homogenize and objectify the diversity of people with autism in relation to "autistic traits" and behavioral idiosyncrasies geneticists and neuroscience seek to map onto gene and brain. The possibility for linking neurological differences to genetic mutations or alleles raises the specter of autism prenatal testing and the attendant eugenic possibilities as autistic differences become reduced to pathological informatics.

In effect, research efforts by cognitive neuroscience and neuropsychology to view and understand the human brain are normalizing to the extent that they generate statistical profiles of normality against which deviance can be measured and analyzed. Images generated from neurological scanning devices assume the status of truth-telling devices for revealing the previously undisclosed substrates of mind. The ultimate goal of these technologies and representational profiles is the visualization of, and potentially control over, human difference and social pathology. These technologies and representations are both objectifying and normalizing. Objectification stems from efforts to reduce the psyche to statistically generated neural profiles that can be used as standards of comparison against which to measure individual deviance. Subjectification occurs as individuals actively draw upon these representations in the course of their everyday lives. The myriad conceptual, methodological, and statistical challenges specific to brain-imaging studies are swept away in relation to a new neurological essentialism and determinism (Peterson, 2003).

GOVERNING DIFFERENCE: SELF-GOVERNMENT, DISCIPLINARITY, AND THE SOCIETY OF CONTROL

The urge to fix, represent, and calculate the range of human differences was explored by Michel Foucault as the empirico-transcendental doublet. Constituted by the empirico-transcendental doublet, modern humans are "perpetually summoned toward self-knowledge" so "man is also the locus of misunderstandings—of misunderstanding that constantly exposes his thought to the risk of being swamped by his own being, and also enables him to recover his integrity on the basis of what eludes him" (Foucault, 1994b, pp. 323–324). Turned back upon itself, and yet cut off from origins, wo/man is in danger of delusion, mystification, misrecognition, and misunderstanding—resulting in still more efforts to capture some elusive transcendental truth. Foucault believed the search for transcendental truth in the context of empirical knowledge has plagued the human sciences generally and psychiatry in particular.

The human and biological sciences together remain locked within this doublet, and societal and individual governmental strategies are affected by their products. The cognitive, affective, social, and developmental norms generated by the human sciences—by psychology, anthropology, sociology, and so on—function as forms of power governing evaluation of the behaviors of self and others. Thus, Foucault described biopower's emergence in the modern period in relation to the "action of the norm" in contrast with the punitive force of the law (1990, p. 144). Diverse social institutions (e.g., workplace, family, school, medicine) drew upon the norms and regularities of human conduct "discovered" by the human sciences to evaluate and govern their populations and, in so doing, produced subjectivities sensitized to, and receptive of, the power of the norm.

Behavioral genetics, psychopharmacology, and cognitive neuroscience provide particularly seductive knowledge formations and technologies of discovery for biopolitical government. Taken together, they operate as a decentralized matrix of ideas, practices, and experts united primarily by a desire to reveal the sources of human difference within a universalizing and objectifying biogenetic framework in order to maximize public health and security, market capitalization, and individual happiness. However, although this dispersed and at times heterogeneous matrix adopts many of the foundational logics of medical genetics, the underlying ontology of personhood varies significantly from the rational, autonomous, choosing subject represented in the genomics and medical genetics materials (see Bunton & Petersen, 2005; Petersen & Bunton, 2002). Where medical genetics typically defines "risky" personhood in relation to an autonomous agent's disease susceptibility, the matrix described here seeks to explain the origins of "risk" in terms of dangerous, deviant, or disabled biogenetic traits and characteristics. Risky traits are seen as threatening to the capacity for optimal self-government and are increasingly represented as demanding biogenetic explanation and intervention.

Risk management is warranted given the economic and social costs calculated in relation to a person's risk for the undesirable end states associated with their riskiness, including alcoholism, depression, psychosis, cognitive impairment, criminality, and so forth (see Rose, 2007). However, contemporary and promised strategies for risk management offered by the genetic-neuro-pharmacological matrix should be studied carefully in terms of potential effects.

The genetic-pharmacological-neuroscience matrix offers a set of strategies for mapping personality, behavioral, and psychiatric differences across the population in a manner focused on explicating and pharmacologically adjusting biological pathologies. However, the specific ways by which behavioral, cognitive, and affective "pathologies" or "difficulties" are medicalized are in large part driven by neoliberal standards of efficiency and calculability, as well as by market incentives for capitalization. Opportunities for developing lucrative commercial products drive research agendas and product developments, marginalizing alternative explanatory frameworks and therapeutic protocols. Although the seductive appeal of pharmaceutical correctives is unmistakable, the genetic-pharmacological-neuroscience matrix poses some significant ethical issues of government.

First, to what extent does this matrix invite new panopticons of biological surveillance coupled with new kinds of (eugenic) biosovereignty? The genetic-pharmacological-neuroscience matrix's ontological logic demands unprecedented surveillance over biological bodies to definitely identify the source of biogenetically inscribed differences. The attendant proliferation of gradients of difference, "abnormality" or "optimization," might usher in forceful exercise of authority to map epidemiological risk and prevent irruptions of disease across the populace. History aptly demonstrates the salience of this concern.

The genetic-pharmacological-neuroscience matrix has the potential to engender technologies of elimination and/or pathologization by inscribing some populations and/or individuals as biogenetically flawed or biogenetically less competitive. New technologies for delineating citizenship or levels of citizenship may derive from the accounts of behavioral genetics (see Kerr, 2003) and neurological profiling.

Given these concerns, a second question must be posed: To what extent does this new matrix render individuals' biology a moral culpability (see Rose, 2007, p. 235) while obscuring social explanations of human misery, mental illness, and criminality? This last question has remained relatively unexplored even while the governmentality scholarship has begun grappling with many of the ethical issues of government stemming from this matrix.

Although biological formulations of intelligence, madness, and criminology may hold some degree of explanatory power, they fundamentally absolve social actors from exploring how everyday social and economic arrangements enable and disable individual subjectivity. The biologically driven criminal madman—the psychopath—captivates attention while the more mundane but pervasive violences of market exploitation/marginalization and everyday sovereign repression are mystified in the public imagination. Accordingly, the empirical fact that African-American populations have less access to economic and cultural resources than Anglo-American populations is "naturalized" by two SNPs, Microcephalin/G37995C and ASPM/A44811G. This kind of research extends a hundred years of research attempting to naturalize social hierarchy on the basis of "racial" differences (see Reardon, 2005). Likewise, Emily Martin (1994) expressed concern, in *Flexible Bodies,* that the popularized idea that people vary inherently in the biogenetic fitness of their immune systems may engender a new kind of social Darwinism.

The natural sciences have in the past pathologized vulnerable populations, legitimizing sovereign repression and disciplining. This pattern can be repeated. Even while contemporary systems of American government—neoliberalism and neoconservatism—purport to govern through freedom, they simultaneously employ diverse forms of power to establish and preserve social order and in so doing govern as much through freedom as they do through domination (see Dean, 2002a). Biological knowledge can readily be utilized to legitimize government through domination. In a dystopian projection of biogenetic possibilities, one could imagine a future in which the imperative to securitize the population would mandate adjusting disruptive or disreputable citizens—pharmacologically perhaps—to "naturally grounded" social orders. Simultaneously, the child or adult lacking the biologically afforded intellectual or emotional skills (e.g., the Down or autistic person) would command little cultural sympathy or public support as he or she would be held liable for his or her own (sub-optimal) existence.

According to Agamben (2000), the contradictions stemming from the operations of liberal democracy are contained by a series of social and geographic exclusions. In order to maintain the fantasy of a society of self-governing individuals, the system must constantly purify itself of those persons and institutions whose very existence belies the fantasy. The "solutions" to demonstrated failures of liberal government are symbolic and/or geographic elimination and/or marginalization of those whose presence mark the ruptures. Biological knowledge has in the past been, and can be in the future, developed and utilized to redress the contradictions posed by liberal democracies.

For the reasons outlined here, the seductive promises of the behavioral genetic, psychopharmacological, cognitive neuroscience biopolitical matrix must be regarded with caution. Although biopower's operations need not result in exclusions and pathologization, the particular formation explored in this chapter demonstrates these capacities. And the strategies of capital accumulation associated with this matrix simultaneously ensure its dissemination throughout the social body and its relative imperviousness to critique even by the most vocal of biosocial activists.

In conclusion, this chapter has highlighted how racist and elitist ideas inflect biopolitical formulations of, and research into, the biology of human behavior and emotion. The chapter has emphasized how forms of biopolitical sovereignty and opportunities for capitalization inhere in, and dictate, research practices, thereby demonstrating the integral connections across biopolitics and economics. Chapter 6 turns to explore a return of more overt expressions of sovereignty in the context of contemporary biopolitical and economic concerns posed by dangerous and/or risky populations.

6 Biopower, Sovereignty, and America's Global Security

The biopolitics of population and the reassertion of the sovereign right to kill and to execute exceptions to the liberal rights of citizenship suggest neoliberal governmentalities are increasingly rent with contradictions. On the one hand, neoliberal government operates from afar through individualized technologies of the self and through dispersed expert/bureaucratic/managerial decision making. Market models of government increasingly replace state-directed ones in the public sphere as social welfare and education are either privatized or operated in accord with "free-market" strategies and technologies. These reforms are viewed as disciplining and/or transforming the inefficient apparatuses of the welfare state. Moreover, contemporary market mechanisms extend neoliberal technologies of government globally through contracts (e.g., international trade agreements and organizations), transnational corporations, and through international finance, securities, and related derivatives. Although market mechanisms involve dispersed sovereignty and disciplines, these tend to be viewed as impersonal and necessary for secure and expansive market operations.

On the other hand, the proliferation of risks associated with barriers to market penetration and derived from the uncertainties surrounding market contingencies seem to require centralized and often state-controlled intervention and government. Risks to market security are posed by energy disruptions or limitations, geopolitical conflict, resistance by nation-states such as Venezuela to neoliberal market operations, and, most recently, terrorism. In the context of these problematics, security exigencies are represented as warranting the reassertion of the sovereign capacity to kill and as legitimizing abnegation of liberal "rights" of personhood.

Consequently, at the beginning of the twenty-first century, public acceptance grows for forms of sovereignty and discipline that might otherwise be viewed as impinging against liberal self-government and liberal notions of privacy. In effect, the ethos of government through freedom is increasingly characterized by "exceptions" whereupon populations are deemed incapable of self-government, warranting the withholding of life, forceful discipline, and/or sovereign repression. Whereas preceding chapters stressed biopower's more pastoral operations and emphasized technologies of the self, Chapter 6 addresses how sovereignty and discipline have been used recently to reduce the risks associated with, or perceived as threatening to, neoliberal and neoconservative principles of government.

Sovereignty is the "underside of the power to guarantee an individual's continued existence" (Foucault, 2004, p. 80). As explained previously, sovereignty is a relatively undertheorized dimension of Foucault's triangular structure of power within the secondary governmentality scholarship. Foucault's relatively infrequent references to modern expressions of sovereignty no doubt resulted from his contention that power in the modern period is caught up with living beings and applied at "the level of life itself" (2004, p. 82). For Foucault, the productive capacities of biopower are more pervasive and insidious than the capacity to "disallow" life expressed as sovereignty (p. 80).

Yet, the sovereign capacity to disallow life, either through death or its gradients in incarceration, torture, starvation, enforced marginalization, and scientific stigmatization, continues to operate upon populations. Moreover, sovereignty is increasingly implicated in (coerced) implementation of neoliberal and neoconservative biopolitical principles of government, particularly in relation to the disciplining of markets. Finally, in the context of everyday life, expert authority and popular sentiment may support authoritarian measures and strategies of government as necessary supplements to government through freedom (see Dean, 2002a). The events delineating the turn of the twenty-first century have generated increased academic interest in sovereign power as the supplement or underside of biopower, as have the complex relations among and across discipline, government, and sovereignty.

This chapter provides a brief genealogy of Foucault's work on sovereignty and addresses the literature surrounding the idea of the exception.

FOUCAULT, AGAMBEN, AND SOVEREIGNTY

Foucault's thoughts on sovereignty are most explicitly developed in the essay "Right of Death and Power Over Life" (2004) and in the posthumously published *Society Must Be Defended*, part of his Lectures at the Collège de France (2003b). Across these texts, sovereignty is considered in relation to the capacities of life and death, race and war. Whereas the essay "Right of Death" emphasizes the contemporary sovereign capacity to let die, *Society Must Be Defended* provides a genealogy of the nation-state founded in metaphors of war and establishment of racialized universalizing identities, linking the sovereignty of the state to violence under the banner of national vitality.

In *Society Must Be Defended*, Foucault (2003b) observed war was initially thought of as "a war between races" in early European history (p. 239)[1]. But over time, the very notion of this war was eventually "eliminated from historical analysis by the principle of national universality" (p. 239). As explained in Chapter 2, universalization of race in the name of the nation-state involved new expressions of sovereignty altering the traditional formulation of the rights of life and death.

Accordingly, Foucault (2003b) described how the state endowed with military institutions emerged after the Treaty of Westphalia. Although sovereignty lacked precise definition in the early modern state, it was characterized in 1606 by the French jurist Jean Bodin as including the power to "'give law,' power of war and peace and the making of foreign alliances, power of taxation, appointing magistrates and coinage" (cited in Orr, 2002, p. 476). Under this new regime of government, police apparatuses administered the population according to the normalizing constraints of law and the exigencies (i.e., imperatives and risks) of commerce and population. The military-diplomatic apparatuses supplemented the power of police and could be used by empowered agents to suppress resistance, often (but not always) under the guise of a state of exception entailing suspension of law.

Resistance was (and is) endemic to state formation and operations. Foucault observed with early state formation, the philosophico-juridical discourse organized around the problem of sovereignty and law was confronted by historical-political discourses challenging the universality of the former discourse of sovereignty. According to Andrew Neal (2004), the ascendant modern discourses of the nation-state ultimately functioned to displace and colonize contestations, such as those posed by historical-political discourses, as a dominant group or nation emerged hegemonic.

Sovereignty was exercised in the strategies and tactics of conflict as particular groups battled for hegemony. For example, in the United States, the interests, values, and perspectives of white landholding men immersed in Enlightenment ideals and laissez-faire capitalist principles ultimately organized and articulated a collective identity and the legitimate forms and operations of political authority; although early colonial life involved people of diverse cultures and religions. The emergence of the American state thus entailed the hegemony of a universalizing and shared identity—the nationalization of a racialized identity—solidifying and unifying the state against external and internal enemies. Coinciding with the birth of biopolitics in the second half of the eighteenth century (Foucault, 2003b), the early American state henceforth looked to cultivate the wealth and health of its populace through police while disciplining and socializing unruly elements (e.g., immigrants) and excising those who posed a threat to the national ideal (e.g., Native Americans; see Hannah, 2000). Racism is thus "inscribed as the basic mechanism of power, as it is exercised in modern States" (Foucault, 2003b, p. 254). In effect, nationalization and extension of the racialized identity of the nation-state entailed sovereignty, discipline, and biopolitical practices internal to the state aimed at pacification and normalization.

What exactly did racism mean for Foucault and how was it linked to sovereignty and conflict? According to Foucault, after the nineteenth century, racism was "primarily a way of introducing a break into the domain of life that is under power's control: the break between what must live and what must die" (2003b, p. 254). Thus, racism fragments the "field of the biological that power controls" (p. 255). Race also entails the idea that one must kill or take lives to live and thereby makes war "compatible with the exercise of biopower" (p. 255). Julian Reid's (2006) work provides a concise summary of the contiguity across race, biopower, and war:

> In a biopolitical context where power is exercised at the level of the life of populations, war occurs in the form of a struggle between populations whose particular existence as the expressions of species life that they are is at stake. The participation of populations in war is therefore reconceived not as the product of a right of seizure, but as a positive, life-affirming act. (p. 136)

Although new understandings of race and nationhood inflect or build upon older ones, modern nation-states continue to wage war against one another to securitize the national identity, the way of life in the name of life itself. Wars between nation-states, or within them, involve distinctions between self and enemy based on racialized norms of identity and ways of life. As Reid argued, biopolitical wars distinguish foes by "their racial differentiation from the norm, and wars are waged by mobilizing populations to defend racial norms against rival populations . . ." (p. 145). Accordingly, Foucault concluded, "the principle underlying the tactics of battle—that one has to be capable of killing in order to go on living—has become the principle that defines the strategy of states" (1990, p. 137).

The sovereign power over death is justified in the modern era to ensure life. Enemies are represented as "threats, either external or internal, to the population and for the population" (Foucault, 2003b, p. 256). The logic holds that eliminating the threat improves the race or species. Foucault asserted: "If the power of normalization wished to exercise the old sovereign right to kill, it must become racist" (p. 256). Thus, when "the State functions in the biopower mode, racism alone can justify the murderous function of the State" (p. 256).

Understood in this context of meaning, sovereignty can be thought of both in terms of the capacities of the biopolitical authorities and forms of expertise to fragment and exploit the biological continuum, and in the institutional capacities of the nation-state and other "sovereign" entities to deny life or to kill (purportedly) to protect and enhance the security of the race. As explored in Chapters 4 and 5, the capacities to delimit normality and thereby label and enable/disable forms of life are found throughout the social field and are executed by a wide array of biopolitical authorities. Sovereignty thus arises in the decision of exceptionality and in the concomitant use of repression to discipline those deemed incapable of self-government. The exercise of sovereignty can be decentered in the practices of everyday life, or it can be centralized in state or institutional authorities who use symbolic and/or corporeal violence to securitize life.

Nineteenth-century biopower operated in the sovereign mode by designating populations as degenerate and/or threatening, leading to their institutional exclusion in enclosed and disciplinary spaces. Twentieth-century biopower sought to engineer the health of the population through hygienic and neohygienic technologies, which eventually stressed technologies of the self. Still, sovereignty operated in the biopower mode in the classification of domestic and foreign populations as "risky"—as requiring supervision and pastoral or authoritarian control. Within the United States, women, poor populations, and populations of people targeted by their nonwhiteness have been subject to sovereign decisionality regarding their exceptionality, as illustrated by the incarceration of Japanese-Americans during World War II and the contemporary practice of incarcerating African-American juvenile offenders. Abroad, the United States exercised state sovereign apparatuses covertly and overtly to pursue markets and/or strategic objectives, including the expansion of markets in Vietnam and the protection of national corporate interests such as ITT and United Fruit in South and Central America.

Over the last two decades of the twentieth century, the extension of neoliberal governmentality has occurred primarily through market mechanisms. The racialized biological identities of the nineteenth and early twentieth centuries have given way (in some locales) to more generic identities delimited by particular market-based practices and market-based technologies of selfhood. The "racialized" identities promulgated at the beginning of the twenty-first century speak to an autonomous, liberal, marketized persona lacking biological specificity. Simultaneously, however, Western, neoliberal constitutions of personhood and market autonomy ground idealized identities against which are pitted constructions of unreasonable, premodern articulations of *others* who are perceived as irrationally resisting the dissemination of neoliberal market principles and personhood. The indigenous peasant and the Orientalized "terrorist" represent such *others*.

Globalization of neoliberal market operations requires security apparatuses that minimize and/or leverage risk. At issue are not those of the nineteenth century seeking to protect a geographically delimited territory. Rather, security is thought of in terms of global circulations of goods, information, and people. Consequently, the modern art of government is not limited to the population and territory of individual states but extends to the larger population of people and things encompassed by the entirety of the world *system*. The well-managed neoliberal state, imagined after a business, strives to exploit global economic opportunities while managing the risks posed by global flows of information, capital, and peoples (Walters, 2004). For the authorities of market and state, the encompassing nature of the emerging world system requires extensive surveillance systems capable of monitoring dispersed locales in order to identify risks that can be leveraged or require management. Authorities must be trained to interpret voluminous data, while still others must be armed with technologies able to influence and administer disclosed risks and opportunities. In effect, neoliberal governmental rationalities—problem solutions, modes of conduct, forms of expertise, strategic interventions—might be understood as colonizing the world system.

As described by Agamben (2001), turn-of-the-twenty-first-century security leads to an opening and globalization in contrast to the closuring and isolating of territories by discipline. Integrally tied up with neoliberal forms of government, security intervenes in processes to direct and regulate disorder but does so in a context of (relative) freedom of traffic and trade. Thus, neoliberal security problematics framed in relation to "circulation" emphasize complex interdependencies and use techno-scientific technologies to calculate and exploit risks (Dillon, 2005, p. 2). Still, disciplines continue to be employed to produce order in enclosed spaces (e.g., refugee camps, corporatized global supply chains, formal immigration bureaucracies).

In essence, analyses of global governmentality suggest the dissemination of neoliberal systems of government most typically involve dispersal of neoliberal market disciplines and technologies of the self, particularly linked to consumption and work-related identities. Power thus centers on life and operates most ubiquitously through the authority of the norm and calculations of risks. The juridical powers of the sovereign state and international governmental agencies adjudicate competing freedoms and liberties. Sovereign power is illustrated in such contexts by the emergent and/or institutionally defined capacity of agents to deny opportunities to pursue life by somehow curtailing others' freedoms or by restricting others' access to the means of life (e.g., through "aid" or privatization).

However, although neoliberal governmentality typically operates from afar, more overt expressions of discipline and sovereign force remain supplementary resources in the context of everyday life and in relations between states, as Foucault observed in his discussion of the biopolitics of race and war (2003b). Scholarship by Barry Hindess and Mitchell Dean are particularly illuminating on the subject of sovereignty in the framework of (neo)liberal governmentality.

In the essay "Liberal Government and Authoritarianism," Dean (2002a) argued persuasively that authoritarian measures are compatible with, and indeed integral to, liberal government. Dean explained the very idea of the liberal norm of the autonomous individual is carved out against forms of life viewed as constituting exceptions, including welfare dependency and statelessness (see also Ong, 2006; Sassen, 2006). Government of exceptions relies more extensively on authoritarian and despotic measures guided by the biopolitical operations of the "liberal police" (made up of biopolitical authorities, forms of expertise, embodied disciplines, etc.).

Hindess (2001, 2006) argued modern states retain the sovereign capacity to use violence and terror, to exercise the despotic power of death over populations. The state's monopolization over violence is legitimized in two foundational myth—one realist and one normative. Both myths explain the formation of the modern world in relation to the concentration of terror in the hands of the state: the realist approach emphasizes the state as a historical outcome of religious conflict in Europe, while the normative approach stresses the contractual emergence of the state's monopoly over violence. Hindess's point in relating these foundational myths rests in their combined capacities to legitimize violence by the state against those internal to the state represented as threatening its peace and security and those external to the state represented as threatening its very existence or the existence of the nation-state system.

States' routine uses of violence against criminals/terrorists and others viewed as threatening the economic and cultural stability of the state or state system is legitimized as regrettably necessary. As explained above, state sovereignty, as practiced through overt state controls and violence, is often vindicated through racialized discourses of national identity cast in terms of foundational mythos.

Giorgio Agamben (1998, 2000, 2005) suggested sovereignty entails withdrawal and suspension of law, in the decision of the state of exception (following Carl Schmitt, 1985). In order to maintain the fantasy of a society of self-governing individuals the system must constantly purify itself of those persons and institutions whose very existence belies the fantasy. Agamben stated, "when, starting with the French Revolution, sovereignty is entrusted solely to the people, the *people* becomes an embarrassing presence, and poverty and exclusion appear for the first time as an intolerable scandal in every sense" (2000, pp. 32–33). The "solution," then, is to "fill the split that divides the people by radically eliminating the people of the excluded" (p. 33). Agamben's paradigmatic example of the state of exception is the concentration camp, but he also applied the concept to explain the U.S. detention of prisoners in Guantánamo: these prisoners have no legal status and are subject "only to raw power" (cited in Raulff, 2004). Additionally, sovereign exceptions may be enacted in the course of everyday life when authorities deem particular subjects incapable of self-government (as defined by particular technologies of government).

Following Agamben, Judith Butler (2004) described sovereignty as a performance enacted in the suspension of rule of law:

> It is not, literally speaking, that a sovereign power suspends the rule of law, but that the rule of law, in the act of being suspended, produces sovereignty *in its actions and as its effect*. This inverse relation to law produces the 'unaccountability' of this operation as sovereign power, as well its illegitimacy. (p. 66)

Butler emphasized the distinction between sovereignty and the rule of law since the former produces a "suspension" of rule of law (p. 66). Moreover, the performance of this suspension is regarded somehow as normative.

Both Agamben and Butler described sovereignty in relation to the power of decision and acts of exclusions, suggesting sovereignty implies exceptionality. However, Andrew Neal cautioned in "Foucault in Guantánamo" (2006) against regarding sovereignty as somehow restricted to extraordinary circumstances, intimating that Agamben-inspired theorizing may risk formulating the exception as distinguished from the norm. Neal noted such theorizing also tends to "privilege a sovereign center" (p. 34) in relation to "formal conditions of sovereignty" or the "metaphysical possibility of the exception" (p. 39). Neal argued instead for exploring the "*dispersal* and *historicity* of the *conditions of possibility* of exceptionalism; to stress that successful and mobilizing declarations of exceptions are only possible because of an already discursive formation of objects, subject positions, enunciative modalities, concepts and strategies" (Neal, 2006, p. 44). Neal's points that sovereign operations should not be regarded as exceptional nor necessarily centered are well taken and raise awareness of the dispersal of sovereign power throughout everyday life.

In "Police, Sovereignty, and Law: Foucaultian Reflections," Mariana Valverde (2007) made a similar argument by observing the state's security apparatuses routinely exercise sovereignty over the population. Valverde suggested the governmentality scholarship's interest in the logic of security has focused disproportionately on police's more pastoral operations, thereby eliding how police apparatuses also invoke sovereign logics in forbidding, disciplining, and punishing. However, while nineteenth-century police apparatuses aimed at normalizing individuals through discipline and punishment, neoliberal and neoconservative police apparatuses work to assess and control public security risks (Garland, 2001; Valverde & Mopas, 2004). The significance of this shift toward risk management is public safety is administered through risk factors rather than through the exclusive supervision of specific concrete individuals. Risk management requires extensive surveillance, engendering the possibility for "targeted governance" of risky spaces, activities, and populations (Valverde & Mopas, 2004, p. 245). But targeting does not involve less government (in the Foucauldian sense); rather, it implies an endless and expansive project of targeting *more*, requiring ever more surveillance. Finally, targeting requires repressive apparatuses to be available for managing and suppressing identified risks.

These analyses raise questions about the utility of the language of exceptionality when studying the operations of sovereignty across everyday life, between states, and in relation to the dispersal of global governmentality. However, Randy Lippert (2004) demonstrated how the language of exception can be maintained without necessitating that exceptionality stand opposed to normativity. Lippert argued, "governmentalities manufacture and defer to sovereign power and create the capacity to make the exception when resistance is encountered in governmental spaces that then become sovereign territories" (p. 543). Further, "both liberal and pastoral rationalities are dependent on the capacity to make the exception, which at times is realized as symbolic salvation but at others as exclusion and coercion" (p. 548). Thus, Lippert's argument contends normativity is manufactured biopolitically in relation to sovereignty and, concomitantly, creates the conditions of possibility for sovereign exceptionality.

In sum, in contemporary neoliberal societies, sovereignty is intimately connected to biopower and operates most insidiously in the capacity to let die as distinguished from the capacity to kill. Sovereign decisions about life and death occur through biopolitical and disciplinary practices delineating normal, desirable, or optimal forms of life from those forms of life viewed as risky, abnormal, undesirable, and suboptimal. Racialized identities are thought of in relation to the technologies and forms of expertise used to divide the bio/cultural continuum of humanity. Individuals and practices viewed as abnormal (e.g., amoral) or undesirable (e.g., risky or dangerous) may be subject to authoritarian measures by petty tyrants, state apparatuses, or privatized "police." The purported "exceptionality" of individuals deemed incapable of self-government legitimizes brute force, authoritarianism, and the invocation of sovereign decision making about life and death. The sovereign capacities to disallow or disable "freedom" and the capacities for life are integrally caught up with biopower. Moreover, the ancient sovereign capability to kill (as distinguished from the modern capacity to disallow life) can be invoked by states and other agents when rationalized by the preservation of life itself. Brute sovereignty meets resistance and there is battle and/or war.

War is not antithetical to neoliberal governmentality. In *The Liberal Virus*, Samir Amin (2004) insisted neoliberalism entails a "permanent war" of military interventions against people at the global market's periphery (p. 24). Amin's expansive approach to war included nearly all police action against resistant populations (see also Giroux, 2004). Even those who view war in more conventional terms (defined in relation to the nation-state) predict proliferating conflicts due to environmental, market, and biopolitical exigencies. Circulating commodities, such as small arms, amplify regional conflicts.

Under neoliberalism, "just wars" are waged to attain resources, to "open markets," and to free individuals from "human rights" abuses (Douzinas, 2003, p. 172) Costas Douzinas observed that wars fought under the guise of protecting human rights entail overwhelming material force often implemented in the form of "police" operations aimed at preventing, deterring, and punishing (purported) criminal perpetrators (p. 172). Offenders are represented as unjust and inhuman, deserving no mercy, although critical examination reveals definitions of abuses, perpetrators, and victims as politically contingent (see Mboka, 2007).

Still, even the most deterritorialized or "just" of wars require that populations be mobilized to support or condone violence. Mobilization of support for violence often entails articulation of a racialized identity, or way of life, represented as threatened by outsiders, criminals, dissenters, and so on. Compelling moral narratives must be drawn upon to fuel cooperation for repression and death (see Cairo, 2006).

Although much can be written about war, conflict, and sovereignty under neoliberalism, in what follows, I focus primarily on how sovereignty operates in and through the formal and ideological technologies of the U.S. state and its outsourced agents in the context of the "war on terror" and the invasion of Iraq. This emphasis is not intended to collapse sovereignty into the state. Across this book, I have demonstrated the biopolitics of petty sovereignty. But the governmentality of the state in and through the biopolitics of population does not exhaust contemporary discussions of power and control.

Thus, this chapter returns to the state to demonstrate that centered forms of brute sovereignty continue to exist. Following Foucault, I address the technologies of government that both constitute sovereign agents, and are employed by them, in the deployment of control over populations. The types of technologies I explore include: (a) "technologies of production"; (b) "technologies of sign systems"; (c) "technologies of power"; and (d) "technologies of the self" (Foucault, 1988, p. 18). First, I address the racialized construction of the American state and its population around the principle of its exceptionality, emphasizing how sign systems unify the population against security threats. I then explore how informatic technologies of production allow the state's police apparatuses to monitor the population directly and indirectly and how the surveillance state produces new technologies of power operating upon, and through, populations. Finally, I conclude by discussing how the state's civilian and military agents exert brute sovereignty over those "othered" as criminal, dangerous, or invisible by America's racialized nationalistic identity.

THE UNITED STATES OF AMERICA: BIOPOWER, RACE, AND SOVEREIGNTY

America's national identity is predicated upon the idea of American exceptionality because the forms of knowledge, thought, and expertise constituting self-understanding have historically stressed America's sovereignty before God in relation to all others.

As mentioned previously, in the United States, the interests, values, and perspectives of white landholding men immersed in Enlightenment ideals and laissez-faire capitalist principles served to organize and articulate a collective identity and the legitimate operations of political authority. Nationalization of a racialized identity, combined with the doctrine of Manifest Destiny (explained in Chapter 2), fueled expansion over North America and, when expedient, justified genocide against Native Americans and the economic exploitation and marginalization of "others," including immigrants (e.g., Chinese railroad workers), slaves, and so on. As explained by Coles (2002):

> The origin of America was rhetorically explained as an act of providence—that is, 'God led people (white Europeans) to America to found a new and superior or exceptional social order that would be the light

onto all nations . . . This chosen nation myth has been the oldest and most continuous creed in American civil religion. (p. 406)

The doctrine of Manifest Destiny rationalized expansion of the American way of life abroad through war and/or intervention (Coles, 2002). Manifest Destiny has served to unify the population against threats both internal and external.

Within the contemporary United States, neoliberal, neoconservative, and conservative Christian principles, practices, and problems of government find legitimacy in appeals to racialized constructions of origins and the doctrine of Manifest Destiny. The U.S. media, judicial courts, history education, and national monuments all contribute to contemporary understandings of the foundational mythos, one characterized by enlightened, entrepreneurial "Founding Fathers" contractually constituting a politically and economically free society. The spread of U.S. territory, from the founding states to the current territorial expansiveness, serves retroactively to prove the essential "correctness" of the doctrine, as does the 1948 Marshall Plan and the implosion of the Soviet Union.

Historical events or phenomena that could potentially rupture the universalization of the mythos are erased or trivialized or are retroactively constituted as "exceptions" to the principles of the benevolent American state and its protections of universal liberal personhood. For example, contemporary acknowledgments of genocide against Native Americans and the internment of Japanese-American citizens during World War II are framed rhetorically as irregularities arising from very isolated historical convergences of events. The more pervasive and mundane practices of exclusion and coercion used against "others"—recent immigrants, women, people of color, laborers—tend toward historical invisibility. American cultural exceptionalism in relation to the global system is vindicated in the popular imagination by the nation's willingness to recognize and learn from the overt and gross "exceptions" to American exceptionalism (e.g., as compared to Japan's unwillingness to claim full responsibility for World War II atrocities).

U.S. foreign policy and industry tactics violating the state's juridical-political principles were, and continued to be, justified in relation to American cultural exceptionalism and the attendant doctrine of Manifest Destiny. Accordingly, covert and overt U.S. military engagements in the Middle East, Southeast Asia, and Central America were explained in relation to the securitization and dissemination of liberal democratic capitalist ways of life rationalized in the 1947 Containment Doctrine, 1957 Eisenhower Doctrine, 1960s Domino Theory, and 1980s Reagan Doctrine, among others (Waldman, 2004). When acknowledged, brute authoritarian force used against dissenting peasants, workers, and rebels in distant lands found legitimacy in the necessities of life. "Enemies" not effectively dehumanized or othered were represented as misguided, naïve, or childlike. Human "collateral costs" were, and continue to be, represented as regrettable necessities in order to preserve the American national way of life: liberal democratic capitalism.

As explained previously, in the post–Cold War context, the American way of life was increasingly cast in relation to neoliberal principles and practices of "freedom" linked in the popular imagination to the historical ideals of America's entrepreneurial, rational, free-market founders. However, although efforts to promote American-style "democratic" capitalism abroad in the 1980s and 1990s typically operated "from a distance," market and biopolitical authorities also sought to map and govern risky individuals using both pastoral and repressive strategies. For example, peasants in Central America protesting neoliberal "reforms" impoverishing populations typically met repressive state force. Poor populations in Nigeria resisting transnational energy corporations exploiting national resources met privatized security. Labor unions in liberal Western democracies protesting outsourcing and flexibilization met technocratic analyses and public apathy. The Seattle World Trade protests of 1999 operated as a site of condensation for organized resistance to neoliberal market imperatives, suggesting opportunities for dispersed forces to gain strength through new alliances fostered and coordinated using new information technologies such as the Internet.

In response to resistance against the effects of neoliberal market strategies and technologies, a wide range of private and public "philanthropic" apparatuses emerged (or became more visible) and promised to foster liberal democratic values and markets abroad. American philanthropic institutions often display their missionary zeal in their statements of "democracy promotion" (House, 2006, p. A26). Among others, these organizations include:

The National Endowment for Democracy

Public funding. "The Endowment is guided by the belief that freedom is a universal human aspiration that can be realized through the development of democratic institutions, procedures, and values. Governed by an independent, nonpartisan board of directors, the NED makes hundreds of grants each year to support prodemocracy groups in Africa, Asia, Central and Eastern Europe, Eurasia, Latin America, and the Middle East." (http://www.ned.org/)

The International Republican Institute

Public and private funding. "A nonprofit, nonpartisan organization, the International Republic Institute advances freedom and democracy worldwide by developing political parties, civic institutions, open elections, good governance and the rule of law." (http://www.iri.org/)

The Center for International and Private Enterprise

Public and private funding. "CIPE provides management assistance, practical experience and financial support to local organizations to strengthen their capacity to implement democratic and economic reforms." (http://www.cipe.org/)

Freedom House

Public and private funding. "Freedom House, a non-profit, nonpartisan organization, is a clear voice for democracy and freedom around the world. Through a vast array of international programs and publications, Freedom House is working to advance the remarkable worldwide expansion of political and economic freedom."(http://www.freedomhouse.org/template.cfm?page=1)

Together, international lending, trade and "democracy promotion" organizations aim to promote and securitize worldwide neoliberal governmentalities by facilitating market penetration while "educating" overseas populations in the principles and practices of marketized, democratic personhood. For example, President Bush's "Millennium Challenge Corporation," created in 2002, sought to ensure "good governance" by making foreign assistance contingent upon compliance with social, market, and governmental policy (M. Phillips, 2006). These discourses of democracy promotion reflect the missionary zeal of Manifest Destiny but are couched in secular frameworks of American-style good governance.

However, the sacred dimensions of Manifest Destiny have been reinvigorated within the discursive alliance of the neoconservative and conservative Christian movements. This union shares neoliberal market values but distrusts government from afar. That is, although the union embraces the idea of a self-regulating global society operating according to neoliberal regimes of government, it demands sovereign intervention to achieve and securitize this ideal domestically and abroad. In particular, neoconservatives view sovereign state authority as necessary to remove barriers to the global flows of capital and to enforce market disciplines upon dependent and/or unruly populations rendered useless by bloated social securities. Neoconservatives favoring expansion of the philanthropic complex to reduce security risks and to shepherd vulnerable and/or ignorant populations empowered Christian "relief" and charitable organizations within the domestic sphere (prisons and welfare operations) and abroad. Neoconservatives and Christian conservatives have also tried to reinvigorate patriotism domestically while fostering the image of a strong state abroad.

As illustrated by the home page for The Project for the New American Century, neoconservative authorities, forms of expertise, and strategies prefer direct state action to enforce dispersion of American liberal-democratic capitalism:

The Project for the New American Century is a non-profit educational organization dedicated to a few fundamental propositions: that American leadership is good both for America and for the world; and that such leadership requires military strength, diplomatic energy and commitment to moral principle.

The Project for the New American Century intends, through issue briefs, research papers, advocacy journalism, conferences, and seminars, to explain what American world leadership entails. It will also strive to rally support for a vigorous and principled policy of American international involvement and to stimulate useful public debate on foreign and defense policy and America's role in the world. ("The Project," n.d.)

Supplementing this introduction is the organization's statement of principles by leading members, which articulates commitments including an explicit need to "accept responsibility for America's unique role in preserving and extending an international order friendly to our security, our prosperity, and our principles" ("Statement," n.d.).

As Norton (2004) argued in *Leo Strauss and the Politics of American Empire*, the Straussian-influenced neoconservative policy agenda has directly shaped U.S. intervention in the Middle East, engineering its policy toward Israel, and its efforts toward regime change in Afghanistan and Iraq (see also Drury, 1999; Postel, 2003).[2] The American religious right strongly favors U.S. support for Israel because of their belief Israel fulfills Biblical prophecy (Higgins, 2006). The convergence of neoconservative foreign policy agendas and evangelical support for Israel shaped U.S. foreign policy under the George W. Bush administration (2001–present). Manifest Destiny oddly embraced Zionism.

George W. Bush's administration strove to revitalize America by reinvigorating patriotism domestically while fostering an image of national strength abroad. The collapse of the Soviet Union had posed an epistemic problem for the United States across the 1990s as it had lost its central, defining adversary (Stephanson, 1995). The global dissemination of (neo)liberal market operations, technologies, and ideologies provided a kind of (secularized) proof of Manifest Destiny but lacked the ideational impact necessary to mobilize populations. Moreover, neoliberal market technologies and ideologies were subject to multiple populist and moralistic discourses of resistance.

The events of September 11 reinvigorated American patriotism while presenting a force against which America's Manifest Destiny could be pitted. "Global terrorism" and "despotic regimes" became the new enemies uniting the nation. Accordingly, at the onset of the twenty-first century, terror and security are the problem spaces occupying neoconservative authorities, and the articulation of these "problems" occurs in the contexts of the imagined spaces of American racial/national/cultural identity and Manifest Destiny. Increasingly, these "problems" occupy the imagination of the broader American public as well.

The historical conditions of possibility for the rise to prominence of these linked problem formulations of terrorism and security stem (at least in part) from past neoliberal governmental policy objectives, including securitization of resources for the state (oil) and capitalist accumulation strategies (open markets). However, although U.S. foreign-policy objectives in the Middle East are fundamentally driven by the neoliberal imperatives of securitizing energy flows vital to the American way of life, they are also inflected and rationalized by a racialized national discourse formalized in the "Lewis Doctrine" (Waldman, 2004, p. A12) and Samuel Huntington's clash-of-civilization thesis (1993a). Together, the Lewis and Huntington doctrines narrate the epic struggle between the forces of modernity and light (embodied in America's Manifest Destiny) and the forces of premodernity and otherness.

The "Lewis Doctrine" was coined by Peter Waldman, a journalist for *The Wall Street Journal*, when describing the political interpretations and policy implications of works by the prominent Middle Eastern historian Bernard Lewis. For at least sixty years, Bernard Lewis provided a looking glass through which Western nations have beheld the Middle East (e.g., Lewis, 1966). In 1978, Edward Said published *Orientalism*, which critiqued Lewis's work for producing a simplifying and colonial construction of the Middle East and its peoples. Despite Said's criticism, Lewis's work continued to define (or legitimize) hegemonic Western interpretations and policy orientations in the region.

Lewis's continued impact is illustrated in Waldman's (2004) article. In particular, Waldman invoked the policy implications of Lewis's idea of Mideastern "malaise." Accordingly, Waldman argued: "Most Islamic countries have failed miserably at modernizing their societies . . . beckoning outsiders—this time, Americans—to intervene" (p. A1). Waldman continued, "Mr. Lewis's diagnosis of the Muslim world's malaise, and his call for a U.S. military invasion to see democracy in the Mideast, have helped define the boldest shift in U.S. foreign policy in 50 years" (p. A1). From this emerges fundamental problematics: how to reduce neoliberal market barriers, contain terrorism, and promote democracy:

> Terrorism has replaced Moscow as the global foe. And now America, having outlasted the Soviets to become the sole superpower, no longer seeks to contain but to confront, defeat and transform. How successful it is at remolding Iraq and the rest of the Mideast could have a huge impact on what sort of superpower America will be for decades to come: bold and assertive—or inward, defensive and cut off. (p. A1)

Waldman cited Paul Wolfowitz as stating: "Bernard has taught us how to understand the complex and important history of the Middle East, and use it to guide us where we will go next to build a better world for generations to come" (p. A12).

Samuel Huntington's idea about the "clash of civilizations," published first in 1993 in *Foreign Affairs*, drew directly upon Lewis's work, particularly *The Atlantic Monthly* essay "The Roots of Muslim Rage" (1990). Huntington's essay was produced as part of the Olin Institute's project on "the Changing Security Environment and American National Interests" (p. 22). It initially received limited attention until it was popularized in the press after the attacks of September 11.

Huntington (1993a) claimed "principal conflicts of global politics occur between nations and groups of different civilizations" (p. 22), primarily between the Western civilizations (including the "European" and "North American" "variants") and Islam (with its "Arab, Turkic and Malay subdivisions"; p. 24), although he also postulated potential conflicts with Confucian, Japanese, Hindu, Slavic-Orthodox, Latin American, and possibly African civilizations. Huntington argued that "fault lines between civilizations" replace Cold War ones. In such clashes, "the question is 'What are you?'" (1993a, p. 27). Huntington focused most exclusively on the "bloody borders" of the "crescent-shaped Islamic bloc" (p. 34) as a source of impending conflict. Huntington (1993b) asserted in "If Not Civilizations, What?" that on important issues, "the West is on one side and most of the other civilizations are on the other" (p. 189). In 1996, Francis Fukuyama referred to Huntington's thesis as the "leading paradigm for post–Cold War world politics" (p. A20).

Huntington claimed "Faith and family, blood and belief, are what people identify with and what they will fight and die for" (1993b, p. 194). Yet, Huntington presupposed his categories of analysis, failing to acknowledge the (bio)politics and sovereign decisionalism implicit in his delineations of distinct "civilizations" and "fault lines" (C. Aradau, personal correspondence, August 6, 2007). The politics of economic development, capital accumulation, colonialism, and the Palestinian conflict are invisible in Huntington's racialized interpretation of cultural conflict (Abrahamian, 2003; Boal, Clark, Matthews, & Watts, 2005; Ibrahim, 2003). Despite invoking stereotyped and homogenizing representations of Middle Eastern people and politics, Huntington's work helped popularize a set of truth statements about the nature of conflict in the world, particularly in the Middle East, shaping perceptions in the United States and other Western nations.

Although neither Huntington nor Lewis actually propounded a Manichean view of the world, their homogenized accounts of Middle Eastern otherness have been grafted upon a preexisting Manichean theology. The American consciousness is steeped in Manichean dualism cultivated across disparate sites, including Hollywood productions (e.g., *Star Wars*) and Cold War political rhetoric (e.g., Reagan's account of the Soviet "evil empire"). The public's perception of a racialized threat of the other is exacerbated by the cultural imaginings of the religious right. Xenophobic fantasies of clashes of civilizations blend oddly with the Armageddon/End-of-Days narrative chronicled in the LaHaye *Left Behind* series. Many Americans believe it is their destiny to challenge the forces of unreason and evil because of America's unique historical and spiritual status. Thus, the seemingly bewildering complexity of Middle Eastern politics is simplified and rendered immediately intelligible through the imposition of these preexisting ideologies.

President Bush's address to a joint session of Congress and the American People on September 20, 2001, dramatized stark conflict between good and evil represented by terrorism:

> Americans are asking, why do they hate us? They hate what we see right here in this chamber—a democratically elected government. Their leaders are self-appointed. They hate our freedoms—our freedom of religion, our freedom of speech, our freedom to vote and assemble and disagree with each other . . .
>
> These terrorists kill not merely to end lives, but to disrupt and end a way of life. With every atrocity, they hope that America grows fearful, retreating from the world and forsaking our friends. They stand against us, because we stand in their way . . .
>
> This is not, however, just America's fight. And what is at stake is not just America's freedom. This is the world's fight. This is civilization's fight. This is the fight of all who believe in progress and pluralism, tolerance and freedom. . . .
>
> Freedom and fear, justice and cruelty, have always been at war, and we know that God is not neutral between them. . . .

Although Bush carefully avoided casting all peoples in the Middle East as terrorist, his binary rhetoric reinforced a Manichean struggle between the forces of good and evil and cast U.S. military actions as "just" protections of human rights (see Coe, Domke, Graham, John, & Pickard, 2004). Bush's repeated warnings of terrorist threats posed by "Islamic extremists" condense and exacerbate general social anxiety (Fletcher, 2006b).

Consequently, as illustrated by Tony Blankley's popular text, *The West's Last Chance: Will We Win the Clash of Civilizations?* (2005), many Americans today believe "Western civilization" is itself threatened with annihilation. The nation, already prepped by a "discourse of fear" cultivated since the mid-1990s by sensationalist media reporting (Altheide, 2002, p. ix), responded to the spectacle of destruction wrought by terrorists with fear and anger. In this context of paranoia, Vice President Dick Cheney offered his "1% Doctrine," which legitimized preemptive action against foreign nations or peoples if there were even a 1 percent chance terrorists could attain "weapons of mass destruction" ("America's Longest," 2006, p. 22).

Cheney's 1 percent doctrine can be understood as formally inaugurating a new formulation of risk. Accordingly, Claudia Aradau and Rens van Munster (2007) stated a dispositif of "precautionary risk" currently governs U.S. evaluation and response to terrorist risk. They compare this "precautionary risk" with "prudentialism," which typically governs neoliberal risk assessment. Whereas prudentialism entails prudent calculation and minimization of risk under contingency, precautionary risk implies catastrophic contingency ("risk beyond risk"; p. 13) and therefore invokes a "dispositif at the limit" (p. 17). Precautionary risk operates as such as a dispositif at the limit because it is premised on the incalculability of risk conjoined with the catastrophic nature of potential effects. Precautionary risk governance thus entails tendencies toward drastic prevention. Whole populations become suspect, leading to limitless surveillance:

> Precautionary technologies change the relation to social groups, to the population as created by the dispositif of insurance. Statistical computation and risk management relied upon the scientific representation of social groups that were to be governed; profiling was an important technology for selecting these groups and targeting them. At the limit of knowledge, this relation to representation becomes an arbitrary connection. 'Suspected' terrorists are arbitrarily gleaned from larger categories, such as migrants or Muslim communities. (p. 15)

The effect is risk assessment becomes "decisional" in the sense that a sovereign decision is made outside of juridical processes because "responsibility is uncertain and *a priori* to the event and therefore impossible to accommodate by the juridical system" (pp. 16–17).

As formulated in the Manichean/clash-of-civilizations thesis, precautionary risk government is absolutely necessary because the American way of life is itself at risk of extinction. Consequently, even the most chilling of measures—including the torture of prisoners at Abu Ghraib and the long-term incarceration of prisoners at Guantánamo Bay—are viewed as justified by the security and ideological imperatives of this epochal struggle for life itself.

The Bush administration drew upon the logic of precautionary risk when justifying the impending invasion of Iraq, as demonstrated by his radio address to the nation: "Our cause is just, the security of the nations we serve and the peace of the world. And our mission is clear, to disarm Iraq of weapons of mass destruction, to end Saddam Hussein's support for terrorism, and to free the Iraqi people" (Bush, 2003). The public, primed by the terrorist acts of 9–11 and conditioned against "those who hate freedom," responded to the invasion announcement by displaying American flags on their person, autos, offices, and houses (Bush, 2002). Fear for the "American way of life" permeated the popular imagination as the public was warned of hidden Iraqi weapons of mass destruction.

By 2004, Bush's rhetoric had shifted away from precautionary risk as weapons of mass destruction failed to materialize in Iraq. Instead, the discourse of Manifest Destiny emerged as retroactive justification for the invasion as Bush described the December 2005 Iraqi elections as a "watershed moment in the story of freedom" (Bush, 2005). Subsequent media reports of staggering civilian fatalities in Iraq soon unraveled the story of freedom. The clash-of-civilizations thesis was subsequently adapted to explaining civil conflict *within* Iraq as the forces of freedom within Iraq were represented as combating the forces of terror and tyranny.

In 2006, the clash-of-civilizations thesis again embraced the entirety of Iraq as Bush represented the United States as engaged directly in "a struggle for civilization" (cited in Rutenberg & Stolberg, 2006, p. 12). Moreover, Bush warned again of a radical Islamic network "determined to bring death and suffering to our homes" (p. 12), thereby articulating the danger as personal and proximate to American citizens removed from the immediacies of war.

Critics' efforts to understand the "truth of the invasion" may reveal neoliberal market imperatives but obscure the reality of the war of the races as experienced in the popular imagination. Many Americans fear for their way of life and for the safety of their families and homes as the rhetoric of terror permeates their daily lives. For them, the clash of civilization is *real* as the fantasy of Manifest Destiny encounters a ferocious but spatially dislocated *other*. Terrorists serve as sites of condensation for displaced social anxieties (e.g., xenophobia, neoliberal market pains, confusion about complex systems), purifying Americans' sense of global purpose in an otherwise complex and risky world.

The regime of truth thriving in this charged political environment tolerates little substantive dissent while masquerading as reasoned discourse (Bratich, 2003, 2004). Simplified understandings prevail while complex accounts implicating American complicity in producing global risks are often rejected as exaggerated, conspiratorial, and/or unpatriotic. According to Jack Bratich, popular discourse encourages moderate skepticism while simultaneously enjoining subjects to reject any discourse of truth that problematizes norms of political rationality. The discourses persisting in problematizing simplified norms and understandings are radicalized and rejected. Thus, the regime of truth operates in a disciplinary fashion as individuals monitor their talk and the talk of social others for the contagion of radicalism and, particularly, conspiracism (Bratich, 2003).

American repressive and surveillance apparatuses have become more apparent, more *visible* in this environment of suspicion and fear. They find justification in the belief by many that extraordinary measures are required to address extraordinary circumstances. The examples developed below illustrate how the ideological and material constitutions of security threats engender and legitimize the resurgence of state sovereignty and police apparatuses in the context of what Ben Chappell (2006) described as "threat governmentality," which refers to the surveillance of space and population in the context of a panopticon of threat (p. 314). Threat governmentality's hegemony stems from particular formulations of risk.

SURVEILLANCE, THREAT GOVERNMENTALITY, AND PRECAUTIONARY RISK

Threat governmentality finds justification in precautionary risk, warranting sovereign decisionality outside of *de jure* juridical processes. In this section I illustrate sovereign decisionality in relation to the state's extension of security apparatuses.

In the context of precautionary-risk government (Aradau & van Munster, 2007), the Bush administration pursued secretive strategies for rendering the populace visible enabled by new surveillance and database technologies. In 2001, the administration launched a clandestine intelligence program monitoring communications between people residing in the United States and other countries when they were was suspected of having terrorist connections (Pincus, 2007). The program was found unconstitutional by a federal judge in 2006 (Liptak & Lichtblau, 2006). The administration also secretly collected the domestic telephone and e-mail records of millions of U.S. businesses and households, violating federal law and/or agency rules more than 1,000 times (Solomon, 2007). The surveillance data were entered into huge databases and analyzed using informatic programs (Gellman & Mohammed, 2006). Data mining has also been used by the Pentagon to target teenagers for military recruiting (Mohammed & Goo, 2006). Widespread surveillance and data mining illustrate the fantasy of informatic, targeted governance (Amoore & De Goede, 2005) while concretely demonstrating how information, once produced, can be used for other and potentially insidious purposes (e.g., targeting recruits or suppressing dissent).

When faced with accusations of privacy abuses, the Bush administration employed juridico-legal means to legitimize its sovereign decisionality. First, they appealed to the U.S. Constitution's vague but broad description of presidential powers (Leonnig, 2006). Then, in 2006, Bush justified the "need" for greater wiretap authority by appealing to changing technologies which demand application of more pervasive surveillance systems: "The nature of communications has changed quite dramatically," Bush warned in an address. "The terrorists who want to harm America can now buy disposable cell phones and open anonymous e-mail messages. Our laws need to change to take these changes into account" (cited in Asthana & DeYoung, 2006, p. A1). In 2007, Bush's administration revised the 1978 Foreign Intelligence Surveillance Act (FISA), which stipulates the conditions under which the government can conduct surveillance. Revisions expanded potential targets for surveillance and warrantless surveillance (Pincus, 2007). Additionally, federal authorities unveiled a new initiative which allowed federal, state, local, and tribal agents to use data from spy satellites for domestic enforcement of civil and criminal law (Warrick, 2007). Precautionary risk management warrants juridical expansion of sovereign decisionality.

Targeted governance and precautionary risk management together have produced a legacy of indefinite detention at Guantánamo and elsewhere. In 2007, *The Washington Post* reported nearly 300 inmates at Guantánamo have never been charged with any crime and lack the right to challenge their imprisonment under habeas corpus. Inmates may appeal to review panels set up by the Pentagon but are denied access to an attorney and to the information used against them ("Spectacle," 2007). Moreover, they are barred by federal judicial order from revealing the details of the "alternative interrogation methods" used upon them (Leonnig & Rich, 2006, p. A1). U.S. war conduct in Iraq has also led to indefinite detentions: detainees numbered 24,500 in August 2007 (Shanker, 2007).

Precautionary risk management of possible terrorist attacks no doubt contributed to the U.S. support of the Israeli invasion of Lebanon aimed at quelling Hezbollah forces, although this dissident group is unconnected to al Qaeda. Amnesty International (2007) reported approximately 1,200 civilians died during that invasion. Additionally, precaution risk management and targeted governance organize the U.S. state's current drive toward an aerial assault on Iran.

Foreign policy is thus inflected by the logic of precautionary risk management, thereby necessitating new strategies for targeted territorial surveillance and control. Arms inspectors, spy satellites, and human infiltrators are supplemented by informatic analysis of currency flows and commodity transactions. Perhaps most bizarrely, precautionary risk management outweighs the potential risks to domestic populations as the government invests extensively in "bioterror" by building classified facilities to research biological weapons (Warrick, 2006, p. A1). As explained by Melinda Cooper (2006), a preemptive logic governs U.S. research on bioterror. Rather than attempting to halt others' dangerous advances, this anticipatory logic mobilizes innovation to preempt potential fallout. However, preemption escalates risk and increases the need for surveillance over one's own and others' innovations.

Consistent with neoliberal market imperatives, much of the work involved in targeted governance and precautionary risk management has been accomplished by private contractors (see Pincus, 2006a, 2006b). Although private contracting exemplifies neoliberal logics, it also points to new opportunities for consolidation of power and control. Particularly ominous in this regard is the U.S. reliance on private security contractors such as Blackwater Corporation, which was employed domestically in the aftermath of Hurricane Katrina and currently enjoys a multimillion-dollar contract with the U.S. State Department for work in Iraq. Blackwater's strong ties to the religious right raise alarm (Scahill, 2007), as does the more general tendency for the state's repressive and foreign-policy apparatuses to be outsourced to market-driven contractors unregulated by legislative and/or judicial oversight (see Hartnett & Stengrim, 2006). In September 2007, Blackwater employees opened unprovoked fire in Baghdad, killing unarmed civilians, raising widespread criticism about contractors' war conduct, especially given their immunity to prosecution in Iraq (Fadel & Hammoudi, 2007).

Securitization of the state has also included a wide and often bewildering array of micropractices, often funded by federal authorities but implemented by local officials. For example, federal money brought surveillance cameras to small towns to protect against terrorist threats (Fahrenthold, 2006). Additionally, the Homeland Security Department created a unit to combat "homegrown terrorists," targeting radicalization at prisons and universities. As the news report reads, "Impressionable students are particularly susceptible to charismatic leaders aiming to 'instill a brand of extreme ideology,'" especially as "extremists 'manipulate social situations to create perceptions of victimization'" (Hall, 2007, p. A4).

Security has also been localized through informal, community-based policing. Immediately following the 9–11 attacks, people were advised to report suspicious individuals, exacerbating cultural xenophobia in an increasingly panoptic society. Individual civilians were interpellated as the first line of defense against the dispersed and circulating networks of "enduring terror," which could purportedly contaminate the safety of any neighborhood in any town (cited in Fletcher, 2006b, p. A1).

As James Hay (2006) described in "Designing Homes to Be the First Line of Defense," American citizens are encouraged by the Department of Homeland Security to securitize their homes using a standardized diagram of preparedness supplemented with the homeowner's personal customization. In effect, civil defense is understood as a kind of "'social security,' a form of welfare articulated as paramilitary preparedness" (p. 357). New, militarized, and prudential understandings of social security replace social-welfare ones (Aradau, personal communication, August 6, 2007) as individual citizens are constituted as "soldiers" (Hay, 2006, p. 374) and are encouraged to self-manage risk, through training and home securitization, since these activities demonstrate civic responsibility and the capacity to self-govern responsibly. Home security not only illustrates government at a distance and the promulgation of a militarized ethos but also effectively simplifies the broader context of international events by hystericizing their significance in terms of threats *to* personal security.

In this context of meaning and action, it is not surprising citizens actively report comments of "suspicious" activities, particularly in high-security locales such as airports, public transportation (trains, subways), and malls. Passage of the Patriot Act in October 2001 expanded legal surveillance while public concern about personal security fostered support for heightened surveillance. Bilge Yesil (2006) observed this amplified scrutiny, particularly in relation to widespread video surveillance, also increased individual angst, leading to more diligent self-surveillance, bolstering the capacity for normalizing government at a distance in the absence of force.

Chappell (2006) argued individuals identified as ethnic minorities are disproportionately caught up in the panopticon of targeted surveillance extended and legitimized by the Patriot Act and other homeland security initiatives. Importantly, liberal notions of citizen rights tend to be outweighed by the epidemiological construction of public security risk, while empowering "petty sovereigns" tasked with protecting public safety. Security apparatuses fail to distinguish between crimes and acts of war and, moreover, often fail to differentiate between criminal offences and minor public-order disturbances (Hörnqvist, 2004).

For all Americans, even those targeted for heightened surveillance, security anxiety, coupled with the individualization of risk and responsibility, encourages personal vigilance and militancy echoing Cold War paranoia (Hay, 2006). Conservative Americans respond particularly vehemently to threat governmentality and precautionary risk, consolidating their alignment with hawkish candidates, especially supporting candidates who espouse a worldview representing Americans as engaged in a "heroic battle against evil" (Pyszczynksi, cited in Begley, 2006d, p. B1). In this discursive milieu, camouflage fashion, *Star Wars*–style media Manichaeism, G.I. Joe–inspired toys, and SUVs and Hummers contribute to a kaleidoscope of militancy into which young children are interpellated. Jonathan Rutherford's (2005) essay "At War" provides a powerful and chilling account of the culture of war at home, including the military's creation of an official war video game, which provides soldiers and citizens alike a "simulacrum of fetishized technology and weaponry, and a frontier land of a collapsing Middle Eastern urbanscape" (p. 633).

This framework of understanding renders intelligible America's popular support for the U.S. invasion of Iraq. American television news networks reported on the war under the "war on terror" heading, legitimizing the invasion even after intelligence links between Saddam Hussein and al Qaeda were acknowledged to be false. America's belief in Manifest Destiny, anxiety about oil, and vague understandings of the cultural and political complexities of the Middle East, coupled with specters of terrorist *others*, converged to solidify continued backing of the war until late in 2006, when rising American casualties and Iraqi civil war began to undermine support. However, since by this time Iraq had *become* a training ground for terrorists, precautionary risk mandated continued involvement to reduce attendant risks.

SOVEREIGN EXCEPTIONALITY

"Once politics is construed as the continuation of war, once war becomes conceived as a condition for the possibility for life, for the pursuit of security and the increase of its being, however that conception may be grounded, the conditions are created whereby life itself becomes the object for various forms of destruction, annihilation, and quiet extermination" (Reid, 2006, p. 149).

Contemporary security exigencies are represented in political discourse and in the popular imagination as warranting the reassertion of the sovereign capacity to kill, and as legitimizing abnegation of liberal "rights" of personhood. Fearing for the national way of life, public acceptance grows for forms of sovereignty and discipline that might otherwise be viewed as impinging against liberal guarantees. Government through freedom is increasingly characterized by "exceptions," justifying the withholding of life, forceful discipline, and/or sovereign repression abroad. Domestically, police apparatuses discard pastoralism in favor of authoritarianism against suspect or dangerous individuals (see Giroux, 2004). Likewise, the conservative Supreme Court has issued rulings limiting citizens' abilities to challenge government and corporate policies, particularly through use of the doctrine of standing (Bravin, 2007) and through the purported protection of state secrets (Sherman, 2007).

Precautionary risk government is used to legitimize sovereign decisionality by executive authorities. For four years, Vice President Cheney has claimed that his office is exempt from federal orders regulating handing of security information; he recently tried to abolish the office responsible for enforcing those orders (Baker, 2007). President Bush has claimed unprecedented presidential authority and has argued he is not subject to bills he authorizes (Weisman, 2007). The 2007 nominee for Attorney General, Mr. Mukasey, echoed the administration's prevailing attitude that the U.S. presidency defines the parameters and applications of law, including constitutional law, stating the U.S. president has the capacity of "putting somebody within the law" (cited in Shenon, 2007, p. A1). However, perhaps the most ominous instances of sovereign exceptionality revolve around ancient biopolitical rights, including habeas corpus.

The Bush administration pursued secret detention and rendition of "terrorist" suspects within the United States and abroad. These suspects, some of whom are citizens of Western "democratic" states such as the United States, Canada, and Australia, often end up in "secret" prisons abroad where they are subject to "aggressive" interrogation techniques, including psychological and corporeal torture (Moore, 2007), and lack access to juridical protections. Journalists seeking to publicize these events have been threatened with censorship and criminal charges, including war-crimes accusations (Stone, 2006). When forced to vindicate illegal extraditions and torture, the Bush administration asserted detainees were war combatants who lack protection by Geneva Conventions (DeYoung, 2007). U.S. judicial authorities stymied efforts by the wrongly accused to challenge detention and torture, arguing judicial review would expose state secrets (Sherman, 2007).

As the recent declassification of the CIA's "family jewels" illustrates, U.S. political actors and petty tyrants knowingly violated the constraints

Biopower, Sovereignty, and America's Global Security 207

of international and national law across the second half of the twentieth century using banned strategies such as press censorship and harassment, targeted assassinations, and torture (DeYoung & Pincus, 2007, p. A1). As revealed by these documents, there is nothing new about the use of sovereign decisionality to strip individuals of all rights and protections, thereby rendering them bare life. The very perseverance and typicality of these operations calls into question the existential viability of liberal protections.

What is new is the transformation of law to legitimize these acts of sovereign decisionality. After the Supreme Court's ruling that enemy combatants were protected by Geneva Conventions, the Bush administration passed new rules in 2006, and again in 2007, for interrogation and prosecution allowing aggressive methods, retroactively protecting American military and personnel who previously tortured suspects, and severely limiting courtroom rights for those defendants fortunate enough to be granted trials (DeYoung, 2007; Fletcher, 2006a). The 2006 rules were justified by their purported role in preventing terrorist attacks:

> This program has been one of the must successful intelligence efforts in American history.... It has helped prevent attacks on our country. And the bill I sign today will ensure that we can continue to use this vital tool to protect the American people for years to come. (Bush, cited in Fletcher, 2006a, p. A4)

Continued allegations of CIA detainee abuse in 2007 met with claims that CIA interrogation programs were conducted "lawfully, with great care and close review, producing vital information that has helped disrupt terrorist plots and save lives" (cited in White & Tyson, 2007, p. A1). The rules passed in the summer of 2007 provided new protocols allowing "harsh interrogation" while offering only the most basic levels of biological protection to prisoners, rendering them simply bare life. Accordingly, a senior administration official stated any future use of "extremes of heat and cold" would be subject to a "reasonable interpretation ... we're not talking about forcibly induced hypothermia" (quoted in DeYoung, 2007, p. A1).

American soldiers in Iraq support the use of torture, particularly in the context of precautionary risk:

> More than one-third of U.S. soldiers in Iraq surveyed by the Army said they believe torture should be allowed if it helps gather important information about insurgents, the Pentagon disclosed yesterday. Four in 10 said they approve of such illegal abuse if it would save the life of a fellow soldier. (Ricks & Tyson, 2007, p. A1)

Fear Up Harsh (Lagouranis & Mikaelian, 2007) chronicled use of torture in Iraq at Abu Ghraib, among other sites, including the use of attack dogs, hypothermia, waterboarding, and beatings. In a National Public Radio segment, Lagouranis (2007) described using torture on a prisoner he did not believe had vital intelligence, stating he was "simply exerting power over this person, trying to topple his will through cruelty and violence." Lagouranis also documented how biopolitical authorities, including army medical doctors and psychiatrists, were employed to "break" prisoners (also see Miles, 2006). Lagouranis acknowledged torture by the United States is not new but argued the "real difference here . . . is that this is being allowed tacitly and explicitly all the way up to/through the Pentagon and to the White House and that's a real shift . . . now we're throwing away Geneva conventions."

Claudia Aradau (2007) recently suggested the practices of torture found in Guantánamo and other locales stem less from sovereign decisionality than from the "necessary consequence of naming the war on terror a different war" (p. 496). Aradau's point was that the law is not suspended by an act of decisionality, but rather it is transformed through its materialization, its sublimation to "concrete situations and representations of spaces and subjects" (p. 496). In response to the supposed exigencies of situation, law thus codifies opportunities for legally creating exceptions to the universalizing discourses of rights.

Aradau's observation reveals the population as always/already subject to sovereign power. We are all bare life. Perhaps this recognition, conjoined with the ascendant war of the races, explains popular nonchalance regarding extraordinary renditions. Elimination of "dangerous bodies" (Cairo, 2006, p. 288) from the global population is believed essential to securitization of the American way of life. A more pastoral biopolitics of population cultivation through foreign aid gives way to a "terroristic" eugenics aimed at excising risk and dangerousness.

This eugenics of terror explains public nonchalance toward civilian casualties in Iraq and Afghanistan. For example, public outrage was muted in response to *The Lancet*'s biopolitical report of 600,000 Iraqi mortalities stemming from the war (Burnham, Lafta, Doocy, & Roberts, 2006). Moreover, the massacre and subsequent cover-up of unarmed civilians in Haditha by U.S. Marines also failed to generate widespread public outrage (Whi, 2007).

In the popular imagination and in the policies of neoconservative authorities, sovereign force over life is warranted by the threats of terrorism, by the clash of civilizations, and by the dispersed micropopulations of individuals who misunderstand and resist the expansion of American markets and values.

SOVEREIGNTY AND LIBERAL GOVERNMENTALITY

In 2007, Amnesty International issued a report online that asserted:

Five years after 9/11, new evidence came to light in 2006 of the way in which the U.S. Administration treated the world as one giant battlefield for its 'war on terror,' kidnapping, arresting, arbitrarily detaining, torturing, and transferring suspects from one secret prison to another across the world with impunity, in what the U.S. termed 'extraordinary rendition.'

Amnesty International's Secretary General insisted, "Nothing more aptly portrayed the globalization of human rights violations than the U.S.-led 'war on terror' and its programme of 'extraordinary renditions' which implicated governments in countries as far apart as Italy and Pakistan, Germany and Kenya," damaging the rule of law and human-rights institutions at national and international levels. Consequently, the world has witnessed a resurgence of ruthless sovereignty:

> Through short sighted, fear-mongering and divisive policies, governments are undermining the rule of law and human rights, feeding racism and xenophobia, dividing communities, intensifying inequalities and sowing the seeds for more violence and conflict. (Amnesty International, 2007)

Although the Amnesty report attaches a kind of pastoral benevolence to the rule of law and human rights that empirical examination might refute (see Mboka, 2007), it points to growing disregard for liberal rights and protections.

Liberal governmentality purportedly operates by means of the production and self-government of "free" individuals. And yet, the ancient capacities of sovereignty, to kill and inflict suffering, remain intact, ready to be executed. Liberal protections including habeas corpus and due process lack existential guarantee. In particular, destruction and annihilation occur when war becomes perceived as the condition for life (Reid, 2006). Life is stripped of rights and dignity, revealed as "bare life" (Agamben, 2005) as the liberal rights of citizens are denied under sovereign decisionality in the state of permanent war.

The rise of the logic of precautionary risk management, coupled with the expansion of the technologies of surveillance, have produced regimes of government that target dangerous and risky individuals using all the technological might and brute force of twenty-first-century repressive apparatuses. Moreover, militant security technologies and logics govern individual practice, producing everyday panopticons of surveillance of self and others.

Totalitarianism and fascism take hold when populations organized around common articulations of national or racialized identity are mobilized by fear and anxiety. Yet, even while liberal rights are stripped, the liberal imagination cannot readily come to terms with creeping totalitarianism. The banality of many domestic sovereign technologies, as illustrated by computerized surveillance, mystifies the consolidation of sovereign power (see Arendt, 1963). Simultaneously, many of the symbolic practices involved in producing biopolitical distinctions between preferred and denigrated or risky forms of life are decentralized ones, promulgated in the neoliberal marketplace of goods and ideas.

It is my argument that totalitarianism always/already haunts liberal governmentalities. First, liberal governmentalities promoting rational subjecthood obscure how understandings of self and other are inflected by economic, political, and often racialized, social relations. This chapter explored how Manifest Destiny informs Americans' self-understandings, shaping perceptions of *others* who fail to conform to, or resist, liberal norms of economic, cultural, and political conduct. In the American popular imagination, deviant, risky, irrational, illiberal others require application of sovereign apparatuses. The deterritorialization of risky persons—their circulation across geographic spaces—heightens fear and demands limitless technological and personal surveillance. Intensified surveillance further amplifies fear, rendering populations vulnerable to authoritarian seductions impinging against liberal freedoms.

Second, market imperatives produce fertile conditions of possibility for state and market authoritarianism. As observed by classical political economy, the self-governing market presupposes the state ensure conditions of possibility for market stability and growth by regulating labor, by guaranteeing resources, and by facilitating expansion. Mercantile problem-solution frames bind states to market formulations of value, prompting colonial undertakings. Neoliberal governmentalities purport to shun state mercantilism, but market interests and state strategic initiatives are served by military undertakings that secure needed resources while producing opportunities for arms dealers, defense contractors, and private security firms.

In sum, although liberal governmentalities profess resistance to centralized and repressive power, they simultaneously rely on them to securitize everyday life and to extend the liberal freedoms of the market. Latent "exclusionary principles" within liberal philosophy and practices legitimize consolidations and executions of power that would otherwise belie liberal sensibilities (see Mehta, 1999, p. 75). Liberal governmentalities are thus haunted by the sovereignty they require to extend and protect liberal operations and fantasies. Neoconservative governmentalities embrace these hauntings while striving to materialize neoliberal imaginings inflected by racialized origins and destinies.

7 "Bad Subjects" and Liberal Governmentalities

Biopolitics addresses the population as a "political problem" (Foucault, 2003b, p. 245) requiring "regularization" (p. 247). It operates in relation to normalizing and/or optimizing corporeal disciplines (anatomo-politics) performed by, and upon, individuals during the course of everyday life. Biopower, as the synthesis of biopolitics and anatomo-politics, stands as the most pervasive expression of power in the modern period.

The expressions of biopower explored in this book are fundamentally conjoined with liberal economic governmentalities. Indeed, liberal ideals about market government emerged in concert with biopolitical strategies for representing and administering the population. Liberal biopolitics and economics are technologies of government that delineate distinct social spheres governed by particular expressions of freedom and discipline, producing self-governing citizens-workers-consumers. Thus, biopower, as described in this book, has operated historically to regularize economic liberalisms.

Yet, it would be a mistake to suggest the aims and effects of biopower always accord with changing economic governmentalities. The goals and consequences of social practices are heterogeneous and cannot be explained in relation to totalizing logics. Consequently, the effects of particular technologies of government can be multiple and produce tensions and contradictions for everyday people pursuing market freedom and personal happiness and for the various (public and private) authorities tasked with shepherding the population's health, expanding and securing market operations, and fostering the wealth and security of the state.

This book has focused specifically upon the biopolitical contradictions and tensions produced by the imperatives and technologies of neoliberal governmentalities. Neoliberal technologies of government privilege market agents, marketized calculi of value, and marketized types of operations. As explored in Chapter 3, capillary neoliberal market (i.e., financial and corporate) technologies of government have extended neoliberal logics and apparatuses throughout the world, transversing geographical, cultural, social, and economic spaces and uniting them within a new society of control governed by market-defined risks and opportunities. The biopolitical problems posed to, and by, populations are increasingly represented, interpreted, and addressed using neoliberal problem-solution frames, which stress enterprise, philanthropy, and personal responsibility while deemphasizing social explanations of human agency.

Neoliberal market logics inflect and transform older social-welfare apparatuses and technologies of government by informing the values, decisions, and practices of individuals operating within "nonmarket" realms of society, including state apparatuses (e.g., public office, public agencies, educational institutions) and "private" life (e.g., families, religious organizations, popular culture). Neoliberal technologies emphasizing government from a distance (supplemented with targeted governance), accountability, and transparency infuse biopolitical and disciplinary practices enacted across the realms of everyday life. For instance, neoliberal economic governmentalities influence how public-health officials represent populations from afar and develop strategies of targeted governance for "at-risk" populations, promising new cost efficiencies while shifting responsibility of health management to privatized, responsibilized individuals. In the new societies of control, market agents, including investors and corporations, draw upon biopolitical statistics to infer market trends, opportunities, and risks and to develop commercially viable strategies for governing corporeal and psychic spaces remotely by using biogenetic formulations.

In one sense, neoliberal governmentalities' production and uses of biopolitical information and technologies can be regarded as serving the objective of government through freedom. However, in another sense, this project of government through freedom is always/already infused with unequal power relations. As Foucault demonstrated, biopolitical knowledge is never neutral but is always inflected by heterogeneous power relations. Chapters 4 and 5 explored how historical and contemporary racialized formulations infused, and infuse, biopolitical understanding. Biopolitical formulations are often organized around normative ideals, against which deviance is measured and targeted for intervention. Moreover, as explained in these chapters, marketized interests and technologies of government increasingly govern types of biopolitical inquiry and treatment regimes. The appeal of market-based technologies of biopolitical government is given in part by neoliberal regimes of fiscal accountability that dictate research agendas by delineating fundable types of problem-solution frames. Market and state authorities reward research demonstrating the capacity to produce commercial products. Responsibilized individuals are mobilized to govern themselves through convenient and promising commercial products and technologies. Yet, as stated above, the personal identities and lifestyles within which these products and technologies are embedded, and which they extend, are not neutral, not devoid of political inflection.

Contemporary biopolitical understandings and products often promote and/or presuppose two distinct kinds of subjects. On the one hand, there exists an implicit formulation of a rational subject capable of monitoring his or her own bodily and psychic health. The monitoring performed by this rational and reflexive subject is always couched in relation to the exigencies of work and private life, the demands of the workplace, and those of privatized relationships. This rational subject selectively peruses the marketplace of ideas and goods for biopolitical strategies that normalize and/or optimize, facilitating the subject's good self-government at work and home. The particular characteristics of this subject are always inflected by the particularities of time and place.

In contrast, biopolitical understandings also carve out formulations of bad subjects, who are judged to be risky and/or are perceived as incapable of rational self-government. Incapable of self-government, or capable only of limited self-government, bad or risky subjects are targeted for increased surveillance and disciplinary normalization. Biopolitical authorities, such as public-health officials or foreign-aid workers, are often called upon to shepherd risky subjects by teaching them preferred technologies of self-government. These biopolitical authorities may be employed by the state or private philanthropy. Irrespective of funding, biopolitical authorities are increasingly answerable to neoliberal regimes of accountability, requiring market efficiencies and calculable outcomes. Moreover, market-based technologies of freedom, including work for former welfare recipients, pharmaceuticals for the mentally ill, and microenterprise for the world's poorest, tend to be pursued as the most desirable remediation. "Bad" subjects who fail to respond to biopolitical reforms are subject to more repressive authorities and/or interventions. Everyday authorities exercise petty sovereignty over those deemed incapable of self-government.

Even in the most privileged spaces of contemporary life, in the efficient and transparent U.S. workplace and in the therapeutic family, neoliberal requirements delineate, ever more sharply, distinctions between those capable and those incapable of self-government. Fear of failing to meet the obligations of self-government presented by the demands of daily living heightens surveillance of self and others. The market-derived competitive logics and demands for accountability infusing so many spaces of everyday life exacerbate the need for continual policing.

These practices of subjectification can have damaging psychic effects as the self is plunged for weaknesses and excesses. As explored so persuasively by a diverse array of social and political observers, social-psychic anxiety is often projected upon societies' most vulnerable or upon those marked as different by biopolitical and/or cultural understandings. Fear of difference and/or vulnerability derives from, and fuels, the policing of self and others. Although liberal governmentalities have historically professed tolerance for difference, perceived economic dependencies and biopolitical risks have always tested the limits of tolerance for liberal imaginations. Simultaneously, liberal frames and technologies of knowledge have often evaded exploration of how liberal technologies of government produce economic and social marginalization.

Fantasmic perceptions of origins that unite populations around common understandings of cultural and biological personhood exacerbate myopia and reveal the limits of liberal tolerances. Although Foucault was hardly the first or last thinker to reflect upon the dangers deriving from symbolic and material constitutions of race and nation, his approach helps explain how racialized understandings of personhood are disseminated in purportedly neutral biopolitical technologies and normalizing disciplines organized around problems of freedom and security.

American liberalisms have for the last hundred years been inflected with a racialized fantasy of origin and purpose that has, for the sake of simplicity, been referenced in this book primarily in relation to the doctrine of Manifest Destiny. Conservative religious authorities and neoconservatives are particularly drawn to the theological and nostalgic dimensions of this doctrine. Manifest Destiny has also assumed relevance within neoliberal formulations of market expansion and global market governance. American invocations of Manifest Destiny animate and spiritualize neoliberal market technologies of government, including market disciplines, securities, and strategies of leverage. Neoliberal market technologies assume prophetic value when proselytized by American authorities as the path for global harmony, good governance, and personal happiness.

American conservative religious and neoconservative authorities share neoliberal adulation of the market but are suspicious of liberal governmentalities that operate from a distance. Neoliberal strategies of targeted governance are perceived by (neo)conservative authorities as inadequate for redressing the moral malaise affecting the national population. (Neo)conservative authorities seek to govern the *entire* population more directly in order to revitalize the national ethos. The pastoral shepherd iconically represents the preferred model of governance necessitated by the moral degradation of the population. Biopolitical knowledge and practices are appropriated by and infused with this moralizing imperative, as illustrated in the biopolitical data and self-help materials described in Chapter 4.

Ideological formulations of origins and nationhood converge with mystified and spiritualized understandings of "the market" in the neoconservative imagination. Neoliberal market logics and technologies demand continuous expansion as new opportunities are identified for colonization and exploitation. While (neo)conservative authorities shy away from market colonization of the inner spaces of the corporeal body/soul, they embrace market colonization of geographically distant spaces, spaces governed by foreign technologies and foreign bodies. Globalization of neoliberal market operations provides neoliberalism and neoconservative governmentalities a common problem-solution frame.

Neoconservative and neoliberal governmentalities favor market and philanthropic technologies for enabling market expansion and for governing the risks posed to and by populations. However, these challenges to market penetration abroad are not readily governed from a distance.

Additionally, global populations marginalized by market operations and/or united by their own mystified constructions of nationhood pose limits to the expansion and operations of market technologies. Philanthropy and microenterprise prove insufficient for redressing environmental, political, and cultural "risks." The events of September 11, 2001, revealed the precariousness of market and philanthropic government from a distance.

The neoliberal fantasy of a global society united by McDonald's and the iPod unraveled. The neoconservative inclination toward authoritarianism was fueled by the specter of uncivilized others. Xenophobic fantasies captured the popular imagination of the American public, reigniting racialized understandings of self and other that had been dampened by the fantasy of the global marketplace.

Sovereignty, the power of death and the power to let die, has always complemented liberal technologies of freedom. The sovereign subjects of liberal democracies have always produced and/or implied others incapable of self-government, in need of sovereign protection and repression. The biopolitical dispersion of sovereignty across everyday life simply decentered sovereign operations, rendering them more mundane, more ubiquitous. However, the dispersion of sovereignty in the subject and in the daily decisions and disciplines of everyday life never eliminated the existence of repressive apparatuses and repressive everyday practices. It was simply that in the liberal imaginations, force and repression were reserved for bad subjects, those incapable of self-government.

In our current era of generalized anxiety, exacerbated by the threat of terror and xenophobic projections, we see an unraveling of particular kinds of liberal governmentalities, especially those historically constituting a private realm of existence for self-governing subjects and those that promised certain types of protections through juridical processes such as habeas corpus. New technological strategies for monitoring corporeal and dividuated (data-defined) populations, coupled with the imperatives of accountability and security, lead to new panopticons of surveillance. Simultaneously, xenophobic projections converge with precautionary risk management, fostering conditions that facilitate abdication of liberal protections and juridical processes. Suspension of liberal governmentalities produces overt and repressive expressions of sovereign power.

The arguments developed in this book set this project apart from so much of the governmentality literature that retains faith in the capacities of liberal governmentalities to redress the problems posed to, and by, populations (populations carved out and governed by liberal technologies of government). Contemporary liberal regimes of truth constrain public discourse about the contradictions posed by extant neoliberal technologies of government. Neoliberal governmentalities are seductive in their promises to maximize personal liberty and happiness but offer limited vocabularies and technologies of government for addressing people, events, and phenomena rupturing liberal fantasies. The failure of private philanthropy, state-sponsored democracy-building initiatives, and free markets and microenterprise to redress biopolitical concerns, including poverty and violence, bewilder the neoliberal imagination even while authorities invoke repressive force to eliminate or control the sources of unreason.

This project fails to offer solutions for redressing the limits of liberal technologies of government; rather, the history of the present produced in this book prompts the reader to reflect upon how liberal governmentalities constrain understandings of technologies of government that privilege and marginalize, enable and constrain, while both objectifying and subjectifying. While there is little question that neoliberal governmentalities offer opportunities for individual expression and market capitalization, the matter remains as to whether they are flexible and responsive enough to represent and address threatened, marginalized, exploited, or alienated forms of life, particularly given market imperatives and liberalisms' constitutions in relation to, and permeation by, racialized constructions of identity. Moreover, sovereignty's historic role as the underbelly of biopower calls into question liberal governmentalities' capacities to obviate totalitarian impulses and movements.

Notes

NOTES TO CHAPTER 1

1. Governmentality is a rather slippery concept that Foucault at times used to describe his *method* of analyzing the governmentalization of the liberal state (2007) and at other times referred more concretely to historically specific arts of government, or governmentalities, linking the individual to social relations of power. These arts of government, or governmentalities, were explicated in Foucault's genealogy of liberalism (1979b). I draw upon both inflections: I differentiate Foucauldian analysis (by its focus and objects) from other approaches to studying social governance, and I describe the arts of government that produce liberal governmentalities including laissez-faire liberalism, social-welfare liberalism, and neoliberalism.
2. Governmentality scholarship has exploded since the publication of Rose's now classic text (see Cruikshank, 1999; Dean, 1999; Deuchars, 2004; O'Mally, 2004; Rose, 1999b). Recent scholarship includes *Governing Globalization: Power, Authority, and Global Governance* (Held & McGrew, 2002), *Globalization, Governmentality, and Global Politics: Regulation for the Rest of US?* (Lipschutz & Rowe, 2005), *Genetic Governance* (Bunton & Petersen, 2005), and *Foucault and the Government of Disability* (Tremain, 2005). Governmentality has also been synthesized with other theoretical traditions, most notably with Cultural Studies (Bratich, Packer, & McCarthy, 2003) in *Foucault, Cultural Studies and Governmentality*, with Marxist scholarship (see Jessop, 1997), and with security and police studies (Dillon & Reid, 2001; Dubber & Valverde, 2006; Garland, 1990, 2001).

NOTES TO CHAPTER 2

1. Lemke uses the phrase *epistemo-political field of visibility* to describe specifically the operations and dispositions of new genetics discourses. I have adopted his phrase for my current context of discussion.

NOTES TO CHAPTER 4

1. Although hospital/clinical-based medical *knowledge* embraced the interiority of the corporeal body, nineteenth-century medical *practice* varied considerably across time and place. For example, "heroic" popular medicine was widely practiced in U.S. rural areas until the second half of the nineteenth

century (Rosenberg, 1977; Starr, 1982). Starr argued hospital-based medical research and state-regulated licensing did not occur widely in the United States until after 1870.
2. See Ariès (1962), Donzelot (1979), Greene (1999), and Hausman (1995) for excellent Foucauldian-inspired analyses of these unities.

NOTES TO CHAPTER 6

1. Importantly, Foucault argued modern understandings of racism emerged in the nineteenth century. Therefore, early modern race wars reflected differences in cultural practices and identities. Race was not understood in biological and scientific terms. See Chapter 5 for discussion.
2. This foreign-policy orientation has raised alarm among traditional conservatives, "realist" policy advisors, and military strategists such as Zbigniew Brzezinski (2004).

References

A Medco survey. (2007, May 16). *The Wall Street Journal*, p. A1.
A new scheme for reducing the laws relating to the poor into one act of Parliament, and for the better providing the impotent poor with necessaries, The Industrious with Work and for the Correction of Idle Poor (2nd ed.) (1737). London. Retrieved August 5th, 2006, from Eighteenth Century Collections Online, Gale Group.
A nominee's abnormal views. (2007, July 10). *The New York Times*, p. 20.
A reader from Los Angeles (n.d.) [online]. Available: (http://www.amazon.com/exec/obidos/tg/detail/-/1853027499/qid=1082226560/sr=8-1/ref=sr_8_xs_ap_i1_xgl14/102-9675413-4828127?v=glance&s=books&n=507846.
Abboud, L. (2005, July 27). The next phase in psychiatry. *The Wall Street Journal*, pp. D1, D5.
Abrahamian, E. (2003). The U.S. media, Huntington and September 11. *Third World Quarterly*, 24, 529–544.
Adams, G. (1787). *Essays on the microscope; containing a practical description of the most improved microscopes: A general history of insects, London*. Retrieved January 27, 2007, from Eighteenth Century Collections Online, Gale Group.
Adams, G. (1931). The golden age of mental hygiene. *American Mercury*, 23, 93–102.
Agamben, G. (1998). *Homo sacer: Sovereign power and bare life* (D. Heller-Roazen, Trans.). Stanford, CA: Stanford University.
Agamben, G. (2000). *Means without ends: Notes on politics* (V. Binetti & C. Casarino, Trans.). Minneapolis, MN: University of Minnesota.
Agamben, G. (2001). On security and terror. *Theory and Event*, 5(4) [online]. Available: http://muse.jhu.edu/journals/theory_and_event/toc/archive.html#5.4.
Agamben, G. (2005). *State of exception* (K. Attell, Trans.). Chicago: University of Chicago.
Aglietta, M., & Breton, R. (2001). Financial systems, corporate control and capital accumulation. *Economy and Society*, 30, 433–466.
Aitken, R. (2006). "The vital force": Visuality and the national economy. *Journal of Cultural Research*, 10, 87–112.
Alexander, F. G., & Selesnick, S. T. (1966). *The history of psychiatry: An evaluation of psychiatric thought and practice from prehistoric times to the present*. New York: Harper & Row.
Alexander, S. (1892). Natural selection in morals. *International Journal of Ethics*, 2, 409–439.
Allen, G. E. (1999). Modern biological determinism: The Violence Initiative, the Human Genome Project, and the new eugenics. In M. Fortun & E. Mendelsohn (Eds.), *The practices of human genetics* (pp. 1–24). Dordrecht, Netherlands: Kluwer.
Altheide, D. L. (2002). *Creating fear: News and the construction of crisis*. New York: Aldine de Gruyter.

Althusser, L. (1971). *Lenin and philosophy and other essays* (B. Brewster, Trans.). New York: Monthly Review.
America's longest war. (2006, September 2). *The Economist, 380*(8493), 22–24.
American Psychiatric Association. (1952). *Diagnostic and statistical manual of mental disorders*. Washington, DC: Author.
American Psychiatric Association. (1968). *Diagnostic and statistical manual of mental disorders* (2nd ed.). Washington, DC: Author.
American Psychiatric Association. (1980). *Diagnostic and statistical manual of mental disorders* (3rd ed.). Washington, DC: Author.
American Psychiatric Association. (1987). *Diagnostic and statistical manual of mental disorders* (3rd ed., rev.). Washington, DC: Author.
American Psychiatric Association. (1994). *Diagnostic and statistical manual of mental disorders* (4th ed.). Washington, DC: Author.
Amin, A. (1994). Post-Fordism: Models, fantasies, and phantoms of transition. In A. Amin (Ed.), *Post-Fordism: A reader* (pp. 1–10). Oxford: Basil Blackwell.
Amin, S. (2004). *The liberal virus: Permanent war and the Americanization of the world*. New York: Monthly Review.
Amnesty International. (2007, May 23). Report 2007: Politics of fear creating a dangerously divided world. [on-line]. Available: *http://news.amnesty.org/mavp/news.nsf/print/ENGPOL100092007.*
Amoore, L., & De Goede, M. (2005). Governance, risk and dataveillance in the war on terror. *Crime, Law & Social Change, 43*, 149–173.
Andrews, E. L. (2005, September 24). For Wolfowitz, poverty is the newest war to fight. *The New York Times*, p. C1.
Angell, M. (2004, July 15). The truth about drugs. *The New York Review of Books, 51*(12) [online]. Available: http://www.nybooks.com/articles/17244.
Aradau, C. (2007). Law transformed: Guantánamo and the 'other' exception. *Third World Quarterly, 28*, 489–501.
Aradau, C., & van Munster, R. (2007). Governing terrorism through risk: Taking precautions (un)knowing the future. *European Journal of International Relations, 13*, 89–115.
Arendt, H. (1963). *Eichmann in Jerusalem; a report on the banality of evil*. New York: Viking.
Ariès, P. (1962). *Centuries of childhood* (R. Baldick, Trans.). New York: Vintage.
Armstrong, D. (1983). *Political anatomy of the body: Medical knowledge in Britain in the twentieth century*. Cambridge: Cambridge University.
Armstrong, D. (1995). The rise of surveillance medicine. *Sociology of Health and Illness, 17*, 393–404.
Armstrong, D. (1999). Bodies of knowledge/knowledge of bodies. In C. Jones & R. Porter (Eds.), *Reassessing Foucault: Power, medicine and the body* (pp. 17–27). London: Routledge.
Armstrong, D. (2002). *A new history of identity: A sociology of medical knowledge*. Houndmills, UK: Palgrave.
Armstrong, D. (2006a, July 11). Financial ties to industry cloud major depression study. *The Wall Street Journal*, pp. A1, A9.
Armstrong, D. (2006b, July 12). *JAMA* to toughen rules on author disclosure. *The Wall Street Journal*, p. D1.
Asthana, A., & DeYoung, K. (2006, September 8). Bush calls for greater wiretap authority. *The Washington Post*, p. A1.
Attention deficit may be tied to smoking, lead. (2006, September 19). *The Wall Street Journal*, p. D3.
Aune, J. A. (2001). *Selling the free market: The rhetoric of economic correctness*. New York: Guilford.
Autism prenatal test. (n.d.). [online]. Available: http://www.autismprenataltest.com/.

Babb, S. (2004). *Managing Mexico: Economists from nationalism to neoliberalism*. Princeton, NJ: Princeton University.
Bakan, J. (2004). *The corporation: The pathological pursuit of profit and power*. New York: The Free Press.
Baker, P. (2007, June 22). Cheney defiant on classified material executive order ignored since 2003. *The Washington Post*, p. A1.
Barry, A. (2002). The anti-political economy. *Economy and Society*, 31, 268–284.
Barry, A. (2006). Technological zones. *European Journal of Social Theory*, 9, 239–253.
Barton, B. (1925). *The man nobody knows: A discovery of the real Jesus*. Indianapolis, IN: Bobbs-Merrill.
Bashford, A. (2004). *Imperial hygiene: A critical history of colonialism, nationalism and public health*. Houndmills, UK: Palgrave Macmillan.
Bateson, G., Jackson, D. D., Haley, J., & Weakland, J. (1956). Toward a theory of schizophrenia. *Behavioral Science*, 1, 251–264.
Bazelon, E. (2007, January 21). Is there a post-abortion syndrome? *The New York Times*, pp. 6, 41.
Beamish, R. (2006, January 30). Religious groups get AIDS grants. *The Arizona Republic*, p. A6.
Beaulieu, A. (2001). Voxels in the brain: Neuroscience, informatics and changing notions of objectivity. *Social Studies of Science*, 31, 635–680.
Beck, U. (2006). Living in the world risk society. *Economy and Society*, 35, 329–345.
Beers, C. W. (1908). *A mind that found itself: An autobiography*. New York: Longmans, Green, & Co.
Begley, S. (1996, Feb. 19). Your child's brain. *Newsweek*, 127(8), 55–61.
Begley, S. (2004a, July 23). How a second, secret genetic code turns genes on and off. *The Wall Street Journal*, p. A9.
Begley, S. (2004b, November 5). Scans of monks' brains show meditation alters structure, functioning. *The Wall Street Journal*, p. B1.
Begley, S. (2006a, September 1). A smaller NIH budget means fewer scientists and 'too-safe' studies. *The Wall Street Journal*, p. B1.
Begley, S. (2006b, January 13). How nurture overrides kids' nature: Or why succotash model fails. *The Wall Street Journal*, p. B1.
Begley, S. (2006c, July 7). Life events thwart scientists' attempts to draw DNA profiles. *The Wall Street Journal*, p. B1.
Begley, S. (2006d, October 13). When terror strikes, liberals and the right vote further apart. *The Wall Street Journal*, p. B1.
Begley, S. (2007, January 19). How thinking can change the brain. *The Wall Street Journal*, p. B1.
Bentham, J. (1776). *A fragment on government; being an examination of what is delivered, on the subject of government in general, in the introduction to Sir William Blackstone's Commentaries*. London. Retrieved June 3, 2006, from Eighteenth Century Collections Online, Gale Group.
Bentham, J. (1796). *Management of the poor: A plan concerning the principle and construction of an establishment, in which persons of any description are to be kept under inspection*. Dublin: James Moore. Retrieved July 2, 2006, from Eighteenth Century Collections Online, Gale Group.
Bentham, J. (1843). *Principles of the civil code*. Edinburgh: Dumont.
Berenson, A. (2006, December 21). Disparity emerges in Lilly data on schizophrenia drug. *The New York Times*, p. C1.
Bernstein, E., & Dooren, J. C. (2007, April 18). Antidepressants get a boost for use in teens. *The Wall Street Journal*, pp. D1, D4.
Berrios, G. E. (1993). European views on personality disorders: A conceptual history. *Comprehensive Psychiatry*, 34, 14–30.

Berrios, G. E. (1996). *The history of mental symptoms: Descriptive psychopathology since the nineteenth centur.*, Cambridge: Cambridge University.
Bianco, A., & Zellner, W. (2003, October 6). Is Wal-Mart too powerful? *Business Week*, 3852, 100–110.
Black, K. R. (1994). Personality screening in employment. *American Business Law*, 32, 69–124.
Blankley, T. (2005). *The West's last chance: Will we win the clash of civilizations?* Washington, DC: Regnery.
Blustein, P. (2005). World Bank reconsiders trade's benefits to poor. *The Washington Post*, p. D1.
Boal, I., Clark, T. J., Matthews, J., & Watts, M. (2005). *Afflicted powers: Capital and spectacle in a new age of war*. London: Verso.
Boies, J. L. (1994). *Buying for Armageddon: Business, society, and military spending since the Cuban Missile Crisis*. New Brunswick, NJ: Rutgers University.
Borden, T. (2003, September 11). Mexico's experience highlights inequalities in free-trade policies. *The Arizona Republic*, pp. D1–2.
Brandes, S. D. (1976). *American welfare capitalism 1880–1940*. Chicago: University of Chicago.
Brandes, S. D. (1997). *Warhogs: A history of war profits in America*. Lexington University Press of Kentucky.
Bratich, J. (2003). Making politics reasonable. In J. Z. Bratich, J. Packer, & C. McCarthy (Eds.), *Foucault, cultural studies, and governmentality* (pp. 67–100). Albany, NY: SUNY.
Bratich, J. Z. (2004). Regime-of-truth change. *Cultural Studies—Critical Methodologies*, 4, 237–241.
Bratich, J. Z., Packer, J., & McCarthy, C. (2003). *Foucault, cultural studies and governmentality*. Albany, NY: SUNY.
Braudel, F. (1981). *The structures of everyday life: Civilization and capitalism 15th–18th century Vol. 1* (S. Reynolds, Trans.). New York: Harper & Row.
Bravin, J. (2007, July 2). Court under Roberts limits judicial power. *The Wall Street Journal*, pp. A1, A12.
Brenner, R. (2006). *The economics of global turbulence*. London: Verso.
Brenner, R. (2007). Structure vs. conjuncture. *New Left Review*, 43, 33–59.
Brotherton, J., & Gilliver, L. (1733). *The Art of nursing: Or the method of bringing up young children according to the rules of physick for the prefervation of health, and prolonging life* (2nd ed.). London: Author.
Brown, W. (2006). American nightmare: Neoliberalism, neoconservatism, and de-democratization. *Political Theory*, 34, 690–714.
Brzezinksi, Z. (2004). *The choice: Global domination or global leadership*. New York: Basic Books.
Bunton, R., & Petersen, A. (2005). *Genetic governance: Health, risk and ethics in the biotech era*. New York: Routledge.
Burchell, G., Gordon, C., & Miller, P. (Eds.). (1991). *The Foucault effect: Studies in governmentality*. Chicago: University of Chicago Press.
Burnham, G., Lafta, R., Doocy, S., & Roberts, L. (2006, October 21). Mortality after the 2003 invasion of Iraq: A cross-sectional cluster sample survey. *The Lancet*, 368(9545), 1421–1428.
Bush, G. (2001, September 20). Address to a joint session of Congress and the American people [online]. Available: http://www.whitehouse.gov/news/releases/2001/09/20010920-8.html.
Bush, G. (2002, August 10). President Bush discusses Iraq remarks by the president to the pool before and after golf—Crawford, Texas Ridgewood Country Club

Waco, Texas [online]. Available: http://www.whitehouse.gov/news/releases/200 2/08/20020810-3.html.
Bush, G. (2003, March 22). President discusses beginning of Operation Iraqi Freedom [online]. Available: http://www.whitehouse.gov/news/releases/2003/03/20 030322.html.
Bush, G. (2005, December 14). Iraqi elections a "watershed moment" in democracy, Bush says [online]. Available: http://usinfo.state.gov/xarchives/display. html?p=washfile-english&y=2005&m=December&x=20051214132201ESnam fuaK0.9026911.
Butler, J. (2004). *Precarious life: The powers of mourning and violence*. New York: Routledge.
Cairo, H. (2006). The duty of the benevolent master: From sovereignty to suzerainty and the biopolitics of intervention. *Alternatives*, 31, 285–311.
Caldwell, A. (2004). Bio-sovereignty and the emergence of humanity. *Theory and Event* 7(2) [online] Project Muse. Available: http://muse.jhu.edu.ezproxy1.lib. asu.edu/journals/theory_and_event/v007/7.2caldwell.html.
Calmes, J. (2005, February 28). In Bush's 'Ownership Society,' citizens would take more risk. *The Wall Street Journal*, pp. A1, A12.
Cambridge Heathtech Institute. (n.d.). Genomic glossaries. [online]. Available: http://www.genomicglossaries.com/content/gene_def.asp.
Cardon, L. R., & Palmer, L. J. (2003). Population stratification and spurious allelic association. *The Lancet*, 361, 597–604.
Carey, B. (2005, October 18). Can brain scans see depression? *The New York Times*, p. F1.
Carey, B. (2006a, March 21). Revisiting schizophrenia: Are drugs always needed? *The New York Times*, p. F1.
Carey, B. (2006b, February 5). Searching for the person in the brain. *The New York Times*, p. D1.
Carey, B. (2006c, November 11). What's wrong with a child? Psychiatrists often disagree. *The New York Times*, p. A1.
Carey, B. (2007, February 15). Charges in the death of a girl, 4, raise issue of giving psychiatric drugs to children. *The New York Times*, p. A20.
Castel, R. (1991). From dangerousness to risk. In G. Burchell, C. Gordon, & P. Miller (Eds.), *The Foucault effect: Studies in governmentality* (pp. 281–298). Chicago: University of Chicago.
Cha, A. E. (2005, April 7). Labs turn DNA into personal health forecasts. *The Washington Post*, p. A1.
Chaddock, G. R. (2003, August 18). U.S. notches world's highest incarceration rate. *Christian Science Monitor* [online]. Available: http://www.csmonitor. com/2003/0818/p02s01-usju.html.
Chadwick, E. (1864). Poor Law administration, its chief principles and their results in England and Ireland as compared with Scotland. *Journal of the Statistical Society of London*, 27, 492–504
Chaker, A. M. (2007, April 14–15). In obesity wars, a new backlash. *The Wall Street Journal*, pp. A1, A8.
Chambers, M., Grew, R., Herlihy, D., Rabb, T. K., & Woloch, I. (1983). *The Western experience* (3rd ed.). New York: Alfred A. Knopf.
Chandler, A. D. (1965). *The railroads: The nation's first big business*. New York: Harcourt, Brace & World.
Chappell, B. (2006). Rehearsals of the sovereign: States of exception and threat governmentality. *Cultural Dynamics*, 18, 313–334.
Cheney, G. (1991). *Rhetoric in an organizational society: Managing multiple identities*. Columbia: University of South Carolina.

Clark, J. B. (1887). The limits of competition. *Political Science Quarterly*, 2, 45–61.
Clarke, A. E., Mamo, L., Fishman, J. R., Shim, J. K, & Fosket, J. R. (2003). Biomedicalization: Technoscientific transformations of health, illness, and U.S. biomedicine. *American Sociological Review*, 68, 161–194.
Clinton, A. (1997, August). Flexible labor: Restructuring the American work force. *Monthly Labor Review*, 120(8), 3–27.
CNN. (2007). Fortune 500 2007 [online]. Available: http://money.cnn.com/magazines/fortune/fortune500/2007/.
Cody, E. (2005, September 22). China warns gap between rich, poor is feeding unrest. *The Washington Post*, p. A16.
Coe, K., Domke, D., Graham, E. S., John, S. L., & Pickard, V. W. (2004). No shades of gray: The binary discourse of George W. Bush and an echoing press. *Journal of Communication*, 54, 234–252.
Coles, R. (2002). Manifest Destiny adapted for 1990s' war discourse: Mission and destiny intertwined. *Sociology of Religion*, 63, 403–426.
Condit, C. (1999). *The Meanings of the gene: Public debates about human heredity.* Madison: University of Wisconsin.
Conlin, M. (2007, February 26). Get healthy or else. *Business Week*, 4023, 60–69.
Conrad, P., & Schneider, J. W. (1985). *Deviance and medicalization: From badness to sickness.* Columbus, OH: Merrill.
Cooke, R. (2002, August 4). Possible link of violence, gene found. *The Arizona Republic*, p. A18.
Cooper, M. (2004). Insecure times, tough decisions: The *Nomos* of neoliberalism. *Alternatives*, 29, 515–533.
Cooper, M. (2006). Pre-empting emergence: The biological turn in the war on terror. *Theory, Culture & Society*, 23(4), 113–135.
Cooperman, A., & Whoriskey, P. (2006, November 15). Christians move to condemn gay sex. *The Washington Post*, p. A1.
Council for Responsible Genetics. (2000). DNA patents create monopolies on living organisms [online]. Available: http:///.actionbioscience.org/genomics/crg.html.
Craig, I. W., McClay, J., Plomin, R., & Freeman, B. (2000). Chasing behavior genes into the next millennium. *Trends in Biotechnology*, 18, 22–26.
Crinson, M. (1996). *Empire building, orientation and Victorian architecture.* London: Routledge.
Crossen, C. (2005, March 16). Broad coalition sought to take the profit out of war following WWI. *The Wall Street Journal*, p. B1.
Crossen, C. (2007, April 30). Before WWI began, universal health care seemed a sure thing. *The Wall Street Journal*, p. B1.
Crowe, M. (2000). Constructing normality: A discourse analysis of the DSM-IV. *Journal of Psychiatric and Mental Health Nursing*, 7, 69–77.
Cruikshank, B. (1999). *The will to empower: Democratic citizens and other subjects.* Ithaca, NY: Cornell University.
Cruikshank, B. (2004). Neopolitics: Policy decentralization and governmentality [online]. Available: http://www.nizw.nl/Docs/Congressen/Neopolitics.pdf.
Curtis, B. (1995). Taking the state back out: Rose and Miller on political power. *BJS*, 46, 575–589.
Curtis, B. (2002). Foucault on governmentality and population: The impossible discovery. *Canadian Journal of Sociology*, 27, 505–533.
Darwin, C. (1859). *On the origin of species by means of natural selection.* London: John Murray.
Darwin, C. (1868). *The variation of plants and animals under domestication.* London: John Murray.

Darwin, C. (1871). *The descent of man*. London: John Murray.
Davies, K. G. (1952). Joint-stock investment in the later seventeenth century. *The Economic History Review*, 4, 283–301.
Davis, B., Lyons, J., & Batson, A. (2007, May 24). Globalization's gains come with a price. *The Wall Street Journal*, p. A12.
Davis, M. (1992). *City of quartz: Excavating the future in Los Angeles*. New York: Vintage.
Davis, M. (2006). *Planet of slums*. London: Verso.
De Giorgi, A. (2006). *Re-thinking the political economy of punishment*. Hampshire, UK: Ashgate.
Dean, M. (1990). *The constitution of poverty: Toward a genealogy of liberal governance*. London: Routledge.
Dean, M. (1999). *Governmentality: Power and rule in modern society*. London: Sage.
Dean, M. (2002a). Liberal government and authoritarianism. *Economy and Society*, 31, 37–61.
Dean, M. (2002b). Powers of life and death beyond governmentality. *Cultural Values*, 6, 119–138.
Deetz. S. (1992). *Democracy in an age of corporate colonization: Developments in communication and the politics of everyday life*. Albany, NY: SUNY.
DeGrandpre, R. (1999, March/April). Just cause? Many neuroscientists are all too quick to call a blip on a brain scan the reason for a behavior. *The Sciences* [online]. Available: http://www.santa.inuk.com/the%20sciences.htm.
Deleuze, G. (1992). Postscript on the societies of control. *October*, 59, 1–7.
Deleuze, G. (1995). *Foucault* (S. Hand, Ed. & Trans.). Minneapolis: University of Minnesota.
DeLong, B. (n.d). Andrew Carnegie. [online]. Available: http://econ161.berkeley.edu/TCEH/andrewcarnegie.html.
Denizet-Lewis, B. (2006, June 25). An anti-addiction pill? *The New York Times*, pp. 6, 8.
Deuchars, R. (2004). *The international political economy of risk: Rationalism, calculation and power*. Cornwall, UK: Ashgate.
De Witt, J. (1971). *Value of life annuities in proportion to redeemable annuities*. Amsterdam.
DeYoung, K. (2007, July 21). Bush approves new CIA methods. *The Washington Post*, p. A1.
DeYoung, K., & Pincus, W. (2007, June 22). CIA to air decades of its dirty laundry. *The Washington Post*, p. A1.
Dillon, M. (2005). Global security in the 21st century: Circulation, complexity and contingency. *World Today*, 61(11), 2–3.
Dillon, M., & Lobo-Guerrero, L. (in press). The biopolitical imaginary of species being and the freedom to underwrite in the molecular age. *Theory, Culture, and Society*.
Dillon, M., & Reid, J. (2001). Global liberal governance: Biopolitics, security and war. *Millennium: Journal of International Studies*, 30, 41–66.
Dodd, E. M. (1936). Statutory developments in business corporation law, 1886–1936. *Harvard Law Review*, 50, 27–59.
Dodge, M., & Kitchin, R. (2005). Codes of life: Identification codes and the machine-readable world. *Environment and Planning D: Society and Space*, 23, 851–881.
Domosh, M. (2004). Selling civilization: Toward a cultural analysis of America's economic empire in the late 19th and early 20th centuries. *Transactions of the Institute of British Geographers*, 29, 453–467.
Donzelot, J. (1979). *The policing of families* (R. Hurley, Trans.). Baltimore: Johns Hopkins.

Dorey, A. K. V. (1999). *Better baby contests: The scientific quest for perfect childhood health in the early twentieth century.* Jefferson, NC: McFarland & Co.
Douzinas, C. (2003). Humanity, military, humanism and the new moral order. *Economy and Society,* 32, 159–183.
Doyle, L. (2001). *The surrendered wife.* New York: Fireside.
Driscoll, G. (2006, November 24). Pastor engages corporate help to fight poverty. *The Arizona Republic,* p. A16.
Driver, F. (1993). *Power and pauperism.* Cambridge: Cambridge University.
Drury, S. B. (1988). *The political ideas of Leo Strauss.* Houndmills, UK: Macmillan.
Dubber, M., & Valverde, M. (Eds.). (2006).*The new police science: The police power in domestic and international governance.* Stanford, CA: Stanford University.
Duffy, J. (1990). *The Sanitarians: A history of American public health.* Urbana, IL: University of Illinois.
DuGay, P. (1996). Organizing identity: Entrepreneurial governance and public management. In S. Hall & P. DuGay (Eds.), *Questions of cultural identity* (pp. 151–169). London: Sage.
Dumit, J. (2004). *Picturing personhood: Brain scans and biomedical identity.* Princeton, NJ: Princeton University.
Dumit, J., & Davis-Floyd, R. (1998). Introduction. In R. Davis-Floyd & J. Dumit (Eds.), *Cyborg babies: From techno-sex to techno-tots* (pp. 1–20). New York: Routledge.
Dunant, S., & Porter, R. (Eds.). (1996). *The age of anxiety.* London: Virago.
Dvorak, P., & Badal, J. (2007, September 20). This is your brain on the job. *The Wall Street Journal,* pp. B1, B3.
Eerlingsson, S. J. (2002). The genomic dream in Iceland (and elsewhere) vs. cystic fibrosis. *Gene Watch* (Council for Responsible Genetics) 15, 4 [online]. Available: http://www.gene-watch.org/genewatch/articles/15-4iceland.html.
Engardio, P. (2007, March 12). Contagion? No, wake-up call. *Business Week,* 4025, 42–3.
Engdahl, F. W. (1993). *A century of war: Anglo-American oil politics and the new world order.* Germany: Paul & Co.
Escobar, A. (2005). Economics and the space of modernity: Tales of market, production and labour. *Cultural Studies,* 19, 139–175.
Esterl, M. (2006, June 26). Great expectations for private water fail to pan out. *The Wall Street Journal,* pp. A1, A10.
Ewald, F. (1991). Insurance and risk. In . In G. Burchell, C. Gordon, & P. Miller (Eds.), *The Foucault effect: Studies in governmentality* (pp. 197–210). Chicago: University of Chicago.
Ewen, S. (1990). *Consuming images: All consuming images: The politics of style in contemporary culture* (rev. ed.). New York: HarperOne.
Fadel, L., & Hammoudi, L. (2007, September 19). Convoy guards unprovoked shooting survivors claim. *The Arizona Republic,* p. A7.
Fahrenthold, D. A. (2006, January 19). Federal grants bring surveillance cameras to small towns. *The Washington Post,* p. A1.
Farmer, P. (2005). *Pathologies of power: Health, human rights, and the new war on the poor.* Berkeley: University of California.
Farrell, C. (2007, March 12). How Alan helped Ben. *Business Week,* 4025, 40.
Farzad, R. (2006, May 23). Emerging markets beat quick retreat. *Business Week* [online]. Available: http://www.businessweek.com/investor/content/may2006/pi20060522_570570.htm?chan=search.
Fialka, J. J. (2004, November 16). Position available: Indestructible bugs to eat nuclear waste. *The Wall Street Journal,* pp. A1, A18.
Financial risk management. (2006). Wikipedia [online]. Available: http://en.wikipedia.org/wiki/Financial_risk_management.

Firth, A. (1998). From oeconomy to 'the economy': Population and self-interest in discourses on government. *History of the Human Sciences*, 11(3), 19–35.
Fisher, J. P. (2007). Tourette's patients are learning to change behavior, suppress tics. *The Arizona Republic*, p. A21.
Fletcher, M. A. (2006a, October 18). Bush signs terrorism measure. *The Washington Post*, p. A4.
Fletcher, M. A. (2006b, September 6). Bush warns of enduring terror threat. *The Washington Post*, p. A1.
Fletcher, R. (1891). The new school of criminal anthropology. *The American Anthropologist*, 4, 201–236.
Fodor, J. (1983). *The modularity of mind: An essay on faculty psychology*. Cambridge, MA: MIT.
Forbes, I. (2006). States of uncertainty: Governing the empire of biotechnology. *New Genetics and Society*, 25, 69–88.
Forego, J. (2007, May 22). Paramilitary ties to elite in Colombia are detailed. *The Washington Post*, p. A1.
Foucault, M. (1965). *Madness and civilization: A history of insanity in the age of reason* (R. Howard, Trans.). New York: Vintage.
Foucault, M. (1979a). *Discipline and punish* (A. Sheridan, Trans.). New York: Vintage Books.
Foucault, M. (1979b). Governmentality. *Ideology and Consciousness*, 6, 5–22.
Foucault, M. (1980a). The politics of health in the eighteenth century. In C. Gordon (Ed.), *Power/knowledge: Selected interviews & other writings* (pp. 166–182). New York: Pantheon.
Foucault, M. (1980b).Two lectures: Lecture 1, 7 January, 1976. In C. Gordon (Ed.), *Power/Knowledge: Selected interviews & other writings* (pp. 78–108). New York: Pantheon.
Foucault, M. (1983). The subject and power. In H. L. Dreyfus & P. Rabinow (Eds.), *Michel Foucault: Beyond structuralism and hermeneutics* (pp. 208–264). Chicago: University of Chicago.
Foucault, M. (1988). Technologies of the self. In L. H. Martin, H. Gutman, & P. H. Hutton (Eds.), *Technologies of the self: A seminar with Michel Foucault* (pp.16–49). Amherst: University of Massachusetts.
Foucault, M. (1990). *The history of sexuality: An introduction* (R. Hurley, Trans.). New York: Vintage.
Foucault, M. (1994a). *The birth of the clinic: An archeology of medical perception* (A. M. Sheridan, Trans.). New York: Vintage.
Foucault, M. (1994b). *The order of things: An archeology of the human sciences*. New York: Vintage.
Foucault, M. (1997a). Security, territory, and population. In P. Rabinow (Ed.), *Ethics: Subjectivity and truth* (pp. 67–71). New York: The New Press.
Foucault, M. (1997b). Technologies of the self. In P. Rabinow (Ed.), *Ethics: Subjectivity and truth* (pp. 235–252). New York: The New Press.
Foucault, M. (1997c). The birth of biopolitics. In P. Rabinow (Ed.), *Ethics: Subjectivity and truth* (pp. 73–85). New York: The New Press.
Foucault, M. (1998). Madness and society. In J. D. Faubion (Ed.), *Michel Foucault: Aesthetics, method and epistemology* (pp. 335–342). New York: The New Press.
Foucault, M. (2003a). *Abnormal: Lectures at the Collège de France 1974–1975* (V. Marchetti, A. & Salomoni, Eds.; G. Burchell, Trans.). New York: Picador.
Foucault, M. (2003b). *Society must be defended: Lectures at the Collège de France 1975–1976* (M. Bertani & A. Fontana, Eds.; D. Macey, Trans.). New York: Picador.
Foucault (2003c). The birth of social medicine. In P. Rabinow & N. Rose (Eds.), *The essential Foucault* (pp. 319–337). New York: The New Press.

Foucault, M. (2004). Right of death and power over life. In N. Scheper-Hughes & P. Bourgois (Eds.), *Violence in war and peace* (pp. 79–82). Malden, MA: Blackwell.
Foucault, M. (2006). *Psychiatric power: Lectures at the Collège de France 1973–1974* (J. Lagrange, Ed.; G. Burchell, Trans.). Houndmills, UK: Palgrave.
Foucault, M. (2007). *Security, territory, population* (M. Senellart, Ed.; G. Burchell, Trans.). Houndmills, UK: Palgrave.
Founders' intent was Christian U.S., poll says. (2007, September 12). *The Arizona Republic*, p. A15.
Frank, T. (2000). *One Market under God: Extreme capitalism, market populism, and the end of economic democracy*. New York: Doubleday.
Friedman, M. (1962). *Capitalism and freedom*. Chicago: University of Chicago.
Friedman, M. (2005). The social responsibility of business is to increase its profits. In S. Collins-Chobanian (Ed.), *Ethical challenges to business as usual* (pp. 224–229). Upper Saddle River, NJ: Pearson.
Fuhrmans, V. (2005, May 31). Health insurers' new target. *The Wall Street Journal*, p. B1.
Fukuyama, F. (1996, November 7). Bookshelf: Still a dangerous place. *The Wall Street Journal*, p. A20.
Fukuyama, F. (2002). *Our posthuman future*. London: Profile Books.
Gabel, M., & Bruner, H. (2003). *Global inc: An atlas of the multinational corporation*. New York: The New Press.
Galton, F. (1871–1872). On blood-relationship. *Proceedings of the Royal Society of London, 20*, 394–402.
Galton, F. (1876). A theory of heredity. *The Journal of the Anthropological Institute of Great Britain and Ireland, 5*, 329–348.
Galton, F. (1889). Kinship and correlation. *Statistical Science, 4*, 81–82, 86.
Galton, F. (1901). The possible improvement of the human breed under the existing conditions of law and sentiment. *Man, 1*, 161–164.
Galton, F. (1904). Eugenics: Its definition, scope, and aims. *The American Journal of Sociology, 10*, 1–25.
Ganesh, S. (2007). Grassroots agendas and global discourses: Tracking a local planning process on children's issues. *International and Intercultural Communication Annual, 30*, 289–316.
Gangemi, J. (2004, December 26). Microcredit missionary. *Business Week*, 3965, 20.
Garland, D. (1990). *Punishment and modern society: A study in social theory*. Oxford: Clarendon.
Garland, D. (2001). *The culture of control: Crime and social order in contemporary society*. Chicago: University of Chicago.
GATT. (n.d.). Wikipedia [online]. Available: http://en.wikipedia.org/wiki/GATT.
Gelderblom, O., & Jonker, J. (2005). Amsterdam as the cradle of modern futures trading and options trading. In W. N. Goetzmann & K. G. Rouwenhorst (Eds.), *The origins of value: The financial innovations that created modern capital markets* (pp. 189–206). Oxford: Oxford University.
Geller, A. (2005, February 10). Wal-Mart to close store that's about to unionize. *The Arizona Republic*, p. D1.
Gellman, B., & Mohammed, A. (2006, May 12). Data on phone calls monitored. *The Washington Post*, p. A1.
Gerson, M. (1996a). Introduction. In M. Gerson (Ed.), *The essential neoconservative reader* (pp. xiii–xvii). Reading, MA: Addison-Wesley.
Gerson, M. (1996b). *The neoconservative vision: From the Cold War to the culture wars*. Lanham, MD: Madison Books.

Girard, K. (2003, July 15). Supply chain partnerships. *CIO* magazine [online]. Available: http://www.cio.com/archive/071503/levis.html.
Giroux, H. A. (2004). *The terror of neoliberalism: Authoritarianism and the eclipse of democracy*. Boulder, CO: Paradigm.
Glick, J. F. (2004). *Holy smokes: Inspirational help to kicking the habit*. New York: Kregel.
Glickman, L. B. (1999). *A living wage: American workers and the making of consumer society*. Ithaca, NY: Cornell University.
Godinho, S. I. H., & Nolan, P. (2006). The role of mutagenesis in defining genes in behavior. *European Journal of Human Genetics, 14*, 651–659.
Goetzmann, W. N. (2005). Fibonacci and the financial revolution. In W. N. Goetzmann & K. G. Rouwenhorst (Eds.), *The origins of value: The financial innovations that created modern capital markets* (pp. 123–144). Oxford: Oxford University.
Gokay, B. (2005). The beginning of the end of the petrodollar: What connects Iraq to Iran. *Alternatives: Turkish Journal of International Relations, 4*(4), 42–56.
Goldstein, J. (2007, August 23). Questions and answers on Risperdal. *The Wall Street Journal*, p. D6.
Goozner, M. (1999). Reform becomes trade group's priority. *The Arizona Republic*, p. A8.
Gordon, C. (1991). Governmentality rationality: An introduction. In G. Burchell, C. Gordon, & P. Miller (Eds.), *The Foucault effect: Studies in governmentality* (pp. 1–52). Chicago: University of Chicago.
Gottweis, H. (1998). *Governing molecules: The discursive politics of genetic engineering in Europe and the United States*. Cambridge, MA: MIT.
Gottweis, H. (2005a). Governing genomics in the 21st century: Between risk and uncertainty. *New Genetics and Society, 24*, 175–193.
Gottweis, H. (2005b). Regulating genomics in the 21st century: From logos to pathos? *Trends in Biotechnology, 23*, 118–121.
Grandjean, P., & Landrigan, P. J. (2006). Developmental neurotoxicity of industrial chemicals. *The Lancet, 368*(9553), 2167–2178.
Greene, R. W. (1999). *Malthusian worlds: U.S. leadership and the governing of the population crisis*. Boulder, CO: Westview.
Greenhouse, S. (2003, November 11). Suit by Wal-Mart cleaners asserts rackets violation. *The New York Times*, p. A12.
Greenhouse, S., & Barbaro, M. (2006, October 2). Wal-Mart to add wage caps and part-timers. *The New York Times*, p. A1.
Greteman, B. (2002, December). An anatomy of our selves. *Time Europe*, 160(23), 98.
Griffith, R. M. (1997). *God's daughters: Evangelical women and the power of submission*. Berkeley: University of California.
Grove, A. (2007, January 22). What business can teach governments about oil. *The Wall Street Journal*, p. A15.
Grow, B., & Epstein, K. (2007). The poverty business. *Business Week*, 4035, 57–67.
Hacking, I. (1990). *The taming of chance*. Cambridge: Cambridge University.
Hall, M. (2007, March 15). Homegrown terrorists' focus of new unit. *The Arizona Republic*, p. A4.
Hanna, K. E. (2006). Germline gene transfer. National Human Genome Research Institute [online]. Available: http://www.genome/gov/10004764.
Hannah, M. G. (2000). *Governmentality and the mastery of territory in nineteenth-century America*. Cambridge: Cambridge University Press.
Hansmann, H., & Kraakman, R. (2001–2000, January). The end of history for corporate law. *Georgetown Law Journal, 89*, 439–468.

References

Hardt, M., & Negri. A. (2000). *Empire*. Cambridge MA: Harvard University.
Harmon, A. (2007, May 9). Prenatal test puts Down syndrome in hard focus. *The New York Times*, p. A1.
Harris, G. (2006, November 23). Proof is scant on psychiatric drug mix for young. *The New York Times*, p. A1.
Harris, G. (2007, July 11). Surgeon general sees 4-year term as compromised. *The New York Times*, p. A1.
Harris, R. (2000). *Industrializing English Law: Entrepreneurship and business organization, 1720–1844*. Cambridge, MA: Cambridge University.
Hart, B. (2003, July 30). Strings attached: Universities look to private money but find it can come with an agenda. *The Arizona Republic*, pp. V1–2.
Hartnett, S. J., & Stengrim, L. A. (2006). *Globalization and empire: The U.S. invasion of Iraq, free markets, and the twilight of democracy*. Tuscaloosa: University of Alabama.
Harvey, D. (1989). *The condition of postmodernity: An enquiry into the origins of social change*. Oxford: Basil Blackwell.
Harvey, D. (2005). *A brief history of neoliberalism*. Oxford: Oxford University Press.
Hausman, B. (1995). *Changing sex: Transsexualism, technology, and the idea of gender*. Durham, NC: Duke.
Hay, J. (2006). Designing homes to be the first line of defense. *Cultural Studies*, 20, 349–377.
Hayek, F. A. (1944). *The road to serfdom*. Chicago: University of Chicago.
Hayek, F. A. (1960). *The constitution of liberty*. London: Routledge.
Hayek, F. A. (1976). *The mirage of social justice*. London: Routledge.
Hayek, F. A. (1988). *The fatal conceit: The errors of socialism*. Chicago: University of Chicago Press.
Hayek, F. A. (1991). *Economic freedom*. Oxford: Blackwell.
Hayles, N. K. (1999). *How we became posthuman: Virtual bodies in cybernetics, literature, and informatics*. Chicago: University of Chicago.
Healy, D. (1997). *The antidepressant era*. Cambridge, MA: Harvard University.
Healy, D. (2004). *The creation of psychopharmacology*. Cambridge, MA: Harvard University.
Healy, D. (n.d.). Psychopharmacology and the government of the self [online]. Available: http://www.academyanalyticarts.org/healy.htm.
Hechinger, J., & Golden, D. (2006, July 8–9). The great giveaway. *The Wall Street Journal*, pp. A1, A8.
Hedgecoe, A. M. (2003). Expansion and uncertainty: Cystic fibrosis, classification and genetics. *Sociology of Health and Illness*, 25, 50–70.
Hedgecoe, A. M. (2004). *The politics of personalized medicine: Pharmacogenetics in the clinic*. Cambridge, MA: Cambridge University.
Held, D., & McGrew, A. G. (2002). *Governing globalization: Power, authority, and global governance*. Malden, MA: Polity.
Herman, E. (1995). *The romance of American psychology: Political culture in the age of experts*. Berkeley: University of California.
Hernnstein, R. J., & Murray, C. (1994). *The bell curve: Intelligence and class structure in American life*. New York: Free Press.
Hicks, J. (1969). *A theory of economic history*. Oxford: Clarendon Press.
Higgins, A. (2006, July 27). A Texas preacher leads campaign to let Israel fight. *The Wall Street Journal*, pp. A1, A11.
Hilt, E. (2006, October). Corporate ownership and governance in the early nineteenth century [online]. Available: www.econ.barnard.columbia.edu/~econhist/papers/Hilt_Columbia.pdf.

Hindess, B. (2001). The liberal government of unfreedom. *Alternatives: Global, Local, Political,* 26, 93–112.
Hindess, B. (2005). Politics as government: Michel Foucault's analysis of political reason. *Alternatives,* 30, 389–413.
Hindess, B. (2006). Territory. *Alternatives,* 31, 243–257.
Hitt, G. (2005, September 22). A kinder, gentler Wolfowitz at World Bank. *The Wall Street Journal,* p. A4.
Hjörleifsson, S., & Schei, E. (2006). DeCODE and the governance of human genetics. *European Journal of Human Genetics,* 14, 802–808.
Hlodan, O. (2000, June). For sale: Iceland's genetic history [online]. Available: http://www.actionbioscience.org/genomic/hlodan.html.
Hobson, J. A. (1972). *Imperialism: A study* (rev. ed.). Ann Arbor: University of Michigan. (Original work published 1905)
Hoenig, J. (1995). Schizophrenia: Clinical section. In G. E. Berrios & R. Porter (Eds.), *A history of clinical psychiatry: The origin and history of psychiatric disorders* (pp. 336–348). London: Athlone.
Home, E. (1814). Observations on the functions of the brain. *Philosophical Transactions of the Royal Society of London,* 104, 469–486.
Horn, M. (1989). *'Before it's too late': The child guidance movement in the United States, 1922–1945.* Philadelphia: Temple University.
Hörnqvist, M. (2004). The birth of public order policy. *Race and Class,* 46, 30–52.
House, B. (2006, July 16). 'Democracy builders' are drawing ire: Some U.S. groups are blamed for weakening foreign regimes. *The Arizona Republic,* pp. A1, 26–27.
Houston, R., & Frith, U. (2000). *Autism in history: The case of Hugh Blair of Borgue.* Padstow, Cornwall, UK: Blackwell.
Hubbard, R., & Wald, E. (1999). *Exploding the gene myth.* Boston: Beacon.
Hudson, M. (2003). *Super imperialism: The origin and fundamentals of U.S. world dominance* (2nd ed.). London: Pluto Press.
Hull, A., & Priest, D. (2007, March 5). It is just not Walter Reed. *The Washington Post,* p. A1.
Human Genome Project (n.d.) [online]. Available: http://www.ornl.gov/sci/techresources/Human_Genome/posters/chromosome/index.shtml.
Human Rights Watch (2002, February 27). Race and incarceration in the United States [online]. Available: http://www.hrw.org/backgrounder/usa/race/.
Hunt, J. (1864). On the Negro's place in nature. *Journal of the Anthropological Society of London,* 2, xv–lvi.
Huntington, S. P. (1993a). The clash of civilizations? *Foreign Affairs,* 72(3), 22–49.
Huntington, S. P. (1993b). If not civilizations, what? *Foreign Affairs,* 72(5), 186–194.
Ibrahim, E. (2003). 11 September and the widening north-south gap: Root causes of terrorism. *Arab Studies Quarterly,* 25, 57–70.
Ilpo, H. (2000). Welfare and its vicissitudes. *Acta Sociologica,* 43,157–164.
Insel, T. R., & Collins, F. S. (2003). Psychiatry in the genomics era. *American Journal of Psychiatry,* 160, 616–620.
Introns and Exons. (n.d.). National Human Genome Research Institute [online]. Available: http://www.genome.gov/Pages/Hyperion/DIR/VIP/Glossary/Illustration/intron.cfm?key=intron.
Ip, G. (2007, January 19). Bernanke raises prospects of 'debt spiral.' *The Wall Street Journal,* p. A.2
Ip, G., & Whitehouse, M. (2007, March 1). Waning appetite for risk poses global challenges. *The Wall Street Journal,* p. A2.

Ireland, P., Grigg-Spall, I., & Kelly, D. (1987). The conceptual foundations of modern company law. *Journal of Law and Society*, 14, 149–165.
Isaacs, S. L., & Schroeder, S. A. (2004). Class—The ignored determinant of the nation's health. *The New England Journal of Medicine*, 351(11), 1137–1142.
Jacker, C. (1966). *Window on the unknown: A history of the microscope*. New York: Charles Scribner's Sons.
Jewson, N. (1976). The disappearance of the sick man from medical cosmologies. *Sociology*, 10, 225–244.
Jia-Ming, Z., & Morss, E. R. (2005). The financial revolutions of the twentieth century. In A. D. Chandler, Jr., & B. Mazlish (Eds.), *Leviathans: Multinational corporations and the new global history* (pp. 203–218). Cambridge: Cambridge University.
Johannsen, W. (1911). The genotype conception of heredity. *The American Naturalist*, XLV(531), 129–153.
Johnson, A. (1898). Concerning a form of degeneracy. *The American Journal of Sociology*, 4, 326–334.
Jones, C. (2004, November 8). Druggists refuse to give out pill. *USA Today* [online]. Available: http://www.usatoday.com/news/nation/2004-11-08-druggists-pill_x.htm.
Jones, K. W. (1999). *Taming the troublesome child: American families, child guidance, and the limits of psychiatric authority*. Cambridge, MA: Harvard University.
Jorstad, E. (1990). *Holding fast/Pressing on: Religion in America in the 1980s*. New York: Greenwood.
Joyce, P. (2003). *The rule of freedom*. London: Verso.
Kahn, J. (2006). Patenting race. *Nature Biotechnology*, 24(11), 1349–1351.
Kalpagam, U. (2000). Colonial governmentality and the 'economy.' *Economy and Society*, 29, 418–438.
Kass, L. R., & Members of the President's Council on Bioethics. (2003). *Beyond therapy: Biotechnology and the pursuit of happiness: A Report of the President's Council on Bioethics*. New York: Dana Press.
Kay, L. E. (1993). *The molecular vision of life: Caltech, the Rockefeller Foundation and the rise of the new biology*. Oxford: Oxford University.
Kellerman, J. (2007, April 23). Bedlam revisited. *The Wall Street Journal*, p. A17.
Kenyon, T. A., Driver, C., Haas, E., Valway, S. E., Moser, K. S., & Onorato, I. M. (1999). Immigration and tuberculosis among children on the United States Mexico border, County of San Diego, California. *Pediatrics*, 104(1), e8.
Kerr, A. (2003). Genetics and citizenship. *Society*, 40(6), 44–50.
Keynes, M. (1926). The end of laissez-faire [online]. Available: http://www.panarchy.org/keynes/laissezfaire.1926.html.
Keynes, J. M. (1965/1936). *The general theory of employment, interest, and money*. New York: Harcourt.
Kim-Cohen, J., Caspi, A., Taylor, A., Williams, B., Newcombe, R., Craig, I. W., & T. E. Moffitt. (2006). MAOA, maltreatment, and gene–environment interaction predicting children's mental health: New evidence and a meta-analysis. *Molecular Psychiatry*, 11, 903–913.
Kintisch, E. (2005). Court tightens patent rules on gene tags. *Science*, 309(5742), 1797–1799.
Kintz, L. (1997). *Between Jesus and the market: The emotions that matter in right wing America*. Durham, NC: Duke University Press.
Klare, M. T. (2004). *Blood and oil: The dangers and consequences of America's growing dependency on imported petroleum*. New York: Metropolitan Books.
Klauck, S. M. (2006). Genetics of autism spectrum disorder. *European Journal of Human Genetics*, 14, 714–720.

Kleinfield, N. R. (2006, January 9). Diabetes and its awful toll quietly emerge as a crisis. *The New York Times*, p. A1.

Koretz, G. (2003, October 13). Russia's huge health hurdle. *Business Week*, 3853, 28.

Kristol, I. (1995). American conservatism: 1945–1995. *The Public Interest*, 121, 80–92.

Kristol, I. (2003, August 25). The neoconservative persuasion. *The Weekly Standard*, 8(47) [online serial]. Available: http://www.weeklystandard.com/Content/Public/Articles/000/000/003/000tzmlw.asp.

Krugman, P. (2007, April 13). For God's sake. *The New York Times*, p. A19.

Kurzweil, E. (1977). Michael Foucault: Ending the era of man. *Theory and Society*, 4, 395–420.

Kyle, R. (1995). *The new age movement in American culture*. Lanham, MD: University Press of America.

Lagouranis, T. (2007, June 5). Fear up harsh. WAMU 88.5 American University Radio [online]. Available: http://www.wamu.org/programs/dr/07/06/05.php#12763.

Lagouranis, T., & Mikaelian, A. (2007). *Fear up harsh*. New York: NAL Hardcover.

Lahart, J. (2007, January 22). Cheap money doesn't explain market puzzles. *The Wall Street Journal*, p. C1.

Lake, R. A. (1984). Order and disorder in anti-abortion rhetoric: A logological view. *Quarterly Journal of Speech*, 70, 425–443.

Lakeoff, A. (2005). *Pharmaceutical reason: Knowledge and value in global psychiatry*. Cambridge: Cambridge University.

Landmark STAR*D depression study offers sobering third-round results. (2006, July 20). *Medical News Today* [online]. Available: http://www.medicalnewstoday.com/medicalnews.php?newsid=46265.

Larner, W., & Walters, W. (Eds.). (2004). *Global governmentality*. New York: Routledge.

Larsen, L. T. (2007). Speaking truth to biopower: On the genealogy of bioeconomy. *Distinktion*, 14, 1–21.

Latham, R. (2000). Social sovereignty. *Theory, Culture & Society*, 17, 1–18.

Latour, B. (1987). Science in action. Milton Keynes, UK: Open University.

Laurence, J., & McCallum, D. (2003). Conduct disorder: The achievement of a diagnosis. *Discourse: Studies in the Cultural Politics of Education*, 24, 307–337.

Lazzarato, M. (2005). Biopolitics/bioeconomics: A politics of multiplicity. Interactivist Info Exchange [online]. Available: http://slash.autonomedia.org/print.pl?sid=05/10/18/0935231.

Lazzarato, M. (n.d.). From biopower to biopolitics. Generation-Online Web [online]. Available: http://www.generation-online.org/c/fcbiopolitics.htm.

Lemke, T. (2001). 'The birth of bio-politics': Michel Foucault's lecture at the Collège de France on neo-liberal governmentality. *Economy and Society*, 30, 190–207.

Lemke, T. (2004). Disposition and determinism—genetic diagnostics in risk society. *Sociological Review*, 22, 550–566.

Lemke, T. (in press). An indigestible meal? Foucault, governmentality and state theory. *Distinktion: Scandinavian Journal of Social Theory*, 15.

Lemov, R. (2005). *World as laboratory: Experiments with mice, mazes, and men*. Hill & Wang: New York.

Leonnig, C. (2006, January 7). Report rebuts Bush on spying. *The Washington Post*, p. A1.

Leonnig, C. D., & Rich, E. (2006). U.S. seeks silence on CIA prisons. *The Washington Post*, p. A1.

Levy, H. (2006, March 17). Caught up in DNA's growing web. *The New York Times*, p. A23.
Lewis, B. (1966). *The Middle East and the West*. New York: Harper & Row.
Lewis, B. (1990). The Roots of Muslim rage. *The Atlantic Monthly*, 266(3), 47–58.
Leyshon, L. A., & Thrift, N. (1997). *Money/space: Geographies of monetary transformation*. London: Routledge.
Liagouras, G. (2005). The political economy of post-industrial capitalism. *Thesis Eleven*, 81, 20–35.
Liebert, M. A., Inc. (2002). Assessment of adenoviral vector safety and toxicity: Report of the National Institutes of Health Recombinant DNA Advisory Committee. *Human Gene Therapy*, 13, 3–13.
Life in the bottom 80 percent. (2005, September 1). *The New York Times* [online]. Available: http://www.nytimes.com/2005/09/01/opinion/01thu2.html?th=&emc=th&pagewanted=print.
Lippert, R. (2004). Sanctuary practices, rationalities and sovereignties. *Alternatives*, 29, 535–555.
Lipschutz, R. D., & Rowe, J. K. (2005). *Globalization, governmentality, and global politics: Regulation for the rest of us?* Milton Park, Oxfordshire, UK: Routledge.
Liptak, A., & Lighctblau, E. (2006, August 18). Judge finds wiretap actions violate the law. *The New York Times*, p. A1.
Lobo-Guerrero, L. (2007). *Emerging securities: A biopolitical genealogy of insurance*. Unpublished doctoral dissertation, Lancaster University, Lancaster, UK.
Locke, J. (1982). *Second treatise of government* (R. Cox, Ed.). Arlington Heights, IL: Crofts Classics. (Original work published 1689)
Long, J. C. (1992). Foucault's clinic. *The Journal of Medical Humanities*, 13, 119–138.
Longworth, R. C. (1998, April 26). International rules being made in secret. *The Arizona Republic*, p. A2.
Lueck, S. (2005, May 24). New kits let you test your own genes, but interpreting the results is trick. *The Wall Street Journal*, p. D1.
Mackenzie, A. (2003). Bringing sequences to life: How bioinformatics corporealizes sequence data. *New Genetics and Society*, 22, 315–332.
Maher, K. (2007a, May 1). Human-rights group flags Wal-Mart. *The Wall Street Journal*, p. A4.
Maher, K. (2007b, January 3). Wal-Mart seeks new flexibility in worker shifts. *The Wall Street Journal*, pp. A1, A11.
Mahler, J. (2005, March 27). The soul of the new exurb. *The New York Times Magazine*, pp. 6, 30.
Marcet, W. (1854). An account of the organic chemical constituents or immediate principles of the excrements of man and animals in the healthy state. *Philosophical Transactions of the Royal Society of London*, 144, 265–283.
Marchand, R. (1985). *Advertising and the American dream*. Berkeley: University of California.
Marchand, R. (1998). *Creating the corporate soul: The rise of public relations and corporate imagery in American big business*. Berkeley: University of California.
Marron, D. (2007). Lending by numbers: Credit scoring and the constitution of risk within consumer credit. *Economy and Society*, 36, 103–133.
Marshall, J. (1864). On the brain of a bushwoman; and on the brains of two idiots of European descent. *Philosophical Transactions of the Royal Society of London*, 154, 501–558.
Marshall, J. D. (1996). *Michel Foucault: Personal autonomy and education*. Dordrecht, Netherlands: Kluwer.

References

Martin, E. (1994). *Flexible bodies: Tracking immunity in American culture—from the days of polio to the age of Aids.* Boston: Beacon.

Massumi, B. (2005, October). The future birth of the affective fact. Conference proceedings of the Genealogies of Biopolitics [online]. Available: www.radicalempiricism.org.

Mathews, A. W., & Abboud, L. (2005, June 29). FDA raises concerns about ADHD drugs. *The Wall Street Journal,* p. D1.

Mathews, A. W., & Kiang, S. (2007, September 21). Media industry helped drug firms fight ad restraints. *The Wall Street Journal,* pp. B1-2.

Maudsley, H. (1870). Relations between body and mind and between mental and other disorders of the nervous system. *The Lancet,* 95, 829-832.

Mbembe, A. (2003). Necropolitics (L. Meintjes, Trans.). *Public Culture,* 15, 11-40.

Mboka, A. (2007). *International responses to gross human rights violations: A comparative content analysis of Bosnia, Iraq, Rwanda and Sierra Leone.* Unpublished doctoral dissertation, Arizona State University, Arizona.

McCallum, D. (2001). *Personality and dangerousness: Genealogies of antisocial personality disorder.* Cambridge: Cambridge University.

McGillivray, D. (2005). Fitter, happier, more productive: Governing working bodies through wellness. *Culture and Organization,* 11, 125-138.

McGlynn, M. (2005). Idiots, lunatics and the royal prerogative in early Tudor England. *The Journal of Legal History,* 26, 1-24.

McWilliams, G., & Martinez, B. (2006, September 22). Wal-Mart cuts drugs to $4. *The Wall Street Journal,* p. B1.

Meckler, L. (2006, November 20). How a U.S. official promotes marriage to fight poverty. *The Wall Street Journal,* pp. A1, A15.

Medawar, C., & Hardon, A. (2004). *Medicines out of control? Antidepressants and the conspiracy of goodwill.* Amsterdam, Netherlands: Aksant.

Mehta, U. S. (1999). *Liberalism and empire: A study in nineteenth-century British liberal thought.* Chicago: University of Chicago.

Micklethwait, J., & Wooldridge, A. (2004). *The right nation: Conservative power in America.* New York: Penguin.

Miles, S. (2006). *Oath betrayed: Torture, medical complicity and the war on terror.* New York: Random House.

Miller, P., & Rose, N. (1990). Governing economic life. *Economy and Society,* 19, 1-30.

Miller, T., & Leger, M. C. (2003). A very childish moral panic: Ritalin. *Journal of Medical Humanities,* 24, 9-32.

Mohammed, A., & Goo, S. K. (2006, June 15). Government increasingly turning to data mining. *The Washington Post,* p. D3.

Moore, M. (2007, June 9). Report gives details on CIA prisons. *Washington Post,* p. A1.

More breaches were discovered at foreign factories last year. (2006, September 6). *The Wall Street Journal,* p. A12.

Moreno, J. D. (2006). *Mind wars: Brain research and national defense.* New York: Dana Press.

Morris, C., Shen, A., Peirce, K., & Beckwith, J. (2007). Deconstructing violence. *GeneWatch,* 20(2) [online]. Available: http://www.gene-watch.org/genewatch/articles/20-2Beckwith.html.

Moss, W. (1794). *An essay on the management, nursing and diseases of children from the birth: And on the treatment and diseases of pregnant and lying-in women: With remarks on the domestic practice of medicine.* London: Longman.

Mumby, D. (Ed.). (1993). *Narrative and social control: Critical perspectives.* Newbury Park, CA: Sage.

Murphy, G. (1937). Personality and social adjustments. *Social Forces*, 15, 472–476.
Nadesan, M. (1997). Constructing paperdolls: The discourse of personality testing. *Communication Theory*, 7, 189–218.
Nadesan, M. (1999a). The discourses of new age corporate spiritualism and evangelical capitalism: Capitalizing on religion in the entrepreneurial age. *Management Communication Quarterly*, 13, 3–42.
Nadesan, M. (1999b). The popular success literature and 'a brave new Darwinian workplace.' *Consumption, Markets & Culture*, 3, 27–60.
Nadesan, M. (2001). *Fortune* on globalization and the new economy: Manifest destiny in a technological age. *Management Communication Quarterly*, 14, 498–506.
Nadesan, M. (2002). Engineering the entrepreneurial infant: Brain science, infant development toys, and governmentality. *Cultural Studies*, 16, 401–432.
Nadesan, M. (2005). *Constructing autism: Unraveling the "truth" and understanding the social*. London: Routledge.
Nadesan, M. (2006). The Make Your Day panopticon: Neoliberalism, governmentality and education. *Radical Pedagogy*, 8, [online]. Available: http://radicalpedagogy.icaap.org/currentissue.html.
Napoli, D. S. (1981). *Architects of adjustment: A history of the psychological profession in the United States*. Port Washington, NY: National University Publications.
National Cancer Institute. (2006). Executive summary of epigenetic mechanisms in cancer [online]. Available: http://dcb.nci.nih.gov/thinktank/Executive_Summary_of_the_Epigenetic_Mechanisms_in_Cancer_Think_Tank.cfm.
National Genome Research Institute (n.d.). Introns and exons [online]. Available: http://www.genome.gov/Pages/Education/kit/main.cfm?pageid=14.
National Genome Research Institute (n.d.). Nucleotides [online]. Available: http://www.genome.gov/Pages/Hyperion/DIR/VIP/Glossary/Illustration/base_pair.cfm?key=base%20pair.
National Genome Research Institute (n.d.). What are the legislative protections? [online]. Available: http://www.genome.gov/10002328.
National Institutes of Health. (n.d.). A short history of the National Institutes of Health [online]. Available: http://history.nih.gov/exhibits/history/index.html.
Neal, A. (2004). Cutting off the king's head: Foucault's *Society Must Be Defended* and the problem of sovereignty. *Alternatives*, 29, 373–398.
Neal, A. W. (2006). Foucault in Guantánamo: Towards an archeology of the exception. *Security Dialogue*, 37, 31–46.
Neal, L. (2005). Venture shares of the Dutch East India Company. In W. N. Goetzmann & K. G. Rouwenhorst (Eds.), *The origins of value: The financial innovations that created modern capital markets* (pp. 165–176). Oxford: Oxford University.
Neiderhiser, J. M. (2001). Conceptual and methodological issues: Understanding the role of genome and envirome: Methods in genetic epidemiology. *The British Journal of Psychiatry*, 178, s12–s17.
Nettleton, S. (1991). Wisdom, diligence and teeth: Discursive practices and the creations of mothers. *Sociology of Health and Illness*, 13, 98–111.
Nordstrom, C. (2000). Shadows and sovereigns. *Theory, Culture & Society*, 17(4), 35–54.
Norton, A. (2004). *Leo Strauss and the politics of American empire*. New Haven, CT: Yale University.
Novas, C., & Rose, N. (2000). Genetic risk and the birth of the somatic individual. *Economy and Society*, 29, 485–513.

O'Driscoll, G. (2007, August 10). Our subprime Fed. *The Wall Street Journal*, p. A11.
Ohlemacher, S. (2007, February 26). Record number in U.S. relying on public aid. *The Arizona Republic*, p. A5.
Olssen, M. (1999). *Michel Foucault: Materialism and education*. Westport, CT: Bergin & Garvey.
O'Malley, P. (1996). Risk and responsibility. In A. Barry, T. Osborne, & N. Rose (Eds.), *Foucault and political reason: Liberalism, neoliberalism and rationalities of government* (pp. 189–208). Chicago: University of Chicago.
O'Malley, P. (2004). *Risk, uncertainty and government*. London: GlassHouse.
O'Malley, P., & Valverde, M. (2004). Pleasure, freedom and drugs: The uses of 'pleasure' in liberal governance of drug and alcohol consumption. *Sociology*, 38, 25–41.
Ong, A. (1991). The gender and labour politics of postmodernity. *Annual Review of Anthropology*, 20, 279–280.
Ong, A. (2006). *Neoliberalism as exception: Mutations in citizenship and sovereignty*. Durham, NC: Duke University.
Orr, D. A. (2002). Sovereignty, supremacy and the origins of the English Civil War. *History*, 87, 474–490.
Ossorio, P., & Duster, T. (2005, January). Race and genetics: Controversies in biomedical, behavioral, and forensic sciences. *American Psychologist*, 60, 115–128.
Palmer, R. R., & Colton, J. (1984). *A history of the modern world since 1815* (6th ed.). New York: Alfred A. Knopf.
Panitch, L., & Gindin, S. (2003). *Global capitalism and American empire*. London: Merlin.
Paradise, J., Andrews, L., & Holbrook, T. (2005). Intellectual property: Patents on human genes: An analysis of scope and claims. *Science*, 307(5715), 1566–1567.
Parascandola, J. (2006). History of U.S. public health [online]. Available: Http://wwwcoausphs.org/phhistory.cfm.
Park, A. (2006, July 10). The perils of cloning. *Time*, 168(2), 56–58.
Parker-Pope, T. (2006, October 31). Web site tallies your risk of disease and tells you what you can do about it. *The Wall Street Journal*, p. B1.
Pasquino, P. (1991). Theatrum politicum: The genealogy of capital—police and the state of prosperity. In G. Burchell, C. Gordon, & P. Miller (Eds.), *The Foucault effect: Studies in governmentality* (pp. 105–118). Chicago: University of Chicago.
Paul, A. M. (2004). *The cult of personality: How personality tests are leading us to miseducate our children, mismanage our companies, and misunderstand ourselves*. New York: Free Press.
Pearce, R. L. (2002). War and medicine in the nineteenth century. *ADF Health*, 3, 88–92.
Penner, E. (2007, August 27). Can the financial markets make a comeback? *The Wall Street Journal*, p. A11.
Perkinelmer (2006). SNPs [online]. Available: http://las.perkinelmer.com/content/snps/genotyping.asp 2006.
Peters, M. A. (2001). *Poststructuralism, Marxism, and neoliberalism: Between theory and politics*. Lanham, MD: Rowman & Littlefield.
Petersen, A. (1999). Public health, the new genetics and subjectivity. In A. Petersen, I. Barns, J. Dudley, & P. Harris (Eds.), *Poststructuralism, citizenship and social policy* (pp. 114–147). London: Routledge.
Petersen, A., & Bunton, R. (2002). *The new genetics and the public's health*. London: Routledge.
Petersen, A., & Lupton, D. (1996). *The new public health: Health and self in the age of risk*. London: Sage.

Peterson, B. S. (2003). Conceptual, methodological, and statistical challenges in brain imaging studies of developmentally based psychopathologies. *Development and Psychopathology, 15*, 811–832.

Petty, W. (1755). *Several essays in political arithmetick* (4th ed.). London: D. Brown. (Original work published 1690)

Pezzolo, L. (2005). Bonds and government debt in Italian city-states, 1250–1650. In W. N. Goetzmann & K. G. Rouwenhorst (Eds.), *The origins of value: The financial innovations that created modern capital markets* (pp. 145–164). Oxford: Oxford University.

Phillips, K. (2006). *American theocracy.* New York: Viking.

Phillips, M. M. (2005, February 28). Bush ties AIDS money to antiprostitution pledge. *The Wall Street Journal,* pp. A1, A4.

Phillips, M. M. (2006, June 30). Controlling carrots and sticks: White House tries to rein in foreign-aid agency it recently created. *The Wall Street Journal,* p. A4.

Pincus, W. (2006a, September 23). As Army adds interrogators, it outsources training. *Washington Post,* p. A14

Pincus, W. (2006b, March 20). Increase in contracting intelligence jobs raises concern. *The Washington Post,* p. A3.

Pincus, W. (2007, April 14). Administration seeks to expand surveillance law. *The Washington Post,* p. A3.

Pitts, J. (2005). *A turn to empire: The rise of imperial liberalism in Britain and France.* Princeton, NJ: Princeton University.

Plant, R. (2004). Neo-liberalism and the theory of the state: From *Wohlfahrtsstaat* to *Rechtsstaat. The Political Quarterly, 75,* 24–37.

Plomin, R. (2001). Epidemiology in neurobiological research. *The British Journal of Psychiatry, 178,* s41–s48.

Poitras, G. (1996, August 25). From commercial arithmetic to life annuities: The early history of financial economics, 1478–1776 [online]. Available: http://www.bus.sfu.ca/homes/poitras/FIN_HIS3.pdf.

Polanyi, K. (1957). *The great transformation: The political and economic origins of our time.* Boston: Beacon. (Original work published 1944)

Pollack, A. (2006, April 13). Genetic technology reshapes the diagnostics business. *The New York Times,* p. C1.

Pontecorvo, G. (1958). The Stock Exchange: Its role at various stages of capitalist development. *The Journal of Finance, 13,* 561–562.

Porter, D. (1999). *Health, civilization and the state: A history of public health from ancient to modern times.* London: Routledge.

Postel, D. (2003, October 18). Noble lies and perpetual war: Leo Strauss, the neocons, and Iraq. Interview with Shadia Drury. Information Clearing House [online]. Available: http://www.informationclearinghouse.info/article5010.htm.

Poterba, J. M. (2005). Annuities in early modern Europe. In W. N. Goetzmann & K. G. Rouwenhorst (Eds.), *The origins of value: The financial innovations that created modern capital markets* (pp. 207–224). Oxford: Oxford University.

Poulantzas, N. (1978). *State, power, socialism* (P. Camiller, Trans.). London: NLB.

Procacci, G. (1991). The social economy of poverty. In G. Burchell, C. Gordon, & P. Miller (Eds.), *The Foucault effect: Studies in governmentality* (pp. 151–168). Chicago: University of Chicago.

Project for the New American Century (n.d) [online]. Available: http://www.newamericancentury.org/.

Rabinow, P. (2005). Artificiality and enlightenment: From sociobiology to biosociality. In J. X. Inda (Ed.), *Anthropologies of modernity: Foucault, governmentality, and life politics* (pp. 181–193). Madden, MA: Blackwell.

Rafalovich, A. (2001). The conceptual history of attention deficit hyperactivity disorder: Idiocy, imbecility, encephalitis and the child deviant, 1877–1929. *Deviant Behavior: An Interdisciplinary Journal*, 22, 93–115.

Rafter, N. H. (2006). H. J. Eysenck in Fagin's kitchen: The return to biological theory in 20th century criminology. *History of Human Sciences*, 19, 37–56.

Rajan, K. S. (2006). *Biocapital: The constitution of postgenomic life*. Durham, NC: Duke University.

Ramus, F. (2006). Genes, brain and cognition: A roadmap for the cognitive scientist. *Cognition*, 101, 247–269.

Raulff, U. (2004). Interview with Giorgio Agamben. *German Law Journal*, 5, [online]. Available: http://www.germanlawjournal.com/article.php?id=437.

Rawls, J. (1972). *A theory of justice*. Oxford: Clarendon Press.

Reardon, J. (2005). *Race to the finish: Identity and governance in an age of genomics*. Princeton, NJ: Princeton University.

Regalado, A. (2006a, April 14). Map quest: New genetic tools may reveal roots of everyday ills. *The Wall Street Journal*, p. A1.

Regalado, A. (2006b, June 7). Plan to build children's DNA database raises concerns. *The Wall Street Journal*, pp. B1, B2.

Regalado, A. (2006c, June 16). Scientist's study of brain genes sparks a backlash: Dr Lahn connects evolution in some groups to IQ. *The Wall Street Journal*, pp. A1, A12.

Reid, J. (2006). War, discipline, and biopolitics in the thought of Michael Foucault. *Social Text*, 24, 127–152.

Researchers learning how young brains grow. (2007, May 19). *The Arizona Republic*, p. A19.

Richards, D. G. (2004). *Intellectual property rights and global capitalism: The political economy of the TRIPS Agreement*. Armonk, NY: M. E. Sharpe.

Ricks, T. E., & Tyson, A. S. (2007, May 5). Troops at odds with ethic standards. *The Washington Post*, p. A1.

Ritter, M. (2003, July 16). Manic-depression gene identified, scientists say. *The Arizona Republic*, p. A7.

Ritter, M. (2007, October 19). DNA Nobel winner's comments about Blacks sparking outrage. *The Arizona Republic*, p. A2.

Rizvi, A. M. (2005). Reading Elden's mapping the present. *Cosmo and History: The Journal of Natural and Social Philosophy*, 1, 177–184.

Rose, N. (1993). Government, authority and expertise in advanced liberalism. *Economy & Society*, 22, 283–299.

Rose, N. (1996). Governing "advanced" liberal democracies. In A. Barry, T. Osborne, & N. Rose (Eds.), *Foucault and political reason* (pp. 37–64). Chicago: University of Chicago.

Rose, N. (1998). *Inventing our selves: Psychology, power, and personhood*. Cambridge: Cambridge University.

Rose, N. (1999a). *Governing the soul* (2nd ed.). London: Free Association Books.

Rose, N. (1999b). Medicine, history and the present. In C. Jones & R. Porter (Eds.), *Reassessing Foucault: Power, medicine and the body* (pp. 48–71). London: Routledge.

Rose, N. (1999c). *Powers of freedom*. Cambridge: Cambridge University.

Rose, N. (2000). Governing liberty. In R. V Ericson & N. Stehr (Eds.), *Governing modern societies* (pp. 141–176). Toronto: University of Toronto.

Rose, N. (2003). Neurochemical selves. *Society*, 41, 46–59.

Rose, N. (2007). *The politics of life itself*. Princeton, NJ: Princeton University.

Rose, N., O'Malley, P., & Valverde, M. (2006). Governmentality. *Annual Review of Law*, 2, 83–104.

Rose, S. (2001). Moving on from old dichotomies: Beyond nature—nurture towards a lifeline perspective. *The British Journal of Psychiatry*, 178, s3–s7 [online]. Available: http://bfp.rpsycho.or/cgi/contents/full/178/40/s3.

Rosen, G. (1993). *A history of public health* (expanded ed.). Baltimore: Johns Hopkins.

Rosenberg, C. E. (1977). And heal the sick: The hospital and the patient in the 19th century America. *Journal of Social History*, 10, 428–447.

Rothschild, J. (2005). *The dream of the perfect child*. Bloomington, IN: Indiana University.

Rothstein, H., Huber, M., & Gaskell, G. (2006). A theory of risk colonization: The spiraling regulatory logics of societal and institutional risk. *Economy and Society*, 35, 91–112.

Rouwenhorst, K. G. (2005). The origins of mutual funds. In W. N. Goetzmann & K. G. Rouwenhorst (Eds.), *The origins of value: The financial innovations that created modern capital markets* (pp. 249–270). Oxford: Oxford University.

Roy, W. G. (1997). *Socializing capital: The rise of the large industrial organization in America*. Princeton, NJ: Princeton University.

Ruskin, L. (2005, September 24). Lawmaker would sell some national parks. *The Arizona Republic*, p. A27.

Rutenberg, J., & Stolberg, S. G. (2006, September 12). In prime-time address, Bush says safety of U.S. hinges on Iraq. *The New York Times*, p. A1.

Rutherford, J. (2005). At war. *Cultural Studies*, 19, 622–642.

Said, E. (1978). *Orientalism*. New York: Pantheon.

Salmon, J. L., & Harris, H. R. (2007, February 4). Reaching out with word—and technology. *The Washington Post*, p. A1.

Sassen, S. (1991). *The global city: New York, London, Tokyo*. Princeton, NJ: Princeton University.

Sassen, S. (2006). *Territory, authority, rights: From medieval to global assemblages*. Princeton, NJ: Princeton University.

Sataline, S. (2007, January 24). To treat cancer, herbs and prayer. *The Wall Street Journal*, pp. A1, A10.

Saukko, P. (2004). Genomic susceptibility-testing and pregnancy: Something old, something new. *New Genetics and Society*, 23, 313–324.

Scahill, J. (2007). *Blackwater: The rise of the world's most powerful mercenary army*. New York: Nation Books.

Schmitt, C. (1985). *Political theology: Four chapters on sovereignty* (G. Schwab, Trans.). Cambridge, MA: MIT Press. (Original work published 1922)

Schultz, D. P., & Schultz, S. E. (1987). *A history of modern psychology* (4th ed.). San Diego: Harcourt Brace Jovanovich.

Schurman, R. A., & Kelso, D. D. T. (Eds.). (2003). *Engineering trouble: Biotechnology and its discontents*. Berkeley: University of California.

Shanker, T. (2007, April 25). With troop rise, Iraqi detainees soar in number. *The New York Times*, p. A1.

Sharp, S. E. (1899). Individual psychology: A study in psychological method. *The American Journal of Psychology*, 10, 329–391.

Shenon, P. (2007, October 19). Senators clash with nominee about torture. *The New York Times*, p. A1.

Sherman, M. (2007, October 10). U.S. justices don't touch Bush policy on secrets. *The Arizona Republic*, pp. A1, A6.

Shorter, E. (1997). *A history of psychiatry: From the era of the asylum to the age of Prozac*. New York: John Wiley & Sons.

Shorto, R. (2006, May 7). Contra-contraception. *The New York Times*, p. 48.

Silver, S., Slater, J., & Millard, P. (2007, January 9). Chávez moves new socialism to faster track. *The Wall Street Journal*, pp. A1, A17.

Simpson, G. R., & Faucon, B. (2007, July 2). Trade becomes route for money tied to terrorism. *The Wall Street Journal*, pp. A1, A6.
Singh, I. (2007). Not just naughty: 50 years of stimulant drug advertising. In A. Tone & E. S. Watkins (Eds.), *Medicating modern America: Prescription drugs in history* (pp. 131–155). New York: New York University.
Slater, J., & Karmin, C. (2007, August 10). Subprime fallout hits new frontiers. *The Wall Street Journal*, pp. C1–2.
Small, A. V. (1895). The era of sociology. *The American Journal of Sociology*, 1, 1–15.
Smart, B. (2003). *Economy, culture and society*. Buckingham, UK: Open University.
Smith, A. (1976). *An inquiry into the nature and causes of the wealth of nations* (3rd ed.; R. H. Campbell & A. S. Skinner, Eds.). Oxford: Clarendon Press. (Original work published 1784)
Smith, D. B. (2007, March 25). Can you live with the voices in your head? *The New York Times Magazine*, pp. 6, 50.
Smith, E., & Hattery, A. (2006). The prison-industrial complex. *Sociation Today*, 4(2) [online]. Available: http://www.ncsociology.org/sociationtoday/v42/prison.htm.
Snyder, J. (2006, July 25). State dollars jump-start autism research. *The Arizona Republic*, p. B1.
Society for Bettering the Condition and Increasing the Comforts of the Poor. (1800). *Hints for those who may be desirous of introducing the manufacture of split straw in country towns, villages, schools, and workhouses*. London: Eighteenth Century Collections Online, Gale Group.
Solomon, D., & Wessel, D. (2007, January 19). Health-insurance gap surges as political issue. *The Wall Street Journal*, pp. A1, A12.
Solomon, J. (2007, June 14). FBI finds it frequently overstepped in collecting data. *The Washington Post*, p. A1.
Spaulding, E. R., & Healy, W. (1914). Inheritance as a factor in criminality. *Journal of the American Institute of Criminal Law and Criminology*, 4, 837–858.
Spencer, H. (2003). *Social statics* and *The man versus the state* (rev. & abridged). Honolulu: University Press of the Pacific.
Spot deep in brain linked to addiction. (2007, January 26). *The Wall Street Journal*, p. B5.
Standaert, M. (2006). *Skipping toward Armageddon: The politics and propaganda of the left behind novels and the LaHaye empire*. Brooklyn: Soft Skull Press.
Starr, P. (1982). *The social transformation of American medicine*. New York: Basic Books.
Statement of principles. (n.d.). Project for the New American Century [online]. Available: http://www.newamericancentury.org/statementofprinciples.htm.
Steinberg, H. (2005). A short history of psychiatry at Leipzig University [online]. Available: http://www.uni-leipzig.de/~psy/eng/geschi-e.htm.
Stephanson, A. (1995). *Manifest destiny: American expansionism and the empire of right*. New York: Hill & Wang.
Stern, A. M. (1999). Secrets under the skin: New historical perspectives on disease, deviation, and citizenship. *Society for Comparative Study of Society and History*, 41, 589–596.
Stringer, K. (2005, January 14). In ad blitz, Wal-Mart counters public image as harsh employer. *The Wall Street Journal*, p. B3.
Stringham, E. (2003). The extralegal development of securities trading in seventeenth-century Amsterdam. *The Quarterly Review of Economics and Finance*, 42, 321–344.

Strohman, R. (2002, April 26). Maneuvering the complex path from genotype to phenotype. *Science,* 296(5568), 701–703.
Sullum, J. (2000, July). Curing the therapeutic state: Thomas Szasz on the medicalization of American life. *Reason Magazine* [online]. Available: http://www.reason.com/news/show/27767.html.
Sylla, R. (2005). Origins of the New York Stock Exchange. In W. N. Goetzmann & K. G. Rouwenhorst (Eds.), *The origins of value: The financial innovations that created modern capital markets* (pp. 299–312) Oxford: Oxford University Press.
Szasz, T. S. (1989). *Law, liberty, and psychiatry: An inquiry into the social uses of mental health practices.* Syracuse, NY: Syracuse University.
Talan, J. (2002, July 19). Scientists link anxiety to specific gene. *The Arizona Republic,* p. A8.
Tanner, L. (2006, May 1). Pediatric group urges doctors to check on family's exercise. *The Arizona Republic,* pp. A1, A7.
The business of giving. (2006, February 25). *The Economist,* 378(8466), 3–5.
The marriage bed: Sex and intimacy for married Christians. (n.d.) [online]. Available: http://www.themarriagebed.com/pages/donate/donations.shtml.
Thornton, E. (2007, May 7). Road to riches. *Business Week,* 4033, 50–57.
Thurow, R., & Solomon, J. (2004, June 25). An Indian paradox: Bumper harvests and rising hunger. *The Wall Street Journal,* pp. A1, A8.
Tobar, H. (2004, April 22). Latin Americans would support dictator if lives better, study says. *The Arizona Republic,* p. A15.
Tomes, N. (1997). The private side of public health: Sanitary science, domestic hygiene, and the germ theory, 1870–1900. In J. W. Leavitt & R. L. Numbers (Eds.), *Sickness and health in America: Readings in the history of medicine and public health* (3rd ed.; pp. 506–527). Madison: University of Wisconsin.
Tomes, N. (1998). *The gospel of germs: Men, women, and the microbe in American life.* Cambridge, MA: Harvard University Press.
Tomlins, C. (2004). Early British America, 1585–1830. In D. Hay & P. Craven (Eds.), *Masters, servants, and, magistrates in Britain and the Empire, 1562–1955* (pp. 117–152). Chapel Hill: University of North Carolina.
Tone, A., & Watkins, E. S. (2007). *Medicating modern America.* New York: New York University.
Torres, C., & Vogel, T. T. (1994, June 20). Some mutual funds wield growing clout in developing nations. *The Wall Street Journal Europe,* pp. A1, A11.
Tremain, S. (2005). *Foucault and the government of disability.* Ann Arbor: University of Michigan.
Tremain, S. (2006). Reproductive freedom, self-regulation, and the government of impairment in utero. *Hypatia,* 21, 35–53.
Trent, J. W. (1994). *Inventing the feeble mind: A history of mental retardation in the United States.* Berkeley: University of California.
Trujillo, K. A., & Chinn, A. B. (1996). Sedative-hypnotics [online]. Available: http://www.csusm.edu/DandB/Sedatives.html#history.
United Nations Human Development Program. (1999). *The human development report 1990–1999.* New York: United Nations.
U.S. Department of Health & Human Services. (2004, March). Innovation/stagnation: Challenges and opportunity on the critical path to new medical products [online]. Available: http://www.fda.gov/oc/initiatives/criticalpath/whitepaper.html#execsummary.
U.S. Food & Drug Administration. (2005, August). Milestones in U.S. food and drug law history [online]. Available: http://www.fda.gov/opacom/backgrounders/miles.html.
Useem, J. (2003, March 3). One nation under Wal-Mart. *Fortune,* 147(4), 64–78.

Uttal, W. R. (2001). *The new phrenology: The limits of localizing cognitive processes in the brain.* Boston: MIT Press.
Valverde, M. (2003). Police science, British style: Pub licensing and urban disorder. *Economy and Society,* 32, 234–252.
Valverde, M. (2007). Police, sovereignty, and law: Foucaultian reflections [online]. Available: www.abf-sociolegal.org/valerdepaper.pdf.
Valverde, M., & Mopas, M. (2004). Insecurity and the dream of targeted governance. In W. Larner & W. Walters (Eds.), *Global governmentality* (pp. 232–250). New York: Routledge.
Vedantam, S. (2003, July 18). Researchers find stress, depression have genetic link. *The Arizona Republic,* p. A10.
Vedantam, S. (2006, March 23). Drugs cure depression in half of patients. *The Washington Post,* p. A1.
Veitia, R. A. (2005). Stochasticity or the fatal 'imperfection' of cloning. *Journal of Bioscience,* 30, 21–30.
Waldman, P. (2004, February 3). Power and Peril: America's supremacy and its limits. *The Wall Street Journal,* pp. A1, A12.
Waldman, P. (2005, December 29). Inside Pentagon's fight to limit regulation of military pollutants. *The Wall Street Journal,* pp. A1, A5.
Walker, M. (2006, July 24). More flexibility by Europe's labor stokes a recovery. *The Wall Street Journal,* pp. A1, A8.
Wallace, H. (2005). Misleading marketing of genetic tests. *Gene Watch: Council for Responsible Genetics,* 18(2) [online]. Available: http://www.gene-watch.org/genewatch/articles/18-2Wallace.html.
Walters, W. (2004). Secure borders, safe haven, domopolitics. *Citizenship Studies,* 18, 237–260.
Warrick, J. (2006, July 30). The secretive fight against bioterror. *The Washington Post,* p. A1.
Warrick, J. (2007, August 16). Domestic use of spy satellites to widen. *The Washington Post,* p. A1.
Waterland, R. A., & Jirtle, R. L. (2003). Transposable elements: Targets for early nutritional effects of epigenetic gene regulation. *Molecular and Cellular Biology,* 23, 5293–5300.
Weaver, L. V. M. (2004). *Fit for God: The 8-week plan that kicks the Devil OUT and invites health and healing.* New York: Galilee Trade.
Webb, S. (1906). Physical degeneracy and race suicide. *Popular Science Monthly,* 69, 512–529.
Wehrle, E. F. (2003). Welfare and warfare: American organized labor approaches the military-industrial complex, 1949–1964. *Armed Forces and Security,* 29, 525–546.
Weintraub, A. (2007, July 2). Lifestyle drug binge. *Business Week,* 4041, 40–41.
Weisman, J. (2007, June 19). 'Signing statements' study finds administration has ignored laws. *The Washington Post,* p. A4.
Weiss, R. (2006, May 12). DNA of criminals' kin cited in solving cases. *The Washington Post,* p. A10.
Weiss, R. (2007, August 6). Death points to risks in research. *The Washington Post,* p. A1.
Welling, J. C. (1888). The law of Malthus. *The American Anthropologist,* 1, 1–24.
Wells, B. (2004). Breast cancer gene discovered with new method. Stanford University School of Medicine [online]. Available: http://mednews.stanford.edu/realeases/1997/janreleases/bcgene.html.
Wells, D. C. (1907). Social Darwinism. *The American Journal of Sociology,* 12, 695–716.
Wessel, D. (2007, October 4). Financial globalization's new power source. *The Wall Street Journal,* p. A2.

Westphal, S. P. (2005, October 14). Human gene patents 'surprisingly high' a new study shows. *The Wall Street Journal*, p. B1.
Whalen, J. (2006, August 23). Armed with new vaccines, drug makers target teenagers. *The Wall Street Journal*, pp. B1, B2.
What can be patented. (n.d.). Building biotechnology [online]. Available: http://dnapatent.com/law/whatcan.html.
Whi, J. (2007, January 6). Death in Haditha. *The Washington Post*, p. A1.
White, J., & Tyson, A. S. (2007, March 31). Detainee alleges abuse in CIA prison. *The Washington Post*, p. A1.
Whitehouse, M. (2007, January 8). Why U.S. should root for dollar to weaken more. *The Wall Street Journal*, p. A2.
Wilson, E. B. (1896). *The cell in development and inheritance*. New York: Macmillan & Co.
Wilson, J. Q. (1995). Capitalism and morality. *Public Interest*, 121, 42–61.
Winslow, R., and Mathews, A. W. (2005, December 21). New genetic tests boost impact of drugs. *The Wall Street Journal*, pp. D1, D4.
Winstead, E. R. (2005). Cancer epigenetics: Beyond genetic mutations. *National Cancer Institute Bulletin* 2, 18 [online]. Available: http://www.nci.nih.gov/ncicancerbulletin/NCI_Cancer_Bulletin_050305/page4.
Winstein, K. J. (2007, October 4). DNA decoding maps mainstream future. *The Wall Street Journal*, p. B3.
Wonacott, P. (2007, May 4). Lawless legislators thwart social progress in India. *The Wall Street Journal*, pp. A1, A13.
Woods, R. P., Freimer, N. B., De Young, J. A., Fears, S. C., Sicotte, N. L., Service, S. K., Valentino, D. J., Toga, A. W., & Mazziotta, J. C. (2006). Normal variants of *Microcephalin* and *ASPM* do not account for brain size variability. *Human Molecular Genetics*, 15, 2025–2029.
Yergin, D., & Stanislaw, J. (1998). *Commanding heights*. New York: Simon & Schuster.
Yesil, B. (2006). Watching ourselves: Video surveillance, urban space and self-responsibilization. *Cultural Studies*, 20, 400–416.
Zamiska, N. (2007, January 30). Thai move to trim drug costs highlights growing patent rift. *The Wall Street Journal*, p. A8.
Zoellick, R. B. (2007, January 8). Happily ever AAFTA. *The Wall Street Journal*, p. A17.
Zoller, H. M. (2003). Health on the line: Discipline and consent in employee discourse about occupational health and safety. *Journal of Applied Communication Research*, 31, 118–139.
Zoller, H. M. (2004). Manufacturing health: Problematic outcomes in workplace health promotion initiatives from employee perspectives. *Western Journal of Communication*, 68, 278–301.
Zuckerman, M. (2005). *Psychobiology of personality* (2nd ed.). Cambridge: Cambridge University.
Zuckerman, S., Lahad, A., Shmueli, A., Zimran, A., Pelag, L., Orr-Urtegar, A., Levy-Lahad, E., & Sagi., M. (2007). Carrier screening for Gaucher disease: Lessons for low-penetrance, treatable diseases. JAMA, 298, 1281–1290.

Index

1% Doctrine, 199–200

A
Abu Ghraib, 200
ADHD, 171
Agamben, G., 11, 35, 181, 184–185, 188, 189–190, 209
anatomo-politics, 8, 21, 23, 25, 66, 73, 93, 98, 211
Aradau, C., 198, 200, 202, 204, 208
Armstrong, D., 97, 98, 99, 102, 103, 105, 111, 136, 152, 171
autism, 131

B
Barry, A., 82
Beaulieu, A., 176
Bentham, J., 53, 63, 65
biosociality, 132–133
biosovereignty 14, 132–133, 163, 180
Bratich, J., 201, 217
Brenner, R., 73, 74, 76, 80, 87, 222
Bretton Woods, 71, 72
Bunton, R., 115, 130, 205, 217
Bush, G., 41, 43, 79, 113, 114, 195, 196, 199, 200–202, 206, 207
Butler, J., 189
Buttonwood Agreement, 50

C
Castel, R., 107, 103
Chandler, A., 56
Chappell, B., 201, 205
Chávez, H., 89–90
cognitive psychology, 159–161
Cold War, 72–73, 118, 115, 155, 194, 198, 205
Company of Merchant Adventurers of London, 48
Cooper, M., 37, 78, 203

Cold War, 72, 73, 115, 118, 155, 194, 198, 205
criminality, 147–148
Cruikshank, B., 31, 33, 34, 41, 217

D
dangerous classes, 87, 147–148
Darwinism: theories, 145–146; social Darwinism, 59, 148, 181
Davis, M., 74, 80
De Giorigi, A., 73, 87
De Witt, J., 49
Dean, M., 8, 9, 11, 18, 19, 26, 28, 33, 34, 35, 51, 66, 181, 184, 188, 217
debt, 48, 49, 74–76, 82–84, 86, 87, 89, 136, 137
degeneracy, 12, 63, 67, 104–105, 138, 140, 143–152, 163, 176, 187
Deleuze, G., 5, 9, 12, 25, 29, 33, 61, 76
Dillon, M., 37, 38, 108, 146, 188, 217
Donzelot, J., 66, 172, 218
Driver, F., 51, 54
Dumit, J., 115, 131, 173, 174

E
Escobar, A., 46
eugenics, 103–105, 117, 129, 130, 140, 145, 147–149, 154, 208
Ewald, F., 49

F
flexibilization, 86
Ford, H., 59, 65
Freud, S., 149–150
Friedman, M., 78
Fukuyama, F., 43, 133, 198

G
Galton, F., 146–148

GATT, 71
genetics
    ambivalence, 123–124
    behavioral, 161–167
    biocapital, 127
    bioinformatics, 118
    capitalization, 133–135
    double helix, 117
    engineering, 126–128
    epigenetics, 122
    heritability, 121–122
    Human Genome Project, 124
    problem space 116–117
    risky, 129–131
    sequencing, 118
    standard understandings, 119–120
    surveillance, 125–126
Geneva Conventions, 206, 207, 208
germ theory, 101, 103, 105, 152
Glass-Steagall Act, 70, 76
globalization, 81, 84, 86, 90, 187, 188, 209, 214, 217
Gokay, B., 71, 72, 75
Gold standard, 61, 62
Gordon, C., 1, 9, 15, 16, 19, 33, 94
gospel of the germ, 67
Gottweis, H., 117, 129, 130
Group of 77, 72

H
habeas corpus, 203, 206, 209, 215
Hacking, I., 49
Harvey, D., 26, 43, 73, 78, 80, 230
Hay, J., 204–205
Hayek, F. A., 30, 32, 78
Healy, D., 169–170
Healy, W., 151
Hedgecoe, A. M., 121, 122, 126
Hindess, B., 11, 28, 36, 188–189
Hobson, J., 60
human rights, 35, 88, 91, 191, 199, 209
Huntington, S., 197–198

I
IMF, 38, 71, 75, 79, 80, 89
Interstate Commerce Act, 58

J
Jia-Ming, Z., 83–85

K
Kay, L. 116–117, 154
Keynes, J., 27, 52, 71

Keynesian, 27, 30, 32, 74, 75, 77, 154

L
laissez-faire, 1, 6, 7, 13, 15, 20, 25, 38, 45, 46, 51, 54, 59, 60, 61, 63–65, 69, 86, 149, 185, 192, 217
Lakeoff, A., 154, 157, 168
Lazzarato, M., 10, 45
Lemke, T., 6, 9, 15, 32, 39, 124, 164, 217
Lemov, R., 68, 117, 154
Lewis Doctrine, 197
Lewis, B., 197, 198
Leyshon, L., 49, 50, 61, 62, 76
Lippert, R., 190–191
Lobo-Guerrero, L., 108, 111, 146
Locke, J., 51
Lupton, D., 107, 115

M
madness, 141–144
Malthus, T., 53, 65, 114, 148
Manichaeism, 198, 199, 200, 205
Manifest Destiny, 38, 41, 42, 43, 61, 192, 193, 195, 196, 197, 201, 204, 210, 214
Marchand, R., 69, 153
Marine Hospital, 100, 101, 102
Marron, D., 74, 82
Marshall Plan, 71, 72
Marxism, 45, 66
Mboka, A., 191, 209
medical police, 24
medicalization, 93, 106, 125, 126, 135, 136, 145, 169, 170, 173
medicine
    epidemiological, 107
    laboratory, 102
    labor force, 96, 99, 103
    social, 93, 94–96, 99, 100, 101, 103
    state, 95, 98
    surveillance, 103–106
    urban, 95, 96, 97
mental hygiene, 149–152
mercantile economy, 47
metrological zone, 82, 84, 87
microenterprise, 81, 90–91, 213, 215, 216
microscope, 101–102, 116
Mopas, 37, 190

N
NAFTA, 79, 85

Uttal, W. R. (2001). *The new phrenology: The limits of localizing cognitive processes in the brain*. Boston: MIT Press.
Valverde, M. (2003). Police science, British style: Pub licensing and urban disorder. *Economy and Society*, 32, 234–252.
Valverde, M. (2007). Police, sovereignty, and law: Foucaultian reflections [online]. Available: www.abf-sociolegal.org/valerdepaper.pdf.
Valverde, M., & Mopas, M. (2004). Insecurity and the dream of targeted governance. In W. Larner & W. Walters (Eds.), *Global governmentality* (pp. 232–250). New York: Routledge.
Vedantam, S. (2003, July 18). Researchers find stress, depression have genetic link. *The Arizona Republic*, p. A10.
Vedantam, S. (2006, March 23). Drugs cure depression in half of patients. *The Washington Post*, p. A1.
Veitia, R. A. (2005). Stochasticity or the fatal 'imperfection' of cloning. *Journal of Bioscience*, 30, 21–30.
Waldman, P. (2004, February 3). Power and Peril: America's supremacy and its limits. *The Wall Street Journal*, pp. A1, A12.
Waldman, P. (2005, December 29). Inside Pentagon's fight to limit regulation of military pollutants. *The Wall Street Journal*, pp. A1, A5.
Walker, M. (2006, July 24). More flexibility by Europe's labor stokes a recovery. *The Wall Street Journal*, pp. A1, A8.
Wallace, H. (2005). Misleading marketing of genetic tests. *Gene Watch: Council for Responsible Genetics*, 18(2) [online]. Available: http://www.gene-watch.org/genewatch/articles/18-2Wallace.html.
Walters, W. (2004). Secure borders, safe haven, domopolitics. *Citizenship Studies*, 18, 237–260.
Warrick, J. (2006, July 30). The secretive fight against bioterror. *The Washington Post*, p. A1.
Warrick, J. (2007, August 16). Domestic use of spy satellites to widen. *The Washington Post*, p. A1.
Waterland, R. A., & Jirtle, R. L. (2003). Transposable elements: Targets for early nutritional effects of epigenetic gene regulation. *Molecular and Cellular Biology*, 23, 5293–5300.
Weaver, L. V. M. (2004). *Fit for God: The 8-week plan that kicks the Devil OUT and invites health and healing*. New York: Galilee Trade.
Webb, S. (1906). Physical degeneracy and race suicide. *Popular Science Monthly*, 69, 512–529.
Wehrle, E. F. (2003). Welfare and warfare: American organized labor approaches the military-industrial complex, 1949–1964. *Armed Forces and Security*, 29, 525–546.
Weintraub, A. (2007, July 2). Lifestyle drug binge. *Business Week*, 4041, 40–41.
Weisman, J. (2007, June 19). 'Signing statements' study finds administration has ignored laws. *The Washington Post*, p. A4.
Weiss, R. (2006, May 12). DNA of criminals' kin cited in solving cases. *The Washington Post*, p. A10.
Weiss, R. (2007, August 6). Death points to risks in research. *The Washington Post*, p. A1.
Welling, J. C. (1888). The law of Malthus. *The American Anthropologist*, 1, 1–24.
Wells, B. (2004). Breast cancer gene discovered with new method. Stanford University School of Medicine [online]. Available: http://mednews/stanford.edu/realeases/1997/janreleases/bcgene.html.
Wells, D. C. (1907). Social Darwinism. *The American Journal of Sociology*, 12, 695–716.
Wessel, D. (2007, October 4). Financial globalization's new power source. *The Wall Street Journal*, p. A2.

Westphal, S. P. (2005, October 14). Human gene patents 'surprisingly high' a new study shows. *The Wall Street Journal*, p. B1.
Whalen, J. (2006, August 23). Armed with new vaccines, drug makers target teenagers. *The Wall Street Journal*, pp. B1, B2.
What can be patented. (n.d.). Building biotechnology [online]. Available: http://dnapatent.com/law/whatcan.html.
Whi, J. (2007, January 6). Death in Haditha. *The Washington Post*, p. A1.
White, J., & Tyson, A. S. (2007, March 31). Detainee alleges abuse in CIA prison. *The Washington Post*, p. A1.
Whitehouse, M. (2007, January 8). Why U.S. should root for dollar to weaken more. *The Wall Street Journal*, p. A2.
Wilson, E. B. (1896). *The cell in development and inheritance*. New York: Macmillan & Co.
Wilson, J. Q. (1995). Capitalism and morality. *Public Interest*, 121, 42–61.
Winslow, R., and Mathews, A. W. (2005, December 21). New genetic tests boost impact of drugs. *The Wall Street Journal*, pp. D1, D4.
Winstead, E. R. (2005). Cancer epigenetics: Beyond genetic mutations. *National Cancer Institute Bulletin* 2, 18 [online]. Available: http://www.nci.nih.gov/ncicancerbulletin/NCI_Cancer_Bulletin_050305/page4.
Winstein, K. J. (2007, October 4). DNA decoding maps mainstream future. *The Wall Street Journal*, p. B3.
Wonacott, P. (2007, May 4). Lawless legislators thwart social progress in India. *The Wall Street Journal*, pp. A1, A13.
Woods, R. P., Freimer, N. B., De Young, J. A., Fears, S. C., Sicotte, N. L., Service, S. K., Valentino, D. J., Toga, A. W., & Mazziotta, J. C. (2006). Normal variants of *Microcephalin* and *ASPM* do not account for brain size variability. *Human Molecular Genetics*, 15, 2025–2029.
Yergin, D., & Stanislaw, J. (1998). *Commanding heights*. New York: Simon & Schuster.
Yesil, B. (2006). Watching ourselves: Video surveillance, urban space and self-responsibilization. *Cultural Studies*, 20, 400–416.
Zamiska, N. (2007, January 30). Thai move to trim drug costs highlights growing patent rift. *The Wall Street Journal*, p. A8.
Zoellick, R. B. (2007, January 8). Happily ever AAFTA. *The Wall Street Journal*, p. A17.
Zoller, H. M. (2003). Health on the line: Discipline and consent in employee discourse about occupational health and safety. *Journal of Applied Communication Research*, 31, 118–139.
Zoller, H. M. (2004). Manufacturing health: Problematic outcomes in workplace health promotion initiatives from employee perspectives. *Western Journal of Communication*, 68, 278–301.
Zuckerman, M. (2005). *Psychobiology of personality* (2nd ed.). Cambridge: Cambridge University.
Zuckerman, S., Lahad, A., Shmueli, A., Zimran, A., Pelag, L., Orr-Urtegar, A., Levy-Lahad, E., & Sagi., M. (2007). Carrier screening for Gaucher disease: Lessons for low-penetrance, treatable diseases. *JAMA*, 298, 1281–1290.

NATO, 72
Neal, A., 190
Neoconservatism, 11, 13, 14, 15, 29, 34, 35, 38–44, 72, 79, 81, 111, 133, 184, 190, 193, 195, 196, 208, 210, 214, 215
Neoliberalism, 1, 3, 4, 6, 7, 9, 13, 14, 30, 31, 32, 35, 38–40, 46, 77–92, 129, 181, 191, 214, 217
neuroscience, 173–177
New Deal, 27, 70, 71
Non-Aligned Movement, 72
normalization, 8, 22, 34, 35, 73, 112, 113, 138, 142, 144, 149–159, 162, 164, 171, 172, 175, 177, 178, 186, 190, 205, 211, 213, 214

O
O'Malley, P., 9, 10, 15, 34, 36, 64, 68, 78, 107, 157
OPEC, 72, 75
Ordo-liberalism, 77–78
Ownership Society, 41, 79, 80

P
Pasquino, P., 45
pastoral power, 3, 8, 9, 14, 16, 23–28, 31, 33, 34–39, 68, 89, 90, 94, 109, 114, 139, 140, 169, 183, 187, 190, 194, 206, 208, 209, 214
personality tests, 156
Petersen, A., 96, 107, 115, 130, 205, 217
philanthropy, 32, 36, 40–42, 66, 81, 90, 95, 137, 212, 213, 215, 216
Phillips, K., 74, 83
Pinel, P., 141–142
Polanyi, K., 46, 60, 62
police, 16, 17, 18, 22, 23, 24, 28, 39, 51, 54, 61, 73, 95, 106, 165, 172, 185, 188, 190, 191, 192, 201, 206, 217
Poor Laws, 54, 64, 65
Porter, D. 14, 54, 93, 96, 106
poverty, 33, 40, 46, 51–54, 66, 67, 75, 80, 81, 89, 90, 104, 112, 169, 189, 216
privatization, 79, 80
Procacci, G., 52
Project for a New American Century, 195–196

protodisease, 109–110
psychopharmacology, 167–173

R
Rabinow, P., 107, 120, 125, 132, 177
race suicide, 104–105, 150
racism, 132, 185–186, 209, 218
Reid, J., 21, 37, 38, 186, 206, 209
Rens van Munster, R., 200, 202
risk
 factors, 107–111, 170, 190
 management, 13, 33, 35, 36, 61, 84, 86, 87, 91, 128, 152, 170, 179, 190, 200, 203, 209, 215
 moral, 112
Rose, N., 1, 2, 9, 12, 15, 25, 26, 27, 29, 33, 34, 35, 37, 59, 104, 106, 115, 125, 129, 131, 139, 152, 154, 155, 156, 158, 165, 166, 168, 177, 179, 180, 217
Rose, S., 163
Rosen, G., 14, 24, 93, 102, 103, 104, 105
Roy, W., 56, 57, 58, 59

S
Said, E., 197
Salomon v Salomon & Co, 57
sanitary science, 22, 94, 96, 97, 100–101, 103, 106
Sarbanes-Oxley, 78
Sassen, S., 73, 75, 76, 77, 82, 188, 242
Securities Exchange Act, 70
sexuality, 10, 41, 42, 44, 54, 95, 108, 112–115
Sherman Anti-Trust, 58
Smith, A., 52
Spencer, H., 64, 65

T
Taylor, F., 59, 66
technologies of the self, 2, 3, 4, 5, 7, 9, 11, 22, 25, 27, 45, 63, 68, 93, 94, 108, 109, 115, 132, 139, 149, 153–154, 170, 183, 187, 188, 192
terrorism, 81, 83, 196, 197, 199, 200, 208
Thrift, N., 49, 50, 61, 62, 76
Tomes, N., 67, 101, 103, 104, 105, 106, 107, 152
totalitarianism, 209–210, 216
Tremain, S., 132, 217
trust, 82

V

Valverde, M., 9, 18, 34, 57, 157, 190, 217

W

Wagner Act, 71

Walmart, 87–89
War on Poverty, 40, 75
World Bank, 71, 75, 80, 81

Z

Zoller, H., 108, 110